New Priorities
for the University

Ernest A. Lynton

Sandra E. Elman

New Priorities for the University

*Meeting Society's Needs
for Applied Knowledge
and Competent Individuals*

 Jossey-Bass Publishers

San Francisco • London • 1987

NEW PRIORITIES FOR THE UNIVERSITY
Meeting Society's Needs for Applied Knowledge and Competent Individuals
by Ernest A. Lynton and Sandra E. Elman

Copyright © 1987 by: Jossey-Bass Inc., Publishers
433 California Street
San Francisco, California 94104
&
Jossey-Bass Limited
28 Banner Street
London EC1Y 8QE

Library of Congress Cataloging-in-Publication Data

Lynton, E. A. (Ernest Albert)
New priorities for the university.

(The Jossey-Bass higher education series)
Bibliography: p. 171
Includes index.
1. Education, Higher—United States—Aims and objectives. 2. Professional education—United States. 3. Educational planning—United States. 4. College graduates—Employment—United States. I. Elman, Sandra E. II. Title. III. Series.
LA227.3.L96   1987   378.73   86-27729
ISBN 1-55542-029-X

Manufactured in the United States of America

The paper in this book meets the guidelines for permanence and durability of the Committee on Production Guidelines for Book Longevity of the Council on Library Resources.

JACKET DESIGN BY WILLI BAUM

FIRST EDITION

Code 8707

The Jossey-Bass
Higher Education Series

Contents

Preface   xi

The Authors   xxi

Introduction: Reexamining the Mission of
Modern Universities   1

Part One: Rethinking Scholarship and Service for a Knowledge Society

1. Broadening the Scholarly Responsibilities of
   the University   16

2. Making Research and Professional Knowledge
   Accessible   30

3. Mobilizing Internally for Effective Outreach   45

Part Two: Meeting the Educational Needs of a Knowledge Society

4. Educating for Competence in Work and Life   56

5. Developing Competence Through Career and
    Professional Programs   69

6. Adapting Programs to New Students and
    Attendance Patterns   86

7. Strengthening the University's Place in a Diverse
    Educational Environment   101

8. Maximizing the Educational Potential of
    Technology   113

        Part Three: Preparing the Faculty to Meet
                    New Challenges

9. Expanding Faculty Roles and Obligations   132

10. Evaluating and Rewarding New Professional
    Activities   146

    Epilogue: Providing Leadership for the New
    University   161

    References   171

    Index   187

Preface

Since World War II a number of fundamental societal changes have had a profound impact on higher education in general and on universities in particular. And the rate of innovation is accelerating. Scientific and technological developments lead more rapidly to new products, to new modes of communication, and to new economic conditions. Global interdependence is growing, and even on a local scale many problems and issues are becoming more complex. These developments have affected both the nature and the importance of knowledge and have thereby significantly changed the role and functions of the American university.

In teaching, as in research, the university needs to forge a closer relationship with the world beyond the campus. Moreover, it should become involved as much in the aggregation, interpretation, dissemination, and application of existing knowledge as in the quest for new knowledge. Internally, the university's mode of instruction and the content of its curricula require adjustment to bridge theory and practice and to help students learn as much from the latter as from the former. And of increasing importance is the need to broaden the university's clientele well beyond the traditional group of young and full-time students.

Both public and private universities in this country enjoy a substantial degree of autonomy that serves as a buffer against

external pressures and ensures reasonable stability in their role
and function. Nonetheless, as societal institutions, universities
are subject to changing societal circumstances and demands.
Some of these challenges can be met and solved without fundamentally affecting the way institutions define and carry out
their mission. But others cannot be dealt with within the existing formulation of university goals and procedures.

   We believe that a reexamination of the modern university
is no longer an option but an imperative necessitated by three
significant changes that have occurred over the past forty years.
First, the substantial growth of the university system has created far more institutions and a much greater number of faculty
than are required to fulfill society's needs for basic research,
indeed than are capable of performing such tasks. Second, the
rapidly changing nature of knowledge and the growing importance of knowledge in modern society, especially of the technological innovation needed to maintain economic development,
have created substantial new needs for individuals who will
transform data into knowledge and will then disseminate the
knowledge so that it can be used and applied. Third, the increase in the number of people participating in higher education—both from the traditional college-age population and from
the older population with previous work experience—has intensified the need to help students achieve and maintain competence
on the job and as members of society. These three developments complement and buttress one another. But the successful
functioning of this tripartite reciprocal relationship depends on
the extent to which certain policies, procedures, values, and
norms are changed within the university itself. This book addresses these critical issues.

   This is not the first work to point out one or more of the
necessary institutional adaptations, nor do we presume that we
will have the final word. What we believe makes this book
unique, however, is its stress on the *mutual interdependence*
and *reinforcement* of these changes. The extension of scholarly
work to include considerably more applied research, the change
in mode and sequence of instruction to relate theory to experience, and the inclusion of more and more students returning to

the classroom after periods of work—all three fit together logically and provide a coherent model for the modern university.

Overview of the Contents

The Introduction stresses the need for new priorities and a broadened conception of the university that will include greater emphasis on the dissemination and application of knowledge and on the education of competent individuals.

The core of the book is divided into three parts. Part One, which consists of Chapters One, Two, and Three, examines the changing function of knowledge in modern society and the new priorities created for scholarship in the university. The first chapter describes the range of scholarly and professional activities needed to move new ideas and new technologies into settings where they can be used. It argues that the prevailing definition of scholarship and professional activity must be appropriately expanded to include applied research, technical assistance, and policy analysis. Chapter Two proposes specific ways of facilitating these outreach activities: making the university more accessible, providing appropriate logistical and procedural support for the development of contracts and other agreements with external clients, and, most importantly, actually delivering the professional activity. This chapter explores each of these aspects in some detail and examines alternative approaches and their respective advantages and disadvantages. Chapter Three describes the internal linkages and procedures needed to facilitate problem-centered, multidisciplinary activities. It argues for a "second stream" of resource allocation and for personnel review that would cut across the traditional departmental and collegiate structure.

The second part of the book, which contains Chapters Four through Eight, deals with new priorities for the instructional tasks of universities. Chapters Four and Five stress that modern society needs not only effective ways of disseminating and applying new knowledge, but also individuals competent to use this knowledge well both on the job and as citizens. Such competence should be the goal of the university in the arts and sciences as much as in career-oriented fields. Competence requires more than the acquisition of knowledge and of technical skills. One essential element in its development is a truly liberal education. Chapter Four describes the implications of this priority for arts and science programs in some detail, indicating the importance of experience. Current efforts to develop scientific literacy are described to illustrate some of the pertinent issues. The chapter further argues that liberal education should be viewed as the capstone rather than the foundation stone of all curricula and recommends closer linkage between the liberal components and the area of concentration through the development of extended majors in which the specialty is placed within a broader context. Chapter Five pursues these arguments with a particular focus on career-oriented and professional fields. It stresses the distinction between liberal education and liberal arts education and suggests that education for competence requires an inextricable mix of liberal education and technical expertise. The chapter examines engineering and management education as two examples. It further describes the growing dissatisfaction voiced by many employers and others with the current state of career preparation and the need for a basic change in the conception of professional practice and therefore also in the approach to career preparation.

Chapter Six describes the new patterns of attendance that are beginning to dominate university education at both the undergraduate and the graduate level. In addition to the growing number of adults returning to universities, younger students are increasingly delaying and interrupting their studies. The chapter examines the implications of this for curricular structure and content and points out how the new patterns reinforce the need for breadth and synthesis at the end rather than the beginning of a degree program. Chapter Six also describes the new element in adult education created by the increasing need for recurrent formal education in order to maintain competence in the face of accelerating change. It discusses the emerging conception of education as a lifelong process and its implications for the traditional continuing education units of our universities. The chapter recommends that all instructional activities be integrated into the core of the university, while retaining the important support services and marketing expertise developed by continuing education units.

Chapter Seven examines the educational role of universities at a time when a growing number of nonacademic sources provide advanced instruction. It maintains that universities continue to have their own, unique areas of instructional responsibility—providing an education that combines technical expertise with contextual and theoretical understanding. Chapter Eight explores the extent to which developments in telecommunication and computer use can help universities meet their expanded educational responsibilities. The delivery of instruction and information to locations remote from the campus can clearly be enhanced by television, the distribution of videotapes and, in the near future, by videodiscs. The chapter also discusses at some length both the potential for and the limitations of microcomputers in higher education and concludes that these devices provide a most valuable supplement to but not a substitute for the more traditional forms of teaching and professional activity.

Ultimately, the faculties must bear the responsibility for carrying out the new priorities. The third part of the book focuses on two essential elements. Chapter Nine describes the new challenges for faculty members who generally need a greater awareness of the applications of their field to the outside world and of the relationship between their area of specialization and cognate disciplines. Both in the classroom and in their professional activity, faculty members must be able to work with practitioners who may have many years of practical experience. Chapter Nine explores the profound implications for the ongoing development of the current professoriate as well as for the preparation of future faculty members. Chapter Ten addresses itself to the all-important issue of incentives and rewards. The new demands on the faculty must become fully integrated into the academic system of values and rewards. Universities need to develop appropriate methods of documenting and evaluating the broader professional activities of the faculty and must ensure that quality performance in these areas is as highly regarded and rewarded as achievement in the more traditional areas of faculty responsibility.

The Epilogue to the book pulls together the various topics discussed in the book and emphasizes once again what has been stressed throughout the book: the mutual reinforcement of the necessary changes in universities. Greater emphasis on application-oriented professional activity both enriches and profits from a curriculum in which theory and practice are more closely related through various clinical and practical components. The presence of a growing number of students returning to the classroom with prior experience helps faculty increase their awareness and understanding of external conditions and their involvement in applied scholarship will make them better teachers of experienced students. Thus, there emerges a coherent, internally consistent model of the new university in which teaching and scholarship are closely tied to each other, each benefiting the other—perhaps to a greater extent than ever was the case in the traditional research-oriented institution. The Epilogue further addresses itself to the implementation of the proposed new priorities. It calls for strong administrative leadership on the campus, for supportive policies at the state and national level, and for the involvement of professional bodies, faculty unions, and national higher education associations in shaping the climate of opinion.

We have chosen not only to stress the need for change but to suggest specific ways of bringing about or at least facilitating the necessary changes. This work describes a variety of structural and organizational adaptations within universities, new approaches to curricular format at both the undergraduate and graduate levels, and substantial changes both in faculty preparation and development, as well as in the system of priorities and rewards for faculty activity. But the book does not attempt to provide a detailed blueprint for all universities. One of the great strengths of the American university system is its marked institutional diversity. The complexity of the future will probably require even more variation among individual institutions. That need is beginning to be recognized even in countries that, to date, have had a highly homogeneous, centrally controlled university system (Organization for Economic Cooperation and Development, 1986). Yet the increasingly important heterogeneity is most useful if it occurs within a unifying conceptual framework. What we set forth is a broadened conception and definition of the basic functions of the university—scholarship, instruction, and professional service—to provide an overall framework within which each institution can find its own optimal and distinct place.

The Audience for This Book

The institutional changes called for in this book will require strong administrative leadership as well as active faculty participation. Thus, it is to these two groups that this book is addressed: to department heads, deans, provosts, vice-chancellors, vice-presidents, and presidents, as well as to leaders of faculty governance boards and faculty unions and to the faculty in all disciplinary fields. Insofar as changes in public policy are also crucial, in terms of accreditation and other external conditions affecting the operation of universities, this book has something to say to key individuals involved in professional associations and in organizations concerned with higher education issues.

Acknowledgments

At one level, this book represents a distillation of our experiences and thoughts during many years of professional activity in higher education. At another, it is the product of a period of intensive research and inquiry. During the former, each of us has benefited from collaboration, discussion, and criticism provided by too large a number of colleagues, friends, and students to be enumerated here. However, each of us has had the good fortune of working with a few individuals who have been our particular mentors and models, who have taught us much, and to whom we are particularly grateful. These include Richard Schlatter, past provost at Rutgers University, and his successor, Henry Winkler, later president of the University of Cincinnati; Robert Wood, past president of the University of Massachusetts; Guy Benveniste and Todd LaPorte, both of the University of California at Berkeley; and Roy Keith, vice-president, University of Maryland. They are erstwhile colleagues and continuing friends.

Much of our intensive collaboration in writing this book was made possible by a generous joint grant from the Carnegie Corporation, the Ford Foundation, and the Lilly Endowment. To these sponsors and to our program officers, Alden Dunhan, Gladys Chang Hardy Brazil, Sheila Biddle, and Laura Bornholdt, our special thanks for their encouragement and support.

As we worked on the manuscript, we benefited greatly from many colleagues and friends both here and abroad. We are particularly grateful to Russell Edgerton and Theodore Marchese, to Susan Fratkin and Nevin Brown, and to Dorotea Furth and George Papadopoulos for opportunities to participate in projects and meetings of the American Association for Higher Education, the National Association of State Universities and Land-Grant Colleges, and the Organization for Economic Cooperation and Development, respectively. These meetings were particularly helpful in showing us the universality of certain critical issues facing universities in different countries. We would like to express our appreciation to Shirley McDade and Marcia Murningham for their valuable research assistance.

In addition, we want to express our special gratitude to a number of colleagues who helped us, well beyond the call of friendship, by reading our manuscript at one or more stages of its development: Patricia Cross, Patricia Crosson, Richard Freeland, Zelda Gamson, Hoke Smith, and Verne Stadtman. Without their critical comments, the flaws of this book would have been greater, its merits less. They bear much of the responsibility for the latter and none for the former. We thank these readers, as well as the anonymous ones who reviewed the manuscript for our publisher and who, with one exception, were as helpful as they were critical. Chapter Ten draws heavily on *Professional Service and Faculty Rewards: Toward an Integrated Structure* coauthored by Sandra E. Elman and Sue Marx Smock, whose continued collaboration is gratefully acknowledged.

Throughout this book we have stressed that professional activity exists within a broader context. Career, family, and society are intertwined, each affecting the other. This holds true for both of us. We are each part of a close family—parents, spouse, children—all of whom provide us with much inspiration and make our work more meaningful. It is for them that we have written this book.

Boston, Massachusetts   Ernest A. Lynton
January 1987   Sandra E. Elman

*To the Lynton family, present and future,
and to my loving mother and father,
Rose and Harry Elman*

The Authors

Ernest A. Lynton is Commonwealth Professor and a senior associate of the John W. McCormack Institute of Public Affairs at the University of Massachusetts at Boston, as well as lecturer at the Harvard Graduate School of Education. After completing his undergraduate and graduate study in physics at Carnegie Institute of Technology and Yale University, he joined the physics department of Rutgers University and was active in low-temperature research, publishing many papers and a monograph on superconductivity that was translated into Russian, German, and French. In 1965 Lynton became the founding dean of Livingston College, a new unit of Rutgers University. He came to the University of Massachusetts in 1973 as the first system vice-president for academic affairs. Resuming faculty status in 1980, he has since concentrated on studying the mission and function of universities. He has lectured extensively on the subject here and abroad and is the author of many articles and book chapters. His book on the role of universities in corporate education, *The Missing Connection Between Business and the Universities*, was published in 1984. His work has been supported by grants from the Carnegie, Ford, and Lilly foundations.

Sandra E. Elman is senior associate of the John W. McCormack Institute of Public Affairs at the University of Massachusetts at Boston. She received a B.A. degree in political science and his-

tory from Hunter College and a Ph.D. degree in higher education administration and planning from the University of California at Berkeley. She is the coauthor of *Professional Service and
Faculty Rewards: Toward an Integrated Structure* (1985, with
Sue Marx Smock) and has conducted several regional confer-
ences on adapting institutional reward systems to accommodate
the professional service activities of the faculty. She has served
as coordinator of policy and planning at the University of Maryland, Central Administration, where she was responsible for
long-range academic and budgetary planning and for research
studies in budgetary and management flexibility. Prior to this,
she was researcher at the Carnegie Council on Policy Studies in
Higher Education. She recently served as a member of the
Mayor's Management Review Committee in Boston. Her current
research interests center on public policy analysis, particularly
as it relates to urban planning, federal-state relations, and university-industry linkages.

New Priorities
for the University

❧ Introduction ❧

Reexamining the Mission of Modern Universities

American universities are facing a new challenge in the last two decades of the twentieth century. They must establish new priorities for their functions because the nature and importance of knowledge in modern society are changing both quantitatively and qualitatively. The need for knowledge has become not only greater but also pervasive, ubiquitous, and continuous. Increasingly, data and information need to be aggregated and interpreted before they can become usable knowledge. Knowledge not only needs to be made available to young people but must be updated throughout life. It must reach all sectors of the economy and all parts of government, again on an ongoing basis. The continuous replenishment and reinterpretation of knowledge are crucial.

Knowledge, and particularly advanced knowledge, constitutes the essence of universities. They are the societal institutions with the specific responsibility to create advanced knowledge, interpret it, and disseminate it. Hence as the role of knowledge in society changes, universities need to respond accordingly. Their task remains the same: to be the prime source of intellectual development for society. But their task environment is

1

changing drastically because more elements of society need to be able to use more forms of that knowledge on a continuous basis. Therefore universities need to change the ways in which they carry out their tasks. While continuing to devote themselves to the ongoing creation of new knowledge, they increasingly need to apply both their resources and their expertise to other components of the complex process through which knowledge is absorbed by society.

In this book we will suggest ways in which the procedures and the values, as well as the structures and policies, of universities should reflect the changing nature of knowledge if these institutions are to effectively carry out their knowledge tasks in the evolving societal environment. We will describe how universities need to revise their priorities so as to broaden the currently accepted definitions of their principal tasks:

First, in scholarship and professional activities, the responsibilities should be extended so as to include what have been described as the external frontiers of knowledge: the many areas where the results of basic research—which is the internal frontier—should be applied. As much value should be placed on interpretation and dissemination of new ideas as on original research. Second, in instructional activities, the definition of specialization needs to be broadened. Individuals need more than special expertise in order to be competent in their occupation. They require, as well, an understanding of its context and a sensitivity to the human and ethical issues involved. In addition, what universities teach should be defined by content, not by clientele, thus extending the student body so as to include adults as well as younger people, those already employed as well as those preparing for their careers, those who need to maintain their present competencies as well as those seeking to acquire new competencies.

To accomplish these extended scholarly and instructional responsibilities, universities must

• broaden their system of values, priorities, and rewards for faculty so as to reflect the wider range of involvement with knowledge-based activities;

- enlarge their instructional and dissemination activities beyond the geographic bounds of their campuses and beyond traditional time frames and formats;
- adapt their traditional structures and procedures so as to accommodate the interrelation of disciplines and the variety of knowledge transfer needs.

Each of these necessary changes has been discussed frequently in recent years, and for each there exist encouraging examples of implementation in different institutions. But, on the whole, the various extensions are being considered and developed separately, in isolation from each other. It is the basic argument of this book that *all these adaptations should be part of a single, overarching conception of the university. They are internally consistent, they reinforce each other, and together they provide a logically coherent model for a set of institutions pursuing a constant goal—meeting the advanced knowledge needs of society—under new and different conditions.* Each of the extended functions contributes to the others, and all of them together must be fulfilled by the aggregate of all universities. Activities and emphases will vary from institution to institution, but the system of universities as a whole must be involved in *all* aspects of this enterprise.

We are suggesting, then, that universities, in their teaching as well as in their other professional activities, relate theory to practice, basic research to its applications, and the acquisition of knowledge to its use. The more faculty become involved in external applications of knowledge through technical assistance, policy analysis, and other extension activities, the easier it will be for them to make the necessary changes in the curriculum and the more qualified they will be to teach students returning to the classroom with workplace experience. In turn, the suggested changes in curricular approaches will facilitate faculty interest and participation in external dissemination of knowledge. The changes in teaching and in professional activity both require the same structural adaptations of the university, the same modifications of the reward system, and the same changes in faculty development.

We are proposing a conception of the university quite different from the pervasive image of a self-contained and fairly isolated campus populated by research scholars engaged in the pursuit of knowledge for its own sake and by young students pursuing undergraduate and graduate studies on a full-time basis. That image has always been an idealization. Today, it has become a myth that constitutes a serious barrier to the university's real objectives. Even the multiversity, in its totality very different from the institutional image just described, remained a "city of the intellect" with "satellite suburbs;" it implied a central, inner-directed core still surrounded by isolating walls (Kerr, 1963, p. 123). We need to tear down those walls as well and arrive at a basic conception of the modern university as a metropolitan region, itself reflecting the complexity and "messiness" of the world around it but capable of bringing to bear any part of its resources as appropriate to the knowledge needs of the society it is supposed to serve. We are speaking here not of a university with an appended set of extensions but of an extended university.

Reviving a Tradition

The conception of the extended university differs from the image promulgated by a long line of individuals, from Aristotle through Wilhelm von Humboldt and Cardinal Newman to Thorstein Veblen, Abraham Flexner, and Robert Hutchins. But it is consistent with a conception almost as ancient, enunciated by Bacon and more recently by Dewey, Whitehead, and many others. Above all, it is really the modern version of what has been the American university tradition from its inception in the nineteenth century. The early presidents of state universities might not have anticipated the new and important role of knowledge in modern society, but they would have strongly endorsed the responsibility of universities to respond to this situation. Decades before the Land-Grant Act of 1862, universities in this country took on more inclusive tasks than did their counterparts in other countries. Particularly in agriculture but in other fields as well, public and private universities in America were for a time not only the principal source of new knowledge by means of basic research but also the major mechanism for the application and dissemination of such knowledge through applied research, technical assistance, and extension services. By insisting on a broad education, they went beyond teaching new generations the emerging skills needed in an industrializing economy. Their responsibility included, as well, the task of providing farmers and others with continuing education and a steady stream of information so as to ensure up-to-date skills and a rapid diffusion and absorption of new ideas. Research, extension, and instruction were seen as inextricably interrelated.

The utilitarian or instrumental conception of the American university as it gradually took shape during the nineteenth century included strong components both of the research orientation characteristic of German universities and of the British emphasis on liberal culture. In its instructional function, the American university focused on career preparation but viewed this as encompassing far more than narrow technical skills. The task of the university was seen as educating high-minded individuals who would bring to their jobs moral precepts and a keen sense of ethical values. Andrew White, the first president of Cornell University, envisioned the graduates of the universities as "pouring into the legislatures, staffing the newspapers, and penetrating the municipal and county boards of America. Corruption would come to an end; pure American ideals would prosper until one day they governed the entire world" (Veysey, 1965, p. 85).

This ideal of providing a broad, humanistic preparation for a career was lost in the growing emphasis on professionalism and the fragmentation of faculties into distinct disciplines. Nonetheless, it is important to remember that the utilitarian view that informed much of the growth of American universities after the Civil War began with a very broad conception of career development that stressed liberal education and placed considerable emphasis on values.

Similarly, the early view of the university's role in disseminating and applying knowledge also encompassed more than outreach. In the earliest days of the land-grant colleges it was discovered that both career preparation and the provision of extension services require research activities (Eddy, 1956). It is quite significant that the Hatch Act, which in 1887 established federal funding for agricultural experiment stations, preceded by twenty-seven years the Smith-Lever Act of 1914, which provided federal financing for cooperative extension. First-rate research as the source of technical assistance became equally important in areas other than agriculture. At Wisconsin the extraordinary successes of applied research in agriculture led its president to promote similar linkages between basic scholarship and practical applications in other fields. In the social sciences, the university recruited several outstanding faculty members who made significant theoretical as well as practical contributions to their field. According to one observer, their research provided the Progressive movement with "the scientific ballast" that earlier political reform movements had lacked (Cremin, 1961, p. 164).

Thus, research, both basic and applied, was recognized as the essential source of the knowledge and techniques that were to be taught in the classroom and disseminated to the public. However, the perspective on scholarship was significantly utilitarian. Rudolph recounts the observations of an English clergyman, who, while visiting the United States in 1907, commented on the distinctiveness of emerging university models in different countries. According to this observer, scholarship was regarded as "a means and measure of self-development" by the British, as "a means in itself" by the Germans, and as "an equipment for service" by the Americans (Rudolph, 1962, p. 356). Indeed, "the believer in a useful higher education . . . valued research and performed a good deal of it. . . . But it remained for him a subordinate goal, [a means toward] some ulterior (and serviceable) purpose, not primarily for the intrinsic rewards of discovery" (Veysey, 1965, p. 76.) A recent British book on universities calls this utilitarian view the quest for "knowledge-as-a-product" as distinct from "knowledge-as-a-process" (Scott, 1984, p. 55).

Thus, in the decades following the Civil War a new conception of the university emerged that was uniquely American and uniquely suited to the demands of a vigorous, changing, and expanding society. The "new university" would have a strong career orientation in its teaching, and it would extend and disseminate knowledge as widely and effectively as possible to collective as well as individual users. Both instruction and extension were to involve the application of research and scholarship. The mutually reinforcing relationship of all these components is the basic American tradition for our public universities. According to Ashby, "the great American contribution to higher education has been to dismantle the walls around the campus. When President Van Hise of Wisconsin said that the borders of the campus are the boundaries of the state, he put into words one of the rare innovations in the evolution of universities" (1967, p. 4).

Clearly, there exists for American universities a well-established tradition for a broad, inclusive definition for their scholarly as well as their teaching functions, one that places as much value on the interpretation and dissemination of knowledge as on its creation and that pays as much attention to providing opportunities for lifelong and recurrent education as to the instruction of the young. Today, the accelerating pace and complexity of change make these extended responsibilities more important than ever before. Yet, the development of American universities after the Second World War triggered a movement toward a different conception of the university that downgraded the earlier tradition and established too narrow a definition of scholarship and too limited a range of instruction.

The Paradox of Postwar Growth: Diversity of Activity

That universities in the aggregate are falling short of their potential just when they are most needed can be attributed in large measure to a basic paradox in the way in which the university sector expanded during the postwar period. This growth resulted in a great diversity of institutions yet created, as well, an astonishing uniformity of values and aspirations.

The diversity is strikingly illustrated by the public university sector, in which the most explosive growth took place. There exist today approximately 300 public institutions that carry the label "university." Of these, 220, or over 70 percent, became universities after the Second World War: 53 were newly created institutions, 167 had been colleges. The Carnegie Council's classification of institutions of higher education, developed in 1973 and revised in 1976, established ten categories based on size, levels of degrees, amount of research support and range of academic fields (Carnegie Council on Policy Studies in Higher Education, 1976). Four of these categories encompass 173 public and private doctorate-granting institutions, further classified into two groups of Research Universities and two of Doctorate-Granting Universities. The 92 Research Universities were, at the time of classification in 1976, among the 100 leading recipients of federal research funds and awarded at least fifty Ph.D.'s in 1973–74. The 81 Doctorate-Granting Universities awarded at least twenty Ph.D.'s in at least five fields in that year. Three hundred and twenty-three additional institutions that contain several professional programs in addition to the liberal arts and usually offer a number of master's programs but have little or no doctoral work are classified as Comprehensive Universities and Colleges I.

As indicated in Table I, these five categories together contain 277 of the 305 public institutions that carry the name of universities. Twenty-four additional ones are in the sixth Carnegie category of Comprehensive Universities and Colleges II because they have only one professional program and do not offer doctoral degrees. Four are in none of the top six categories. The striking fact is that 60 percent of the public universities are in the categories labeled "comprehensive" rather than "doctoral" or "research" and that almost all these institutions were created or designated as universities during the postwar period.

Sponsored research is substantially concentrated in relatively few universities. The combined total of sponsored research in the ten universities receiving the most nonmedical research support in 1979–80 constituted almost 30 percent of the total received by all public universities that year. The pat-

Table 1. Distribution of Public Universities.

Carnegie Classification	Number of Institutions	Percentage of Total
Research I	29	9.5
Research II	32	10.5
Doctorate I	38	12.5
Doctorate II	19	6.2
Comprehensive I	159	52.1
Comprehensive II	24	7.9
Other	4	1.3

Source: Carnegie Council on Policy Studies in Higher Education, 1976.

tern persists throughout the public and private sectors. Of the 563 colleges and universities, public and private, receiving research support from the National Science Foundation in 1980–81, the top 90 received 80 percent of the total, the top 130 received 90 percent. As one might expect, there is a strong correlation between research support and institutional age. Excluding medical research support, 16 among the top 20 public and private institutions granted federal research funds in 1979 were also among the 20 leaders in research activity in 1950, with most being recipients as far back as 1920 as well. Twelve of the 14 original members of the Association of American Universities (established in 1900 as an organization for research-oriented institutions) are now among the top 20 recipients of federal research funds (Kerr, 1983). By contrast, in 1980 4 out of 5 postwar universities received less than $5 million of research support from any source (National Science Foundation, 1985a).

The diversity among private institutions bearing the label "university" is even greater. Some states have little or no control over what private institutions choose to call themselves. The result is a number of marginal and decidedly unusual "universities." For example, the *Higher Education Directory* (1985) lists six "universities" in California with enrollments under 100. But even if one focuses on more traditional institutions, the situation in both the public and the private sectors is quite similar. The universe of universities in the United States today consists

of a broad continuum that ranges from a group with a strong research orientation, mainly comprised of prewar institutions, to
a number of small, struggling campuses at the other extreme.
The largest single group makes up the middle range, categorized
as Doctoral II and Comprehensive I and II by the Carnegie
Council.

Indeed the diversity is so great as to lead many knowledgeable observers of higher education to apply the term *university* only to about 150 institutions—essentially those in the Carnegie Research I and II categories, along with a few in Doctoral
I. All other institutions, regardless of the label they carry, are
viewed by these observers as colleges. This notion is exemplified
in a recent publication by the National Institute of Education
(1985) with four essays that describe the major sectors of
American higher education: the community colleges, the liberal
arts colleges, the state colleges, and the research universities.
The last of these essays focuses explicitly on a limited number
of universities, so that all other institutions carrying that label,
including many in the doctoral and essentially all in the comprehensive categories, are relegated to the "state college" group.

There is much to be said for making such a sharp distinction between those universities that clearly are primarily engaged in research and all other institutions. Yet to do this is to
achieve homogeneity of classification at one end of the continuum at the cost of even greater diversity at the other. The
majority of institutions called universities occupy the broad
middle range. Everyone in higher education is familiar with institutions such as San Diego and San Francisco state universities
and Memphis State University in the public sector, Baylor University, Adelphi University, and Hofstra University in the private sector. These universities may not fit into the top Carnegie
categories, but surely they differ even more drastically from an
institution that is primarily an undergraduate college, public or
private, and that combines a liberal arts curriculum with one or
two career-oriented programs.

These universities constitute a major intellectual resource
that has not, as yet, been fully utilized. They typically have a
strong faculty with doctoral degrees from prestigious universi-

ties. They are fully qualified both to provide excellent undergraduate and graduate education and to engage in a variety of
scholarly and professional activities. Their potential role is of
particular importance at the local and regional level, where they
can be the providers of preparatory as well as continuing education, applied scholarship, technical assistance, and public information, and can make substantial contributions to economic
development. Indeed, these "regional universities," as they are
sometimes called, can be the principal sources of intellectual
and cultural vitality, technological advance, and economic renewal for their communities. Their educational potential is eloquent-
ly described in a recent article that describes these institutions
as "potential synthesizers of liberal and professional education."
They can become a new institutional model, one that "embraces both intellectual elitism and social egalitarianism" (Smith,
1978, p. 470) and strikes "a dynamic balance between the theoretical and applied studies leading to education for professional competence and leadership" (p. 471).

Uniformity of Values and Aspirations

A major barrier thwarting the potential of regional universities is partially self-imposed: *all* universities adopt the goals
and measures appropriate for the few larger institutions with
ample research funding. In spite of the considerable diversity
among the universities described in the previous section, the internal hierarchy of values, the measures of academic respectability, and the faculty reward and incentive systems are astonishingly—and distressingly—uniform. Nearly two decades ago,
Jencks and Riesman (1968) commented on the monolithic status system in American universities—a system based on the
model of the large, research university. A subsequent survey
provided data on institutions and faculty attitudes that lend
"support for the idea that there is a monolithic status system in
American higher education and that its base is in research and in
the 'national reputation,' both for the person and for the institution, that research (and a rapid increase in graduate programs) apparently can bring" (Hodgkinson, 1971, p. 17). Such

a "single-status system works to homogenize higher education" (p. 18); "the diversity which is one of the strengths of American higher education becomes weakened by an urge toward isomorphism" (Ashby, 1971, p. 43). The situation has not changed during the past fifteen years. Prestige in American universities continues to derive from narrowly defined criteria. The resulting pressures are particularly strong at this time of growing public insistence on excellence in education because "lay persons and academics alike are inclined to equate prestige with quality" (Astin, 1985, p. 5).

The striving for prestige is understandably greatest among the large number of new universities created after the Second World War. Many of these had been transformed, at least in name, from former teachers colleges and other four-year institutions. These new universities inevitably saw themselves in the shadow of the older, better established institutions and as a result felt that they had to imitate these institutions to gain academic respectability (Dunham, 1969). In 1956, Riesman described the "snakelike procession" in which each institution tended to follow the path taken by the head (p. 35). A recent study of the system of American universities again underscored the importance of prestige in the academic world and the widespread striving for parity of esteem (Clark, 1983). The tendency of the new institutions to accept the norms of the research university was intensified by the fact that the preponderance of their newly recruited faculty held recent Ph.D.'s from a relatively small number of older institutions, the values and goals of which they imposed in their new environments (Trow, 1975, p. 5).

These orientations heightened the contrast between "greater academicism in [the university's] intellectual values and greater instrumentalism in its social relationships" (Scott, 1984, p. 75). As a result, there exists almost no connection between the internal views and the external expectations as to the role and functions of our universities. The existing, narrowly defined mold into which almost all universities have tried to cast themselves is not adequate to the expanding needs of our contemporary, knowledge-based society. A large number of institutions are failing to realize their full potential because their internal system of values, priorities, and aspirations primarily emphasizes and rewards traditional modes of teaching for which the clientele is shrinking and basic research for which most of these institutions cannot receive adequate support. This has resulted in a real crisis of purpose (Lynton, 1983a). By believing themselves to be what they are not, these institutions fall short of being what they could be. This not only deprives society of the substantial intellectual services that these universities could provide. It also constitutes a real danger to the institutions themselves. Unless they clearly establish their missions and realize their capacity to be more than undergraduate teaching institutions, they risk losing their university status in terms of funding and faculty work loads. In a number of states, pressure already exists to treat the flagship campuses differently from the other public universities (Jordan, 1985).

Instead of downgrading the comprehensive universities, we should use *all* universities more effectively. If no alternative providers would fill the void left by the universities, there would be less urgency for change. However, the knowledge needs of modern society have already reached a magnitude that has caused nonacademic organizations to pick up the slack. Employers are dissatisfied with the preparation of newly hired university graduates. They also find most universities rigid, slow, and unresponsive in providing continuing instruction for employees. As a result, there now exists a major system of employer-sponsored education in which academic institutions play but a minor part (Lynton, 1981, 1984; Morse, 1984; Eurich, 1985). One can document many other ways in which nonacademic "suppliers" are meeting the external demand for interpretation and dissemination of knowledge. Universities cannot and should not under any circumstances have a monopoly in these areas. The totality of needs far exceeds the capability of all our schools, colleges, and universities put together, and it is appropriate to have a permanently disaggregated system of educational providers. Nevertheless, in many areas universities should play a more important role than they do.

A Framework, Not a Blueprint

If our universities began to implement a broader and more inclusive mission, this would go far toward mobilizing the full capacity of these institutions in meeting the advanced knowledge needs of society. What we are advocating is not a uniform blueprint for all universities but rather a common framework within which each institution can determine its appropriate mix of activities. Universities *collectively* should retain the primary responsibility for a broad range of knowledge-related instructional and scholarly activities. As a group, they need to involve themselves not only in the production of intellectual raw material through basic research but also in the synthesis, interpretation, distribution, and ingestion of knowledge so that it indeed becomes absorbed by society.

The overarching conception, then, is that the system of universities should address itself to this entire process of knowledge manipulation. Each institution can choose how to combine the broad array of tasks and activities that are part of that process. Some universities will continue to focus strongly on basic research, while others may emphasize the interpretation and dissemination of knowledge. The students served at some institutions will continue to be primarily younger, full time, and residential; at others they may be older, part time, and commuters. Even within a single university, different colleges and schools may vary in the emphasis they place on the various components of the knowledge process. Given the substantial diversity among universities, a corresponding variation of tasks is appropriate and indeed advisable as long as the entire spectrum of scholarly and professional activities and the whole range of modes and audiences of instruction are seen as equally important and as consistent with the extended conception of what a university should be.

A monolithic status system is likely to remain the norm in the academic world. We therefore believe that it is both appropriate and necessary to move toward a broader definition of the mission of *all* universities and of the standards by which they are to be measured.

The extended model of universities is fully applicable to our most prestigious institutions. The universities in the top Research categories of the Carnegie classification scheme will undoubtedly continue to be heavily engaged in basic research and to enroll a predominantly traditional student body. Recently, however, many of these institutions have begun to collaborate closely with major corporations in applied research and development. In addition, some of these universities are quite heavily involved in outreach and extension at both the national and international levels. Several enjoy increasing demand for their prestigious continuing education programs for managers, executives, and government officials.

The extended conception of the university mission is equally applicable to the large number of institutions included by the Carnegie Council in its Doctoral and Comprehensive categories. Thus it can provide for all universities a single model broad enough to accommodate a wide variety of institutional activities and priorities. This extended, more inclusive conception would—perhaps for the first time—build upon the diversity among American universities while providing a greater sense of coherence and complementarity in the system as a whole. It would go far toward creating the conditions needed to make full use of the substantial potential of these institutions.

This book attempts to articulate such an extended definition of the role and function of universities. The chapters that follow will describe the broadened scholarly and instructional tasks that universities need to undertake and will explore, as well, the principal organizational, procedural, and policy adaptations needed to bring this about.

❧ 1 ❧

Broadening the
Scholarly Responsibilities
of the University

❧❧❧❧❧❧❧❧❧❧❧❧❧❧❧

Most institutions classified by the Carnegie Council (1976) as Comprehensive universities as well as those in the Research and Doctoral categories differ from all other postsecondary institutions in their potential for scholarship. Their faculties have the academic qualifications, the reduced teaching load, and the academic support facilities such as libraries that make it possible for them to engage in scholarly activities traditionally defined as the creation, interpretation, and dissemination of knowledge. Any changes in the nature and function of knowledge have an impact on the nature of the scholarly activities that university faculties pursue. It is therefore appropriate to begin this book on universities by exploring the nature of knowledge in contemporary society.

The plethora of recent books and articles about our "knowledge society" have made us all aware of the extent to which our economy and indeed many other aspects of our daily lives have become knowledge intensive. The importance of knowledge manifests itself in a number of different ways:

- The economic vitality and global competitiveness of indus-

trialized nations increasingly depend on a steady influx of
technological innovations.

- The resulting new ideas and new techniques must be understood and absorbed by all sectors of society through effective and rapid technology transfer and knowledge diffusion.
- The proliferation of data and the veritable glut of information place a growing premium on the aggregation, synthesis,
and interpretation of knowledge.

Each of these affects both the opportunity and responsibility
of universities to exercise their scholarship function. Though
each manifestation is discussed separately in subsequent sections, it is important to keep in mind that they are closely interrelated and reinforce each other.

Technological Innovation

Given the increasingly global context for the production
and distribution of material products as well as of intangible services, the United States will have a comparative advantage in the
years to come only if it gains and maintains a head start in the
creation and use of new technologies such as robotics, successive generations of computers, and genetic engineering.

A first requirement in this effort is a continuing and indeed growing emphasis on basic research, which has for so long
constituted the principal component of scholarship in universities. More than ever, it is important that our universities carry
out research that has no other predetermined goal than to gain
new insights. Because research costs money, much of it will inevitably be directed toward areas of particular interest to funding agencies. This has always been the case. But the very essence
of fundamental research is the unpredictability of its outcomes.
Hence it is also essential to maintain conditions that allow a
substantial amount of totally undirected exploration.

However, such research by itself is not enough to ensure
technological innovation. Knowledge must be organized for action (Baker, 1983). Research is only one component in a far
from unidirectional process, which is sometimes driven by mili-

tary necessity, as in the development of atomic weapons, and sometimes by the prospect of financial gain, as currently in much of the work on biotechnology. Under either circumstance, for basic research to result in high-technology applications there is a need for a "rich mix" of pure science, of scientists and engineers eager to apply it, and of venture-oriented small firms or government agencies able to develop applications. Furthermore, the process is inherently interdisciplinary and involves engineering as much as science (Shapley and Roy, 1985).

Until recently, American universities have placed excessive emphasis on basic, nondirected research. On the whole, most academic institutions have neglected the next step—applying research findings in ways that would benefit the overall economy. This has been attributed to a widespread misunderstanding and misapplication of Vannevar Bush's report, *Science —The Endless Frontier,* written in 1945 at the request of President Franklin Roosevelt as a plan for the development of postwar science in the United States (Bush, [1945] 1960). Shapley and Roy comment: "In our view, the Bush report contains a much broader message [than the importance of basic science] that was ignored for the most part in the evolution of postwar science institutions. This message concerned ... the *interconnectedness* of basic research with other parts of the process, along a spectrum from basic research to applied science, to engineering, to technology, to public, national needs. The people who came after Bush and his colleagues, who set up the system and trained the current generation of scientists, narrowed the definition of what science is, how it should be done, and why. Unwittingly, they set in motion a chain of events that today has isolated much of the U.S. basic research community, especially many university researchers, from the larger problems of the country" (1985, pp. 7–8).

A recent study of university-industry collaboration in research and development describes the issue in terms of "The subtle but important distinction between the 'pull' vs. the 'push' of technology. During the postwar period, at least, the advent of large pure research universities seemed to confirm the merit of ideas being pushed into the marketplace by researchers in the laboratory—most of which were lavishly funded by federal dollars. But in recent years, a new view is coming to prevail. Ideas must be 'pulled' out of the university in response to immediate and definable needs of the marketplace" (Dimancescu and Botkin, 1986, p. 21). The authors quote a university official as explaining that technology cannot be pushed, because it "is like a cooked noodle. It transfers by pulling" (1986, p. 36).

The interconnection of basic research with its applications and the growing need to pull the "cooked noodle" are particularly prevalent in the so-called high-technology area. " 'High tech' . . . refers to the application of science to products that are at the state of the art in terms of their function and design" (Botkin, Dimancescu, and Stata, 1982, p. 20). In fields such as biotechnology and computer applications, this has led to "the extraordinary shortening of the time between the development of an idea and its useful application. The time between the development of the principles underlying the combustion engine and their application in automobiles was relatively long, and the life of the industry thus spawned has also been relatively long. But the period required for the advancement of electronic computing from an idea into a major industry has been only a few decades. Scientific principles and ideas are now moving to useful applications in only a few years and to product manufacture in only a few years more" (Adamany, 1983, p. 427). That is one of the most striking aspects of the relationship between science and technology today, and it clearly intensifies the need for a complex interactive process between researchers and users, scholars and practitioners.

Research-related contacts between universities and industry have existed for many decades, most of them consisting of direct or indirect corporate support for university-based research, usually through one-on-one relationships between a university and a corporation. In recent years, initiatives by the National Science Foundation have led to the creation of a number of cooperative ventures through which a group of industries support university research in a certain field (National Science Foundation, 1984). But in the past there have been very few instances of truly collaborative interaction in research design and management (Peters and Fusfeld, 1982).

Quite recently, a number of research and development

consortia have been created in order to bring about effective partnerships focused on applied research and product development. These usually involve various areas of engineering together with basic sciences. A recent overview of such cooperative arrangements, based on fourteen case studies (Dimancescu and Botkin, 1986), shows a wide variety of relationships and emphases. For example, Project Athena joins MIT with two principal corporate partners, IBM and Digital Equipment, in experiments to integrate a wide variety of interactive computing facilities on a campus. By contrast, Stanford University's Center for Integrated Studies works with about twenty corporations on a broad agenda of research on integrated circuit design and fabrication. Some consortia have been stimulated by statewide initiatives such as the Benjamin Franklin Program in Pennsylvania and the Advanced Technology Centers in New Jersey, while others have relied on corporate funding alone. The Robotics Center at Carnegie Mellon University is strongly oriented toward applications; the Center for Advanced Optical Technology at the University of Rochester focuses on basic research in advanced optics.

In spite of the wide variety of approaches and emphases among the consortia described in this study, they all pose the same basic challenges to our universities: the need to focus as much on technology as on basic science, the need to adapt the disciplinary structure of the institution to the inherently interdisciplinary nature of applied research and development, and the need to provide appropriate incentives and rewards for faculty involvement. In addition, the consortia raise other issues that affect employers as well as educators: the need for new approaches to management, for better preparation for entry-level jobs, and for greater stress on lifelong learning (Dimancescu and Botkin, 1986). These issues will be discussed in greater depth in subsequent chapters.

Another common feature of existing university-industry collaboration is that, to date, much of what has happened involves only a few prestigious universities that either work with large corporations or help to incubate newly spawned high-technology ventures. Significant opportunities exist for many more academic institutions to become engaged in applied research and development, particularly in partnership with, or under contract from, medium and small enterprises. A good example of what can be done for these enterprises is provided by Carnegie Mellon's Robotics Center, where state funds under the Ben Franklin Partnership program allow small companies to "buy in." Another such model is provided by the Manufacturing Engineering Application Center (MEAC) at the Worcester Polytechnic Institute. At MEAC, "what is going on is not basic research but, rather, the critical art of taking an existing technology and expanding it to perform new tasks. The goal is to apply new technology to old needs . . . students, faculty, and full-time engineering staff work with company engineers to solve shop floor application problems" (Botkin, Dimancescu, and Stata, 1984, pp. 232, 234). MEAC works with large and medium-sized enterprises, each of which contributes $50,000 per year to the operation of the center.

The Benjamin Franklin Partnership program in Pennsylvania also provides opportunities for many of the smaller academic institutions in the state to participate in projects at any one of the four advanced technology centers, including the Robotics Center at Carnegie Mellon. Only by involving a broad range of universities in cooperative research projects can we ensure that these institutions will keep abreast of technological developments. If more opportunities for such participation in cooperative efforts with external partners are not created, there is a real danger of a widening two-tier system of education (National Research Council, 1986). Science and engineering units in one set of universities will remain at the forefront of development, while those in the second group will increasingly fall behind.

Technology Transfer and Knowledge Absorption

But working closely with the corporate sector at the cutting edge of innovation constitutes only a portion of the knowledge needs to which universities should address themselves. There exist substantial opportunities for the entire range of uni-

versities to cooperate with industry as well as with government
and other external constituencies in ensuring the rapid transfer
and absorption of innovation into all segments of the economy.
Economic vitality cannot be sustained by the high-technology
industry alone. Both large and small enterprises in this area have
created many new jobs in recent years and are likely to do so in
the future, but they alone will not be able to produce high employment and a healthy economy. Technological and other advances must become part of the mainstream of the economy,
and new knowledge must be absorbed by existing enterprises if
they are to survive. The cutting edge of science and technology,
at best, produces only a new set of tools. Such tools need to be
put to use. They need to be absorbed into the workplace,
whether that is an assembly line or an office. A whole range of
transfer activities are needed. In some cases, new ideas and new
devices should be transformed into new products: high-technology research must evolve into high-technology industry. The
innovations also need to be brought to bear on already existing
enterprises; low-technology activities must be coaxed into a
high-technology mode. A clear example of the latter is the need
to introduce robotics and related innovations into our traditional manufacturing industries so as to make them more com-
petitive. The giants of industry can undertake this process by
themselves, but the medium-sized and smaller enterprises need
technical assistance and management advice.

The cumulative impact of involving a large number of
universities in this effort could be extraordinary: "Imagine all
the expertise sitting in 200 or 300 engineering departments
throughout the country. If you could put it to use, you would
bring to bear a massive amount of brainpower on the low-technology, old companies" (Botkin, Dimancescu, and Stata, 1984,
p. 237). In all, there are over 400,000 scientists and engineers
employed in higher education (National Science Foundation,
1985b). Mobilizing such academic resources to participate in
the transfer and dissemination of technological innovation is
part of the new conception of scholarship made imperative by
the changing role of knowledge in modern society. A distinguished nuclear physicist made this point very forcefully. Using

Vannevar Bush's image of science as the endless frontier, he pointed out that science has both external and internal frontiers. The internal frontiers are "those boundaries where human knowledge is pushing most vigorously toward the unknown." The external frontiers, characterized as "no less important," are those that border on the many areas of applications of science: "the federal government, the educational establishment, the private sector, national security and defense, world science and technology, the developing world, and U.S. society itself" (Bromley, 1982, p. 1035).

One can expand this metaphor by pointing out that only a small fraction of our universities and only a portion of the faculty in those institutions in fact contribute significantly to pushing back the *internal* frontier, but that just about every university and the vast majority of faculty members could be productive and effective at the *external* frontier. A recent survey commissioned by the American Association of State Colleges and Universities (Chmura, 1986) describes a number of encouraging examples of activities at the external frontier carried out not only by leading research institutions but also by less prestigious universities. Examples from the study will be cited in the next chapter.

The potential contributions by the majority of universities to the knowledge needs of society become even more apparent when one considers that current technological innovations involve much more than the introduction of new devices and equipment. They pervade all aspects of society and affect almost every element of our social and economic structure. The impact of technology is changing the way in which we must operate our business enterprises as well as our governmental agencies; it changes relationships between individuals, between constituencies, between regions, and between countries. The political process has been altered, and this has posed new ethical and moral issues. A wide variety of private enterprises, as well as public agencies and organizations, now find themselves having to cope with the implications of new technologies and new knowledge. Almost all of them require assistance in this process. The opportunity for university involvement ranges from basic and applied research to technical assistance, policy analysis, and—last but certainly not least—a great deal of continuous updating of individual skills and understanding.

Every component of our universities can and should contribute to this effort: the social sciences, the humanities, and the professional schools, as well as the science and engineering units. Faculty in all these fields can take part in a wide range of activities, from individual consultation and short-term analyses and projects to long-term, interdisciplinary applied research. The opportunities are legion. At the same time as prestigious research institutions explore pertinent issues at a fundamental and universal level, faculties in all universities can apply state-of-the-art knowledge and insights to local and regional issues.

The totality of universities represents an enormous potential that could be mobilized if a substantial portion of faculty in a substantial number of these universities were more actively involved in technology transfer and knowledge diffusion. To approach this goal is perhaps the most important challenge faced by the university sector of higher education.

Transforming Information into Knowledge

A participant at an international meeting on the future of higher education in industrialized countries aptly described another aspect of knowledge transfer and extension: "In the coming decades, the assimilation and synthesis of more and more complex bodies of knowledge will be a more important service [of higher education] to society than ever before. And, along with the synthesis, will be the urgent need to transmit it much more effectively, not only to future generations of young people, but also to the broader society. Inundated as we will continue to be by information, our most crucial need will be to learn to sort, assimilate, and use it effectively" (O'Keefe, 1983, p. 68).

This component of scholarship is not receiving adequate attention and emphasis. When we speak of knowledge as a central resource of a modern society, we are referring to *usable* knowledge that can be applied by the practitioner to an actual problem or task (Lindblom and Cohen, 1979). This kind of knowledge is more than information or raw data. It is astonishing, for example, how frequently advertisements for personal computers stress the accessibility of data bases, in view of the fact that the majority of these are impenetrable to most potential users. It takes an expert to use a data base, and even experts will be familiar only with certain fields.

To the public-at-large, access to vast amounts of undigested facts is of little value. Society already suffers from a glut of data, an overabundance of information, which is usually fragmentary and often inconsistent. For knowledge to be useful, the bits and pieces of information need to be aggregated and synthesized into more coherent ideas, with apparent contradictions explicated. Furthermore, useful knowledge needs to bring together all the pertinent aspects of a situation and not deal only with one field of specialization. Issues and activities of different kinds are becoming increasingly interdependent; for example, technical solutions increasingly need to be considered in light of their economic, social, political, and cultural contexts.

Many examples can be cited to illustrate the limited usefulness of raw data. Economic analysis and forecasting certainly require more than undigested facts for any kind of understanding. Daily newspapers provide a constant stream of disconnected data: the percentage change in automobile sales from one month to another, the inflation rate during the past month, the revised growth rate of the gross national product, or this or that projection for the months ahead. Some of these figures may indicate moderate growth, others may suggest stagnation or even a downturn. The situation is complex even for experts; it is quite bewildering to the lay person without at least some explanation of the limited meaning of the data and some discussion of other factors likely to be pertinent to the economic situation.

Part of the confusion inherent in unexplicated data derives from the frequent mixing of absolute and relative figures. The percentage growth of an economic index or some other quantity means little without some knowledge of the prior situation. Conversely, absolute changes need to be compared with the magnitude of the quantity in question. A very similar shortcoming arises in the area of risk assessment. Newspaper accounts of chemical waste disposal, of nuclear accidents, or of the carcinogenic aspect of certain foods are usually devoid of comparisons that would provide a degree of perspective. How does this radiation level, or that concentration of chemicals, compare with the amount that exists under normal circumstances? Does it constitute a significant change or only a minor fluctuation?

The need for interpretation is particularly pressing in the political arena. Legislators and the general voting public must grapple with issues of great complexity and often frightening implications. All too often, at the local, national, and international levels, decisions are made on the basis of inadequate understanding and as a result of political demagoguery. Universities cannot reverse the trend toward greater uncertainty and greater complexity. But they can offer invaluable assistance in coping with this trend by providing needed background information and explication of complex issues. They can help to offset the prevailing tendency to view all questions in terms of absolutes—in terms of dichotomies that do not reflect reality.

In order to be of real use, universities need to establish their credibility as disinterested institutions. A clear distinction can and should be made between providing essential information and pertinent explanations regarding complex issues, on the one hand, and taking a partisan position on the resolution of such issues, on the other hand. But the neutrality of universities on public issues does not require silence in the face of ignorance. On the contrary: The responsibility of universities to their society includes a determined effort to be sources of information, knowledge, and understanding. That effort must be viewed as an important part of their scholarly function.

The *Harvard Education Letter* (*HEL*), published bimonthly by the Harvard Graduate School of Education, provides an excellent example of what a university can do to keep policy makers as well as the general public well informed. Widely disseminated and highly regarded, *HEL* describes recent research results and provides background information and analysis on important current issues. The president of the American Federation of Teachers calls *HEL* "a major resource in national debate" from which "the public can get an in-depth discussion of important educational issues presented in a way which is useful to both the professional and the general public" (Shanker, 1986). In the same way, a number of medical schools, including Harvard's, publish periodic informational bulletins on health-related matters. Similar efforts are needed in many different fields, and particular attention should be paid to local and regional issues.

Society's hunger for better understanding of issues and phenomena is evident in the proliferation of magazines and special newspaper sections that provide popularizations of science and technology. Magazines such as *Discover, Omni,* and *Psychology Today* have circulations of over a million. *Scientific American* has more than 700,000 readers, and there are several other such publications with circulations over 100,000. In addition, the trend started by the *New York Times* in publishing a weekly section devoted to science has now been followed by a number of other newspapers. Clearly there is great demand for useful information. Yet, it is important to note that with the exception of *Scientific American* and *Natural History,* these various publications make only limited use of university faculty. In this regard university resources are certainly not being tapped, particularly at the regional level. There exist a large number of local newspapers and a growing number of cable networks that provide local programming. Together these create substantial opportunities to carry out an important part of the universities' mission to disseminate knowledge and to help increase the number of "savvy citizens . . . not bewildered or intimidated by the introduction of new technologies or the arrival of new scientific languages" (Prewitt, 1983, p. 53).

Rediscovering Extension

Universities must recognize that the effective attainment of their scholarly mission calls for a complex and interactive process with their constituencies that goes beyond carrying out basic research. There is no question that such research continues to be important, yet by itself it has limited societal value and impact. Such scholarly work needs to be part of a variety of interrelated activities that link the research efforts to their eventual applications and that produce a two-way flow of continuous feedback and adaptation. These integrated activities need to become an integral part of the mission of universities if they are to continue to be the principal source of knowledge for society.

Responding effectively to the challenge of knowledge transfer does not require a change in the mission of universities but rather necessitates an understanding that the methods needed to engage in knowledge transfer will have to be adapted as external conditions change. Knowledge has been described as the "material" of universities, and research and teaching as "the main technologies" (Clark, 1983, p. 12). It is these "technologies" that must evolve to meet changing needs and circumstances. Universities can no longer concentrate primarily on the initial creation of the material of knowledge. The knowledge-intense nature of our economy, the general knowledge needs of society, and the diminishing time lag between the generation of new knowledge and its application all combine to demand that universities become more involved in the direct distribution and absorption of that knowledge.

Linking internal and external frontiers (Bromley, 1982) precisely parallels the linking of extension and outreach to basic research, which was described in the previous chapter as the basic characteristic of the emerging American university around the turn of the century. What we need today are a rediscovery and renewed implementation of the fundamental concept that underlay the land-grant institution: combining extension with research. The needs of our knowledge society today are strikingly similar to those of our agricultural society a century ago. Then, as now, there was a need for new scientific as well as technical advances. But then, as now, there was also a need to bring the results of the research efforts to the workplace, a process that became the task of cooperative extension. This structural development ensured that new discoveries and new inventions were rapidly and effectively adopted and absorbed by agriculture. Extension and research were closely intertwined, and the flow of information proceeded in both directions, so that at all times the course of research was influenced by a knowledge of the issues and problems facing the working farmer. There is no doubt that the spectacular development of modern agriculture in the United States is substantially due to the impact of the unique character of the land-grant institutions (Eddy, 1956).

The need to recapture the basic concept of the land-grant institution is gaining salience. Here and abroad, "technology transfer" has become a new motto. To date, the term has often been narrowly interpreted to mean university-industry cooperation in research and development. But there exists growing recognition that scientific and technological innovations are tools, useful only to the extent to which they are absorbed and used in traditional portions of the economy, such as the textile and automobile industries. This more pervasive kind of technology transfer requires the mutually interdependent combination of research, instruction, and extension that characterized the traditional land-grant college. If the potential of modern technology is to be fully realized, there is little doubt that the basic idea of extension should be resurrected.

However, the implementation of this idea is far more difficult in the contemporary context than it was for agriculture at the beginning of the century. Everything is vastly more complex. We need to deal not with one broad area—agriculture—but with a whole range of interrelated fields of knowledge, and we must work with a very heterogeneous collection of interacting constituencies. Operationally, the past has little to teach us: neither the mechanism of extension agents nor the relatively simple funding pattern through federal legislation is adequate to current and future needs. The next chapter will describe a number of transfer mechanisms that exist in many universities and will explore general guidelines with regard to the organizational and procedural approaches needed for an effective renaissance of the idea of extension.

❧ 2 ❧

Making Research and Professional Knowledge Accessible

❧❧❧❧❧❧❧❧❧❧❧❧❧❧❧❧❧❧❧

The previous chapter described the growing importance of scholarship and professional activity along the external frontier of knowledge: that is, at the interface between universities and their external constituencies. Along these boundaries, the number and variety of opportunities for "organizing knowledge for action" (Baker, 1983, p. 110) are both unprecedented and continuously expanding. The scope of tasks is so vast that every university can make an effective contribution. Indeed, it would be difficult to find any university without some examples of appropriate outreach. Yet in almost every instance, such efforts are peripheral to the institution as a whole. More often than not, they involve only a small fraction of the faculty or, in some cases, only special staff. Even the multiversity, as pointed out earlier, though engaged in a great deal of externally oriented activity, tends to relegate it to the "satellite suburbs," with minimal involvement of and change in the central "city of the intellect" (Kerr, 1983).

We believe that this orientation needs to change for two reasons. In the first place, the need for externally oriented scholarly activities is of such proportion and so varied as to necessitate involvement of substantial portions of all units within our universities. To maximize the scope and effectiveness of activity along the external frontiers, it is important that faculty and other professional staff throughout the institution be accessible to and communicate with external clients and become involved in a variety of professional activities with a minimum of procedural constraints. In addition, as will be indicated in subsequent chapters, such across-the-board participation is important in creating the intellectual climate conducive to necessary educational changes. Active involvement of faculty from many disciplines in a variety of applied and externally oriented professional activities is the best way—indeed perhaps the only way —to bridge the current pedagogical gap between theory and practice and to bring about a greater integration in the curriculum between specialized skills and liberal education. It is this mutually reinforcing relationship between a broader definition of scholarship and a more instrumental educational process that provides the central rationale for our conception of an extended university.

But broader engagement of universities along the external frontiers will not happen by itself. A number of current academic policies and procedures do not encourage such activities, and some even pose serious obstacles to realizing this goal. The new functions will require new forms. In essence, if universities are indeed going to become actively engaged in a broader range of scholarly activities, including applied research and development, technology transfer, and knowledge dissemination, then they must establish an appropriate and viable infrastructure to support these efforts. Changes are needed in three areas:

- A variety of linkages and bridging mechanisms are needed to ensure easy communication between external constituencies and all components of the university, to handle the procedural and administrative details of various contractual relationships, and to oversee the prompt and effective delivery of high-quality services.
- Within the university, internal procedures and organizational modifications should be adapted to facilitate and indeed to

encourage activities that cut across departmental and collegiate boundaries.
- Significant changes in the current system of priorities, values, and incentives are needed if the new categories of scholarly work of the faculty are to be adequately documented,
  evaluated, and rewarded.

The first two issues will be addressed in this and the following
chapter; the third issue will be treated in Chapter Ten.

Bridges to the Outside

The development of a multimillion dollar partnership between a university and a major corporation requires mobiliza-
tion of the executive leadership in both organizations. The
points of contact and the channels of communication can be
established relatively easily, especially since collaborations of
this type are often the outgrowth of prior joint activities. Any
procedural or legal issues usually receive special attention by
appropriate top officials. In addition, these highly visible arrangements have in a very short time gained a considerable
degree of acceptance both within and outside the academic community. That is perhaps not surprising in view of all the incentives: the industrial partners are likely to be sufficiently prestigious, and the amount of money involved is likely to be
considerable—at a time when the more traditional sources of
research support are decreasing and many of the scholarly and
professional activities are at the cutting edge of their respective
fields and pose stimulating intellectual challenges.

But the need for new forms of scholarship includes a
vast amount of technology transfer and knowledge diffusion
that is likely to be on a smaller scale, more transient, less glamorous, less visible, and with less prestigious corporate or public
partners. The majority of desirable projects will focus more on
the absorption and implementation of new ideas rather than on
their creation and, like the projects at Worcester Polytechnic
Institute cited earlier, will consist mostly of "applying new
technologies to old needs." It is important, as well, that the substantial resources of *all* universities be mobilized for these pur-

poses, including those universities that, to date, have had little or no experience with external contacts. For this to happen, each university needs a set of effective bridging mechanisms to link it with a range of users who could benefit from applied research, technical assistance, and usable information. Many such mechanisms already exist. Structurally, they vary as widely as the institutions in which they are located and the circumstances and conditions to which they are responding. Some have existed for a long time, others were established recently. Some are in purely technical areas, others exist in the social sciences; some focus on the private sector, others on public agencies. There exists no single model, and, indeed, each university should develop the methods and organizational patterns most suited to its circumstances.

In this effort it is important to keep in mind the three basic functions that must be accomplished for effective extension:

1. The *information and communication function,* which gives potential clients information about pertinent resources of the university, informs faculty of external demands and opportunities, and effects the proper match between external needs and internal expertise
2. The *brokering and negotiating function,* necessary for all except short and perfunctory contact, through which appropriate administrative details and contractual arrangements are worked out
3. The *delivery function,* which actually provides the desired professional and scholarly activity

We will take up each of these in turn.

Information Function: Making the University More Transparent

Perhaps the single most important—and most difficult—task in establishing effective extension is to help prospective users of the university's expertise and scholarship find the appropriate resources within the institution. A contemporary university is, even to an insider, a complex and at times confusing conglomerate of schools and colleges, departments, institutes, and centers. More often than not, it contains several departments in different schools with very similar titles. Furthermore, the vocabulary used by academics to describe their scholarly interests usually differs substantially from the language in which outsiders express their problems and questions.

The first step then is to provide appropriate contact and entry points through a combination of various mechanisms. These can include one or more appropriately staffed information centers, telephone hotlines with toll-free numbers, and inventories of faculty expertise and available instrumentation. Such inventories can be in printed form, or they can be made available as computerized data banks. Campus-based information centers can be supplemented in various ways. Universities can set up booths at industrial fairs, they can open storefront offices, and they can also use the modern equivalents of extension agents: individuals assigned to work with specific agencies or groups of potential clients. A particular means of communication may be structurally more appropriate and financially more feasible for one university than for another. The functional utility of all of them depends on at least two critical factors: (1) awareness of the mechanism's existence on the part of the potential user, and (2) the extent to which the available information is comprehensible to the user.

Potential clients, it goes without saying, cannot utilize an available university resource if they do not know of its existence. Whether the university provides a hotline or issues extensive printed directories and computer inventories is of little value unless individuals within and outside the university are able to avail themselves of the service. Publicizing the existence of hotlines, contact offices, and other forms of linkage is a difficult and time-consuming task and one that cannot be accomplished quickly. Appropriate marketing techniques and strategies for informing various constituencies must be carefully developed and coordinated in cooperation with key individuals in designated campuswide offices as well as with organizations and agencies in the external community. This requires a concerted effort over time, with much emphasis on both internal and external network building.

It cannot be overemphasized that information about resources must be conveyed in language that is understandable to potential clients. Descriptions of a faculty's areas of expertise, as well as of the kinds of data bases, instrumentation, and services available, must be communicated in terms of the client's problem or the kind of service the client needs, not in terms of the academic specialization of a particular faculty member or the technical language of the instrument that eventually will be used. It is very important to have a small staff—initially even one part-time person may suffice—of knowledgeable individuals who are capable of translating into the potential client's vocabulary the kinds of expertise available and of linking up the client with the appropriate experts or data bases. These "communicators"—recruited from among existing staff or newly hired— would play a role similar to that of a reference librarian. The latter really is the catalyst that makes it possible for the resources of a library to be effectively utilized by students, faculty, and, indeed, by external users as well. By the same token, the effectiveness of the communicator will determine the extent to which potential clients effectively utilize other intellectual resources of the university.

Brokering and Negotiating Function

Modern universities have become complex bureaucracies, with a web of procedures and policies that are further complicated, particularly in the case of public institutions, by state and federal regulations. Professional relationships with external clients that involve a fee for service or some other kind of formal agreement call for paper work to be done, policies to be clarified, contracts to be drawn up, legal issues to be resolved. These administrative operations can constitute a major barrier to outreach. It is essential, therefore, to institute effective ways of taking care of them quickly and with a minimum of inconvenience to the client, faculty member, chairman, or dean.

The brokering functions closely resemble the traditional

responsibilities of an office of grants and contracts. Most universities have found that a unit of this kind is needed not only to
provide logistical support for faculty who seek research funding
on their own initiative but also to encourage more faculty to
seek external research support. The broader and more inclusive
definition of scholarship and professional activity given in the
previous chapter requires a new kind of office of grants and
contracts that would be proactive in providing expert advice,
administrative support, and special encouragement to faculty
throughout the university. The unit's tasks need to be extended
so as to include relationships not only with outside funding
sources but with all prospective clients. As in the case of traditional grants and contracts activities, the brokerage function
would not involve any control or responsibility over the content of the activity, except to make sure that it complied with
any pertinent statutes or regulations.

Delivery Function

Actual delivery of the applied research, technical assistance, policy analysis, or other professional service is the final—
and crucial—step. Some universities may choose to keep this
function entirely decentralized at the departmental level. Contact between a potential client and the department may have
been made through an informational unit, and negotiations regarding the nature, scope, and cost of the services may have
been carried out with the help of a brokering unit. But once
an agreement has been reached, the designated academic unit
assumes full responsibility for the quality and timely completion of the project.

Although such a fully decentralized mode has some advantages to which we will return presently, many universities
have chosen to create one or more organizational units for the
specific purpose of delivering professional and scholarly services
to external clients. These units assume responsibility for the
content and substance of programs, and it is also their duty to
ensure high standards. Faculty and others involved in a specific
project are considered staff of the delivery unit, working for

and responsible to it, regardless of whether they are loaned by a department on a temporary and part-time basis or they have a long-term affiliation with the center or institute in question.

Specifically designated units for the delivery of professional services exist in various sizes, scope, mission, and organizational loci. A statewide university system may set up a single delivery mechanism for all campuses—as used to be the case for the extension divisions at the University of California and the University of Wisconsin. In both systems these functions have been substantially decentralized to the campus level in recent years. The State University of New York has established the Rockefeller Institute, located in Albany, to work with the entire system in a variety of public service activities. Campuswide delivery units exist in some universities. Many more have centers, institutes, or programs linked primarily to a single college or school, with the traditional cooperative extension service the best-known example of this kind. The model of extension has also been applied to nonagricultural technology and engineering. The Pennsylvania Technology Assistance Program (PENN-TAP) at Pennsylvania State University is generally regarded as one of the country's outstanding technology outreach programs. It works on a one-to-one basis with a large number of small and medium-sized enterprises through a network of transfer agents, programs of continuing education, and a library information system (Chmura, 1986). Another example of effective technology transfer by a leading research institution is the industrial extension service provided by Georgia Tech; this service maintains twelve field offices throughout the state. The University of Maryland at College Park sponsors a smaller but similar program.

Penn State, Georgia Tech, and the University of Maryland are among our most prestigious and research-oriented institutions, but they by no means hold a monopoly on effective technology transfer activities. As we have stressed throughout this book, less research-oriented universities can also provide highly important and valuable professional services. A recent survey of collaborative activities of universities with industry and public and private agencies turned up the names of such schools as the University of Texas at San Antonio, San Jose State University, and George Mason University. As a further example that advances the thesis of this book, it also described how several components of the University of Alabama at Tuscaloosa, a middle-range institution, provided multifaceted technical assistance to a local General Motors assembly plant (Chmura, 1986).

The many examples of delivery mechanisms in a wide variety of universities show that there exists no unique approach: what works well at one institution may not be appropriate for another. Much will depend on the nature and level of administrative leadership; thus, initiative on the part of a president or a provost may well lead to a campuswide mechanism, while an enterprising dean may be responsible for a college-based unit. Historical circumstances, such as the prior existence of a center or institute affiliated with a specific school or college, also affect the situation, as do the nature and the extent of external demand.

Certain trade-offs exist among the range of possible delivery mechanisms. A highly centralized unit can more easily gain visibility on and off campus and establish close working relationships with external constituencies and clienteles. However, it may do so at the cost of some degree of isolation from the academic departments. Decentralized units are closer to the faculty and are likely to be more readily accepted among them. But these units will find it difficult to develop interdisciplinary projects and programs that cut across departmental and collegiate boundaries.

Most institutes or centers are either issues centered or client centered. The former focus on a particular set of related issues, such as drug and alcohol abuse. In such instances, all the services and projects undertaken relate, to varying degrees, to the identified issue area. By contrast, a client-centered organization attempts to respond to many different needs of a particular constituency. For example, the traditional agriculture-oriented Cooperative Extension programs address a wide range of services and projects aimed at a particular population group and may deal with issues in home economics as readily as with the application of new plant genetics.

Each university must also make a fundamental policy decision as to whether the delivery of professional services should be client driven or resource driven. Essentially, the question is whether the services are to be limited to those areas in which all or at least most of the necessary expertise is drawn from within the university or whether activities will be undertaken in response to the client's articulated needs even if this requires substantial reliance on external professional resources. Our own view is that the provision of professional services by a university should be strongly resource driven. We are arguing throughout this book that the basic challenge faced by universities today is to make their existing intellectual resources more widely available to external constituencies. That implies that each university should overall rely more heavily on its own internal capability than on outside sources. To do this does not preclude the utilization of some external resources in cases where internal expertise does not suffice. Nonetheless, just as universities rely primarily on their own faculty and staff for formal instruction, so too should they rely primarily on their own scholarly resources for professional outreach.

Closely related to this question is the delicate, at times troublesome issue of whether there are intrinsic limits on what a university can and should do in this area. Embarking on a variety of applied, extended professional activities may have negative repercussions. External expectations can rise quickly and may soon exceed what the university can in fact deliver. Resources are not unlimited, and at some point demand will exceed supply; thus, the university will not be able to accommodate every request for assistance. Beyond the issue of sheer overload is a more complex dilemma: namely, that of advocacy. In many situations, the professional service rendered by a university to external constituencies becomes a factor in some external controversy and is used for advocacy purposes by the university's clients—that is, by community groups, corporations, or government agencies. There is nothing inherently wrong with that. However, universities should avoid becoming direct participants in the debate: professional assistance implies maintaining optimal objectivity; it is not the role of university experts to render judgment.

Funding and Staffing

Each institution should have clearly enunciated fiscal policies and practices for collecting fees for professional services
rendered to external clients. These procedures may vary considerably from one university to another and may require a variety
of approaches, depending on the nature of the institution and
its relationship to external constituencies. But in all instances
a number of basic questions need to be resolved in advance so
as to avoid misunderstandings and unfulfilled expectations: Are
any services to be offered without remuneration? Which clients,
if any, are to be granted services pro bono? Are there certain
kinds and categories of services for which requests will be de-
nied? Should need be a guiding principle in setting fees? Should
more prosperous clients be charged fees greater than cost so as
to provide services without charge to those with fewer resources? In the case of public universities, are public agencies to
be treated differently from potential private clients? What is the
cutoff point with regard to quantity of service at which fees are
instituted: a single phone call, an hour's worth of time, a day's,
a week's?

Effective external scholarly and professional outreach activities depend on a certain level of continuity; they cannot be
performed on an on-again, off-again basis. There needs to be at
least a minimal permanent administrative staff to manage the
outreach operation, as well as reasonable continuity in the staff
responsible for programs. Clients, as well as participating faculty, must be able to count on a reasonably stable commitment
from the institution. Any center or institute within a university
that delivers professional services requires an ongoing infrastructure so as to be able to cope with temporary fluctuations in
activity, to provide an appropriate level of pro bono services,
and, when necessary, to refuse requests that do not fall within
the guidelines for the unit. Hence, regardless of the extent to
which the unit in question can obtain fees for the services it
provides from its external clients, it also needs reasonable assurance of core funding, as part of the university budget, as a
direct legislative appropriation, or from a permanent endow-

ment. Continuity of effort is also enhanced if at least a portion of any external fees and overhead charges collected for services are kept by the delivery unit in some kind of revolving fund rather than reverting to general university accounts.

The staffing of an institute or center raises a basic question with regard to the balance between using faculty who are "borrowed" or "rented" from a department and using full-time professional staff employed directly by the unit. On the one hand, using principally professional staff limits the capability of the delivery unit to the area of expertise of the staff and does not optimize the use of the scholarly resources of the university. Furthermore, engaging professional staff on long-term contracts may lock the unit into certain categories of activity for a longer period of time than demand actually exists. On the other hand, relying entirely on faculty engaged by the center or institute on an ad hoc, project-by-project basis severely limits the ability of the unit to plan ahead or to take certain program initiatives. Directors of existing centers and institutes tend to agree that a unit can function most effectively with a core of full-time professional staff, buttressed by a number of faculty affiliated with the unit for prolonged periods of time and devoting varying amounts of time to professional service, with additional faculty engaged, as needed, for specific projects.

Faculty participation in delivery mechanisms poses a fundamental issue that is closely related to the problem of faculty rewards—namely, should faculty be assigned to professional service activities, much as they are given their instructional assignments, or should they be used only on a voluntary basis? The answer ultimately depends on the extent to which participation in professional service activity gains legitimacy and is accepted as part of a faculty member's responsibility. This issue will be explored in Chapter Ten.

Consultation

The most traditional way that universities provide scholarly and professional services to external constituencies is through individual consultation by faculty members. A recent

report indicates that such activity is widespread, although there
are no reliable indicators for differentiating between paid and
unpaid consultation or to separate consultation from other activities that lead to supplemental faculty income (Boyer and
Lewis, 1985).

Faculty consultation is a highly desirable way of bringing
the intellectual resources of a university to bear on the knowledge needs of external constituencies. Consulting activities
often can be arranged on an ad hoc basis, with a minimum of
paper work or delay and without the involvement of any institutional bureaucracy. In addition to monetary remuneration,
consulting affords faculty opportunities to keep up-to-date in
their fields. It also enhances their ability to relate theory to
practice, to incorporate appropriate material into their classes,
and to improve their recognition of the relationship of their
own specialty to cognate fields.

Consultation, however, does have some limitations and
disadvantages. Since it is not institutionally based, it does not
have an infrastructure and support system of the kinds discussed in the preceding sections. Faculty members usually operate as individuals and on projects of limited scope, unless they
work through a large consulting firm that in effect provides the
communication and brokering services that we are advocating
universities should develop. Independent consultation also pre-
cludes or at best makes it difficult to involve students in outreach activities. Perhaps most importantly, although faculty
consultation carries substantial benefit to its parent institution,
there are real costs as well (Lynton, 1984; Boyer and Lewis,
1985). When an external client employs a faculty member as a
consultant, it obtains the services of this individual "at marginal
cost and without having to pay the indirect, overhead expenses
of the institution that furnishes the faculty member with a
basic salary, office and research facilities, health insurance, and
other fringe benefits" (Lynton, 1984, p. 85). Institutions need
to think about implementing such alternative means as "practice plans" for accommodating consultation activities. Used by
many medical schools, practice plans offer a vehicle by which
payments for consulting services, like payments for patient

treatments, are shared in a designated way by the faculty member and the institution.

Student Participation

Student participation in professional service has extraordinary unexplored potential. Direct student involvement in professional service epitomizes the central theme of this book: the reciprocal reinforcement of applied scholarship and professional service, on the one hand, and the improvement of the educational process, on the other. Though often an overlooked resource, students can both contribute to and benefit from involvement in professional service activities. The next part of this book will discuss the need in both undergraduate and graduate education to relate theory more closely to practical experience and to make the latter a source of learning rather than merely an occasion to "practice" the application of theory. There is a great opportunity to do this by involving students in actual technology transfer and other professional outreach activities.

This can occur at a variety of levels. Graduate students can be given considerable independence to carry out substantial projects as the basis for dissertations. Advanced undergraduates can engage in more limited activities under closer faculty supervision for senior theses. And even at an early stage in their curriculum many students can assist in a faculty project. Student participation in these extended scholarly and professional activities is quite analogous to, and as potentially valuable as, their involvement in the more traditional forms of basic research. But the success of such activities cannot be left to sporadic individual initiatives. Both administration and faculty must be seen as interested and supportive, and one or more individuals need to take the responsibility—and have the necessary resources—to act as catalysts in bringing students and faculty together (MacVicar and McGavern, 1985).

However, student involvement in professional service activities differs in one important respect from most kinds of research participation. The activities in question are likely to be problem centered and to cut across a number of disciplines. This characteristic can create difficulties not only for student participation but even more important for faculty participation as long as universities are organized exclusively along disciplinary, departmental lines. The following chapter will describe the need for, and a possible approach to, creating administrative linkages that cut across these lines so as to facilitate multidisciplinary professional activities on the part of all members of the university community.

𝕳 3 𝕳

Mobilizing Internally
for Effective Outreach

As universities begin to broaden their linkages with their external constituencies and offer them new vehicles for defining and
solving policy problems, they need to adapt their *internal* arrangements as well. The image of the multiversity notwithstand-
ing, universities today continue to have a central core that has
not changed a great deal over the years in its priorities or in its
basic structure. The research-oriented disciplinary organization
continues to dominate the fabric of the institution. Yet, as discussed in Chapter One, it is increasingly important that the
modern university extend its scholarly activities beyond basic
research to include a wide range of applied work, technical assistance, interpretation, and dissemination. Such projects are
inherently problem oriented and cut across disciplinary lines.
The prevailing institutional procedures and structures do not
facilitate such work. Furthermore, the next chapter will indicate that degree programs, as well as other instructional offerings of universities, will also increasingly require not just contributions from different disciplines but active collaboration
among departments and colleges if coherent multidisciplinary
programs are to be developed.

45

A multidisciplinary activity—whether it is a program committee in charge of an interdisciplinary curriculum or a unit engaged in problem-centered research and outreach—is usually not
part of the university's principal system of internal resource
allocation. The activity must either obtain funds from an external source, such as a federal grant, charge fees for services, or
manage to obtain a position or two and some operating funds
out of a dean's or provost's discretionary fund. Most of the participating faculty continue to be supported totally from departmental funds, and more often than not the time they spend on
the interdisciplinary activity is looked upon as time lost to their
department. Thus to the extent that a multidisciplinary project
does not have its own source of funding, it must subsist on the
charity of departments.

The second barrier is a reflection of the first: the flow of
personnel recommendations in almost all universities is structured along the same, one-dimensional, departmental base as is
the flow of resources. Furthermore, the criteria used for advancement focus strongly on traditional, disciplinary research
that leads to scholarly publication. As a result, the participation
of junior faculty in multidisciplinary programs places them at
considerable risk with regard to their chances for reappointment, promotion, and tenure. Teaching in interdisciplinary programs or participation in problem-centered projects is usually
not viewed as contributing to the priorities of the department.
Furthermore, the formal or informal system that a department
uses to evaluate the quality of faculty performance in teaching
and research usually does not take into account nondepartmental activities. Thus they are given little or no weight in the
faculty reward system. In one view, "our present faculty ap-
pointment procedures, departmental organization, and curriculum development do little to establish a correlation between
courses and even less to encourage and protect the creative
teacher beyond the sometimes narrow range of departmental interests. In some instances such teachers are seen as disloyal and
unsound. We need to develop structures to support and reward
the builders of departmental bridges" (Rhodes, 1985, p. 80).

A Dilemma to Resolve

If a university is to meet needs that require effective collaboration among different disciplines, departments, and schools, then the system of resource allocation, as well as faculty evaluation and reward procedures, should be accordingly adapted. The last chapter discussed the need for external mechanisms. Clearly, the modern university also needs new internal structures to meet its new missions. Yet the traditional missions of the university continue to be of great importance. Foremost among these is a continuing involvement in basic, undirected, and disinterested research—not in the pursuit of knowledge for knowledge's sake, but because there is no way of predicting what useful results will arise from pushing at the internal frontiers. Some of the resources and energies of universities must continue to be devoted to such research to ensure that we will continue to generate new knowledge and deepen our understanding of the world around us. For these traditional purposes, the disciplinary structure, as well as the existing system of academic values and faculty rewards, continues to be effective. The disciplines do constitute appropriate ways of organizing knowledge and provide the best basis for the development of future scholars and researchers.

Furthermore, disciplines are deeply ingrained in higher education today. It would be foolish to overlook or to underestimate the extent to which the traditions, values, and priorities of faculty members are linked to their various disciplines. Every description of contemporary higher education stresses that the typical faculty member identifies more strongly with her or his discipline than with the institution: "Give the academic worker the choice of leaving the discipline or the institution, and he or she will typically leave the institution" (Clark, 1983, p. 30).

In spite of a number of valiant attempts during the sixties to develop alternatives to the departmental structure (McHenry and Associates, 1977), the University of Wisconsin at Green Bay appears to be the only university-level institution currently organized on a thematic, nondisciplinary basis, with some vestiges of this approach remaining as well at the University of California at Santa Cruz.

Another reason for not simply substituting some problem- or theme-oriented organization for the traditional disciplinary model is the need for many different combinations of faculty. These groupings depend on the particular problem or issue being pursued and are bound to change and to evolve as internal interests and external needs change. The organization of the university should retain enough flexibility to allow not only the *formation* but also the *termination* of multidisciplinary programs and projects. By setting up a quasi-permanent interdisciplinary organization as a replacement for the traditional disciplinary one, universities would merely substitute one rigid structure for another.

Thus both the intrinsic value of the discipline as a way of organizing research in the pursuit of advanced knowledge and the strong disciplinary identification of university faculties suggest that it would be unwise to create a new university structure that would entirely eliminate disciplines and departments. It would endanger the ability of a university to pursue its traditional mission and, as a result of faculty disaffection, would probably fail to enhance its ability to meet new objectives. Nevertheless, it is very clear that implementing the new missions of the university faces serious barriers as long as the allocation of resources, not to speak of the evaluation and reward system for faculty, places much greater priority on disciplinary than on interdisciplinary activities and greater value on basic research than on the interpretation and dissemination of knowledge. How is this dilemma to be resolved?

Some will argue that it is best to continue the status quo and to muddle through with the approach of the multiversity: leaving the core of the university unchanged and meeting new needs by adding on a variety of peripheral units. They will say that there is no point in trying to impose on any university a high degree of structure in a vain attempt to bring about organizational rationality. Academic institutions necessarily have ambiguous goals (Cohen and March, 1974) and loosely coupled structures (Weick, 1976, 1983). Moreover, faculty members can be mobilized only in opposition to drastic changes (Baldridge, 1971). Hence, it is probably wrong to try to go too far in changing institutional structure. Yet to do nothing under present circumstances may be even more dangerous. The external demands are too strong, the available resources too limited, the growing competition to universities too threatening. The issues of university organization, structure, and reward systems cannot be ignored even though they need to be approached with caution.

Developing a "Second-Stream" Approach

The basic challenge is to find ways of supporting and rewarding faculty activities that cut across disciplinary and departmental lines while at the same time retaining much of the current one-dimensional organization in which the principal flow of resources and the channel for personnel evaluation and rewards follow the single line that links the department through the school or college to the central campus administration. That challenge might best be met by the addition of a crosscutting flow of resources and a concomitant second channel for personnel actions. To a limited extent higher education already has a "matrix structure" that provides two bases of faculty grouping: the disciplinary dimension, on the one hand, and the institutional one, on the other (Clark, 1983, p. 31). However, in the great majority of institutions this matrix structure is highly asymmetrical. As was noted in the preceding section, it provides few incentives and little support for faculty activities that cut across disciplinary boundaries. The two dimensions of the current matrix crosscut at the department level; departments retain control and evaluation of faculty assignments and remain the locus of resources and rewards. As a result, a nontenured faculty member undertakes nondepartmental assignments at considerable risk.

Two recent analyses of university organization pointed out that "instead of integration of the missions [of the university] through organizational structure, the multiple-function professional faculty member is expected personally to make the necessary connections" (Bess, 1982, p. 209). Moreover, "in the development of initiatives transcending departmental lines, the research university depends on dedicated (and often unconventional) individual faculty members rather than on organizational structure or administrative leadership" (Alpert, 1985, p. 263).

The need is for a more effective matrix organization that would provide structural support for the many faculty activities in teaching and research that transcend departmental and disciplinary boundaries. Such a model would offer "a starting point for universities wishing to redefine their roles in either the local or the national context. It [would] reveal some of the features of both the internal and the external environment that have constrained efforts to redefine organizational goals" (Alpert, 1985, p. 276). In what follows we will set forth the basic organizational and procedural characteristics of a workable matrix structure that could establish and maintain a more equal balance between the disciplinary emphasis and crossdisciplinary support. It requires a basic modification both in the flow of resources and in the process of personnel evaluation and rewards.

In the first place, the basic resources available for the instructional activities of a university would be divided into two *unequal* portions. The larger one would be allocated, in the usual way, by the chief academic officers to the deans of the colleges and schools, and by them in turn to the academic departments for the traditional disciplinary courses and programs. This *first stream* of resources would constitute a substantial portion of the total available resources—perhaps as much as 75 or 80 percent—but it would not be quite enough to provide colleges and departments what they need for their traditional functions. For example, in an arts and science college with 180 fulltime equivalent faculty positions, only 150 might be provided for in this fashion. The other 30 would constitute a *second stream* of resources, to be made available to the college only for interdepartmental and intercollegiate instructional activities. In an institution in which the average teaching load consists of six courses per year, this would mean that on the average each faculty member would teach one course per year within a nondepartmental context. Of course, the average would vary from department to department and from individual to individual. The numbers, as well, are somewhat arbitrary. The important thing is to put enough resources into the second stream so as to make the "first stream" by itself not quite adequate to meet departmental needs. In this way department chairpersons will have a substantial incentive to engage in interdepartmental activities. Furthermore, resources in that second stream would be allocated for only as long as the nondepartmental activities continued and were deemed pertinent and desirable.

Such a second stream in fact already exists in most universities. Most provosts or academic vice-presidents, and in turn most deans, have some discretionary funds and some nonallocated positions with which they can encourage and support nondepartmental activities. But the existing second stream is usually only a trickle as compared with the flow of resources in the first stream, and furthermore it is commonly allocated on an ad hoc basis. The magnitude and visibility of the second stream need to be enhanced in order to signal, internally as well as externally, the growing importance of interdisciplinary, nondepartmental programs and to stimulate their growth by gradually augmenting the fraction of funds in the second stream. The provost or chief academic officer of the university would have principal responsibility for the allocation of the second-stream resources as the individual who takes an overview of the entire academic enterprise of the institution and who can best allocate resources among competing programs and projects.

A second stream of funding is a necessary but not sufficient condition to redirect the resources and energies of our universities to meet the emerging needs of society. There must also be a second stream for *personnel actions* to link the program committees, centers, institutes, and other units involved in interdisciplinary and interdepartmental activities with the central academic administration of a campus. Each unit would function like an academic department in evaluating the contributions of a faculty member and in initiating recommendations for salary adjustments, reappointments, promotions, and tenure on the basis of the pertinent portion of the faculty member's work. These recommendations would further peer review by a second-stream personnel committee. On a relatively small campus there might be one such committee for all multidisciplinary activities, while large campuses with a wide variety of nondepartmental units might require several. For activities spanning a number of disciplines within one college, the traditional collegiate personnel committee would function as the reviewing body.

The recommendations put forth in the second stream would be forwarded for central review and action at the same time as evaluations and recommendations regarding the discipline- and department-based activities of the faculty member. The two flows would merge at the level of the chief academic officer—provost, dean of faculty, or academic vice-president—who would have the responsibility to reconcile the two, aided by the advice of the usual campuswide committee.

Such a two-stream system of peer review and faculty reward is essential if multidisciplinary, nondepartmental activities are to gain the necessary professional legitimation. Evaluation by peers is one of the central characteristics of the academic profession. Nondiscipline-based faculty activity has been severely handicapped by the absence of an appropriate evaluation mechanism. Thus, such activity has either been ignored or viewed as a kind of civic good deed, not to be taken too seriously. Setting up a second stream for personnel actions as a supplement would remedy this without replacing the traditional, discipline-based system. Many past proposals have suggested a teaching track for personnel recommendations as an alternative to a research-based track (see, for example, Locke, Fitzpatrick, and White, 1983), with the implication that a faculty member is primarily involved either in teaching or in research. The two streams suggested here, by contrast, envision every faculty member as being involved in both departmental and nondepartmental teaching and professional activities. Every faculty member would continue to be firmly based in his or her discipline and would be evaluated in part for pertinent teaching and scholarly work. In addition, many faculty members would also participate in one or more multidisciplinary units and have their work evaluated by their peers in those groups.

Challenges and Benefits

The organizational and procedural details of a "two-stream" system are likely to vary widely from university to university, depending on local circumstances. In any form it would have a great advantage over the present, purely department-based procedure by giving a substantial amount of visibility, leverage, and credibility to the many new missions of universities without diminishing the importance of traditional objectives. There exists, however, an obvious disadvantage: the inevitable increase in complexity of a "two-stream" organization as compared to the traditional, one-dimensional, discipline-based structure. Recent history indicates how much of a hurdle such an increase creates. During the sixties, the State University of New York at Buffalo, the University of California at Santa Cruz, and Rutgers University each in its own way attempted to balance the dominance of disciplinary departments with a crosscutting collegiate structure. In each of these institutions, some or all of the faculty were members both of a department and of a college. Resource allocation, curriculum development, and personnel decisions required varying degrees of cooperation and conflict resolution between college dean and departmental chairs.

Obviously, these structures created administrative difficulties not found in the one-dimensional departmental organization of the traditional university, and they were much resented not only by discipline-oriented faculty members but also by many middle-level nonacademic administrators who were not involved in discussions of educational policy and therefore saw only the problems and not the possible advantages of the complex organization. By the end of the seventies, the colleges at Buffalo had all but disappeared, and those at Rutgers and Santa Cruz had essentially lost whatever autonomy they had had with regard to budget, faculty appointments, and program development. The scrapping of these three organizational innovations attests to the difficulty of maintaining a relatively complex structure if the reasons for its existence are not understood by members of the university administration and are not consonant with the "emerging and reconsolidated values of the central faculty" (Clark, 1983, pp. 224-225).

Yet the current situation and current needs differ in several important ways from the conditions and motivations that triggered changes in the sixties. At that time great emphasis was placed on the dichotomy between teaching and research. As a result, most faculty members perceived the principal objectives of crosscutting organizational components at universities like Buffalo, Rutgers, and Santa Cruz to be the improvement of undergraduate education. This placed the essentially "local" priorities of the institution into direct opposition and confrontation with the "cosmopolitan," discipline-based values of the faculty (Gouldner, 1957). Furthermore, resources were still plentiful and pressures for adaptation few and weak.

By contrast, most of the new missions that universities are presently called upon to respond to are much more closely related to the faculty's professional interests. They may not be discipline based, but they involve both advanced instruction and a variety of professional activities that overlap at least in part with "cosmopolitan" priorities. Thus they tend to expand and modify but not to oppose intrinsic faculty values. At issue now are activities such as applied research and technical assistance, professional education, opportunities for interaction with the workplace, and relationships with practitioners. These matters may not lie at the core of faculty concerns and priorities, but one can hope that they lie sufficiently close to those concerns and priorities to diminish faculty opposition to organizational adaptations.

Furthermore, there is much evidence of faculty dissatisfaction with the status quo (Bess, 1982; Locke, Fitzpatrick, and White, 1983; Clark, 1985; Bowen and Schuster, 1986). Thus one might expect that a substantial portion of university faculties would enjoy greater involvement in interdepartmental, multidisciplinary activities and might support appropriate organizational changes. In fact, the potential attractiveness of problem-oriented, external professional activities to university faculty members is one of the key premises on which the recommendations of this book are based. We believe that especially in universities in which faculty members do not feel themselves to be at the cutting edge of basic research, the new opportunities for stimulating and productive scholarship will become a source of personal satisfaction. We would expect that with appropriate logistical and organizational support by their institutions, and with the modifications of the reward system to be discussed in Chapter Ten, faculty will come to view professional activity and professional involvement not as an additional burden or as a civic duty, but rather as enriching and enjoyable work. Furthermore, they will derive new satisfaction from their teaching because they will experience reciprocal relationships and reinforcement between their applied professional activities and their classroom activities. The next chapters will describe the need for a qualitatively as well as quantitatively different approach to the function of practical experience in both the arts and sciences and career-oriented curricula.

✂ 4 ✂

Educating for Competence
in Work and Life

Education at its best has always fostered a sense that knowledge in itself is a source of enjoyment and satisfaction. Such an outcome remains highly desirable and indeed necessary, but it is not sufficient in today's world. If individuals are to function effectively as citizens, as members of a social group, and in their occupations, they must be able to cope with complex realities and rapid change, to tolerate and deal with considerable uncertainty and ambiguity, to make sense of a flood of disjointed and often contradictory data, to assess risks, and at times to choose among competing humane and ethical values. The real world is messy. Political rhetoric to the contrary, there are few situations and problems that lend themselves either to a clear definition, to an unequivocal identification of the "good guys" and the "bad guys," or to a straightforward and unequivocal solution.

"Perhaps no word has been used more frequently in recent years with less precision than *competence*" (Grant and others, 1979, p. 2). In this book we are using the term in its very broadest sense. Competence to us is the ability to function effectively in complex and ambiguous situations, to have a sense

56

of being in charge, to be—at least to some extent—master of one's fate, not a helpless and passive victim of external forces. We see competence as an overarching goal for all education. It can be achieved by many pedagogical approaches, including but not limited to the particular educational methodology known as *competency based.*

We believe that education aimed at the achievement and maintenance of competence constitutes the essence of true liberal education. It reflects Whitehead's view that all higher education is "the acquisition of the art of the utilization of knowledge" (1949, p. 16) and that its whole aim is the production of "active wisdom" (p. 48). It closely resembles what Gamson calls *liberating education,* defined as having three central aspects: (1) leading students to broad critical awareness, (2) helping them to apply what they learn to everyday life, and (3) increasing their sense of power (Gamson and Associates, 1984).

Several recent commentaries on the state of undergraduate education make consistent suggestions. The report of the Study Group on the Conditions of Excellence in American Higher Education (1984) calls for "curricular content directly addressed to the development of capacities of analysis, problem solving, communication, and synthesis" (p. 43). Since then, Newman (1985) has urged that education foster "a sense of civic responsibility." He points out that education is increasingly important because contemporary realities have enhanced the importance of informed civic participation and of applying critical thinking to complex political and social issues. These statements, like Whitehead's and Gamson's, view the purposes of general and liberal education as basically utilitarian and instrumental. They suggest that in the arts and sciences, as much as in explicitly career-oriented programs, the overarching goal is for individuals to become effective and competent in all their activities. In the United Kingdom, one of the leading advocates of change in the universities has similarly called for "Education for Capability" (Ashworth, 1982, 1986).

To make this kind of effectiveness the principal goal of liberal education is not at all to exclude other purposes (see, for example, Gaff, 1983, for an excellent summary of these other purposes). In fact, competence automatically subsumes most other stated objectives. The development of critical thinking, for example, is clearly essential to the acquisition of competence. To cope with a complex and multifaceted environment requires the acquisition of a variety of intellectual skills. One must be able to think and write clearly and effectively. In an age dominated by science and technology, one must also possess a degree of analytical skill as well as what has come to be known as scientific literacy. But competence also requires an awareness of the limitations of quantitative analysis and a sensitivity to the role of values and of moral and esthetic considerations. Competence on the job and competence as a member of society both involve risk assessment and risk taking, as well as the ability to strike a balance between competing values. They require that the emphasis be shifted from answering questions to deciding which are the right questions to ask. Both of these kinds of competence need to assume "responsibility for the affective as well as the cognitive, for process as well as content, for interactive and other workplace skills" (Hahn and Mohrman, 1985, p. 11).

Competence to deal with one's social, political, and economic environment is also much enhanced by a knowledge of history and a sense of one's cultural heritage. Competence requires, as well, an understanding of the moral and ethical principles that allow one to make value judgments. Such elements are considered by many educators to be "an essential core of knowledge that should be taught" (Gaff, 1983, p. 4). Thus these objectives of general education also have an important place in any program that wants to teach participants to cope effectively with present and future circumstances. But the inclusion of pertinent curricular components should be seen as means to a greater end: the past is used to illuminate the present and to provide clues to the future; different cultures are compared to gain a better understanding of the values of others; the study of ethics is applied to the many dilemmas one faces in real situations. The study of essentialist subjects should contribute to the students' ability to utilize knowledge in ways that enhance their ability to cope with the world in which they will live and be active.

Role of Experience in the Arts and Sciences

The best way of making the connection between that world and education is by the appropriate use of practical experiences as part of arts and science curricula. In these programs —especially those in the social sciences and the humanities— internships and other real or simulated practical components should assume a more important and central function than has been the case to date. In liberal arts as in career-oriented curricula, experience needs to become a primary learning tool, a way of providing a broader context for theory and illuminating its pertinence, its limitations, and its relationship to other fields.

The necessary conditions for this are quite similar to those that pertain to career education. In the first place, experiential activities must begin early in the curriculum so as to provide ample opportunity for subsequent reflection and analysis and thus facilitate a better understanding of theory. Classroom instruction that follows such activities should use them as starting points and build on them as a foundation for the development of general principles and methodologies. That is tantamount to a very basic shift in the prevailing pedagogical approach in higher education, which is a strongly deductive one. The most common way of presenting a subject is to begin with statements of theory and basic principles and then to apply these to a variety of situations. The sequence reflects a view that learning precedes doing. This approach needs to be reversed if practical experience is indeed to become a basic source of learning rather than being merely an illustration and application of theoretical principles. Instruction should become more inductive, reasoning from the particular to the general and using the singular experience to suggest broader principles.

The integration of real as well as simulated experiences into the arts and science curriculum can also contribute substantially to enhancing student involvement in the learning process. Such involvement is viewed by many current critics as essential to effective education, yet it is noticeably absent in most of our colleges and universities. Astin emphatically states that "students learn by becoming involved" and devotes much of his recent book to this subject (1985, p. 133). Newman also urges

that students become more actively involved in their own learning (1985). The previously cited report of the Study Group on
the Conditions of Excellence in American Higher Education
(1984) identifies student involvement as the first of three "conditions of excellence." The report lists a number of means to
achieve such involvement, including student participation in faculty projects, internships and carefully monitored experiential
learning, simulations, and use of practitioners on the faculty.
Here, then, is a further set of reasons to link theory and practice
and to incorporate into the curriculum substantial opportunities
to learn from hands-on experience.

Chapter Six will describe the trend toward increasingly
intermittent attendance by students of traditional college age
and will discuss the implications of the fact that more and more
adults are returning to higher education after years of practical
experience. For those enrolled in career-oriented curricula, the
prior activities may or may not have a direct relationship to
their future occupation. But for those enrolled in arts and science majors, *all* previous experience must be considered ger-
mane. It is therefore very important that arts and science courses
be taught in ways that help these individuals reflect on their
prior experience and help them generalize from the particular.

Of course the faculty can accomplish this only to the extent to which they themselves are familiar with the relationship
and the applications of their discipline to external problems and
issues. Thus, the involvement of faculty members in a variety of
applied scholarly activities can reinforce their ability to relate
classroom instruction to external issues and to make constructive use of practical experiences in the curriculum.

Science and Technology in Liberal Education

The importance of using practical components and an inductive approach to teaching is illustrated by some of the recent
developments incorporating science and technology in liberal
education. Individuals in their capacities as legislators, managers, editorial writers, and voters are confronted with political,
social, economic, and ethical choices and decisions that are in-

fluenced by technological and scientific factors. To be liberally educated, we believe, means to have acquired a reasonable degree of effectiveness and competence in making intelligent and informed judgments. What skills, knowledge, and understanding of science and technology are needed to this end, and how should these be incorporated into liberal education?

Until fairly recently, the widespread call for scientific literacy was usually translated into a distribution requirement intended to ensure that all undergraduate students take one or more introductory science courses. The student would become familiar with basic scientific concepts and also learn "how a scientist thinks." Some enthusiastic advocates viewed an understanding of the second law of thermodynamics as being of equal importance to having read Shakespeare. Computer literacy, similarly, was to be acquired by a course in how a computer works or by a course in computer programming.

Such an emphasis on the acquisition of knowledge rather than on the ability to use it would be questionable even if one could be reasonably certain that the knowledge was, indeed, acquired. But basic scientific concepts are very difficult to teach—much more so than is imagined by most scientists. A simple but illuminating experiment was recently carried out at the University of Chicago. A number of nonscience professors were invited to be "students" during two days of intensive lecture and discussion sessions provided by two members of the physics department considered to be master teachers. It was an ideal setting, one would imagine, in which to learn some basic concepts of physics without all the usual barriers: "youth, lack of confidence, unsophistication, inability to concentrate—except for the one barrier, newness to the field" (Tobias, 1986, p. 36).

Yet the outcome was as disappointing as it was enlightening. Tobias quotes one faculty member who participated: "I was surprised by . . . how very interesting I found what I was able to understand and . . . by how quickly when I failed to understand *immediately* my usual feelings of mind-lock, frustration, panic, and helplessness surfaced. . . . I lacked any framework of prior knowledge, experience, or intuition that could have helped me order the information I was receiving. . . . I

could not tell whether I understood or not. Nothing 'cohered' "
(Tobias, 1986, pp. 38–39). This was the reaction of a scholar,
someone who was mature, experienced, and self-confident. How
then does the average undergraduate nonscience major really
feel after taking the usual introductory science course in order
to satisfy a distribution requirement?

It would thus appear that exposure to basic science
courses may not be the best way to increase the competence of
individuals to cope—as lay persons—with science- and technol-
ogy-related questions. Even if such courses really led to the
acquisition of knowledge, there is just too much to know: "Scientists and engineers like to argue that I should know all sorts
of things they consider basic to their fields. But their list of
basics looks to me like a lifetime assignment. I have learned to
respect my microwave oven without knowing beans about
radioactivity" (Edgerton, 1986, p. 5). Instead, there should be
courses that provide students "with the feeling of being in control" and giving them "a toehold of self-confidence about their
ability to understand and master things technological" (p. 5).
Edgerton's objectives have elsewhere been described as giving
people "the sense that they had a say in their own lives" (Riesman, 1979, p. 33) and providing them with "the resources,
skills, and personal qualities necessary to control [their] own
fate" (Gamson, 1984, pp. 67–68).

An essential element in bringing about this kind of empowerment is to make students aware of the impact and consequences of science and technology: "The citizen who takes at
face value the 'knowledge for its own sake' metaphor is doubly
disenfranchised. . . . Unless it becomes clear . . . that the purposes of science . . . are commercial, strategic, and bureaucratic,
there can be no democratically involved populace. . . . Scientific
literacy . . . encompasses an understanding of the nonscientific
purposes of science" (Prewitt, 1983, p. 58).

Fortunately, a promising approach to the development of
a reasonable degree of lay competence in technical areas has begun to emerge in recent years. A growing number of colleges
and universities are introducing courses that concentrate on
technology rather than on science and stress the utilization of

scientific findings as well as assessment of their impact. Students are involved in actual hands-on projects—real or simulated —such as an assessment of the "turn right on red" traffic regulation. From such an exercise they learn how to estimate orders of magnitude, to judge the pertinence of a variety of components, and to appreciate the interconnected economic and sociological implications of any technological decision. The courses emphasize *technology assessment* and focus on helping students to understand "technology's characteristics, capabilities, and limitations" and to appreciate that in "most socio-technological problems, there is no clearly correct answer, but there are bases from which better opinions can be formed" (Truxal, 1986, pp. 12, 16).

We consider such courses to be models for truly liberal education. In the first place, they begin and end with practice. They use real or simulated cases as primary learning experiences from which generic approaches and principles can be induced and stress as outcomes the ability to apply these to complex issues in the students' everyday experiences. Factual knowledge and methodological skills are introduced when and to the extent to which they are needed. Furthermore, such courses are inherently multidisciplinary and emphasize the reciprocal relationships and connections between a variety of subjects. Most importantly, these courses are very explicitly designed and taught as a way of fostering what Edgerton (1986) and Prewitt (1983) call a "street-smart" kind of savviness rather than theoretical knowledge for its own sake. In short, these courses develop *competence*.

Liberal Education as a Capstone

The type of course in technology assessment described in the previous section is likely to be most effective toward the end rather than at the beginning of the undergraduate curriculum. It should help students pull together the many separate pieces of disciplinary knowledge acquired previously. Throughout this chapter, we have stressed our conviction that competence to deal with complex situations is an essential outcome of liberal education. Acquiring such competence is inherently a synthesizing, multidisciplinary activity, bringing together the insights and methodologies of several pertinent disciplines. Whether liberal education is seen as helping professionals understand the context in which they function in their occupation or enabling individuals to exercise their civic responsibilities in a knowledgeable and rational fashion, the central need is to be able to bring a variety of perspectives to bear on complex issues.

To be liberally educated, therefore, is not just to have satisfied some distribution requirements by taking a few courses in a variety of fields. It is to have acquired, in Whitehead's words, "the art of the utilization" of different disciplines and fields; it is to be able to bridge the gap between theory and practice in one's field of concentration; and it is to be able to apply what has been learned about ethics, sociology, history, and economics to the complex problems and issues faced on the job and as citizens.

Thus, we believe that the pertinent courses should be taken toward the end rather than at the beginning of the undergraduate curriculum as a synthesizing capstone rather than as a foundation for specialization. Here we distinguish sharply between liberal education and such essential skills as literacy and numeracy, the ability to read and to express oneself clearly. The latter must be acquired as early as possible because such basic skills constitute a necessary means toward a broader end. But liberal education is concerned with relationships and complexity, with exercising judgment and dealing with conflicting values. It is best achieved in the later rather than the earlier stages of an individual's development.

The need to shift the curricular components providing liberal education toward the later stages of a degree program is heightened by the trend toward intermittent attendance as well as the growing number of adults returning to higher education. Individuals who have moved in and out of the university classroom, who have spread their degree programs over many years, or who have attended several institutions need even more help than the traditional student in putting the pieces together and in achieving some measure of coherence and synthesis in what they have learned. We return to this in Chapter Six.

What we have described amounts to the need to develop in all higher education a real synthesis between breadth and depth. Many of the current statements that imply that career education cannot be liberal because the first is narrow and the second broad would do well to remember a pertinent statement by the former president of Columbia University: "The issue . . . is not the specious one of 'breadth' versus 'depth,' which implies a nonsensical choice between superficiality and competence. The central problem is rather relevant breadth versus a limited and dangerously irresponsible competence" (Truman, 1968, p. ix).

Holding on to that "specious" distinction has resulted in a nearly universal pattern for the undergraduate curriculum that can be described as a pyramid: proceeding from a broad base to an increasingly narrow and specialized point. By and large, "breadth" and "general education" are relegated to the first two years. When upperclassmen seek courses outside their major, either out of curiosity or in order belatedly to fulfill distribution requirements for graduation, they often have no other choice than to take freshman- and sophomore-level introductory and survey courses.

Instead, we advocate that more breadth be provided after, not before, students have begun to specialize and/or after they have spent some years in the workplace. That would seem to be the most effective way of encouraging reflection on prior experiences and on the functions and limitations of the area of concentration. It would, we think, provide the "relevant breadth" suggested by Truman. In essence, we are advocating a move toward a more inclusive definition of concentration, placing the area of specialization into a broader context and developing what elsewhere has been called an "extended major" (Lynton, 1982) in which relevant breadth illuminates necessary depth.

The Extended Major

Extended majors can be fashioned in many different ways, and we certainly do not intend to provide a blueprint for doing so. But some general features can be described. In essence, an extended major as we envision it contains three components in addition to the basic skills:

1. The progressive acquisition, throughout the course of study, of reasonable expertise in the area of concentration, with more emphasis than in the past on utilizing practical experiences in order to induce generalizations
2. As an integral part of the curriculum, at least one substantial clinical experience at a sufficiently early stage to allow subsequent reflection, analysis, and utilization in course work
3. Contextual and integrative capstone courses during the final years

We can illustrate in very general terms the appropriate types of practical experiences and capstone courses for several broad categories of majors. In the social sciences, there exists a wide variety of possible internships and clinical periods closely related to areas of concentration, such as, for example, working with a legislator or government official for majors in political science or assisting in a human service agency for majors in sociology and psychology. Capstone courses would use cognate disciplines so as to provide different perspectives on topics such as the economics of human service delivery systems, the diverging philosophical approaches of scholars like Rawls and Nozick to societal responsibilities, and the historical development of certain categories of social institutions.

Majors in the *physical and life sciences* should acquire both a sense of how their discipline applies to a variety of practical problems and what Prewitt (1983) calls an essential element of scientific literacy, that is, an understanding of the nonscientific purposes of science. An appropriate experiential component might well consist of asking students to undertake intensive laboratory work toward a specific utilitarian goal, such as, for example, obtaining a certain degree of precision in some category of measurement. They would themselves have to decide on ways of achieving this outcome and design experiments to verify their ideas. Capstone courses would center on technology assessment, the history and philosophy of science and technology, and economic and other issues in science policy, as well as on the ethical and moral aspects of scientific development.

Philosophy curricula should reduce their emphasis on methodology and focus more on asking questions about fundamental activities and practices in our daily lives, in our jobs, and as citizens. Programs in philosophy should culminate in a number of seminars that involve faculty and students, as well as practitioners in other fields. Medical students and faculty and practicing physicians would be involved in exploring the complex ethical issues facing physicians today; those in education would join in discussing such fundamental questions as "for whose benefit are the young educated; for themselves, their families, the polity, future generations?" Seminars with colleagues from human services might ask, "Who are the ultimate clients of such services" (Rorty, forthcoming).

This sketchy outline of possible extended majors clearly indicates an essential condition for setting up such majors—active cooperation across departmental and collegiate boundaries within a university. There is no way to bring about a mutually reinforcing relationship between breadth and depth under the arrangements currently prevailing in just about every university. The course sequence and content of the concentration, which furnish the depth, are viewed as purely departmental responsibilities, limited only by distribution and other general requirements set at the collegiate or campus level. Breadth, as represented by these requirements, is usually specified with little or no regard to the details of specific concentrations, except for the usual debate about how many credits may be required for the major. This dominance of the department is particularly pronounced in specifying upper-division and graduate programs, both of which are viewed as the exclusive domain of the particular department or discipline.

That approach maintains a dysfunctional separation between breadth and depth, which can be overcome only if the entire curriculum, but particularly at the upper-division and graduate level, is viewed in its totality and in as unified a way as possible. Groups representing both the core discipline as well as other subjects must together discuss how the concentration can best be supplemented and reinforced by contextual courses in order to achieve Truman's "relevant breadth." The necessary cross-departmental and cross-collegiate cooperation will reinforce the need for the second-stream organizational structure discussed in Chapter Three. And, as we will note in the next chapter, that structure needs to cut across both the arts and sciences as well as the professional units of a university.

5

Developing Competence Through Career and Professional Programs

If competence as defined in the previous chapter is an appropriate goal for education in the arts and sciences, it is an even more crucial outcome in professional and other career-oriented subjects. These fields have come to dominate undergraduate education—as, for a long time, they have already dominated at the postbaccalaureate level. Thus, 65 percent of all baccalaureate degrees and 79 percent of all master's degrees awarded in the academic year 1983–84 were in professional and other career-oriented majors. The preponderance of vocational majors is as indicative of the changing role and functions of contemporary universities as are the demands for a broader definition of scholarly and professional activities discussed in Chapter One. That the majority of students major in areas other than the traditional liberal arts is, whether we like it or not, one of the new realities resulting from the astonishing growth that has taken place in higher education since the Second World War. Chapter One noted the relationship between the large number of existing universities and the concomitant implications of having a large system of universities for the *scholarly* activities of these institutions. The *educational* mission of the university system is

69

also strongly affected by its size. About six million students now attend universities, or approximately 20 percent of the college age cohort. Such a participation rate suggests that the dominant motive for going to a university has become preparation for a career, particularly at a time when structural unemployment in the United States has risen to 7 percent from the 3 percent level at which it stood for so long. Unemployment levels for young people are considerably higher—though this may soon improve somewhat for demographic reasons—and the recent recession is still a vivid memory. Under these conditions it is inevitable that the majority of university students will come to view their education as preparation for a career. In a 1984 Carnegie Foundation survey of students, occupational training and skills were identified by the largest percentage of respondents (75.2 percent) as the most important objective of going to college (Carnegie Foundation for the Advancement of Teaching, 1986). A poll of freshmen entering higher education in the fall of 1985 indicated that 71.8 percent, up from 55.8 percent in 1973, agree that "the chief benefit of a college education is that it increases one's earning power" (ACE/UCLA, 1986, p. 1).

Such career orientation is further reinforced by the fact that during the past decades, a growing number of occupations became professionalized. An appropriate college degree containing a certain amount of specialized knowledge is expected for more and more jobs. Furthermore, the relationship between education and the economy, as well as the growing value of "human capital" and of "working smart," has been emphasized in a score of books, articles, and newspaper accounts (Carnevale, 1983; Lynton, 1984). If so many others make the connection between study and work, why should one expect students attending a college or university to pursue knowledge for its own sake?

We do not share the frequently expressed regret over these pervasive qualitative changes in higher education. Many critiques of "excessive vocationalism" are flawed by a strong undercurrent of nostalgia, a desire to turn the clock back to a past that seems rosier in retrospect than it ever really was. Actually, higher education has always been viewed from the outside as preparation for a career. In 1968, Jencks and Riesman addressed themselves to the then frequent complaint that "the nation's colleges have been corrupted by vocationalism." They dismissed the belief that "in the good old days . . . colleges were pure and undefiled seats of learning [where] students came to get a liberal education." They pointed out that "like other pastoral idylls, this myth serves all sorts of polemical purposes, good and bad. But it is a myth nevertheless. Young men of college age worried about their future careers in the colonial era just as they do today, and this affected . . . the kind of things they did once they arrived [in college] " (1968, p. 199).

Much of the current criticism of alleged vocationalism is also caused by an artificial and unnecessary dichotomy between career orientation and liberal education (Cheit, 1975; Riesman, 1981; Jones, 1986). There is no a priori reason to view a preponderance of majors in professional areas as signaling the demise of all the cherished values associated with a liberal education. To do so is to confuse a liberal education with majoring in one of the liberal arts subjects. Those two are quite distinct. Majoring in history, in physics, or in economics certainly does not guarantee a liberal education. Many participants in the educational debates of the 1980s tend to forget the widespread criticism expressed during the 1960s of the professionalization of undergraduate programs in the so-called liberal arts. Jencks and Riesman aptly pointed out then that almost all the undergraduate units of our universities, as well as many freestanding liberal arts colleges, had become "university colleges . . . whose primary purpose is to prepare students for graduate work of some kind—primarily in the arts and sciences" (1968, p. 24). As part of this process, undergraduate curricula in the arts and science disciplines turned increasingly into preprofessional preparation, loaded with more and more specialized courses in methodology, which are as narrowly vocational for one kind of career as a course in accounting is for another.

The professionalization of the curriculum in the arts and sciences reflects the extent to which, in many disciplines, methodology has become an end in itself. As was pointed out recently in a collection of essays on "The Institution of Philosophy,"

"We [philosophers] are good at discussing whether answers to the question 'How should one/we/I live?' are objective, or whether they can be rationally justified. But we are not good at actually examining the details of competing substantive answers to that question, tending as we do to move straightway to methodological issues. So quickly do we make that move that we rarely even ask questions about the most basic and fundamental features that shape our lives" (Rorty, forthcoming).

In short, it is important to distinguish between the label attached to a curriculum, on the one hand, and its content, on the other. An excessive focus on methodology is as narrowly vocational when it occurs in philosophy, history, or literature as it would be in management, engineering, and nursing. But courses in philosophy, history, or literature that do "ask questions about the most basic and fundamental features that shape our lives" are as appropriate and indeed as necessary in career-oriented curricula as they are in liberal arts majors. The real challenge is to make sure that all curricula in higher education—including those in the arts and sciences—combine as much as possible the objectives both of preparing for a career and of obtaining a liberal education. The competence that we view to be the common outcome of all higher education melds breadth and depth. It requires a depth of knowledge in some field of specialization, an understanding of that field's application to external realities, and an awareness of the complementary perspectives that are needed to illuminate the context in which the specialized expertise is applied. An excellent summary of the broad capabilities needed for management competence is provided by Johnston in a recent book (Johnston and Associates, 1986) that stresses the need to combine liberal and career education.

Current Criticism of Career-Oriented Education

A number of specific professions are currently looking for ways to improve preparation for practice. The similarity of diagnosed weaknesses in a wide variety of career-oriented fields is striking (see, for example, Stark, Lowther, and Hagerty, 1986). Critics see both undergraduate and graduate programs as having curricula that are too narrowly confined to technical skills, with too much of a gap between theory and practice, too much emphasis on purely cognitive and analytical material, too much abstract classroom work, and too little hands-on experience. Most of these comments echo earlier criticism. Turning again to Jencks and Riesman (1968), we find that they pointed out almost twenty years ago the low correlation between course grades and occupational success. They described at length how the affiliation of professional schools with universities has, over the years, tended to deemphasize the schools' occupational commitments and encouraged "a more academic and less practical view of what . . . students need to know" (Jencks and Riesman, 1968, p. 252; see also Riesman, 1979). They spoke of "the divergence between professional training and professional practice" and suggested that, just as undergraduate liberal arts units during the postwar years became "university colleges" whose curricula prepared students for graduate work in the disciplines, so also have professional schools focused more on "turning out men with skills appropriate to teachers [of the professional]," simply taking for granted that "these skills will also be appropriate to the practice [of the profession] " (Jencks and Riesman, 1968, p. 253). Changing the name of several engineering and business schools to colleges of "engineering science" and "management science" was a striking symptom of this strong trend toward more academic and abstract kinds of career-oriented curricula.

Schein and Kommers similarly commented on the narrowing and indeed the fragmentation of professional curricula. They stated that the professions had become so specialized that they were now "unresponsive to certain classes of social problems that require an interdisciplinary and interprofessional point of view.

"Professional education provides no training for those graduates who wish to work as members of and become managers of intra- and interprofessional project teams working on complex social problems.

"Professional education generally underutilizes the applied behavioral sciences, especially in helping professionals to

increase their self-insight, their ability to diagnose and manage client relationships and complex social problems, their ability to sort out the ethical and value issues inherent in their professional role, and their ability to continue to learn throughout
their career" (1972, p. 60).

The divergence between theory and practice and between
professional preparation and professional practice, the narrow
specialization, the excessive emphasis on technical skills and
cognitive factors, and the lack of breadth—all these criticisms
are once again being heard. Johnston and Associates (1986, pp.
215-217) provide an excellent bibliography for the current discussion about management education. These shortcomings of
career preparation have become more serious because of the
new demands and new dimensions of contemporary society.
The changes in the nature of knowledge, along with an ever
faster rate of obsolescence, have substantially intensified the
need for a more practice-oriented approach, with less emphasis
on accumulating facts and more emphasis on preparing students
to deal with external realities. Practitioners must be prepared to
handle the new and more difficult job requirements that exist
today in almost every occupation because of the rapid changes
and complexity of modern society.

Engineering provides a good example of the unprecedented
educational challenges posed by this complexity and by technological advances. The current demands on engineers clearly indicate the need to achieve a convergence of "vocational" and "liberal" education. Competent engineers need much more than
scientific and technical skills. They must become increasingly
familiar with the way in which science and technology operate
in society. They need to realize that the ramifications and implications of their decisions have far-reaching consequences, many
of which may be uncertain or even unpredictable. As technical experts they may be able to forecast with some degree of accuracy
the first-order implications of a particular course of action, but
that is not enough. Their analysis must also take into account
the second- and third-order consequences that affect individuals, the environment, and perhaps the political or economic
structure. But to do this is very difficult. In addition to being

only partially predictable, the second-order effects usually require choices among competing values and objectives. Prewitt speaks of the "bittersweet" principle of technological change: "to innovate technologically is not just to offer new social benefits; it is also to impose social costs" (1983, p. 61). Even small projects often undermine some social value, harm some social interest, penalize some groups. At a minimum, most new construction requires some dislocation; most new techniques take away some jobs. These and other such effects are the unintended and inevitable second-order consequences of the introduction of the products of technology into society. Competence as an engineer must include an awareness of this. Engineers should be educated to think about these matters and to develop a mind set that allows for a fusion of technical and other factors, including ethical considerations. It is not enough for engineering students to master *technical skills,* they need to develop *technical judgment* (Jerath, 1983).

The competent engineer must also cope with the ever accelerating obsolescence of technical and scientific knowledge. The changes that are taking place occur more and more at a basic conceptual level. Not only are new theories and paradigms constantly introduced but there are even, at times, discontinuous changes in technology. As a result, independent learning and on-the-job training, however important they may continue to be, are no longer sufficient to keep engineers and individuals in many other advanced professions up-to-date. Increasingly, ongoing competence for these occupations requires recurrent periods of formal instruction (Bruce and others, 1982; Lynton, 1983b). We will return to this topic in the next chapter.

For managers, as well, competence requires considerably more than mastery of an array of technical skills. For one thing, there is virtual unanimity regarding the importance of interpersonal and affective abilities (Lynton, 1984). It is also increasingly important that supervisors and managers acquire a better understanding of the context in which they function. Like engineers, they should learn to assess the second- and third-order effects of their decisions. The need for this is growing even at lower levels of the managerial hierarchy because of the current trend toward a "flatter," more decentralized organizational style in which there is more delegation of authority and more shared decision making. A survey conducted by the Conference Board reported widespread agreement among corporate leadership that managers at all levels require these competencies (Lusterman, 1981):

- An awareness that events in the business environment significantly affect company interests, and an alertness to particular threats and opportunities
- Sensitivity to how company decisions will affect, and be perceived by, others
- Attentiveness to the opinions, values, and interests of others
- An ability systematically to monitor and analyze the business environment and integrate the data developed into strategic planning processes

Another reality of contemporary society of particular relevance to the education of managers is the growing internationalization of commerce and industry. Obviously this suggests not only more emphasis on training in languages but, perhaps more importantly, on acquiring some understanding of and sensitivity to different cultures (Burn, 1986).

A further dimension of managerial competence derives from the changes in management style recently recommended by many authors (Hayes and Abernathy, 1980; Peters and Waterman, 1982; Reich, 1983; Piore and Sabel, 1984). All blame much of the decline of this country's international competitiveness on an adherence to the traditional, rigid principles of "scientific management." The modifications and remedies suggested by these authors differ in vocabulary and to some extent in substance. But throughout their writing there runs a common thread: the call for a management style that is more intuitive and more flexible, that tolerates ambiguity and accepts "messiness." Piore and Sabel speak of the need for "flexible specialization," and Reich advocates the substitution of what he calls a "flexible-system" model of production for the outdated method of standardized mass production. He states that "flexible systems can adapt quickly only if information is widely shared within them. There is no hierarchy of problem solving, solutions may come from anyone, anywhere. In flexible-system enterprises, nearly everyone in the production process is responsible for recognizing problems and finding solutions" (1983, p. 135). Hayes and Abernathy stress the need for "insight into the subtleties and complexities of strategic decisions" (1980, p. 70), and Peters and Waterman (1982) call for the ability to manage ambiguity and paradox.

It is quite evident that the traditional heavy emphasis in management programs on quantitative analysis and cognitive skills is no longer adequate. Ackoff, one of the founders of operations research, recently wrote that "the future of operations research is past" and that "managers are not confronted with problems that are independent of each other, but with dynamic situations that consist of complex systems of changing problems that interact with each other. I call such situations *messes*" (1979, p. 90). He continued, "Managers do not solve problems: they manage messes" (p. 100). A poll of 600 senior corporate executives conducted for a national magazine indicated that 86 percent agreed with the statement: "Business schools teach students a lot about management theory but not much about what it takes to run a company" (Nussbaum and Beam, 1986, p. 64).

A New Conception of Practice

It is clear, then, that the new demands on the practitioner require educational changes that go beyond a mere reshuffling of the curriculum. Broadening programs by including a larger number of pertinent liberal arts subjects and by adding problem-centered, multidisciplinary courses will be necessary, but it will not be sufficient. To help students acquire the kind of judgment that is required for good practice, along with the ability to take into account higher-order implications and to deal with the resulting complexity and ambiguity, calls for a rethinking and revision of the basic approach to career-oriented education. In spite of wide use of clinical and other practical components, the pervasive emphasis today continues to be on *content* rather than on *process,* on the *acquisition* of a body of knowledge rather than on the ability to *use* it. That emphasis needs to change.

The current educational approach reflects the traditional view of professional practice as the systematic application of a set of standardized concepts and analytical methods to a recurrent problem in order to arrive at a unique solution. (Moore, 1970). This positivist view has become the hallmark of the professions. During the past decades, more and more occupations have been striving to achieve professional status by adopting this approach. It sets up a hierarchy of knowledge and a corresponding hierarchy of activity. Schein and Kommers (1972) have described the three components of professional knowledge as follows:

1.   An underlying basic science or discipline component that provides the fundamental principles of the practice
2.   An applied science or engineering component that furnishes many of the diagnostic and problem-solving procedures
3.   A skills component that consists of acquiring the ability to utilize the basic and applied knowledge in actual practice

The application of (1) yields (2), and in turn that leads to (3). Schön has further pointed out that "the order of application is also an order of derivation and dependence. Applied science is said to 'rest on' the foundation of basic science. And the more basic and general the knowledge, the higher the status of its producer" (1983, p. 24).

This hierarchy of status and values is equivalent to the prevailing but invalid assumption discussed in Chapter One that basic research is necessarily the precondition for technological innovation and development (Shapley and Roy, 1985). The traditional view of professional practice is reflected in the basic structure of current career-oriented programs. Even in fields that can advance only a marginal claim to professional status, the curriculum usually begins with what are viewed as the pertinent basic sciences, followed by a number of applied science and technology courses. The curriculum ends with clinical experiences intended to provide opportunities to develop skills of application (Schein and Kommers, 1972). The approach throughout is that *learning precedes doing* and that *practice is the application of theory*. This is the model that, particularly since the Second World War, has become normative for almost all career education.

There are good reasons to believe that this traditional, positivist approach is no longer adequate. When Ackoff speaks of "managing messes," he is describing situations for which no technique provides a single and direct path to a unique solution. In most cases there are likely to be several alternatives, each with its combination of advantages and disadvantages. Applying "technical judgment" or "managerial judgment" to such situations is a rather different process from the traditional application of a predetermined paradigm. Furthermore, the majority of situations faced daily in most occupations cannot be readily reduced to the application of standardized problem-solving methods. Thus, problem definition and clarification, rather than problem solving, emerge as the major task.

Schön believes that an effective practitioner approaches each problem "as a unique case. He does not act as though he has no relevant prior experience, on the contrary. But he attends to the peculiarities of the situation at hand. [He does not behave] as though he were looking for cues to a standard solution. Rather [he] seeks to discover the particular features of his problematic situation, and from their gradual discovery, designs an intervention" (1983, p. 129). The title *The Reflective Practitioner* describes the basic theme of Schön's book: Successful practitioners learn while doing. They engage in what Schön calls "reflection-in-action" as they interact with their client or with the situation they are facing. During this time, they continuously reflect on their activity and adjust each successive step on the basis of this reflection. It is, in essence, an ongoing feedback process of successive approximation, an exercise in "artistry" of which the architectural design process is an excellent example (Schön, 1983).

This radically different view of professional activity also suggests the need for a substantial change in career education. The crucial need is to use simulated as well as real experience in very different ways from what is currently done. Instead of being a matter of "practicing"—that is, of merely acquiring the skill to apply prior theoretical learning—the experiential components of the curriculum should become themselves *primary* learning devices. In a sequel to his earlier book, Schön (1986) addresses himself to the education of the "reflective practitioner" and discusses characteristics of the "reflective practicum." Learning ought to be related to and derived from doing, instead of preceding it. Greater emphasis should be placed on inductive reasoning and the power to generalize. Both the sequence and the hierarchy of the curricular components of career education must change, with the clinical and other experiential parts coming to occupy both a more pervasive and a more important place.

There is nothing new in experiential learning. It was the hallmark of the progressive education movement, reflecting the pedagogical ideas of John Dewey and others (for an excellent discussion, see Cremin, 1961). Abraham Flexner was a strong advocate of Dewey's ideas (Ludmerer, 1985), and in his famous report on medical education (Flexner, 1910) poured scorn on didactic instruction. Years later he expressed concern about the enormous amount of factual information a medical student was even then expected to master (Flexner, 1925). Today, even more is being crammed into medical curricula; and, in most of these, as in other health-related programs, clinical work is delayed until the later stages of the curriculum and continues to be an opportunity to apply prior theoretical knowledge rather than constituting a primary source of learning in itself. The case method used in many other career-oriented programs comes closer to being such a source, yet it only simulates experience and usually does so with considerable simplification. Some critics view its use in business training as too narow and too superficial for imparting complex management concepts (Nussbaum and Beam, 1986).

Relation of Teaching and Professional Activity

One of the principal traditional arguments for an emphasis on basic research in universities is its beneficial impact on both undergraduate and graduate instruction. If faculty are involved in research, their teaching will presumably reflect the state of the art in their disciplines. An analogous argument can be made within the context of the extended university's responsibilities. Increasing the emphasis on practice and using prior or concurrent periods of clinical experience as primary learning sources obviously require that the faculty itself be familiar with practice. But that is precisely what happens when faculty engage in applied research, technical assistance, and the other externally oriented professional activities that should become part of the extended tasks of universities. In turn, more emphasis on practice in the curriculum is likely to make faculty members more willing to engage in an extended range of scholarly activities and to increase their ability to do so.

In addition, a more applied orientation in the curriculum would require greater use of practitioners on a part- or full-time basis. The recent report entitled *Engineering Undergraduate Education* (National Research Council, 1986) recommends that engineering schools establish positions for "professors of professional practice" to be filled by practitioners, preferably on a full-time basis for a specific period of time. The dialogue and interaction between such individuals and traditional faculty members will not only enrich the curriculum in which they are jointly involved but will also enhance the ability of academically oriented professors to engage in various applied activities.

Student participation provides yet another close link between the new needs in instruction and the extended definition of professional involvement. As was mentioned at the end of Chapter Three, professional involvement is likely to offer substantial opportunities for undergraduate as well as graduate projects that can in turn strengthen the practice-oriented aspects of the curriculum.

Thus, there exists a strong reciprocal reinforcement between the extended definition of scholarship, on the one hand, and emerging instructional needs, on the other. It seems to us that it is precisely this two-way interaction that provides an inner logic and a substantial coherence to the model of the extended university. The necessary adaptations in each area relate to each other; each is made easier by the other.

Implications for Assessment

If simulated and real experiences are to become major sources of learning in career education instead of being merely the "practicing" of theory, if a principal goal of such education is to enhance the competence of individuals in the practice of their occupations, if *process* is to become as important as *content,* then the assessment of student progress and achievement should reflect these broadened objectives (Elman and Lynton, 1986). At this time most assessment in career education, as well as in the arts and sciences, is of the traditional kind: written examinations that test the students' grasp of basic principles and pertinent facts. Such paper-and-pencil exams tend to be used even in clinical courses. A typical example is the treatment of "negotiation" in the majority of business programs. These programs often include the topic as a separate course, usually with several opportunities for active student involvement in simulated negotiating sessions. In many institutions these are videotaped and provide a useful source of self-assessment. But when it comes to assigning a grade to the student for the course, most instructors rely on testing knowledge of textbook material. Much the same situation exists in the clinical components of other career programs, such as patient interviewing and diagnosis in social work and medical education, or moot court activity in legal education.

Traditional assessment of factual knowledge and analytical skills must remain an important part of career education. But there needs to be, as well, substantial assessment of experiential performance. It is not enough to test students' capabilities; we also need to assess them: "Testing can tell us how much and what kind of knowledge someone *has.* Assessment gives us a basis for inferring what that person can *do* with that knowledge" (Loacker, Cromwell, and O'Brien, 1986). Thus what is needed in career education—as in all other kinds of education— is to move away from a virtually exclusive emphasis on testing and to begin including a substantial amount of assessment.

Such a move might well be the cause rather than the effect of important changes in curricula. Modes of testing and assessment have always tended to define the objectives of educational programs and thereby to have great influence on content and on pedagogical approach. This is of particular importance in career-oriented education because of the existence of licensing requirements in many occupations. In many cases, the completion of an accredited degree program constitutes the requirement for eligibility. In others, state boards or similar bodies apply their own assessments, which are almost entirely content oriented. A shift in the eligibility requirements toward greater emphasis on experiential assessment—more assessment in the Loacker sense and less testing—would provide a major impetus toward substantial revisions in career-oriented education.

Competence and More

We want to end this chapter by returning to the point made at the beginning of the previous one: education should lead to the enjoyment of knowledge. A utilitarian or instrumental approach such as the one we are advocating here strikes some observers as starkly limited, neglecting the sheer joy of knowing. But that is not at all the case—quite the contrary. When Whitehead defined education as "the acquisition of the art of utilization of knowledge," he was not taking a narrowly pragmatic view. In his treatise on *The Aims of Education,* in which he discussed the role of professional schools within the university, he contended that "the justification for a university is that it preserves the connection between knowledge and the zest of life" (1949, p. 97).

Whitehead considered the inclusion of professional schools in academic institutions as entirely appropriate and consistent with the general educational functions of a university. Using business schools as an example, he went on to say, "We need not flinch from the assertion that the main function of such a school is to produce men with a greater zest for business. . . . In the modern complex social organism, the adventure of life cannot be disjoined from intellectual adventure" (1949, p. 98).

Writing nearly sixty years ago, Whitehead anticipated in almost every detail what current studies of education are rediscovering as elements essential to effective education. An "imaginative grasp" of the social, political, and economic context of one's job, an ability to deal with the complex human interactions that are part of almost every occupation, even "a sufficient conception of the role of applied science"—it is all there in Whitehead's definition of what constitutes a true "vocational" education. The necessity of technical skills is so obvious as to be taken for granted, but preparation for competence on the job—almost any job, and certainly those jobs for which a college education has come to be expected—must go much further. Whitehead makes it very clear that these additional and essential components of competence for a businessman are those that constitute a liberal education.

The essence of Whitehead's statement is that, ultimately, education is about intellectual growth and excitement, about the *enjoyment* as well as the *utilization* of knowledge. What better way of enriching the lives of individuals than to make them recognize their occupation as more than a way of making money, to make them interested in the history of their trade or profession, to make them view what they do in relation to society and as a contribution to society? Francis Bacon recognized this four centuries ago when he wrote in *The Advancement of Learning* that "it may be truly affirmed that no kind of men love business for itself but those that are learned . . . only learned men love business as an action according to nature, as agreeable to health of mind as exercise is to health of body, taking pleasure in the action itself" ([1605] 1955, p. 169).

The challenge to education is to make men's and women's occupations intellectually rewarding and exciting to them so that these occupations can indeed "hold or detain their mind[s]", as Bacon recommends. They must learn to recognize their jobs as being considerably more than the proficient exercise of technical skills. Extending and enriching the career-oriented curriculum can achieve this. But precisely the opposite is likely to happen if we continue to maintain a separation between general or liberal education, on the one hand, and career preparation, on the other. The result of that can only be to reduce an individual's occupation to a purely materialistic and mechanical activity. Frank Rhodes, president of Cornell University, stated the issue very clearly: "We must replace excessive vocational training with professional education. Professional education is broad and expansive and, in the spirit of liberal learning, sees skills as a means to a larger end. It embraces meaningful attention to liberal education, not as an add-on, but as a vital component of professional study. It is concerned not with the job, but with life, with the social goals a profession promotes and the ethical standards it demands. Vocational training, on the other hand, is narrow and restrictive, developing specific skills for routine tasks, sometimes very technical or specialized in nature. It involves knowledge for specific ends, raising no questions of larger significance; it is impervious to social context, oblivious to moral choice. Liberal learning is nurtured in professional education; it soon withers in the presence of vocational training" (1985, p. 80). Francis Bacon and Alfred North Whitehead would have agreed.

❧ 6 ❧

Adapting Programs
to New Students and
Attendance Patterns

❧❧❧❧❧❧❧❧❧❧❧❧❧❧❧❧

In Part One of this book we suggested that, in order to be responsive to current conditions and needs, universities should substantially expand the traditional definition of their scholarly role. The first two chapters in Part Two described how universities should also change the content and methodology of instruction. Now we turn to yet another fundamental development in the role and functions of universities, one that is in fact already well under way but that to date has not been recognized explicitly—namely, the changing pattern of student attendance.

Not so very long ago, the vast majority of university students enrolled on a full-time basis right after graduating from high school, continued without interruption toward their baccalaureate degree, and, if they went on to graduate and professional schools, did so immediately. Furthermore, formal higher education was usually completed before the start of an individual's career. A "front-loaded," full-time, continuous mode of attendance was the norm. Adults came to colleges and universities either for enrichment and self-improvement or because they had not had a prior opportunity to do so. In recent years, however, two changes have become evident. In the first place, younger students are now increasingly delaying and interrupting their studies (Lynton, 1986). Secondly, adult education has acquired a new dimension. A growing number of older individuals are turning to various sources of formal education in order to keep up with changes in the nature and the content of their jobs (Lynton, 1983b, 1983c).

In the sections that follow we will discuss these two trends separately. Both trends, however, are part of the same phenomenon: a change in the pattern of advanced study that constitutes a fundamental change in the characteristics of higher education. Instead of being full time and continuous, it is becoming spread out, recurrent, and increasingly part time. Instead of being "front loaded," with learning preceding doing and the knowledge required for a lifetime of work gathered prior to the start of a career, higher education is becoming continuous and lifelong, with learning and doing interspersed.

It is encouraging to note an essential convergence and internal consistency between the necessary adaptations to the new pattern of attendance and the previously suggested changes in content and pedagogy. Intermittent and recurrent involvement in formal learning both reinforces the need for and facilitates the implementation of the changes discussed in Chapters Four and Five. In the first place, it will be increasingly important to bring about a closer relationship between theory and practice if the attendance pattern results in more frequent alternation between work and study. Students who drop in and out of college, as well as older persons returning to update their knowledge and skills, will insist on that relationship, but at the same time such individuals will bring to the classroom their own experiences and thereby make it easier to bridge the gap. By the same token, even a minimum of work experience will make many younger students aware of what most adults already know: real-world situations are too complex to be soluble by technical expertise alone. Many faculty members who have taught experienced, older students have noted that they are more receptive than younger students to liberal education, to learning about context, and to obtaining a broad perspective.

The intermittent pattern is also likely both to require and to result in a more inductive approach to teaching. Persons with prior experience will want to learn from what they had been doing on the job. They will want to generalize from the specific and indeed will want to reflect on their prior actions in ways that resemble the process suggested by Schön and commented on in the previous chapter. Instruction will increasingly have to begin with a description and analysis of the participants' prior experience. Such an approach will help to accomplish yet another desirable goal: that is, it will involve students more actively in the learning process.

The greatest challenge created by the new pattern is to achieve reasonable coherence, continuity, and cumulation of learning. Without this, degree programs pursued intermittently will degenerate into a mere collecting of credits until the requisite number for a degree has been "bagged." Indeed that already happens all too frequently. Even continuously attended courses of study—undergraduate or graduate—often constitute a whole that is considerably less than the sum of its parts. The model of the extended major can counteract such fragmentation to a considerable extent. By constantly and consistently stressing the reciprocal relationships of diverse curricular components, by repeatedly emphasizing how different subjects supplement each other, and in particular by pulling topics together at the end through appropriate capstone courses, even a much interrupted program of study can achieve a considerable degree of internal coherence.

Coherence, continuity, and cumulation are equally important for individuals who are updating their knowledge. They, too, are badly served by fragmented, disconnected snippets of learning, a workshop here and a seminar there, each piece focusing on some narrow topic or skill. Thus there exists also a great need to provide adult learners with seminars and short courses that pull the pieces together and relate changes in technical skills to changes in context and environment.

Intermittent Attendance Among Younger Students

The transformation taking place in the attendance pattern of younger students (Lynton, 1986) was noted in the recent report of the Study Group on the Conditions of Excellence

in American Higher Education, which pointed out that "enrollment patterns have changed. One in three of our freshmen has
delayed entry into college after high school, more than two in
five undergraduates attend college part-time, and over half of
the bachelor's degree recipients take more than the traditional
four years to complete the degree" (1984, p. 7). A national profile of undergraduate students based on a recent survey by The
Carnegie Foundation for the Advancement of Teaching illus-
trates this change. In a large sample consisting of approximately
equal numbers of freshmen, sophomores, juniors, and seniors,
30 percent of the respondents indicated that they had dropped
out for at least one semester since starting college (Carnegie
Foundation for the Advancement of Teaching, 1986).

Intermittent attendance patterns are also indicated by the
aging of the student body and by the growing proportion of
part-time students. Data in Table 2 show the recent trends
among students enrolled in credit courses nationwide. The latest
figures released by the Census Bureau show that in 1982 the
majority of all *undergraduate* students were over twenty-one.
The Carnegie Foundation survey disaggregates this data by type
of institution and indicates that, as might be expected, community colleges have the highest proportion of older students
and four-year liberal arts colleges the lowest. What is most striking is that across all categories of universities, fully one-third of
all undergraduates are twenty-three or over, and one in five is
twenty-five or older. (Carnegie Foundation for the Advancement of Teaching, 1986). Inasmuch as these averages include
the most prestigious—and largely residential—private and public

Table 2. Distribution of Undergraduate Enrollment by Age and Status.

	1972	1982	1992 (est.)
24 and under	69%	61%	51%
25 and over	31	39	49
Full-time	66	58	52
Part-time	34	42	48

Source: Trends in Adult Student Enrollment, 1985.

universities, the proportion of older students in the many
urban, commuter universities is likely to be considerably higher.

Several concurrent trends are causing this change in the
traditional pattern of undergraduate attendance. Some are financial. In recent years there has been a steady increase in the
proportion of loans relative to total student financial aid. As
recently as 1980, loans constituted only 40 percent of all student support; by 1984 the percentage had increased to about 53
percent (Wilson and Melendez, 1985; see also Newman, 1985).
In order to avoid too large a debt burden, many students either
delay or interrupt their studies; many others enroll on only a
part-time basis. The anticipated further decline in federal financial aid over the next few years will probably intensify this
trend.

These developments are reinforced by unprecedented
demographic changes. The age profile of the population is shifting upward as the bulge due to the baby boom of the 1960s
progresses through the various age groups (see Table 3). During
the 1970s the greatest increase in population occurred in the
age group between fifteen and twenty-nine; during the current
decade the principal increase has shifted to those between
thirty and forty-nine; and during the last ten years of the century it will occur for the age group between fifty and sixty-nine.

Table 3. Percent Change in Age Groups.

| | Age Groups | | |
Period	15 to 29	30 to 49	50 to 69
1970–1980	+26.7%	+16.4%	+15.0%
1980–1990	− 6.3	+35.9	− 0.3
1990–2000	− 2.5	+13.9	+16.1

Source: Masnick and Pitkin, 1982.

These demographic changes, of course, have a substantial
impact on the age distribution of the country's work force (see
Table 4.) Between 1980 and 2000, the percent share of the
working-age adult population between fifteen and thirty years
old will drop from 40 percent to 30 percent. Furthermore, dif-

Table 4. Percent Share of Working-Age Adult Population.

	Age Groups		
Year	15 to 29	30 to 49	50 to 69
1980	39.12%	34.25%	26.63%
2000	29.89	44.32	25.79

Source: Masnick and Pitkin, 1982.

ferential birthrates among ethnic groups will bring about a
growing proportion of inner-city, minority youth within this
age group (Hodgkinson, 1982). They will have difficulties in
getting jobs both because they come from weak secondary
schools and because they face continuing prejudice. Overall,
therefore, there is going to be a drastic decrease during the coming years in the number of adequately educated and readily employable young people entering the labor market. Employers
and the armed forces will compete with higher education for
this shrinking cohort of new talent with offers of higher wages
and other benefits. Any employable young person opting to
pursue full-time study instead of taking a job or enlisting will
probably give up a lucrative opportunity. This is the so-called
opportunity cost of full-time study. Consequences of the demographic shift may well increase this opportunity cost to a point
at which an ever greater proportion of employable young people will take full-time jobs instead of completing their undergraduate education on a continuous, full-time basis. Within a
few years there is likely to be a real need for universities and
colleges to offer programs through which full-time employees
and members of the armed forces can complete their undergraduate degrees, just as there already exist many opportunities to
complete graduate degrees in this fashion.

At the graduate level, the impact of the growing opportunity costs of continuing one's studies is already evident. Applications for graduate and professional schools are decreasing at
what appears to be an accelerating rate. As of June 1986, law
school applications were 7 percent lower than in 1984–85 and
14 percent lower than in 1983–84 (*Law School Admission Data*

Bulletin, 1986). Medical school applications are also decreasing, and dental school applications peaked in 1980 (American Association of Medical Colleges, 1985). According to a survey of the Harvard College class of 1985, 29 percent of the students indicated they were planning immediate graduate study, as compared with 52 percent in 1975 (Harvard University Office of Career Services, 1985). In engineering, the competition for technically trained individuals in computer science and other high-technology fields has led industry to offer nearly irresistible starting salaries to students with bachelor's degrees. The resulting decrease in full-time graduate students has drawn national attention and resulted in increased graduate student stipends and fellowships in an attempt to offset the opportunity cost of full-time study (*Signs of Trouble and Erosion,* 1983).

In the areas of business and management, uninterrupted progress toward an advanced degree is being discouraged or even ruled out by a number of the most prestigious graduate business schools. They are setting a pattern for the entire profession by requiring a minimum of two to four years of practical experience before admitting prospective students into their M.B.A. programs. In 1985, less than 1 percent of the almost 800 students admitted into the Harvard M.B.A. program had completed their baccalaureate degrees that same year (Adams, 1985, p. A6).

An additional factor likely to accelerate the trend toward deferred and interrupted study at the undergraduate as well as the graduate level is one that has little or nothing to do with economic or demographic conditions. It is a consequence of the basic paradox that over the past decades young people in this country have matured physically and have become emancipated socially at ever younger ages, while at the same time the school-leaving age has steadily increased. Many years ago, a presidential commission published a report (Coleman and others, 1974) that severely criticized, on psychological and sociological grounds, the existing pattern that continues full-time, age-stratified schooling well past the age of physical and social maturation. The report recommended the development of alternative patterns in which young people could intersperse work and study. A recent article contrasted the more rapid physical maturation of adolescents with their continuing dependency in formal, full-time school settings, a situation that lessens "motivation, self-discipline, enthusiasm for learning, and a capacity for sustained attention" (Woodward and Kornaber, 1985, p. A31)—attributes essential for successful learning. The authors concur with other educators who are calling for postponing postsecondary education and instituting some kind of national service after high school graduation.

These various economic, social, and psychological factors are almost certain to intensify the trend that has already considerably reduced the traditional prevalence of full-time, continuous study after high school. Soon the norm even for young people may be a pattern of delayed, intermittent, and part-time higher education. Clearly, the mode of attendance will vary considerably among institutions. Small liberal arts colleges and the most selective, largely residential universities will continue to have an undergraduate student body of which the great majority attends full time and on a continuous basis, although even in these institutions the phenomenon of taking a year off has become quite common. Transfers after the freshman or sophomore year are also more frequent even among students in elite institutions. But the greatest change in attendance patterns will occur in the many other universities with more flexible admissions policies, particularly those in metropolitan areas with many commuting students. In these, relatively few students are likely to enter as freshmen immediately after high school graduation, and even fewer will graduate after four years of uninterrupted study and from the same institution. These universities are also likely to be most affected by the second trend that is pushing higher education into an essentially lifelong pattern: the growing number of individuals who are returning to the classroom in order to maintain their competence.

A New Dimension of Adult Education

In essence, the accelerating obsolescence of knowledge is creating a whole new dimension of adult education (Lynton, 1983b). Traditionally, courses and programs for older students fell into two categories. The first kind of adult learning, arising in the 1880s, focused on individual enrichment and self-fulfillment, as exemplified by the short courses provided by the University of Wisconsin and by the Chautauqua educational programs, which were aimed particularly at rural adults. The second mode of adult education concentrated on providing adults with belated opportunities for upward mobility. It grew out of settlement houses and other sources of language and civic training for immigrants. These categories of adult education continue to be important, but something quite new has been added: it has become necessary to return frequently to the classroom just in order to keep up with evolving conditions and circumstances. Most people find themselves on a treadmill of change; they have to continue to learn in order to stay in place. Many of the changes are sufficiently fundamental and sweeping as to require some kind of formal instruction rather than individual study alone.

Categories of jobs are changing on a time scale that is much shorter than the working life-span of an individual. New types of employment are appearing, and others are becoming obsolete, sometimes quite rapidly. Certain computer-related jobs provide striking cases in point. Just a few years ago, a number of specialties involving the use of mainframe computers were in great and continuing demand. But the advent of microcomputers has rendered many of these occupations obsolete.

As important as the ongoing shift in types of work is the certainty of continuing changes in almost all existing jobs, even though their nomenclature may remain the same. Today's requirements for competence as a bank manager, a nurse, or a secretary are substantially different from what they were just a few years ago. The understanding and skills required to perform these and most other jobs, from entry level to the highest executive ranks, are likely to continue to change with time.

Chapters Four and Five emphasized *competence* as the dominant educational objective. If changes in the workplace are pervasive and rapid, then the need for recurrent and indeed lifelong education to *maintain and to renew the competence* of individuals becomes as important as their *preparation for compe-*

tence (Lynton, 1983b; 1983c; 1984). Maintaining competence on the job requires much more than keeping up with changes in necessary technical skills. As a recent report on engineering education (Bruce, Silbert, Smullin, and Fano, 1982) pointed out, new scientific and technological developments are often more than mere extensions of previous ones. They constitute categorical advances that require new scientific and mathematical knowledge. New generations of engineering students are learning basic principles that differ from those previously taught: "Thus [older] engineers are faced with the problem of learning, during their professional lives, what new generations of engineers are currently learning in school" (pp. 11-12). And for most engineers, learning new fundamentals requires formal instruction. Similar statements can be made about other professions and occupations.

In addition, everything that was said in Chapter Five about the importance of breadth and of combining liberal and vocational elements in preparing individuals for careers is equally pertinent to the maintenance of effectiveness on the job. The social, economic, and political context in which an engineer, a manager, or a physician operates is likely to change as much and as rapidly as do the technical elements of their particular fields. For example, we suggested in Chapter Five that competent engineers need to be aware of the ways in which science and technology operate in society and to be sensitive to potential second- and third-order consequences of technical developments. Over time, these environmental elements are bound to change as much as technology itself evolves. Thus engineers need to update their understanding of these contextual matters in order to maintain their competence. Similarly, it is as important for managers to maintain their scientific and technological literacy, as described in Chapter Four, as it is for them to update their specialized skills in marketing or financing. In both cases, maintaining competence requires continuous updating of individuals' understanding of the context in which they are functioning as much as it requires learning about innovations in the area of their technical expertise.

But the ongoing and accelerating changes in modern society affect every aspect of life, not only the workplace. Thus the maintenance of competence is essential if an individual is to be effective as a citizen and as a member of a societal group. As Rudolph has recently commented, "I have been haunted by the degree to which we all in one way or another are destined to inherit one set of values and circumstances, required to grow up with another, all the time preparing for an unclear future that will impose yet another" (1981, p. 61). Individuals must continue to learn in order to remain effective and knowledgeable in civic affairs as well as in their occupations. "Civic education," as Boyer and Hechinger point out (1981, p. 48), "is not just a one-shot affair. If Americans are to be more adequately informed, *education for citizenship must become a lifelong process.*" Throughout life there will now be a need for the inclusive kind of education that combines liberal and technical elements.

Thus we seem to have reached the point long predicted by the advocates of adult education: the maintenance of competence as a citizen and on the job should be recognized as a continuous and coherent process through lifelong learning, in which successive phases of organized instruction alternate or are intertwined with periods of work. The previously cited report on engineering education calls for replacement of "the present discontinuity between full-time study and full-time work by a gradual transition extending through most of . . . professional life. [There needs to be] intermixing of work, study, and teaching with the active support of employers [and] close collaboration between faculties and their industrial colleagues" (Bruce, Silbert, Smullin, and Fano, 1982, p. 32). This recommendation applies to all occupations.

Universities have an opportunity—as well as an obligation —to play a significant role in the lifelong maintenance of competence. They can do this in several ways. In the first place, universities can intensify their efforts to meet the educational needs of adults. It is hardly necessary to repeat that this requires the kind of adaptations in content and methodology of instruction that have been the subject of this chapter and the two preceding ones. In addition, universities must handle issues of format, location, and timing of instruction with great flexibility and must adapt, as well, many day-to-day procedures so as to facilitate access by working adults. In addition to these efforts to provide education to individual adults, universities should also try to increase their participation in an appropriate fashion in employer-sponsored instruction, as well as in other components of the disaggregated system of learning that we will discuss in the next chapter.

Another dimension further underscores the basic coherence and reciprocal reinforcement of the institutional changes that we are advocating throughout this book. Universities can contribute substantially to lifelong educational maintenance by means of many of the professional outreach activities described in Chapter Two. We envision a real continuum of university activity, ranging from basic research at one end to formal classroom instruction at the other, with a variety of outreach activities in the middle that combine technical assistance and instruction.

Dilemma of Continuing Education

It is obvious from the preceding sections that no clear distinction any longer exists between "continuing education" and what might at one time have been thought of as "regular education." We saw that at least half of all undergraduates interrupt their studies for a minimum of one year, that the proportion of part-time enrollment in colleges and universities is steadily increasing, and that the average age of students on our urban, commuter campuses is now twenty-seven or twenty-eight. The "nontraditional" student is becoming the norm. In addition, the accelerating obsolescence of knowledge increasingly requires that we see education as a recurrent and lifelong process, involved as much with the maintenance of competence as with its initial development. Hence, the traditional distinction between education of the young and education of adults is becoming blurred, as is the difference between those who continue postsecondary studies immediately after high school and those who return to the classroom at some later stage. Furthermore, credits and credentials are likely to lose significance, with emphasis shifting to other ways of assessing and demonstrating the maintenance of competence.

What then is the function of the traditional institutional branch of learning called "continuing education"? What are the structural and organizational implications of the changes that are taking place? Does it still make sense to have certain individuals in a university administration with specific responsibilities for an activity that has become part of, and perhaps indistinguishable from, the central instructional mission of the institution?

Our answer to this question is affirmative. We believe that universities should merge the activities that used to be subsumed under the label "continuing education" into the mainstream instructional organization of the institution so as to make them a central and integral part of the institutional mission. But universities should make every effort to retain the full benefit of the experience, the expertise, and the enterprise of individuals who have been involved in continuing education in the past. Precisely because "regular education" is becoming indistinguishable from "continuing education," each institution needs to make the fullest possible use of continuing education experts.

Continuing education is becoming part of the institutional mission in a manner very similar to that of research. In a university, research and other professional and scholarly activities are seen as part of the responsibilities of every academic unit and of every faculty member. These activities, therefore, come under the purview of academic administrators—provosts, deans, and department chairpersons—who have line authority. Yet almost every university has senior officials with a *staff* responsibility for research or possibly for research and graduate work. Such individuals may be called deans, associate provosts, or, in some cases, even vice-presidents or vice-chancellors. Their responsibility, on a staff basis, is to stimulate research and graduate activities and to provide various kinds of staff support. In addition, they also have substantial responsibility for quality control. In some large institutions, the central officials with this responsibility may be supplemented by counterparts at the level of school, college, or even department.

Much the same approach would seem to be optimal for continuing education. In the central academic office of a university there should be a senior individual, with appropriate staff, clearly responsible for providing guidance, stimulation, staff support, and quality control for the extension of instructional activities beyond the traditional on-campus classrooms and regular daytime hours. That individual should be the principal catalyst for stimulating such activities; his or her office would also be the principal boundary-spanning mechanism for relating the university to clienteles other than traditional high school graduates. Those functions can be supplemented, as appropriate, by similar positions in schools, colleges, or departments.

The integration of continuing education into the core of the institution of course implies that instruction formerly provided under that rubric would now be subject to the same academic review and procedures as the "regular" programs. That is not without its risks and potential disadvantages. Until now, "continuing education has been a marginal activity in educational institutions . . . and in its operations it amply demonstrated the uses of marginality . . . [it] has been successful in large parts because of marginality" (Gordon, 1980, pp. 173, 174). There indeed exists a considerable risk that absorption into the institutional mainstream may inhibit many of the characteristics that have made continuing education so successful to date: entrepreneurship, innovation, flexibility, speed of response, and placing the student, rather than the discipline, at the center. As discussed in considerable detail in Chapter Four, the challenge for universities is to review and revise many of their current procedures and policies so as to reduce this danger (Lynton, 1984). We will return to this issue in the next chapter.

Absorption of continuing education into the mainstream instructional activities of a university has a further, very important implication. In continuing education, as in other kinds of professional outreach, universities must decide whether these activities are to be resource driven or client driven. As noted in Chapter Two, the former would limit instructional offerings to the areas of expertise of the regular faculty. Adjunct faculty might be used if quantitative demand exceeded capacity, but the regular faculty would be responsible for quality as in traditional instruction. In contrast, client-driven activities would involve the university in areas of instruction in which the faculty does not have expertise and cannot exercise their academic responsibility. We believe quite strongly that this option is inappropriate to a university.

But the question of whether to rely primarily on the existing expertise of the faculty is just one of the issues that must be faced in defining what a university should teach. The instructional tasks of universities can no longer be defined by *who* is taught. Because of the changes described in this chapter, neither age, pattern of attendance, nor employment status can under current conditions be used to characterize the "typical" university student or to delimit what instruction is appropriate to a university. Furthermore, colleges and universities no longer have a monopoly on higher education, which is increasingly available as well from other sources. In the next chapter, therefore, we will examine the instructional role of universities in an increasingly disaggregated system of education.

7

Strengthening the University's Place in a Diverse Educational Environment

Contemporary society is characterized by a highly disaggregated and heterogeneous system of education and training. A wide variety of sources provide different types of instruction, from the most basic to the most sophisticated and advanced levels. In one sense this is not a new phenomenon. Schools, colleges, and universities have never had a monopoly on education. Churches, libraries, museums, fraternal and professional associations, and many other institutions have provided learning opportunities for decades. In the past, however, these offerings could on the whole be easily distinguished from typical college and university courses. But more recently not only has the number of nonacademic providers increased considerably but so has the range of the instruction that they offer. Alternative sources now make available a substantial amount of advanced instruction, some of it even beyond the equivalent of the baccalaureate degree. Hence it is becoming increasingly difficult to define the proper instructional "turf" of universities.

Nonacademic Systems

The nonacademic educational system that has received most attention (Lynton, 1981, 1984; Morse, 1984; Eurich,

1985) has been the massive "shadow educational system" (Dunlop, 1975) of formal instruction created by the corporate sector for its employees. Although some employer-sponsored education and training programs have existed for many decades (Fisher, 1967), corporate education has expanded greatly in recent years, particularly at postsecondary levels of instruction intended for managers, supervisors, technical personnel, and other professionals. At this time, total out-of-pocket expenditures by corporations for employee education are estimated at $20 to $40 billion, not counting on-the-job training or the appreciable value of employee time devoted to instruction off the job (Carnevale and Goldstein, 1983; Carnevale, 1986). The magnitude of this corporate instructional system is comparable to the combined appropriations of all states for higher education, which in 1981-82 totalled $22.5b (*Digest of Educational Statistics, 1985-86,* 1986, p. 166). Colleges and universities are estimated to supply only about 6 or 7 percent of employee education (Lusterman, 1981). Increasing this share by only a few percentage points would substantially add to the activities of academic institutions.

A number of unions have also become involved in employee education. District 37 of the American Federation of State and Municipal Employees has for many years insisted that employers contribute to an educational fund as part of their contracts. The monies are used for a wide variety of courses, some of which are provided directly by the union, others by local colleges and universities (Barton, 1982). More recently, the United Automobile Workers obtained educational contributions from a number of major automobile manufacturers. These funds are primarily intended for programs that retrain dislocated workers for new jobs.

Other parallel educational systems aimed at the maintenance of competence have emerged in recent years. In most of the licensed professions, from law and medicine to undertaking, practitioners have ready access to a wide variety of workshops, lectures, packaged materials, and other means of updating their technical skills. This is particularly true of the large number of licensed and registered occupations for which some form of organized instruction is now state mandated as a condition for renewal of certification (Phillips, 1986; Lowenthal, 1981). Professional units in our colleges and universities provide only a small portion of this instruction. Most of it is either organized under the auspices of the related professional association or is provided by a growing number of proprietary enterprises. The latter make up a growing "training industry" that also sells a variety of training programs to corporate sponsors.

Another system of higher education is sponsored by the government, and particularly by the armed forces. The vast array of activities here range from short informational sessions to full-fledged residential programs and probably rival the corporate and traditional educational systems in magnitude, although there exists as yet little reliable information about these activities. Some of the advanced education of government personnel is provided by cooperating colleges and universities, but a substantial amount is generated within the armed forces and other government agencies without academic involvement except perhaps for the use of faculty consultants.

It is clear, then, that vast sums of money are spent each year by public- and private-sector employers for a wide range of instruction intended to maintain the competence of their work force in the face of changes in job categories and job content. The combined scope of these employer-sponsored systems is evidence of the real need for such maintenance and also shows that many sectors of society have recognized that professional development now must be considered a recurrent and lifelong process. Unfortunately, most colleges and universities were slow to gain this understanding. The reluctance and lack of urgency with which academic institutions by and large have reacted to these opportunities are striking indications of the gap between external societal needs and the internal priorities of higher education (Lynton, 1983a). There indeed exists a "missing connection" (Lynton, 1984).

What Universities Should Not Do

In recent years, many academic institutions have rushed to fill this gap, but not always in an appropriate fashion. For universities it is particularly important to make a careful determination of which instructional tasks are appropriate to their general mission and which are not. In making this choice, they should keep in mind that the existence of nonacademic systems for the maintenance of employee competence is not, in and of itself, a source of concern for higher education. It would be neither possible nor desirable for colleges and universities to provide most of the instruction required to maintain the competence of all public- and private-sector employees, members of the armed forces, and independent professionals. So much needs to be done that there is ample opportunity for many categories of providers. Furthermore, the maintenance of competence includes a great deal of instruction that is product and industry specific and can best be provided in-house. Even in many of the more generic topics, the optimal approach to employee development is likely to be one that focuses more on "knowing how," or training, than on "knowing why," or education. Usually the goal is to prepare employees as quickly and as efficiently as possible to cope with some change or innovation. Universities by and large are not very good at training and probably should not engage in it at all (Branscomb and Gilmore, 1975).

The reason for the preponderance of training in nonacademic instructional systems is, of course, that these systems maintain the competence of employees primarily for the benefit of the employer, not that of the individual being taught. A clear distinction exists "between the role of corporate education and that of the more traditional institutions. Because the corporate classroom is ultimately concerned about productivity and performance, its goals are apt to be specific, even narrow" (Boyer, 1985, p. xiv). Employers in both the private and the public sector spend substantial sums on employee training in order to protect their investment in human resources. This is especially true when labor market conditions, collective bargaining contracts, or civil and military service regulations preclude the alternative of bringing in new hires who acquired the requisite skills elsewhere (Lynton, 1984; Carnevale, 1986). In the same way, professional associations are interested in maintaining the standards of their profession. Hence both employers and professional associations sponsor various educational efforts as a means of furthering their self-interest. By contrast, academic institutions view individual development as an end in itself.

It is important, therefore, that as colleges and universities search for alternative sources of enrollment and revenue, they do *not* rush in and attempt to provide "quick fix" workshops, seminars, and courses that are designed to meet short-term needs for data and skills. Campuses should not "turn themselves into educational supermarkets with a view toward mere fiscal survival" (Boyer and Hechinger, 1981, p. 58). Yet there is a real danger that "in a bid for survival, higher education will imitate its rivals . . . as colleges pursue the marketplace goals of corporate education. If that happens, higher learning may discover that, having abandoned its own special mission, it will find itself in a contest it cannot win" (Boyer, 1985, p. xiv).

What Universities Should Do

The responsiveness of universities to the need for employee education should be based on their inherent strengths and capabilities. They should concentrate on education, on "knowing why." The obligation to link theory and practice goes both ways. We have in previous chapters cited criticisms of universities for focusing on theory to the exclusion of practice. It would be even less appropriate for universities to provide practice without relating it to a theoretical framework. There exists a great need—although as yet a limited demand—in employee education and in professional development for such theory-related teaching. As we noted in the previous chapter, in every occupation there occur times when it becomes necessary to absorb new theories, new paradigms, and new concepts in order to understand and apply new techniques. That calls for the kind of seminars and courses that universities, in principle, are well qualified to provide—but only if they change their tradition of teaching theoretical concepts abstractly and in isolation from their practical application.

Universities can also increase their participation in employee education by working with employers to update employees' understanding of the social, political, and cultural environment in which they are working. Once again we state our opinion that such knowledge is essential to competence on the job. The more advanced the position, the greater the need for contextual understanding, which needs to be kept up-to-date as much as any technical skill. Again, this is the kind of instruction that universities are well qualified to provide.

Thus if employers begin to recognize these broader needs that go beyond the quick acquisition of a narrowly defined skill, the demand for university participation in employee education will increase substantially. Even now, that participation could be considerably greater than it is. For example, employers as well as professional associations provide instruction in many subjects listed in university catalogues. These include scientific and technical subjects, from introductory chemistry and basic calculus to the most advanced aspects of biochemistry and state-of-the-art engineering. This category of instruction also covers language training and a variety of other communication skills.

At present, corporate and other nonacademic sources provide numerous courses of these kinds. Both the American Council on Education on a nationwide basis and the New York State Board of Regents evaluate such offerings and publish periodic guides that recommend academic course and credit equivalents for several thousand noncollegiate offerings. (*Regents Guide,* 1980; *The National Guide to Educational Credit for Training Programs,* 1982.) A random sampling of the volumes shows a wide variety of collegelike courses, such as "An Introduction to Finance" and "Calculus I and II" offered by General Electric to its employees, "Materials Engineering" and "Modern Structural Analysis" offered by General Motors, "Accounting" and "Money and Banking" by Manufacturers Hanover Trust, and "Multivariate Analysis" and "Statistical Foundations" by the New York Telephone Company. In each case, the level and extent of the course are considered the equivalent of one to three college credits.

The similarity between some kinds of employee instruction and higher education is also attested to by the accredited graduate and undergraduate degree programs offered by noncollegiate institutions such as Arthur D. Little, a major consulting firm in Cambridge, Massachusetts, and the American Banking Institute (Hawthorne, Libby, and Nash, 1983; see also Lynton, 1984; Eurich, 1985). Several of the institutions often listed as "corporate colleges," such as the Wang Institute in Lowell, Massachusetts, are substantially or totally independent of their original corporate sponsors. Furthermore, taken together, they constitute only a miniscule portion of the total system of employee education. However, these entities clearly demonstrate the growing overlap between the offerings of the corporate instructional system and the courses of traditional higher education.

Another promising area for university involvement is among smaller enterprises. As one might expect, in-house corporate instructional programs are far more prevalent in medium-sized and large businesses than in smaller ones (Lusterman, 1977; Lynton, 1984; Carnevale, 1986). Only larger enterprises have employees who are charged with the specific task of organizing such programs, and there must be enough employees needing a certain kind of instruction at any given time to make this cost effective. For the same reason, programs for public employees are more likely to exist at the national than at the state and local levels. Private and public employers with a few hundred employees either have to rely substantially on prepackaged courses from external vendors or do nothing at all. Many of them are likely to welcome help from academic institutions.

The Necessary Adaptations

Thus, universities do have a very appropriate and as yet only partially filled role to play in employer-sponsored instruction. But bringing these opportunities to fruition will require a number of basic changes in the procedures and attitudes of our academic establishment and also in the way in which employers view their human resources (Lynton, 1984).

First, our colleges and universities need to become considerably more flexible and nimble in their response to external demands. When employers, particularly those in the private sec-

tor, order something, they want rapid delivery. That is as true
for an instructional program as it is for supplies and equipment.
Corporate clients will not wait patiently as the lengthy process
by which new academic programs typically move from conception through development to approval evolves. Colleges and universities here face a real dilemma: the continuing education unit
operating outside the regular academic approval process is usually able to respond quickly and effectively to external requests.
However, for the reasons described in the last chapter, it is increasingly important that all the instruction provided by academic institutions be viewed as an integral part of the institution's mission and be treated in comparable ways with regard to
faculty involvement and oversight. Thus, it is essential to find
ways of expediting the traditional approval process rather than
to continue to bypass it. This could be accomplished by having
new offerings reviewed by a standing faculty committee that
meets frequently and has authority from the principal faculty
governance body to grant approval. Alternatively, new courses
and curricula could be subject to a kind of postaudit procedure;
that is, they could be given automatic approval for one or two
years and then reviewed for permanent approval.

There is also a need for flexible and rapid admissions procedures that take into account the wide variety of backgrounds
and, in many cases, the very remote time of prior formal education of the applicants. The easiest approach is to grant provi-
sional admission to such applicants, with matriculation as degree candidates made conditional on successful completion of
two or three courses. In the corporate area, it is important to
provide counseling and guidance services to employees to help
them identify personal needs and priorities and deal with the inevitable ambiguity and possible divergence between the interests
of their employer and themselves.

In addition to responding more rapidly to external needs,
colleges and universities need to be much more flexible with regard to format, location, and timing of instruction. The next
chapter will discuss the extent to which educational technology
—particularly as a delivery mechanism—can facilitate such
movement. Greater flexibility is also needed in faculty assign-

ments and work loads. Insofar as all learning needs do not come packaged into forty-two fifty-minute segments, so too faculty teaching assignments cannot continue to be measured in terms of a certain number of semester-long courses.

Greater involvement in employee education will intensify the new pedagogical demands on faculty. Interviews of employers frequently reveal that they tried using a local college or university for employee programs but stopped doing so because the enrolled personnel were taught as if they were teen-aged college students. In addition, any move by academic institutions beyond providing instruction in straightforward fundamental skills requires that faculty understand the relationship of their discipline and their area of expertise to the external world. Once again this is a matter of being able to bridge the gap between theory and practice, and once again the main burden falls on faculty members. Faculty members will have to be familiar with the application of their area of specialization and understand its relationship to other disciplines and subjects. Unless they know how to relate theory and practice and have a broad perspective on their field of specialization, the courses they provide will not meet the needs of employee education. It will be necessary for them to teach more inductively, to help students generalize from the specific, and, in general, to provide intellectual guidance to much more active and more demanding learners.

Examining these demands on the faculty, one again finds considerable internal consistency within the emerging model of the expanded university. The knowledge needs of modern society require that university faculty become more involved in broader areas of scholarship, in the aggregation, synthesis, interpretation, and application of knowledge, and in outreach and extension. In short, faculty must come to be in active contact with the world outside academia. But that is also what they will have to be in order to respond to the new lifelong educational needs of employees and professionals. Thus we find once again, as in traditional universities, a fundamental relationship between the scholarly activities of faculty and their teaching. It used to be that research, narrowly defined, was seen as important to effective teaching within the confines of the discipline. Now we begin to recognize that scholarly activity in the broader sense is essential to the larger perspectives and experiences that must inform and illuminate teaching in the modern university. And of course there exists a reciprocal relationship. Intense participation of faculty members in employee education in turn will make it easier for them to become involved in various applied professional activities.

Faculty collaboration with professionals in industry and government in outreach activities will also facilitate the most crucial adaptation for the academic community if it is to participate in employee education—namely, moving toward a real sharing of authority in identifying educational needs of employees and in developing ways to meet these. Employers complain about the "arrogance" of academics in presenting corporate clients with instructional programs without a serious attempt to elicit the clients' input. The other extreme is just as inappropriate; universities must not merely respond passively to requests for proposals in which all details of content and outcomes are specified. Cooperative activities indeed should become what they imply: real *joint* ventures.

Adaptation by Employers

But the burden of adaptation lies not only on the universities and on their faculties. Basic changes are needed as well on the part of employers. Employee education is still limited to a small proportion of the labor force in spite of the billions of dollars spent on it. It is primarily supervisors, managers, and other professionals who participate in it. And on the average, their involvement amounts to less than thirty hours per year, or little more than 1 percent of their total time at work (Lusterman, 1977). In smaller enterprises the participation rate may be zero. For the most part, employers are still not fully convinced of the need to regard their work force as a human capital investment (Carnevale, 1983; Lynton, 1984). Even the corporations most dedicated to human resource development allocate far less each year to the maintenance of their employees' performance and skills than to the maintenance of their physical plant and equipment. The amount of money spent is not necessarily the best measure of the priority accorded by employers to maintaining the competence of existing employees, yet it does indicate that the prevailing tendency is still to cope with change by hiring new people who already have the prerequisite skills.

This attitude is also evident in the very limited extent to which human resource considerations enter into corporate long-range and strategic planning. The cost of labor is usually a major factor in decisions about where to locate plants, as is the availability of appropriately trained workers. But it is rare to find systematic attempts to determine the skills that will be needed to deal with changing products and technologies. Instead, "time and again a changing external environment has caught corporations ill prepared to accept change, much less to lead it" (Branscomb and Gilmore, 1975, p. 227). As a result, many employee education programs are created at the last moment, in reaction to imminent changes. This simply reinforces the tendency to require immediate responses from providers, which in turn contributes to employer dissatisfaction with the slow response of academic institutions.

The short time perspective of many employers is also often reflected in the content of employee instruction, most of which is directed at meeting immediate needs through short periods of highly specific training. Much of this kind of instruction is indeed very necessary and appropriate and is properly provided either by nonacademic providers, on an in-house basis, or by lower-level academic institutions. Universities, as we stated earlier, should not rush in to fill demands that they are ill equipped to meet. Instead, they should make every effort to convince employers that it is in the latter's own self-interest to have their employees receive more than narrow technical training. That will be a difficult task. One hears a good deal of rhetoric on the part of many chief executive officers about the value of a liberal education, and indeed top executives cherish an opportunity to attend an Aspen or Dartmouth humanities seminar. But for much of employee education, the emphasis is on filling immediate skill needs in the shortest possible time.

This attitude is part of the general tendency of American managers to focus on short-term returns. Many recent articles and books have criticized the lack of a longer-range perspective as contributing to the obsolescence of so much of this country's manufacturing industry. One can only hope that these critical commentaries will have some impact and that employers will come to realize that a greater emphasis on education rather than on ad hoc training can in the long run be the most cost effective. As part of such a longer-range view, one would hope that employers will become increasingly willing to include in employee education the kind of content that universities are best able to provide.

The Need to Move . . . but in the Right Direction

There exist some hopeful signs that employers are recognizing the shortcomings of an excessive emphasis on narrow technical and analytical skills in employee development. The larger corporations in particular are increasingly realizing that if they want their employees to have the insight and ability to weigh alternatives, then they need to provide a longer-range and broader educational approach. In principle, this poses a major opportunity for universities to increase their involvement in employer-sponsored education. There are, in fact, many examples of successful collaboration in which academic institutions really concentrate on the kind of intellectual development that is, or should be, their strength. More universities should move aggressively in this direction rather than trying to compete with nonacademic providers in such areas as short-term training and skill development. There still exist many opportunities for universities to provide the broader and more cumulative education that is their proper domain and through which they can assume their proper share of responsibility for the maintenance of employee competence. But other providers, including the corporations themselves, are also on the move, and that "window of opportunity" will not be open very much longer.

❦ 8 ❦

Maximizing the Educational
Potential of Technology

Much of what has been discussed in the preceding chapters extends the activities of universities well beyond their campus boundaries. The expanded definition of scholarship, as well as the changing pattern of attendance in higher education, calls for substantial outreach. To engage in technical assistance, technology transfer, and, in general, effective dissemination of knowledge and to meet the instructional needs of an increasingly diverse clientele on a recurrent and lifelong basis, universities must begin to make their intellectual resources available to individuals, organizations, and enterprises at locations remote from the campus and must be able to do so with considerable flexibility.

Current developments in educational uses of technology can significantly help in meeting certain extended functions of universities and can, furthermore, affect modes of instruction both positively and negatively. Two broad areas of development are of particular importance:

First, using telecommunication as a *delivery mechanism,* universities can substantially increase their ability to provide instruction at off-campus locations and augment their potential to deliver certain informational and professional services.

113

Second, using computers as an *instructional tool* holds great promise to increase the flexibility and individualization of instruction and thus to help universities meet the varying needs of an increasingly heterogeneous student body. Computer-based simulation and games also have considerable potential, as do the capabilities of computers in graphics and in structuring and manipulating texts. At the same time, however, computers lend themselves more to the absorption of facts and to straight deductive teaching than to speculative and inductive modes of learning. The use of computers may, therefore, affect instruction in both positive and negative ways. Used in conjunction with various modes of telecommunication and with the appropriate equipment, any campus-based increase in computer utilization also becomes available to off-campus instruction. Hence, both the advantages and the possible problems of using computers affect all the instructional activities of the extended university. In addition, the development of campuswide computer networks together with modes of telecommunication can significantly increase external access to the noninstructional resources of a campus. In the aggregate, therefore, computerization is likely to have a major impact on the expanded functions of universities.

Using Telecommunication

Telecommunication, or communication at a distance, has experienced an enormous expansion both in scope and in kind in recent years. Because electronic signals can be sent at ever higher frequencies, we can today encode and transmit information at increasing rates and volumes. That has made possible the move from the telephone and radio to television. In addition, information in digital form can now be handled in large quantities at enormous speeds, and that capacity continues to increase. As a result, various means of high-frequency or broadband telecommunication are now available to transmit numerous video and voice signals simultaneously with a large amount of digitized data. Telecommunication has thus moved from the horse and buggy stage to that of the jumbo jet in a very short time.

We must, however, distinguish between *broadcast* and *narrowcast* telecommunication. The former is exactly what its name implies: an electronic signal broadcast in all directions that can be received by anyone with a generally available receiving device. Conventional radio and television are both broadcast. Narrowcast telecommunication, by contrast, is transmitted in such a way that it can be received only by a specific audience. This can be accomplished by transmitting through a network, as is the case with telephone and cable television. For both of these one has to be a subscriber to obtain the signal. It can also be accomplished by transmitting a signal only to a specific receiving antenna, as is done in point-to-point microwave transmission, or by sending out a scrambled signal that can be picked up only by means of a special device. Limiting access by narrowcasting has the advantage of restricting the audience to those for whom the transmission is intended. That could be individuals who have paid a pertinent fee or tuition or professionals in particular fields.

A number of recent developments have substantially increased the possibilities of both categories of transmission. Communication satellites are rapidly expanding the geographical span of transmission, and the development of fiber optics is increasing the potential bandwidth and transmission capacity of wired telecommunication. At the same time, substantial changes in the economics of communication have been brought about both by the breakup of AT&T and by the decreasing cost of equipment. As a result, there are a growing number of competing communication systems. Private corporations as well as public institutions have found it increasingly advantageous to create their own captive networks. Several statewide university systems as well as universities with satellite campuses link their components by means of appropriate networks. In some states, complex electronic networks have been created to link a variety of institutions for educational purposes. Moreover, there are now a number of regional, national, and even worldwide computer networks, some dedicated to specific purposes, others available at a fee to a broad range of users (Jennings and others, 1986).

As a result of these developments, distance is no longer a barrier to the rapid transmission of large volumes of information. Telecommunication already provides many remarkable ways of making available to anyone, anywhere, and at any time both the spoken and written word, still as well as moving pictures, and data of all sorts. This capability will steadily increase while, in all probability, the cost will decrease. There is no doubt, therefore, about the potential importance of the new technologies as delivery mechanisms for university instructional and informational services to remote locations.

Off-Campus, Distance Learning. Indeed, the new technologies have already had a marked impact as a medium of instruction for off-campus or "distance" learning. Audiocassettes have been used in various ways for many years, but students' attention span for listening to the spoken word is limited. The advent of videocassettes thus has added substantially to the educational potential of technology. A number of colleges and universities and many commercial enterprises produce tapes of material that range from basic skills to highly sophisticated graduate-level instruction, and these are available for either lease or purchase. Studio production has the advantage of allowing use of various resources to enliven content. Cameras can move, and a wide variety of illustrative material can be employed. Of course, such productions are costly and time consuming and require considerable adaptation by faculty members. These barriers limit both on- and off-campus use of television.

One can avoid these problems by instead videotaping regular classroom instruction, although this requires a classroom equipped with lights, cameras, and an adjoining director's booth. Recording in a live classroom, with minimal production facilities and costs, has a number of obvious advantages over more elaborate, studio-based productions. The televised material can be changed as easily as the classroom course, and faculty usually find it easier to address an actual class than to "perform" in a studio. The result, however, is most suited for relatively advanced subjects aimed at sophisticated and motivated audiences.

Stanford University was among the first to use this method to provide advanced engineering courses at high-technology

industrial plants in nearby Silicon Valley. This pioneering effort entailed using local tutors chosen from the company's staff
or from a local educational institution, who received brief
training sessions in the use of televised materials, the conduct
of discussions, and other pedagogical issues. The showing of the
tape can be interrupted at any time for questions and discussion (Gibbons, Kincheloe, and Down, 1977). Other institutions,
such as the Illinois Institute of Technology (Guralnik, 1981),
ensure interaction with students by means of a telephone hook-
up back to the campus. In addition, a courier service ensures
regular collection of assignments and examinations with fast
turnaround times.

The potential of televised instruction for distance learning is substantially enhanced when it is combined with the use
of telecommunication as a delivery mechanism. The physical
transport of tapes is cumbersome, slow, and costly and has increasingly been supplanted by narrowcast microwave transmission, in most cases using the so-called ITFS channels that for
many years have been reserved for educational use. Some regions and states have developed substantial microwave networks
for educational purposes. The growing availability of satellites
has created the opportunity for national and even worldwide
distribution of this kind of televised instruction. The Association for Media-Based Continuing Education in Engineering
sponsors the National Technical University, which in 1984 began to offer two complete graduate curricula in engineering
through videotaped courses created in participating institutions
(Fitch, 1982; Eurich, 1985).

The use of narrowcast videotapes of classroom instruction, supplemented by telephone hookups, local tutors, and the
availability of pertinent reference material, has major implications for universities. All current indications are that these
"televised classrooms" work well with advanced students who
are studying fairly sophisticated material. The mode would
therefore appear to become more and more useful as universities move toward an increasingly intermittent pattern of instruction and focus their attention on more mature students who are
continuing their education.

Broadcast Instruction. A parallel development in distance

learning involves broadcasting the instructional material rather than targeting it to a limited audience. Radio lectures are one of the earliest forms of that technology and still provide instruction in a wide variety of subjects to large audiences, particularly in developing countries (Perry, 1984). The advent of television, of course, initiated the use of that medium for instruction. One of the pioneers was New York University with its "Sunrise Semester," for which thousands of avid viewers got up early every day. This venture and many other early uses of televised instruction relied on the "talking head" approach: the broadcast consisted quite literally of the image of the lecturer's head, although it was occasionally "enlivened" by a glimpse of the blackboard. Since then, both the sophistication and the cost of production of much televised instruction have increased manifold.

Examples include a number of major television productions that have become very popular in this country in recent years. Series such as "The Ascent of Man" and "Cosmos," which cost many millions of dollars to produce, were seen by millions of viewers here and abroad. The number of viewers for "Cosmos," about 10 million, was approximately equal to the total enrollment in higher education in the United States (Dirr, 1983). Clearly these ambitious projects demonstrate the enormous potential of television as a cultural and informational medium. A much smaller number of viewers used them as part of a college-level degree program. A book and other printed instructional material and study guides were available for each of the series, and a large number of community colleges and other higher education institutions allowed individuals to register for a course and obtain credit upon passing an examination based on the televised material.

As a means of widespread dissemination of information and knowledge to the public-at-large, these projects are very useful. Participation by university faculty members should be encouraged. But it is not clear whether elaborate productions represent an effective use of technology for the formal instructional responsibilities of a college or university. The format of these programs restricts them, by and large, to fairly introductory surveys of a subject, and the need to amortize their high cost makes it essential to use the same "course" for many thousands of students over a long period of time.

Somewhat greater flexibility and individualization are possible with the growing number of telecourses produced by consortia of colleges, such as the Coast Community Colleges in California. These telecourses are developed specifically for instructional purposes and use an intermediate level of production sophistication. They are bought or rented by academic institutions for local broadcasting at certain set times. Anyone can tune in and watch them, but only students who have registered and who take a final examination can receive academic credit. Use by many institutions throughout the country is intended to reduce initial costs in a sufficiently short time so as to allow periodic updating and other changes at reasonable intervals. Both these categories of telecourses are broadcast as part of the regular schedule of a local station. This means that the only viewer equipment required is a regular television set, but there are also some major disadvantages to telecourses. Stations provide only limited time slots for telecourses so that only a few of them can be provided at any given time. In addition, a student must either view the programs at the time they are broadcast or use a recording device.

Those limitations exist as well when broadcast instruction is used in conjunction with modern versions of traditional correspondence schools. The British Open University is the best-known example of the correspondence model at the university level (Perry, 1977). Its considerable success could not have happened without the imaginative use of technology to enhance written material. However, it is important to keep in mind that the Open University relies primarily on printed material and assesses student progress by mailed exchanges of assignments and self-administered tests. In addition, it makes much use of local tutorial centers where students can receive personal help as well as access to reference material. Each semester also includes a week of residence at the Open University's central campus.

The experience of the Open University shows that well-

conceived and well-produced radio and television courses can
have a very substantial impact on student interest and motivation, on the one hand, and on public interest and acceptance of
the institution, on the other. The British Open University would
not have gained its reputation and its success without judicious
use of technology. While direct broadcast has the considerable
pedagogical limitation of proceeding at a rate that cannot be
controlled by the student, this can be remedied by the use of a
videotape recorder, which allows replays. Tapes are usually also
available at regional tutorial centers and similar locations.

Even with replay, however, videotape remains a fairly
passive medium that by itself provides no opportunity for student interaction. That is why the newest major venture in this
category, the Dutch Open University, which opened in 1984, is
placing much emphasis on the use of programmed interactive
videodiscs. The potential of these devices has barely been
touched (Beeman, 1986; Kurland, 1987). They not only combine text and illustrations, both still and moving, but are also
highly interactive, allowing a variety of programmed sequences
depending on question and answer dialogue with the viewer. In
effect, the programmed, laser-read videodisc is a highly sophisticated and much more versatile version of old-fashioned programmed instruction.

The utilization of telecommunication has significantly
increased competition in the educational marketplace. Many
enterprising universities and colleges have begun using telecommunication in order to provide educational programs beyond
the borders of the state or region in which they have degree authority and accreditation. This has raised a number of difficult
policy issues that are currently being examined (Goldstein,
1983). The new technologies have also made it considerably easier for nonacademic providers of instruction to enter the market. Higher education faces growing competition, one in which
it will lose all advantage if it tries to duplicate what external
vendors produce rather than sticking to what it can do best.
Many commercial enterprises are quite good at producing and
marketing videotapes that provide short periods of training in
specific skills. Universities should not try to compete in this

area. Instead, as we urged in the earlier discussion of employee education, the best strategy for universities is to concentrate on broadly based educational programs that relate theory and application.

Using Computers

Judging from the flood of recent publicity, the computer age appears to have arrived on our campuses. A number of institutions have begun to require that every entering undergraduate own a microcomputer (Turner, 1985), although there is considerable controversy concerning the appropriateness of such a requirement (Waldrop, 1985). Almost all colleges and universities make personal computers easily available to students, faculty, and staff. A few universities have undertaken major development projects, usually in close collaboration with one or more computer firms, to enhance the utilization of computers (Tucker, 1984). Brown University and Carnegie Mellon University, for example, are devoting substantial efforts to the evolution of what has come to be called the "scholar's workstation": a personal computer with substantially increased memory, processing speed and capacity, as well as enhanced visual display (Waldrop, 1985; Crecine, 1986). Two recent issues of *Science* (1985, 1986) contain several articles devoted to the use of computers in different disciplines for both research and instruction.

In principle, microcomputers can greatly enhance instructional flexibility and can be adapted to a wide variety of individual needs. When a computer becomes the sole or at least the primary source of learning, each student can proceed at his or her own pace, can skip ahead or back, and can switch programs. The computer, therefore, could significantly enhance the ability of a university to meet the varied needs of a highly diversified student body. The key question, then, is the extent to which the computer can indeed become the primary teaching source. Can this happen in all subjects and at all levels, or only for certain categories of instruction? On this, opinions vary considerably. There are those who believe that the computer will soon revolutionize education, that the development of adequate software is only a matter of time and effort, and that it might make traditional classroom instruction, on or off campus, obsolete. Others view the computer as a further link in that progression of instructional support systems, from the printed book through the typewriter and microfiche to videocassettes, that have affected and enriched the educational process without changing its fundamental nature. But the jury is probably still out: "The PC and its associated information technology seem to be triggering some profound changes in the educational process and in higher education as an institution—although no one is quite sure yet what those changes will be" (Waldrop, 1985, p. 438).

One of the most informative and measured assessments of the prospects of computers in university instruction is contained in a recent annual report by President Derek Bok of Harvard University. He concludes that "with all the exaggerated claims and the media hype, we can still look upon the new technology with cautious enthusiasm" (Bok, 1985, p. 8).

One substantial benefit of the introduction of computers has been renewed attention to the process of learning and teaching. The development of computers and, in particular, the current focus on artificial intelligence have intensified thought and research about the cognitive process at a very basic level (see, for example, Walsh, 1986). In addition, in scores of institutions throughout the country faculty are actively pursuing ways of introducing computers into their courses and are developing or adapting software for that purpose. That inevitably has renewed their awareness of and interest in what happens in the classroom.

To assess the potential impact of microcomputers on the teaching of subjects, from basic writing skills to advanced science laboratories, let us consider four pedagogical categories of computer applications that are already widely used (Schwartz, 1982): (1) word processing and text feedback, (2) drill and practice, (3) simulations and games, and (4) tutorials. These categories are used here only as a convenient simplification. They overlap to a considerable extent and form a continuum quite analogous to that characterizing all pedagogy—a continuum that ranges from directed instruction providing a carefully structured lesson plan in which each student plays a relatively passive role to open education in which students exercise substantial control over the content of their own learning (Jackson, 1986; see also Jackson, 1987).

Using a microcomputer as a *word processor* provides a relatively painless way of editing a piece of writing, and that in itself can be a great boon at almost every level of language instruction. Increasingly, programs are also available that provide feedback on the basis of text analysis: they will flag misspellings and grammatical errors and will even provide a "readability index" based on the average number of words per sentence. But there are also limitations to this approach. Although Robinson (1983-84) mentions an experimental IBM program capable of drawing the user's attention to homophones, commercially available programs currently cannot distinguish between "lose" and "loose" or "to" and "too," to say nothing of "principal" and "principle." Furthermore, Raben (1985) fears that students using these programs are less likely to consult dictionaries. Existing programs also place a premium on simple, declarative sentences that may not necessarily constitute the optimum in writing. The programs are useful in drawing attention to serious errors, but they are a danger if they replace individual judgment.

Drill and practice applications of computers are widespread and have great advantages if properly used. Students can proceed at their own pace and use the program for self-diagnosis of progress. For many individuals, particularly adults returning to formal education, the use of computers in this mode avoids the embarrassment of making mistakes in front of their fellow students. Drill and repetition programs basically use multiple-choice questions, but the more sophisticated versions can do much more than the traditional printed text. They can provide successive sets of clues or hints and keep track of how many of these the student had to use before arriving at the right answer. Some programs also automatically choose material at the appropriate level of difficulty after a few initial diagnostic questions. Still, even the most sophisticated drill and practice programs have the inherent limitation of any such question and answer approach: there is only one "right" answer, and alternative responses are usually not accepted. These programs, therefore, should be "chiefly used to learn facts, basic routines (as in mathematical computations), or collections of rules" (Bok, 1986, p. 146).

Simulation and game playing constitute one of the great potentials of computers in teaching. They are of particular importance in helping to bring about a closer relationship between theory and its applications and to provide opportunities to reflect on and learn from practice. There are many ways of applying this mode. Computers can be used to simulate chemical processes and physical interactions and thus allow a student to observe the importance of pertinent variables without having to carry out an actual experiment. Computers are also increasingly used in the social sciences and in areas such as management to simulate complex situations and to observe the consequences of different choices among possible decisions. A large number of programs are commercially available, and there is even an international journal entitled *Simulation and Games.* The sophistication of available programs is constantly increasing, and they provide a very valuable instructional tool that has the further advantage of encouraging teamwork. But this computer application is subject to a limitation analogous to that of the drill and practice mode: the program of necessity contains a unique, causal relation between any choice and its consequences, which clearly is a simplification of reality.

A characteristic of each of these applications of computers, therefore, is that while they can supplement and indeed change the relationship between teacher and student, they do not eliminate the need for the basic interaction between the two that is the essence of formal education. Using the computer can eliminate much drudgery and routine work for the instructor and can help a student to make much more effective use of his or her study time. But ultimately computers are "new tools [that], however useful, do not change the fundamental role of the teacher" (Tucker, 1984, p. 5). Involvement of the teacher with a student remains essential. In fact, proper use of the computer can intensify this interaction in a most effective way. If their computers could communicate with each other, faculty members and students could at any time leave questions and comments on one another's machines. Frequent review and prompt reaction to all incoming messages and queries can, in principle, provide a very versatile and convenient means of student-faculty communication. Indeed, such "electronic mail" has been used successfully on a limited basis (De Sola Pool, 1983-1984). It remains to be seen whether the necessary dedication of faculty and students to frequent monitoring and rapid responses would also happen on a large scale.

Some observers anticipate a more basic impact of computers—namely, that someday the need for the mentor-learner relationship will be significantly reduced through the development of a true *tutorial mode* of computer application. One of the earliest pioneers and enthusiasts of instruction by computer predicted twenty years ago "that in a few more years millions of [students] will have access to what Philip of Macedon's son Alexander enjoyed as a royal prerogative: the personal services of a tutor as well-informed and as responsive as Aristotle" (Suppes, 1966, p. 206).

As part of the growing body of research into artificial intelligence (AI), much work is currently being done on tutoring by computers (Anderson, Boyle, and Reiser, 1985). However, the development of an effective tutorial system for university-level instruction is, at best, still remote (Walsh, 1986). Tutoring, as distinct from drill and practice, consists of a dialogue in which each successive element depends on an interpretation of what has preceded it. Both the subtleties of such interpretation and the rapidly escalating number of possible combinations of responses in the case of sophisticated subjects are well beyond the capabilities of present computers. That does not entirely rule out the use of the computer as a tutor but restricts it to situations in which the number of possible responses to any pertinent question is limited (Bok, 1986; Schwartz, 1982).

Tutorial systems are closely related to so-called expert systems that combine some of the characteristics of simulation with those of a tutorial mode (Anderson, Boyle, and Reiser, 1985). Some of the earliest examples of expert systems were developed for medical diagnosis and consist of a large number of rules that prescribe what questions should be asked if a certain symptom is observed and what subsequent questions or tests are appropriate depending on the answers to the first. The interesting aspect of these rules is that most of them are based on interviews with physicians. In other words, they are derived from individual diagnostic judgment in an area in which unique, one-to-one relationships between cause and effect usually do not exist. However, such expert systems are coming ever closer to simulating the "messiness" of real situations not only in medicine but also in complex social, political, or economic situations. Ultimately, the ability to do this might be of great help in bridging theory and practice and could have substantial impact on the content of higher education curricula. It might also be used very effectively in providing at least a simulation of real situations to faculty who are isolated from actual practice.

Two further categories of computer utilization are likely to become important, particularly for the "nonhard scientist" (Beeman, 1986). With the sophisticated work stations currently under development, scholars as well as students will have the capacity to manipulate texts, narrative materials, and illustrations in many different ways. They will be able to juxtapose the text of an original document or piece of writing with various commentaries and explications or display, side by side, written material and pertinent illustrations from other sources. They will also have available a great variety of highly sophisticated graphic tools for the display as well as the comparison of complex bodies of data.

The Wired Campus

Earlier sections of this chapter described how telecommunication enhances the ability of universities to provide data, information, and even some professional services at remote locations. The most straightforward uses are those in which a single source of information or a single device on campus is hooked up through an appropriate form of telecommunication to a remote location. An external user, for example, can tie into a large computer on campus by a simple telephone connection. This is currently of particular interest because of the installation of so-called supercomputers—fifth-generation machines with very high speeds and capacities—on a number of university campuses. These are made available to external users on a contractual or fee-for-service basis (Turner, 1986). Similarly, remote access is in principle also readily available to campus libraries with computerized catalogues and also to whatever national search and reference services and data bases the university may be connected with.

Certain categories of research and other modes of professional cooperation can be furthered by having participants communicate with each other by means of a computer and in some cases by using on-line computers tied directly into an experiment that delivers the observations to various remote locations. A variety of long-distance interconnections have been used for many years within the academic community; they are used, for example, to link researchers in various astronomic observatories to each other. In recent years such networks have increasingly been extended to industrial laboratories (Jennings and others, 1986).

These various connections of universities with the outside world through telecommunication may, in the near future, come to include what has been called the "wired campus." In a sense, of course, our campuses have been wired ever since the advent of electric lights and the telephone. Additional wired networks appeared on campuses in recent years, including a variety of interconnections for instructional television and networks for computer access and time sharing. In most cases these networks remained separate, with some installed and owned by the university, others by a telephone or other utility company. But it is now possible, with a high initial investment, to install a single institutional network, most likely using the technique of fiber optics, that can do much more than all the previous pieces combined. The technical problems of having a great variety of different computers talk to each other are proving to be formidable (Waldrop, 1985; Sanger, 1986). One of the principal objectives of Project Athena at the Massachusetts Institute of Technology is to develop what it calls "coherence" in a highly heterogeneous computer system by making it as hardware-inde-

pendent as possible and facilitating the uniform sharing of data
and work among all users (*Project Athena,* 1983).

The value of ubiquitous access to data bases, computing
facilities, and electronic mail differs for different constituencies
both on and off campus. The potential administrative benefits
and cost savings of an all-inclusive, high-capacity campus network are substantial (Steele, 1983). The educational potential,
however, remains more questionable. Advocates of the wired
campus anticipate a way of linking all the microcomputers on
every faculty and student desk and all the computers in the library, research laboratory, and computer center so as to provide
everyone with (1) virtually universal access to data bases, biblio-
graphical searches, and other information sets from all the campus libraries as well as from outside information sources connected to the network (Williams, 1985); (2) virtually universal
communication among all members of the campus community
by electronic mail; and (3) virtually universal access to central
computing and graphics facilities as well as the clustering of
micro- and minicomputers for greater capacity.

All access available on campus can be readily extended to
any off-campus location; from the outside it is as easy to tie
into a totally wired campus as it is to a single computer. Hence,
in principle, the wired campus suggests the ultimate in extending the university: for the categories of activity enumerated
above, it has no geographical boundaries at all.

All this is likely to be very desirable for researchers and
students as well as for external clients of sophisticated professional services, particularly in the hard sciences and engineering.
These are also fields in which external funding for computer acquisition and maintenance is quite readily available. But the
wired campus may be of much less value to many other users,
on and off campus, for whom present modes of access are quite
adequate for their more limited and intermittent needs. Thus,
paradoxically, it may well be that "if computers are to be a permanent feature of academic life, they must justify themselves in
education and research terms in those social sciences and humanities for which no external support is ever likely to arise"
(Beeman, 1986, p. 36). Hence, when the novelty of networking

wears off, hard questions will have to be asked about costs and benefits (Tucker, 1984).

The New Technology and the Extended University

The potential computerization of the university campus has been discussed in this chapter at some length because, as has been mentioned repeatedly, the educational use of new technology is very pertinent to the extended functions of the university. There are both benefits and risks here.

On the one hand, it is very evident that the combination of computerization and telecommunication quite literally eliminates the physical boundaries of the university and enables it in principle to extend many of its functions to any desired location while at the same time maintaining, electronically, considerable contact and communication with on-campus faculty. Both the instructional and the scholarly activities of the university can thus be much more easily extended. In addition, the technology also enhances a university's ability to tailor both instruction and certain professional services to the specific needs of a wide range of different clients. Thus, overall, there is no question that computerization together with telecommunication can make it much easier for universities to bring about many of the changes advocated in this book and in principle to have a beneficial effect on the mode and intensity of interaction between instructor and student.

Yet, on the other hand, the reduction of the geographical bounds of the university also means that any downside risks with regard to the use of educational technology similarly affects activities both off- and on-campus. And, in fact, substantial dangers are inherent in the rapid development of telecommunication and computers. By their very nature, the new technologies place a premium on simplicity, on direct causal relationships, on unambiguous, yes-or-no situations, on hard facts and figures. Subtleties, conditional relationships, multiple interactions are much more difficult to represent than, say, illustrations of Newtonian mechanics or numerical information. In general, "the computer cannot contribute much to the learning of open-ended subjects like moral philosophy, religion, historical interpretation, literary criticism, or social theory—fields of knowledge that cannot be reduced to formal rules and procedures" (Bok, 1985, p. 5).

Televised material can *illustrate* some aspects of these subjects and indeed does so very successfully in many Open University courses as a supplement to reading and discussion. But used by itself, it is likely to lead to dangerous simplifications. That risk is real, because one cannot be sure that the applications of technology will remain limited to fields for which it is appropriate. Means often become the end. The glamor of new technology, and the expectations raised once substantial investments of time and money are made in its development, both lead to strong pressures to extend its use too far. Statements by enthusiasts and the hyperbole associated with the sweeping introduction of computers on some campuses all carry the implication—and increase the probability—that new technologies are to be applied to everything. It is all too easy to place excessive emphasis on material that is quantifiable and programmable, and all too tempting to ignore that which is more ambiguous, speculative, and qualitative. A recent biography of one of the pioneers in computing warns that "the issue is not whether the computer can be made to think like a human, but whether humans can and will take on the quality of digital computers" (Bolter, 1984, p. 150).

This very real problem is further intensified by the enormous capacity of the new technology for information retrieval. On the whole, this potential constitutes a great boon. The relative ease with which it is now possible to do extensive literature searches by computer and the availability of a large variety of data bases are very important to many students and faculty (Williams, 1985) and can also enhance the professional services rendered by the university to external clients. Yet this very accessibility places a premium on the accumulation rather than the selection of information, on amassing data rather than on the interpretation and synthesis. It reinforces the prevailing trend to confuse data and information with knowledge and understanding instead of ensuring that "information literacy rather than computer literacy [is] the goal" (Steele, 1983).

Lastly, one must also keep in mind that the use of technology will make access to many university activities dependent on having the necessary equipment and means of communication. That requirement may make such activities *less* available to individuals, organizations, and enterprises that cannot afford the necessary gadgetry. Thus the increasing use of computers and telecommunication may, paradoxically, raise rather than lower barriers to access for some potential clients of university services (see, for example, Wagner and Lynton, 1987).

To point out the dangers of excessive reliance on the new technologies is not to reject their use but to call for discrimination and perhaps some caution in their application (Lynton, 1987). On the whole, we agree with the assessment that "the balance of benefits and risks seems to favor the new technology" (Bok, 1985, p. 7). In particular, the proper use of the new technologies will greatly enhance the ability of universities to carry out their expanded responsibility as described in this book. The combination of telecommunication and computers, in effect, allows universities to bring a substantial portion of their instructional and professional resources to clients, instead of having them come to the campus. But these same technologies can also be used by other providers of instruction, information, and technical assistance. Not using the technologies, or using them improperly, will make the universities increasingly vulnerable to this competition.

9

Expanding Faculty Roles
and Obligations

Many of the changes that universities must undertake to meet
evolving societal needs create important tasks for trustees, for
academic administrators, for the leadership of professional associations, and for state and federal policy makers. But at the
heart of all reform and essential to its success is active participation by the faculty. The major challenge is to place the faculty
at the center of any process for change, to provide them with
appropriate incentives and rewards, and to make it possible for
them to acquire the knowledge and skills needed to perform
new and expanded tasks. These are the most critical steps in extending the role and functions of universities.

At the most basic level, the task of university faculty continues to be a principal dedication to and involvement in advanced knowledge. That is the common element in the activities
of all professors (Clark, 1983). But as Chapter One pointed out,
contemporary society has vastly expanded, as have its different
needs for knowledge. Hence, changing external needs and conditions, coupled with the vast growth of the university sector, call
for new priorities and emphases on the part of the faculty.

In their scholarly activities, university faculty members

need to concentrate as much on the interpretation and dissemination of knowledge as on its generation. If the knowledge-related function of universities changes and expands in fundamental ways, it follows that there should be a concomitant broadening of the definition of professorial practice and of the role of faculty members. This role must shift from an exclusive emphasis on the accumulation of factual data resulting from research projects to include the dissemination of aggregated, interpreted, and usable knowledge. All portions of the broadened range of scholarship and professional services required by contemporary society, as we argued in Chapter One, deserve to be accorded parity of esteem as well as reward not only because they are of comparable importance but also because they are intellectually as challenging as most of the more traditional forms of scholarship.

The earlier discussion of the evolving instructional tasks of the modern university provided ample evidence that the kind of teaching necessary to educate competent individuals also is considerably more challenging than the traditional exposition of theory. In career-oriented as well as in arts and science programs, at both the graduate and the undergraduate level, more has to be expected from faculty than an *ex cathedra* transmission of knowledge, with the student as a passive recipient. Every current discussion of higher education calls for more active involvement of students in the learning process, with faculty acting more as catalysts than as dispensers of knowledge. Chapters Four and Five further described the need for teaching that relates theory and practice, emphasizes relationships and complementary elements among disciplines, and helps students define questions rather than merely solve problems. Those are pedagogical challenges that make the instructional task in the modern university exceedingly difficult.

An enumeration of what a faculty member needs to be able to do in order to be effective in terms of the expanded definition of the professorial role clearly indicates how demanding it is:

In the first place, faculty members must of course remain up-to-date on the results of basic research in their field, although this can be accomplished without their being actively engaged in such research. Second, as knowledge moves closer to its application, it becomes increasingly problem oriented and multidisciplinary. Hence, faculty members require a clear understanding of the relationship between their own disciplines and cognate areas. They need to make an effort in both the preparatory and subsequent stages of their academic careers to transcend narrow specialization if they are to be active in the application of knowledge and if they are to help their students to become more than narrow specialists.

Third, they also need knowledge of, and preferably some professional experience in, the world outside of the university to gain an understanding of the applications of new ideas and methodologies, the relationship of theory to practice, the limitations of the former, and what can be learned from experience.

Finally in all their didactic activities, whether formal instruction, consulting, or providing public information, the faculty will need to be able to help others understand complex issues. Their audience, in the classroom and elsewhere, will span a wide range of ages and backgrounds, and thus faculty will increasingly require a sensitivity to a variety of learning modes.

All this is asking a great deal of faculty and shows that if universities are to respond more systematically to external knowledge needs, they must *raise,* rather than *diminish,* the intellectual standards and challenges both for their institutions as a whole and for participating faculty members. This book's advocacy of an extended definition of faculty scholarship differs quite fundamentally from what has been called the "clergy model" of faculty (Lovett, 1986)—a model that calls for individuals who are primarily teachers of undergraduates and are basically generalists. For universities to carry out their expanded scholarly function and to provide competence-oriented teaching, faculty must be *more* than scholars in a discipline, not *less*; they must be scholars with a broad perspective on the interrelationship of disciplines and their practical applications. As Lovett points out, in a growing number of disciplines good teaching will require that faculty "will not necessarily have to make original contributions, but they *will* need to keep up with a formidable volume of theoretical and applied research. We can hope that they will be broadly educated men and women; we cannot hope that they will be generalists" (1986, p. 8).

The need to remain up-to-date, as well as to be broadly educated, is at least as important for effective involvement in applied professional activity as it is for the development and teaching of coherent and comprehensive curricula. Von Humboldt, in his sweeping reform of Prussian universities in the beginning of the nineteenth century, insisted on integrative scholarship (Sweet, 1980). In a very real sense, the new definition of faculty excellence is closer to this definition than to the prevailing emphasis on original research.

To bring about these changes is a formidable task. It cannot be accomplished by fiat, nor will it happen quickly. It requires a gradual process, but a pervasive one. Progress can only be made a step at a time, but if many small steps are taken by many people in many places, the cumulative effect will be considerable.

The steps that are needed fall, broadly, into two groups:

1. A variety of activities to help current faculty adapt to new external opportunities and pressures, together with ways of preparing future generations of faculty
2. Basic changes in the existing system of values, incentives, and rewards in order to bring about parity of esteem and equality of treatment for the full range of professional activities

The remainder of this chapter addresses the first set of issues. It should be read with the realization that to bring about changes in the reward system is an essential precondition for improving faculty development. When the academic scale of respectability and rewards acknowledges the importance—and the difficulty— of the synthesis, interpretation, and application of knowledge as equivalent to that of carrying out a set of original measurements, then needed faculty development is likely to evolve.

Conversely, in the absence of a decisive change in the value and reward system, little is likely to happen. The next chapter will address itself to that crucial issue.

Helping Current Faculty Meet New Challenges

The current age distribution of faculty members in American universities reflects their concentrated growth between 1955 and 1965. A large number of new Ph.D.'s in their mid twenties entered the system during those years. In 1980, a survey by the Carnegie Council on Policy Studies in Higher Education indicated that about 34 percent of tenured faculty members were between the ages of forty-six and fifty-five, with about 20 percent in the bracket from fifty-six to sixty-five. The survey predicted that by 1990, 46 percent of tenured faculty will be between forty-six and fifty-five, and about 31 percent between fifty-six and sixty-five (Carnegie Council on Policy Studies in Higher Education, 1980). Today, therefore, the professoriate contains a substantial fraction of individuals who can anticipate another decade or more of active service. Thus, to expand the mission of the university, the most immediate need is to help this group, as well as their younger colleagues, to adapt to an expanding task.

There is no intrinsic reason why this cannot be done. Current problems are due neither to inadequate ability nor to inadequate interest—both are amply available. Many faculty are very much aware of the gap that now exists between prevailing practices and real needs. Indeed, hundreds of them already are actively and successfully engaged in professional outreach. However, many more should become involved. Institutional action is needed to reduce the existing barriers to such activities. The following are some of the ways in which faculty can be assisted in becoming more active and more effective in carrying out their expanded teaching and professional responsibilities:

1. A clear commitment to the expanding role of universities by the academic leadership of the institution is probably the most important factor in bringing about a redirection of faculty energies. Presidents, academic vice-presidents, and deans

can set the tone by encouraging and supporting a variety of activities through which the tenured faculty can broaden their disciplinary perspectives and gain a better understanding of the potential applications of their areas of specialization.

2. Academic administrators should exert their influence to ensure that faculty involvement in extended scholarly and professional activities receives parity of esteem and reward with more traditional forms of scholarship. They should also insist on adequate documentation and rigorous evaluation, as will be discussed in the next chapter.

3. Faculty in different fields can learn a great deal from each other. Groups of faculty from different disciplines and indeed from different colleges should be appointed to engage in intensive curriculum development. What is needed is not the usual abstract discussion about "general education," which does not reflect the basic interests and background of most faculty members. Rather, these joint explorations should focus on the knowledge needs of specific occupations. For example, what are the needs of an engineer, a manager, or a government official in order to be competent and effective on the job? What understanding of history, political processes, economic forces, and social systems is pertinent at various stages of professional development? How can such issues best be included in the curriculum? What are the principal ethical issues the practitioner will encounter? Discussions of this type will teach faculty members a great deal not only about other fields but also about their own.

4. Much benefit can also be derived from interaction with practitioners. The effectiveness of many degree programs would be enhanced by involving more individuals with practical experience. Yet experience alone is not a sufficient condition for effective teaching; practitioners need to reflect on their experience and derive generalizations from it. That is a process that should involve faculty as well as practitioners: each set of participants would help the other by applying complementary skills to the situation. In that way practitioners can relate their experience to a methodological framework, and faculty can better understand the relationship of theory to practice.

5. Administrative leadership is essential for encouraging the exchange of qualified professionals between the campus and external places of work. The academic labor market is far too separated from other sectors (Lovett, 1986). Moreover, there is a great need to enhance a two-way flow of individuals between the campus and the world outside not only in professional areas but also in the liberal arts. Efforts are needed not only to increase the appropriate use of practitioners as full-time or adjunct faculty but also to encourage tenured faculty to spend periods of time in settings external to the campus. In addition to fostering this by implementing appropriate leave policies, institutions should explore all possibilities of formal exchange agreements both with private industry and with public agencies.

6. An inescapable responsibility of all university faculty is to remain abreast of the latest developments in their fields, but there are ways of encouraging this other than by insisting on original basic research. The more isolated and less research-oriented the institution, the more value can be derived by expecting every faculty member at regular intervals to summarize the state of the art in his or her field in written or oral form as a presentation for colleagues in other departments and/or the public-at-large. The quality of such activities can be judged quite easily.

The Next Generation of Faculty

In ten years, American colleges and universities will need to replace a large number of their current faculty. A recent study (Bowen and Schuster, 1986) estimates that even during the impending enrollment decline between now and 1995, at least 30,000 and perhaps as many as 100,000 new faculty members will be needed to replace those who will be retiring. From 1985 to 2010, the need is likely to range from 70,000 to 130,000 new full-time faculty in each five-year period. The individuals who will be hired during the nineties are about to embark upon their own undergraduate education and will begin their advanced training by the end of this decade. We have just a few years of lead time to reflect on the preparation of new faculty and to explore possible alternatives to our current practices.

Perhaps the most basic need is to broaden the curricular content of the course of study that prepares future university faculty. They need more than mastery of a narrowly defined specialty in order to carry out their extended and diverse responsibilities in the modern university. Indeed, of all professions it is the academic one that needs a truly liberal career preparation. Much of this, of course, should have been achieved during the undergraduate years, but it is especially important that during the graduate years of specialization future faculty also obtain broad perspectives on their own disciplines. The necessary breadth of knowledge to be emphasized as part of the doctoral program has been summarized as follows (Dunham, 1970; Dressel, 1982):

- A thorough knowledge of the fundamental aspects of a discipline or field of study and the ability to relate this knowledge to current issues and problems
- The ability, by means of case studies as well as practical experience, to relate the essential ideas, concepts, and principles of that discipline to cognate fields and to understand how these need to be combined in analyzing complex situations
- A reasonable understanding of the nature and processes of human learning, acquired by some appropriate combination of course work and teaching internships, and some familiarity with educational methods and technology
- A measure of perspective on the current status and the probable future of higher education gained through study of its history and an understanding of its societal role

The first three of these points echo what has been discussed in the earlier sections of this chapter. An additional comment is in order with regard to the fourth. The academic profession on the whole is astonishingly ignorant of "the province of [its] own commitment" (Clark, 1983, p. 1). Its limited knowledge of the history of higher education and its inadequate over-

view of the educational system as a whole diminish its ability to
exercise an adequate measure of control over its own destiny.
With only fragmentary knowledge of the continuing changes
that have taken place in the evolution of universities, many faculty members do not recognize the extent to which it is inevitable that their institutions will continue to evolve and to adapt
in response to changing external circumstances. Without that
understanding, members of the professoriate either drift along
as passive participants in changes triggered externally or tend to
resist all change to preserve what they believe to be immutable
institutions. If faculty are to play an active and constructive
role in helping to shape (and indeed to moderate) adaptation
and change, they need to know more about past developments
in higher education. We applaud the Study Group on the Conditions of Excellence in American Higher Education for rec-
ommending that "graduate deans and department chairs should
help prospective faculty in all disciplines . . . to learn about the
history, organization, and culture of American higher education" (Study Group on the Conditions of Excellence in American Higher Education, 1984, p. 65).

Of course time and resources are limited, and broadening
the content of a doctoral program in some directions necessarily
requires some curtailment in others. The extent and nature of
this trade-off should be as flexible and as individually adjustable
as is compatible with the application of uniformly high standards of excellence. Within this limitation there should be as
much opportunity as possible for self-selection and choice on
the part of doctoral candidates. This is beginning to happen, to
some extent, in such professions as medicine and law. The individual clearly committed to a career in basic research would be
identified early in his or her career and would be encouraged to
pursue the traditional path toward a Ph.D. Others might be
more interested in synthesis and explication, in problem-oriented
applied work, or in formal teaching. Each should be able to find
some modification of curriculum and some culminating project
that might differ from a traditional research-based dissertation.

Closely related to extending and broadening the content
of the education for a faculty career is the issue of its pattern

and timing. To be prepared for applied work and for direct extension and dissemination of knowledge, faculty require considerable experience in and understanding of the world outside the campus. The current pattern of uninterrupted study from nursery school to the first academic job is hardly conducive to developing someone's capabilities to apply his or her expertise to complex real issues and to work directly with clients and students from highly diverse backgrounds. A major effort should be undertaken to introduce a period of practical experience into the process of preparing future faculty members.

Again there is no one way of bringing this about. One could imagine an approach analogous to that now taken by an increasing number of business schools, which require a minimum of two years of pertinent practical experience before admission into MBA programs. Perhaps a similar stipulation, requirement, or strong recommendation might be applied to doctoral programs. Alternatively, or perhaps in addition, periods of internships and other practical experience could become part of the doctoral program itself. The University of Chicago includes a graduate internship in its doctoral programs (Groneman and Lear, 1985), and some institutions use the model of cooperative education at this level. For such advanced programs the same holds as for undergraduate programs: experience needs to be recognized as more than a matter of opportunities to apply theory. Experience is itself a source of learning and understanding, indicating the limitations of theory and the relationship of cognate fields and different methodologies. Hence reflection on practice and learning from the standpoint of experience should become part of the formal curriculum.

Introducing such practical interludes into the preparation of future faculty is also likely to decrease the extraordinary, self-imposed separation of the academic profession from all other career paths (Lovett, 1986). A doctoral degree is, on the whole, viewed as preparation only for an academic career, and the Ph.D. alone opens the door to a faculty position in a university. Both limitations are open to serious questions. In recent years the shortage of faculty positions has forced many Ph.D.'s into nonacademic jobs in which most of them—perhaps to their

own surprise and that of their employers—have done very well
(Groneman and Lear, 1985). At the same time, in universities
across the country, in liberal arts colleges as well as in professional schools, non-Ph.D.'s are making significant contributions
both as teachers and as scholars.

In addition to the inclusion of practical experience into
doctoral preparation for an academic career, alternatives to the
current research dissertation as a requirement for the Ph.D.
might also be considered as a way of reflecting the more varied
scholarly functions expected from faculty in the contemporary
university. Doctoral requirements, for instance, could include
one or more of the following:

- Carrying out a thorough impact analysis of a proposed policy or project
- Writing an extensive review and critique of a field that ex-
  plains its principal methodological and paradigmatic debates
  in terms understandable to a nonexpert
- Developing a complete annotated and critical bibliography
- Designing an innovative course outline and syllabus combining pertinent materials from different disciplines
- Developing significant new software for educational use of
  computers and other technology

All these rely on secondary sources rather than requiring
first-hand observations and measurements. Therefore, as compared to a more traditional thesis project, these alternatives may
not provide the student opportunities to gain a firm grounding
in the methodology utilized in basic research. Nevertheless, such
tasks may ultimately better prepare future faculty to meet the
new knowledge needs of society and will enhance their teaching
skills as well.

Alternatives to the Ph.D.

In the past, the many expressions of dissatisfaction with
the preparation of college and university faculty focused primarily on the lack of emphasis on teaching skills. Many critics

believed that adaptation of the traditional doctoral degree would not go far enough and that a different degree was needed. As a noted critic of higher education aptly observed: "For college teaching, graduate programs produce competencies, values, expectations, and a reward system that are simply incompatible with undergraduate liberal education. The research Ph.D. degree is inappropriate for most college teaching jobs in this country, especially at the lower-division level" (Dunham, 1970, p. 506).

Dunham strongly advocated establishing the doctor of arts (D.A.) degree, a new type of graduate program recommended by the Council on Graduate Schools in 1970 that was designed "to prepare graduate students for a lifetime of effective teaching at the college level" (1970, p. xx).

Carnegie Mellon University was the first university to offer such a degree. The most recent survey (Dressel, 1982) lists twenty-four institutions offering the D.A. degree. By 1982, approximately 900 such degrees had been awarded in fields ranging from English and history (by far the most common) to physics, chemistry, and mechanical engineering, on the one hand, and music education, foreign language instruction, and medical technology, on the other. The range of topics mirrors the range of institutions, which includes Carnegie Mellon University, the University of Michigan, the Claremont Graduate School, Middle Tennessee State University, the University of Northern Colorado, and Simmons College. There are also marked differences in degree requirements, as pointed out by Dressel: "Diversity, whether desirable or undesirable, makes it difficult to characterize the D.A. except that it is not a Ph.D. and therefore acquires either the advantages or disadvantages of this status, depending upon the critic" (1982, p. 10).

On the whole Dressel welcomes reasonable diversity but recommends that all D.A. programs have a number of common characteristics, which include "extradepartmental and interdisciplinary courses or seminars that require that the student relate his or her field of major study to other fields so as to enhance his or her insights into the significance of the major field and foster the ability to make it more meaningful to students of diverse interests and abilities" (1982, p. 25). He also advocates a teaching internship and "a dissertation, research, or evaluation effort that provides a demonstration of the prospective teacher's ability to interpret a disciplinary base to students in ways that facilitate broad behavioral learnings rather than rote recall of facts" (p. 25).

The D.A. program was introduced just at the time when both higher education administrators and state officials were belatedly recognizing demographic realities and were coming to see that the postwar period of growth had come to an end. In public universities thoughout the country, new graduate programs were severely curtailed or hit by a complete moratorium. The limited number and aggregate enrollment of existing D.A. programs, therefore, do not provide a fair measure of the intrinsic merits and appeal of this new degree. Yet it is likely that even had growth continued, D.A. programs would not have come to represent a substantial portion of the preparatory programs for university faculty. The D.A. in its present form is specifically aimed at teaching institutions. Chapter Two made clear that universities are not prepared to view themselves as teaching institutions, regardless of how limited their involvement in graduate work and research is. Indeed the major thrust of this book is that all universities have a responsibility for the interpretation, dissemination, and application of knowledge—a responsibility that includes but transcends classroom teaching.

For the preparation of future university faculty one would therefore have to modify the current conception of the D.A. so as to retain more connection with and emphasis on scholarly activities other than formal instruction. The question can really be viewed as essentially a tactical one: given the inherent conservatism and inertia of the academic world, can one realistically expect modifications in the organization and the degree requirements of the traditional Ph.D. program? Or is there a greater likelihood of success by introducing a new degree? Our own position is to favor changes in the current approach to the Ph.D. degree, reflecting our view that the university must continue to be a place of scholarship, albeit with a broadened conception of this term.

Whatever the strategy, change is crucial. At present, the

academic profession is virtually alone among all occupations in not taking a hard look at its own methods of preparation and overall practices. To be sure, there are plenty of academic critiques regarding inadequate faculty preparation and development. Many sessions of recent American Association for Higher Education meetings and of other professional associations have focused on the need for change. But as yet little or no attention has been directed at this issue by those associations that set the tone with regard to graduate study and the preparation of future academics. There is an urgent need for bodies such as the Council on Graduate Schools and the American Association of Universities to address themselves to these issues.

✣ 10 ✣

Evaluating and Rewarding
New Professional Activities

The previous chapter described the need to expand faculty roles and activities by giving as much emphasis to the synthesis, interpretation, and transmission of advanced knowledge as to its generation. Such a broadened definition can be implemented only through basic changes in the priorities that determine faculty values, incentives, and rewards (Lynton, Elman, and Smock, 1985). In virtually all universities—in strongly research-oriented institutions as well as in the broad middle range of doctoral and comprehensive universities—existing priorities focus heavily on the traditional and limited definition of scholarship: basic research that leads to publication in refereed, scholarly journals.

In the Introduction we described the uniformity of values and aspirations that pervade universities, in spite of the substantial diversity of activity within them. This uniformity is strikingly illustrated by the prevailing faculty reward system. In conducting an informal survey that elicited responses from more than one hundred institutions, we found that virtually every university—small or large, research oriented or not—uses substantially identical language both in its formal statements of criteria for faculty appointments, promotion, and tenure, and

146

in its informal description of how these criteria are actually applied in personnel processes. The emphasis on traditional scholarship is pervasive, and almost without exception all other categories of professional activity are lumped together with campus committee work and civic activities under the rubric of service. And service, although always listed as one of the three principal factors to be considered in the faculty reward system, actually never has parity of esteem and reward with scholarship.

To achieve what is being advocated throughout this book—namely, that the range of professional and scholarly activities of faculty be expanded—the reward system needs to encourage the participation of all faculty members, tenured or not. At this time, most existing outreach activities are carried out either by tenured faculty or by special professional staff not on a tenure track. Junior faculty run a considerable risk if they spend more than a small fraction of their time in the less traditional kinds of scholarship. When these faculty are reviewed for reappointment, promotion, and tenure, externally oriented, applied projects, no matter how excellent, generally carry considerably less weight than traditional scholarly publication, even of a fairly routine nature. Limited involvement by nontenured faculty matters little at this time because of the prevailing high proportion of tenured individuals. But during the next decade, a substantial number of new faculty will be hired (Bowen and Schuster, 1986). Increasingly, a university's ability to provide the necessary knowledge-based services to its external constituencies will depend on using younger, nontenured faculty.

Service or Scholarship?

The broad range of professional activities described in this book are often categorized as *public service*. One can take the position that there exists in American higher education a long and proud tradition of public service (Crosson, 1983) and that this mission should be strengthened and given more emphasis (Crosson, 1985; University of California at Davis Committee on Public Service, 1985). We, on the contrary, believe that one can more successfully encourage a wider range of professional activities if these are recognized as valid components of *scholar-ship*. We take this position both because we think that the aggregation, interpretation, and application of knowledge are in fact scholarly exercises and because we do not believe that service will ever be taken as seriously as scholarship.

Service is a term that has the inescapable overtone of "good citizenship," implying, as it does, a kind of philanthropic activity in which one ought to be engaged for the good of the institution and the community. The term is appropriate to serving on campus committees, being on the local library board, giving volunteer tutorial help to high school students, and many similar civic activities. But the same label should not be applied to professionally based technical assistance and policy analysis for a local government or community group. There exists a fundamental difference. Technical assistance and policy analysis constitute direct applications of the faculty member's professional and scholarly expertise. By contrast, civic involvement, on or off campus, engages the faculty member as a participant within a community but is usually not explicitly based on her or his professional capacity. It is of utmost importance to make a distinction between faculty members' activities as scholars and professionals, on the one hand, and what they do in their capacity as citizens of the institution and community, on the other. The kind of professional activity discussed in this book refers exclusively to work that draws upon one's professional expertise and is an outgrowth of one's academic discipline (Elman and Smock, 1985). It is as serious and demanding an activity as teaching and traditional scholarship. It requires faculty to apply their expertise directly to an issue or problem or to the public dissemination of information.

Hence professional activity is an *extension* of traditional scholarship, not a *substitute* for it. The institutionalization of a reward structure for faculty engaged in such activity does not imply a reduction in the importance of traditional scholarship. Rather, it elevates to a comparable level of importance and esteem—and subjects to a comparable level of quality control—a broad continuum of knowledge-related scholarly activities. We believe that the quality of the academic environment will be enhanced through close reciprocal relationships between strong teaching, traditional scholarship, and externally oriented professional activities, with the whole being greater than the sum of the parts. We are also convinced that the expanded and multiple knowledge needs described in Chapter One require that there be considerable flexibility of movement along the continuum of scholarly activities for individual faculty members, for units within a university, and for the institution as a whole. Traditional scholarship and professional activity should not be posed as dichotomous, mutually exclusive undertakings. This would establish two echelons of faculty, one engaged in traditional scholarship, the other in externally oriented professional activities. At any given time, some faculty members may concentrate on traditional scholarship, others on professional outreach. On the whole most should engage in a mix that is likely to vary with time, as interests, opportunities, and needs change.

An excellent way of clarifying this and of providing assurance to the faculty that no one will be expected to be simultaneously involved in the entire spectrum of professional activities is to institute a yearly or biyearly review of individual work loads for each faculty member (Lovett, 1986). The University of Louisville is one example of an institution that does this in order to arrive at periodic reciprocal agreements between faculty member and dean or provost as to assignments and expectations, with the clear understanding that these can be modified at subsequent reviews, depending on external needs, internal priorities, and personal circumstances. The mix of traditional scholarship and applied professional activity will vary from faculty to faculty. The important task is to insist on equivalence of quality, on parity of esteem and reward, and on ongoing linkages and communication. Applied work and extension ought to reflect the state of the art of the pertinent disciplines, and basic research should in turn be informed by external problems and issues.

The current situation is actually quite paradoxical. Many of our most prestigious universities in fact strongly encourage their faculty to engage in technical assistance and outreach. We all know the ancient joke about the similarity between certain

well-known institutions and the Strategic Air Command: both
have one third of their staff in the air at any given time. Some
major state universities, as well as such private institutions as
Harvard, MIT, and Stanford, have for many years been substantial providers of professional expertise to governmental agencies
as well as to the private sector. More recently, many of them
have developed strong collaborative relationships with industry
in applied research. To be sure, there is something intrinsically
prestigious about consulting for the State Department or the
National Security Council, entering into a cooperative venture
with IBM or Digital Equipment, or writing for the *New York
Times* or a national newsmagazine. It is much less glamorous to
work with state and local governments, to cooperate with the
small, low-tech enterprise down the road, or to explain issues of
nuclear waste disposal in a local newspaper. This distinction is
unfortunate. Outreach activities at the local level can be just as
intellectually challenging as those in the national or international arena. Moreover, such local and regional issues are precisely
those in which the majority of universities can and should play
an important role. Unfortunately, they do not. The prestige is
not there, and middle-range universities are engaged in a sometimes desperate search for academic respectability. As a result,
they often insist on academic purity in order to show that they
are "real universities" that give priority to traditional research
and scholarly publication.

Adapting the Reward System

Without a substantial adaptation of the faculty reward
system, all efforts at greater university outreach and expanded
faculty activities will continue to be what they have been in the
majority of institutions: a matter of well-intended but ineffec-
tive rhetoric. It is not enough simply to say that these changes
ought to occur. It is necessary to address in a pragmatic and
realistic way how they can be made to occur. Most important,
ways should be found of assuring that the broader range of
faculty professional activity comes to be taken just as seriously as the more traditional scholarly engagements with regard

both to evaluation and rewards. Because we are not talking about civic duty or philanthropy but rather are addressing ourselves to the professional activities of faculty members, it is essential to insist on the same standards of quality as are used in the more traditional areas of scholarship. Means are needed of *documenting* the professional activity and then of *evaluating* it (Elman and Smock, 1985). Without them, the faculty will not place any value on outreach activities and will continue to denigrate them as "public service," measured only by quantity, as in the case of committee membership or student advising.

In the remaining sections of this chapter we will suggest some practical ways for dealing with a number of pertinent issues:

- What are the categories of professional activity in which greater faculty involvement should be encouraged?
- What is it that a dean, a chairperson, or a promotion and tenure committee needs to know about such activities in order to evaluate and, if appropriate, to reward them?
- How does one define and recognize the crucial element of applying professional expertise that must characterize all such activities?
- What are the criteria by which these activities are to be evaluated: originality? impact? replicability?

Categories of Professional Activity

The effective institutionalization of an equitable reward structure requires that all relevant actors clearly understand what professional activity encompasses. It is not an all-inclusive concept. As set forth here, professional activity consists of the application of high-level expertise in an attempt to relate the results of basic research to their utilization. These conditions provide severe limitations on what can be called professional activity, yet they encompass a wide variety of scholarly work that ranges, at one extreme, from applied research virtually indistinguishable from the traditional mode of basic research to, at the other extreme, informational activities closely resembling traditional teaching. In between there is a continuum that includes the following activities:

1. Directed or contracted research
2. Consultation, technical assistance, policy analysis, technology assessment, and program evaluation
3. Targeted briefing and other didactic activities
4. Informational and explanatory activities for a general audience

Directed or Contracted Research. As a result of the shrinking time lag between basic research activities and their application, the traditional distinction between pure and applied research has largely lost its meaning. It has become more useful to distinguish between nondirected research carried out at the initiative of the investigator and research carried out under contract or in response to a request for proposal and thus initiated by the potential user of the research results. Even that distinction is a blurred one, but it has some utility in the current context because there exists a tendency to classify the latter kind of research as less valid or less respectable than the former. Yet both are important.

Directed or contracted research exists in virtually every discipline. It can consist of developing and testing new materials, of carrying out ecological, meteorological, and other environmental studies, of conducting market and opinion research and other kinds of social science surveys, of applying ethical and moral criteria to complex situations, and of designing modes of assessment and evaluation. It might involve the design of a sophisticated computer program to optimize certain complex operations, of a protocol to assess the effectiveness of a new therapy, of an evaluation instrument to test a new mode of classroom instruction. The list of examples could fill many pages. Regardless of the specific issue under inquiry, the defining characteristic of this kind of research is that it focuses on immediate problems and attempts to provide results within a reasonable period of time. Its concern is with the here and now.

Consultation and Technical Assistance. The broad category of technical assistance, consultation, policy analysis, technology assessment, and program evaluation may well constitute the most valuable and yet most underestimated form of professional activity that a university can offer. Through these activities, businesses, governments, nonprofit organizations, and community agencies can avail themselves of needed expertise and obtain "answers" to a wide range of policy-related problems relatively quickly or in some cases immediately. In this age of rapid technological development, almost every university can help private enterprises and public agencies absorb new technology and other innovations, providing them not only with technical expertise but also with assistance in dealing with concomitant human, financial, and organizational problems. Furthermore, there are a wide variety of ways in which faculty members can assist local, state, and federal agencies and commissions in dealing with specific and often pressing problems. Their work might involve economic analysis of the impact of alternative tax proposals or the application of operations research to traffic control or the location of firehouses. It might mean evaluating programs, analyzing census data, testing for pollution, and so on. The list is open-ended. Yet, to date, faculty expertise in this arena remains largely untapped.

Targeted Briefing and Other Didactic Activities. Somewhat overlapping with the previous category are a large variety of professional activities through which university faculty can provide background information and briefing material to specific targeted groups in both the public and private sectors. A number of universities now do this on a regular basis. For example, Harvard's Kennedy School of Government, the Eagleton Institute at Rutgers, and the McCormack Institute at the University of Massachusetts at Boston each regularly conduct sessions for newly elected national, state, and local government officials, respectively, at which these individuals discuss especially prepared background papers and are briefed on current issues. These schools or institutes, as well as similar units in many other universities, also organize seminars and panel discussions on topics ranging from radioactive waste disposal to regional demographic projections. The McCormack Institute publishes a journal on regional issues specifically targeted at practicing professionals and policy makers in the private and public sectors, and the PENNTAP program at Penn State regularly issues brief bulletins on matters of interest to the state's business community. Much more can and should be done, particularly at the local and regional level in the public sector and for smaller enterprises in the private sector. Both usually lack adequate staff support and could profit substantially from the expertise of university faculty.

Public Information for General Audiences. There exists an enormous opportunity for university faculty members to help the public-at-large to better understand the various complex issues that confront it. This form of professional activity has the potential of serving a wide audience. In an age when we rely so heavily on television, radio, and our daily newspapers for diverse kinds of information—information that goes beyond the perfunctory reporting of local accidents, crises, and developments—faculty expertise constitutes a major resource for the analysis and examination of different issues. Through cable television programs and newspaper articles and feature stories that draw upon the scholarship of faculty, knowledge can be disseminated in a useful and efficient way. Newsletters and bulletins can also be useful. In this area, as in the other three categories of professional activity, great opportunities also exist at the local and regional level. Faculty members can provide material for local newspapers and local radio, television, and cable stations, and they can also offer courses, seminars, and lectures for adult schools, community organizations, and the general public.

The Issue of Compensation

Discussions of faculty involvement in external professional activities at some point always turn to the question of whether faculty should be rewarded institutionally for work for which the client has already granted them compensation. Many academics contend that in such cases faculty should not be rewarded in terms of tenure, promotion, or salary increments. We consider this to be a specious argument. In the first place, a great deal of traditional scholarly activity results in additional compensation. Summer salary from a grant, an honorarium from an endowed lecture series—indeed, to push this argument to its extreme, a MacArthur Fellowship or the Nobel Prize—all constitute additional compensation for scholarly work. The same is true for income from royalties or license fees derived from scholarly activities. Yet no one would argue that this kind of work should not also be counted in the faculty member's evaluation for promotion and tenure. Furthermore, the basic academic reward system should judge the quality, the importance, and the appropriateness of a faculty member's professional activity. Whether it is done for additional compensation or pro bono, whether for a token honorarium or a substantial consulting fee usually depends on factors that have little relevance to the intrinsic merit of the activity. In sum, whether or not the faculty member receives additional compensation for professional activity, it is critical that such work be documented, evaluated, and rewarded institutionally.

Need for Documentation

If professional activity is ever to be equitably rewarded within the university structure and gain credibility as a legitimate form of activity, it is essential that it be subject to the same elements of measurement as are teaching and traditional scholarship: documentation and evaluation. If the work itself must be of the same quality as that expected in traditional scholarship, then the same procedure for evaluating the level of quality must be used. To utilize different structures and different mechanisms would set professional activity apart from scholarship, which is antithetical to our objectives.

The first requirement is to institutionalize the documentation of all professional activity just as routinely and as completely as is now the case for traditional scholarship. This needs to happen at the time of the activity, not when a performance or tenure review takes place, perhaps at a much later time. As a matter of course, every instance of substantial professional activity should be buttressed by some form of written, explanatory documentation. The maxim that should guide university leaders and personnel committees is: if the work cannot be documented, it cannot be evaluated; if it cannot be evaluated, it does not merit reward (Elman and Smock, 1985).

The primary responsibility for providing documentation for such professional work rests with the individual faculty member. Faculty members should be encouraged to place into their personnel files a written record of their work even if such material has not been requested in the contract or agreement with the client. With such documentation on file, the faculty member can at the very least be assured that there is a record of the work performed. The procedures for providing a written record of the professional work need to be incorporated and explained in detail in the institution's faculty handbook. Just as individual faculty members are responsible for submitting a written record of their work if they wish to have it evaluated for purposes of tenure, promotion, and salary decisions, so too are department chairs responsible for making certain that faculty, especially incoming junior faculty, are given explicit information regarding documentation procedures. This is frequently neglected. Faculty often do not have clear-cut role expectations or knowledge of procedures for attaining even the most crucial rewards.

The written record should, of course, describe what was done, the process that was used, how the outcome was used, and what purposes it served. It must include copies of any written product and also of the contract or other written understanding under which the work was carried out. But because professional activity can take place in such a wide variety of settings, under such different circumstances, and for such different clients and audiences, it is essential that the record of the work also explain who the clients or audience were, as well as the context and conditions under which it was carried out. In addition, when the written document is submitted, any appropriate evaluation or feedback on the activity should be included if possible. For some didactic activities involving direct contact with an audience—live or via telecommunication—the documentation might include evaluations and critiques elicited from the participants.

In short, there are many ways of providing adequate documentation for professional activity, and each university can develop the guidelines and procedures most appropriate to its needs and circumstances. But it is critical that the documentation make sense to the external reader and provide enough information for evaluation. Once the documentation process has been institutionalized and is routinely implemented at the time the professional activity is carried out, it should not prove to be unduly time consuming.

Criteria for Excellence

One of the principal objectives of the evaluation process should be to foster excellence in all forms of professional activity. The stringency of the evaluation component of the institutional reward structure is particularly important. If professional activity is to achieve recognition as legitimate academic work, standards must be developed that recognize and differentiate between different degrees of quality.

A proper evaluation process should be of value not only to those who are conducting the evaluation but also to the individual faculty members whose work is being evaluated. The details of the evaluation structure need to be designed in concert with the specific needs and norms of each university and each college, wherever applicable, within the university. Details of the criteria used in the evaluation are likely to depend on the particular areas of activity as well as on the context in which the work was carried out. Yet one can enumerate some generic evaluative questions broadly applicable to all professional activity, from contract research to public information:

1. How complex, difficult, or intricate is the problem or situation to which the work addresses itself? How much skill was needed to relate theory with practice and to transfer knowledge from an abstract setting into a concrete context?
2. Does the work use state-of-the-art knowledge and methodology, the most recent data bases, and other up-to-date components?
3. To what extent are the approaches and techniques utilized

in the work original and innovative, to what exent are they perfunctory and repetitive? Do they break new ground, and are they applicable in other contexts? By the same token, has the applied work influenced the faculty member's traditional teaching and research pursuits?

4. Does the work represent a comprehensive and thorough analysis of the problem(s) under inquiry? Did it take into account all relevant factors in formulating conclusions and recommendations? Did the analysis identify issues, policy alternatives, and related critical problems of which the client may have been unaware?

5. Is the work objective in presenting alternative approaches and the relative advantages and disadvantages of each?

Many of these questions can be asked, as well, about traditional scholarship. One additional criterion for evaluating professional activity that does not have an equivalent in evaluating traditional scholarship is the need for the final document to be written in language understandable to the client and all others who might use the results. The final document must convey the author's findings, ideas, and conclusions to an audience who may not be familiar with or tolerant of professional jargon and discipline-bound terminology. There must be direct and functional communication; all must be clear, brief, and understandable by the lay reader.

Most forms of externally oriented professional activity, from contracted research projects to the providing of public information, lend themselves very well to student involvement. In fact, these activities can contribute greatly to an improvement in university instruction at all levels, in part because of the opportunities they provide for student participation. Thus additional criteria for excellence include the extent to which opportunities for student participation have been utilized, along with the quality of the guidance and supervision provided by the faculty member.

A few more measures can be added. As with traditional scholarship, one of these is quantity of output, provided that this does not lead to a decrease in quality. Another, to be used with caution, involves the "ranking" of the contractor and the size and scope of the project. We previously remarked that developmental assistance at a local and regional level should be taken as seriously as a World Bank contract for work in a less developed country. Yet a multimillion dollar project for the latter can be quite appropriately weighted more heavily than a short-term effort for a neighboring county.

The Process of Evaluation

Determining who actually does the evaluation should be fairly easy to decide once the criteria have been established. With clearly enunciated guidelines, it should be possible to evaluate many of the new modes of scholarly activities in the same way as more traditional forms of scholarship are assessed. But there is one important issue that requires special attention. Many of the instances of technical assistance, policy analysis, technology assessment, and public information will be problem or issue centered and will cut across disciplinary boundaries. In Chapter Three we advocated a second stream of budget allocation to support activities that do not fit readily into the vertical, department-based system currently prevailing in almost all universities. We stated that, by the same token, it may also be necessary to have a second, parallel stream of personnel review, evaluation, and reward for faculty engaged in multidisciplinary activity. The evaluation of such activities might best be carried out by means of collegewide or even campuswide personnel committees that may better be able than departments to apply appropriate standards of excellence to problem-centered scholarly activity.

Because of the practice-oriented nature of much of this kind of work, it may also be appropriate to involve practitioners or other external evaluators. This needs to be determined by each individual institution in regard to each situation. External evaluators can play a valuable role by posing certain questions to the faculty member with respect to the finished product and developing a set of questions for the client at the initial stages of the professional work that may help not only direct the project itself but also set up some concrete guidelines by which the outcomes can be assessed (Elman and Smock, 1985).

The Bottom Line:
Greater Demands and Greater Satisfaction

This book repeatedly highlights a substantial increase in the demands placed on faculty members in the modern university. In addition to expertise in their specialty, they also should know how it relates to cognate fields, how it is applied to practical situations, and how such applications are affected by their context. They also require substantial pedagogical skills. Indeed, few members of the faculty are likely to attain all the knowledge and capabilities that have been enumerated. Nor is it necessary for the entire professoriate to reach the ideal. What is essential is a pervasive system of values and priorities that prizes breadth and multiplicity of talents and provides incentives for everyone to strive to attain them.

In addition, we firmly believe that the extended activities and responsibilities described in this book will bring heightened and more lasting satisfaction to faculty members as they follow their profession. The greater variety of possible tasks offers many more opportunities for change and growth. It enables a faculty member to move periodically from one aspect of scholarship to another, and through such a change to vary his or her instructional emphasis. Such possibilities should go far toward enhancing the attractiveness of a lifetime career as a university faculty member.

❧ *Epilogue* ❧

Providing Leadership
for the New University

❧❧❧❧❧❧❧❧❧❧❧❧❧❧❧❧❧

This book has described how a variety of factors have triggered the need for new priorities for modern universities, leading to substantial adaptation of their role and function. It suggests a new conception of universities extending beyond the model of the research university that has dominated the academic world's rhetoric as well as its procedures and policies during the past decades. Our conception of a university is much removed from the classical vision of an ivory tower, an internally oriented, isolated "city on a hill" engaged in pursuing knowledge for its own sake and in transmitting the import and need for that quest to its students. It differs, as well, from the multiversity of the postwar years, that central, still quite isolated "city of the intellect" surrounded by many "satellite suburbs." Our geographic metaphor for the modern university suggests something similar to a metropolitan region, with no single center but many points and concentrations of activity. This university is a network or web of many nodes, each closely connected to all the others, and it engages in continuous two-way interaction with its environment. It is an institution that still has a clear identity as a whole but is less defined and less compartmentalized than the traditional university.

161

Internally, our extended university retains its vertical structure of departments and colleges or schools, but contains, as well, organizational, budgetary, and procedural linkages that cut across components of that structure. These elements provide a variety of flexible and changing horizontal connections in research and professional activities and also in the design and delivery of instruction. There need to be, as well, bridges to the outside that enable all components of the institution to maintain strong ties with various sectors of society. These bridges have procedural functions, but, more importantly, they serve as conduits for the transmission of knowledge. In its scholarship and professional activities, as in its instruction, the modern university is characterized by a constant interplay, a reciprocal interaction between the specific and the general, theory and its application, action and reflection. Basic research is linked to its applications; questions posed by practical situations generate new research initiatives. New ideas flow beyond the borders of the campus; new conceptual and methodological issues, in turn, are explored within the academy. The model of the extended contemporary university that we envision is really a modernized version of the uniquely American land-grant and state university tradition in that the institution as a whole is dedicated to a broadly defined utilitarian, instrumental purpose.

The "new" university is an institution less clearly delineated than the traditional one; it is more closely interrelated with its surroundings, and it is in fact a part of the context in which it operates. It is extended in terms of its student body, which can no longer be uniquely defined in terms of age and full- or part-time status, or even in terms of whether they are matriculated degree candidates or not. The new university is extended as well in terms of its instructional objectives. It focuses on developing and maintaining a kind of competence that requires more than narrow technical expertise, more than abstract theory. Instruction in the new university encompasses practical experiences as an integral part of the curriculum and focuses as much on generalizing from the particular as it does on the more traditional mode of deducing specific applications from broad principles. Its faculty will include practitioners who have learned to incorporate their experience into a theoretical framework, and conversely it will ensure that its academically trained professors will have opportunities for first-hand practical applications of their theoretical knowledge. And, most importantly perhaps, the extended university as a whole will define its scholarly and professional responsibility so as to give equivalent weight, value, and prestige to the entire range of professional work, from basic, nondirected research through applied work to technical assistance and public information.

Perhaps the most striking feature of the modern university is the mutual reinforcement and complementarity of the three dimensions along which it extends. The faculty's involvement in applied work and other outreach activities will increase their ability to bridge the gap between theory and practice, to help students reflect on and generalize from their prior and concurrent experiences, and to assist young and old alike to gain and maintain the kind of real competence that is based on comprehending the relationship among disciplines and dealing with complex issues. This enhanced capability of the faculty will be further reinforced by using practitioners as colleagues and by including involvement in practical, professionally relevant experiences as part of the preparation for an academic profession. In turn, active collaboration in developing and teaching problem-centered, multidisciplinary curricula with colleagues from other fields, along with close intellectual interaction between those in the liberal arts with those in the professional areas, will enhance the faculty's ability to engage in externally oriented professional activities. This mutually reinforcing circle of interactions is brought to closure through the broader mix of students. The growing presence of older and more experienced individuals in the classroom will assist faculty as well as the younger students in bridging theory and practice and dealing with complex realities.

The model of the extended university subsumes a great variety of instructional and professional tasks. However, we cannot emphasize strongly enough that no one university should become involved in the entire span of activities. Each institution needs to determine its unique configuration and priorities. Just

as no two metropolitan regions are alike, so no two universities
are or need to be alike. No one university can be all things to all
people. Each must set its own priorities, building on its strengths
and assessing the principal needs of its region and its constituencies. Each will be composed of its distinctive student body
and its particular mix and balance of scholarly and professional
activities. What we consider to be essential is that the particular
choices of a given institution not be skewed in one direction because certain categories of students, certain modes of instruction, and certain kinds of professional services are assumed to
be "less academic" or "less respectable" than others. We would
also urge that each institution move more in the direction of
satisfying its extended responsibilities by expanding professional activity, relating theory and practice in the curriculum, and
broadening the student body. The three reinforce and supplement each other, and all are necessary to bring about the coherence and inner logic of the extended university.

Much progress has already been made in many universities, particularly in increasing applied research and other forms
of professional activity and in diversifying the student body.
The latter has often taken place almost inadvertently. Many universities find that the average age of their students is increasing
even though there has been no explicit attempt to attract more
adults or any effort to accommodate their special needs. Cooperation with industry in research and development has very rapidly become one of the most talked about subjects in higher
education. It even has acquired its very own accronym: UIRR,
for university-industry research relationship. Rhetoric still exceeds reality by a considerable amount, but much collaboration
has taken place during the past few years. In addition, a growing
number of universities have created centers or institutes to provide technical assistance and policy analysis to external clients,
particularly public agencies. Visits to lesser-known campuses
more often than not show these focal points of external interaction to be the most intellectually vibrant elements of the institution.

But however much has happened, and however respectable higher education–industry relationships have become,

much more remains to be done if the extended concept of the university is indeed to become the norm. Very little structural or pedagogical change has as yet taken place in either undergraduate or graduate education in response to changing needs and mounting external criticism of universities. Furthermore, and more importantly, faculty values and reward systems remain substantially unchanged, as does the mode of preparation for the academic profession. Until significant change takes place in these areas, universities on the whole will continue to fall significantly short of realizing their full potential.

Throughout this book we have emphasized the critical role of faculty in implementing the necessary changes in the mission and function of universities. However, faculty commitment and involvement, though essential, are not sufficient. Individual universities and the system as a whole are not likely to change priorities and values without effective leadership both locally and nationally.

Within institutions, such leadership is needed particularly at the collegiate and campus levels. Deans and provosts need to be strong advocates of broadening the definition of scholarship and adapting procedures to document, evaluate, and reward new forms of professional activity. They are also the ones to take the lead in developing a second stream of personnel review and budgetary allocation to encourage and support crossdisciplinary and intercollegiate projects and curricula. The role of deans and provosts is particularly important here in showing that it is possible and worthwhile to cope with the inevitable increase in administrative complexity and ambiguity brought about by the second stream.

Ultimately, as a number of recent studies and commentaries have indicated (Kerr and Gade, 1986; Riesman and McLaughlin, 1984), it is the leadership of the president or the chancellor of a university that is most important and that alone can set the tone for the institution. Central leadership is of particular importance in changing the priorities of the university and extending their activities. One of the key characteristics that distinguishes our conception of the university from the currently prevailing model is that much of its scholarship, professional activity, and instruction requires active collaboration among several departments and schools. Thus the university needs to have a strong collective, institutional identity and to be a whole considerably greater than the sum of its disciplinary components.

Leadership at the national level is also of great importance. We mentioned in Chapter One how strongly most universities are affected by national models and expectations. Priorities and values in an individual institution will change more rapidly the more such changes are discussed and encouraged at the national level. The rapid acceptance throughout the university system of the need for strong ties with industry in research and development has been largely due to the prominence given to this issue at meetings of higher education associations. Analogous attention given to the other dimensions of the evolving nature of universities could have a similar impact.

Faculty unions, both locally and nationally, constitute a key element, either as facilitators or as barriers, in bringing about the changes that we are advocating. Flexibility in interpreting faculty work loads and willingness to adapt established criteria and procedures for personnel review will be essential if universities are to respond to the growing diversification of instructional tasks and to the need for a broader range of professional activities. Many of the necessary changes involve matters in which professional societies and their accreditation processes play a vital role. A number of associations are indeed exercising such leadership by undertaking basic reexamination of curricula and accreditation requirements.

While we strongly advocate that universities move toward a more extended model in their professional activities and in their instruction, we are fully aware that there are considerable risks in such a development. First, in the absence of a combination of self-restraint and clear ground rules regarding response to external pressures, some institutions may indeed try to become "all things to all people," stretching their limited resources past the breaking point and ending up doing nothing very well (Keller, 1986). That risk exists unless each university assesses what it can and what it cannot do, establishes its own limits as explicitly and as clearly as possible, and continues to review and reevaluate those guidelines as internal resources and external needs change.

Implicit in the model of the extended university is the need for multiple funding sources, and here again there are risks. We believe that faculty in most universities should engage in applied research, policy analysis, and technical assistance for both public- and private-sector agencies. Payments for such services can constitute an important source of financial support that will, inevitably, influence the research agenda of an institution and its faculty. That influence is even greater when potentially lucrative license and patent rights may result from the work. A recent survey of research in biotechnology, for example, indicates that such commercial considerations do influence faculty choices of research projects (Blumenthal and others, 1986). There is a risk that this tendency may go too far (Wofsy, 1986). It is essential that short-term external demands not monopolize the institutional research agenda to the extent of squeezing out nondirected, long-term research for which the university system in the aggregate is the foremost societal mechanism. By definition, the outcomes of such work are unpredictable, and we must maintain this kind of exploration precisely because we do not know where it may lead.

Last, but not least, there is the risk that universities will lose their sense of detachment. Universities constitute the principal societal mechanism for objective analysis and critique of societal activities. They are not social agencies, but rather instruments of society that cannot remain isolated, as in the past they have tended to be, but must instead maintain a measure of detachment and autonomy. We believe this to be possible in the extended university, but it will require ongoing vigilance and clear criteria as to the appropriate limits of activities. As long as these limits are maintained, greater university involvement in external activities can, in fact, make the institutions much more effective in their critical role.

We are not discounting these downside risks, nor are we trying to minimize them. But we believe that we need to take these risks because not changing the basic conception of universities carries even greater risks with more negative consequences.

First, unless universities across the board accept and act on a broader definition of their role, we believe that about two-thirds of the institutions presently calling themselves universities will degenerate into substantial mediocrity, with negative effects on their teaching as well as on their scholarly activities. We will be left with a binary system in which about 150 institutions will be regarded as research universities in the traditional sense; all others will be cast with four-year state colleges and similar institutions into quite a different category. To a considerable extent this is already the way in which many observers of higher education classify the university system. The most recently published summary of public and private institutions derived from U.S. Department of Education data lists 155 universities and 1,870 four-year colleges (*Digest of Educational Statistics, 1985–86,* 1986). To widen this perceived gap even further would in our opinion constitute a great waste of valuable intellectual resources. We believe that the vast majority of existing universities can and should contribute to meet the multiple, expanding, and complex knowledge needs of society. This is all the more important because a substantial fraction of career and professional education at the baccalaureate and master's level occurs in universities other than the leading research institutions. Unless the intellectual vitality of the nonresearch oriented universities is maintained by active involvement in the spectrum of applications and outreach described in this book, many of our future teachers, our future managers and our future engineers (National Research Council, 1986) will have received a mediocre education.

Second, while the status of the leading universities is less endangered, their dominant role with regard to basic research is likely to diminish unless they explicitly address themselves to filling the gap between long-range research and short-term development. If this does not happen, industry may turn increasingly to direct working relationships with government laboratories and enhance, as well, their own basic research efforts. In the area of instruction, the dominant role of these universities in professional education will be upheld for a long time by virtue of the institutional prestige and the job opportunities they provide. But in the long run the leading universities cannot remain immune to the mounting clamor for change.

We want to conclude by emphasizing that we advocate the extended university not only because it is a more useful and responsive institution. It is also likely to be a more exciting, a more effective, and a more rewarding place to teach, to learn, and to be educated. As we think of the wide range of existing universities, we are certain that extending their role and functions as we have described in this book constitutes the best—indeed perhaps the only—way of making them places that "preserve the connection between knowledge and the zest of life."

References

AACSB. "Factory of the Future Gains Early Success." *Newsline,* 1983, *14* (2).

ACE/UCLA Cooperative Institutional Research Program. "1985 Freshman Survey Results." Los Angeles: Higher Education Research Institute, University of California at Los Angeles, 1986.

Ackoff, R. "The Future of Operations Research Is Past." *Journal of Operations Research Society,* 1979, *30* (2), 90-104.

Adamany, D. "Science and the Urban University." *Science,* 1983, *221,* 427-430.

Adams, J. M. "Harvard Business School—Ticket to the Top." *Boston Globe,* Sept. 8, 1985, pp. A1, A6.

Alford, H. J. (ed.). *Power and Conflict in Continuing Education.* Belmont, Calif.: Wadsworth, 1980.

Alpert, D. "Performance and Paralysis: The Organizational Context of the American Research University." *Journal of Higher Education,* 1985, *56* (3), 241-281.

American Assembly of Collegiate Schools of Business. "Factory of the Future Gains Early Success." *Newsline,* 1983, *14* (2), 11.

American Association of Medical Colleges. *News Release.* Washington, D.C.: American Association of Medical Colleges, Nov. 1985.

Anderson, J. R., Boyle, C. F., and Reiser, B. J. "Intelligent Tutoring Systems." *Science,* 1985, *228,* 456-462.

Ashby, E. "The Case for Ivory Towers." Paper delivered at the International Conference on Higher Education in Tomorrow's World. University of Michigan, Ann Arbor, Apr. 26–29, 1967.

Ashby, E. *Any Person, Any Study.* New York: McGraw-Hill, 1971.

Ashworth, J. M. "Reshaping Higher Education in Britain." *Journal of the Royal Society of Arts,* 1982, *130,* 713–729.

Ashworth, J. M. "Tomorrow's Universities: Ivory Towers, Frontier Posts or Service Stations?" *Journal of the Royal Society of Arts,* 1986, *133,* 464–479.

Astin, A. W. *Achieving Educational Excellence: A Critical Assessment of Priorities and Practices in Higher Education.* San Francisco: Jossey-Bass, 1985.

Bacon, F. *Advancement of Learning.* Chicago: Encyclopaedia Britannica, 1955. (Originally published 1605.)

Baker, W. O. "Organizing Knowledge for Action." In Langfitt, T. W., and others (eds.), *Partners in the Research Enterprise.* Philadelphia: University of Pennsylvania Press, 1983.

Baldridge, J. V. *Power and Conflict in the University: Research in the Sociology of Complex Organizations.* New York: Wiley, 1971.

Barton, P. E. *Worklife Transitions.* New York: McGraw-Hill, 1982.

Beeman, W. O. "The Future of Campus Computerization: Humanists and Social Scientists May Hold the Key." *Connection —New England's Journal of Higher Education,* 1986, *1,* 34–37, 55.

Bess, J. L. *University Organization: A Matrix Analysis of the Academic Profession.* New York: Human Sciences Press, 1982.

Blumenthal, D., and others. "University-Industry Research Relationships in Biotechnology: Implications for the University." *Science,* 1986, *232,* 1361–1366.

Bok, D. *Beyond the Ivory Tower.* Cambridge, Mass.: Harvard University Press, 1982.

Bok, D. "The President's Report, 1983–84." Cambridge, Mass.: Harvard University, 1985.

Bok, D. *Higher Learning.* Cambridge, Mass.: Harvard University Press, 1986.

Bolter, D. J. *Turing's Man: Western Culture in the Computer Age.* Chapel Hill: University of North Carolina Press, 1984.

Botkin, J., Dimancescu, D., and Stata, R. *Global Stakes.* Cambridge, Mass.: Ballinger, 1982.

Botkin, J., Dimancescu, D., and Stata, R. *The Innovators.* New York: Harper & Row, 1984.

Bowen, H. R., and Schuster, J. H. *American Professors: A National Resource Imperiled.* New York: Oxford University Press, 1986.

Boyer, C. M., and Lewis, D. R. *And On The Seventh Day: Faculty Consulting and Supplemental Income.* Washington, D.C.: Association for the Study of Higher Education, ERIC Research Report no. 3, 1985.

Boyer, E. L. "Foreword." In N. P. Eurich, *Corporate Classroom: The Learning Business.* Princeton, N.J.: The Carnegie Foundation for the Advancement of Teaching, 1985.

Boyer, E. L., and Hechinger, F. M. *Higher Learning in the Nation's Service.* Princeton, N.J.: The Carnegie Foundation for the Advancement of Teaching, 1981.

Boyer, E. L., and Levine, A. *A Quest for Common Learning.* Princeton, N.J.: The Carnegie Foundation for the Advancement of Teaching, 1981.

Branscomb, L. M., and Gilmore, P. C. "Education in Private Industry." *Daedalus,* 1975, *104,* 222–233.

Bromley, A. D. "The Other Frontiers of Science." *Science,* 1982, *215,* 1035.

Bruce, J. D., Silbert, W. M., Smullin, L. D., and Fano, R. M. *Lifelong Cooperative Education.* Report of the Centennial Study Committee. Cambridge, Mass.: MIT Press, 1982.

Burn, B. B. "The Training of, and U.S. Business Needs for, International Specialists." Conference Proceedings, University of Massachusetts, Amherst, 1986.

Bush, V. *Science—The Endless Frontier.* Washington, D.C.: National Science Foundation, 1960. (Originally published 1945.)

Carnegie Council on Policy Studies in Higher Education. *A Classification of Institutions of Higher Education.* Revised edition. Princeton, N.J.: The Carnegie Foundation for the Advancement of Teaching, 1976.

Carnegie Council on Policy Studies in Higher Education. *Three*

Thousand Futures: The Next Twenty Years for Higher Education. San Francisco: Jossey-Bass, 1980.

Carnegie Foundation for the Advancement of Teaching. *Carnegie Survey of Undergraduates.* Washington, D.C.: Carnegie Foundation for the Advancement of Teaching, 1986.

Carnevale, A. P. *Human Capital: A High-Yield Corporate Investment.* Washington, D.C.: American Society for Training and Development, 1983.

Carnevale, A. P. "The Learning Enterprise." *Training and Development Journal,* 1986, *40* (1), 18–26.

Carnevale, A. P., and Goldstein, H. *Employee Training: Its Changing Role and an Analysis of New Data.* Washington, D.C.: American Society for Training and Development, 1983.

Cheit, E. F. *The Useful Arts and the Liberal Tradition.* New York: McGraw-Hill, 1975.

Chmura, T. *The Higher Education-Economic Development Connection.* Menlo Park, Calif.: SRI International, 1986.

Clark, B. R. *The Higher Education System.* Berkeley: University of California Press, 1983.

Clark, B. R. "Listening to the Professoriate." *Change,* 1985, *17* (4), 36–43.

Cohen, M. D., and March, J. G. *Leadership and Ambiguity: The American College President.* New York: McGraw-Hill, 1974.

Coleman, J., and others. *Youth: Transition to Adulthood.* Chicago: University of Chicago Press, 1974.

Council of Graduate Schools. *Scholarship for Society.* Report of Panel on Alternative Approaches to Graduate Education. Princeton, N.J.: Educational Testing Service, 1973.

Crecine, J. P. "The Next Generation of Personal Computers." *Science,* 1986, *231,* 935–942.

Cremin, L. A. *The Transformation of the School: Progressivism in American Education, 1876–1957.* New York: Knopf, 1961.

Cross, K. P. "Taking Teaching Seriously." Paper presented at annual meeting of the American Association for Higher Education. Washington, D.C., Mar. 11, 1986.

Crosson, P. H. *Public Service in Higher Education: Practices and Priorities.* ASHE-ERIC Higher Education research report.

Washington, D.C.: Association for the Study of Higher Education, 1983.

Crosson, P. H. "Strengthening the Public Service Mission." *Thought and Action,* 1985, *1,* 109-122.

De Sola Pool, I. "Academic Practices, Freedoms, and the New Technologies." *Current Issues In Higher Education,* 1983-1984, no. 1, 19-24.

Digest of Educational Statistics, 1985-86. Washington, D.C.: U.S. Department of Education, 1986.

Digest of Educational Statistics, 1986-87. Washington, D.C.: U.S. Department of Education, 1987.

Dimancescu, D., and Botkin, J. *The New Alliance: America's R&D Consortia.* Cambridge, Mass.: Ballinger, 1986.

Dirr, P. J. "Television in Higher Education." In P. J. Tate and M. Kressell (eds.), *The Expanding Role of Telecommunications in Higher Education.* New Directions for Higher Education, no. 44. San Francisco: Jossey-Bass, 1983.

Dressel, P. L. *College Teaching as a Profession: The Doctor of Arts Degree.* New York: Carnegie Corporation, 1982.

Dunham, E. A. *Colleges of the Forgotten Americans: A Profile of State Colleges and Regional Universities.* New York: McGraw-Hill, 1969.

Dunham, E. A. "Rx for Higher Education: The Doctor of Arts Degree." *Journal of Higher Education,* 1970, *41,* 505-515.

Dunlop, J. T. *Human Resources: Toward Rational Policy Planning.* Report no. 669. New York: Conference Board, 1975.

Eddy, E. D., Jr. *Colleges for Our Land and Time.* Westport, Conn.: Greenwood Press, 1956.

Edgerton, R. "Abilities That Last a Lifetime: Alverno in Perspective." *AAHE Bulletin,* 1984, *36* (6), 3-4.

Edgerton, R. "Feeling in Control." *Change,* 1986, *18,* 4-5.

Elman, S. E., and Lynton, E. A. "Assessment in Career-Oriented Education." In C. Adelman (ed.), *Assessment in American Higher Education.* Washington, D.C.: U.S. Department of Education, 1986.

Elman, S. E., and Smock, S. M. *Professional Service and Faculty*

Rewards: Toward an Integrated Structure. Washington, D.C.: National Association of State Universities and Land Grant Colleges, 1985.

Eurich, N. P. *Corporate Classrooms: The Learning Business.* Princeton, N.J.: The Carnegie Foundation for the Advancement of Teaching, 1985.

Fisher, B. M. *Industrial Education: American Ideals and Institutions.* Madison: University of Wisconsin Press, 1967.

Fitch, J. T. "A Consortium for Engineering Education." In *Communications Technology in Education and Training.* Silver Spring, Information Dynamics, 1982.

Flexner, A. *Medical Education in the U.S. and Canada.* Princeton, N.J.: The Carnegie Foundation for the Advancement of Teaching, 1910.

Flexner, A. *Medical Education, A Comparative Study.* New York: Macmillan, 1925.

Fusfeld, H. I. "Overview of University-Industry Research Interactions." In T. W. Langfitt and others (eds.), *Partners in the Research Enterprise.* Philadelphia: University of Pennsylvania Press, 1983.

Gaff, J. G. *General Education Today: A Critical Analysis of Controversies, Practices, and Reforms.* San Francisco: Jossey-Bass, 1983.

Gamson, Z. F., and Associates. *Liberating Education.* San Francisco: Jossey-Bass, 1984.

Gibbons, J. F., Kincheloe, W. R., and Down, K. S. "Tutored Videotape Instruction: A New Use of Electronic Media in Education." *Science,* 1977, *195,* 1139–1146.

Goldstein, H. "Using Data on Employee Training from the Survey of Participation in Adult Education (C.P.S.)." Proceedings of the ASTD National Issues Forum. Washington, D.C.: American Society for Training and Development, 1983.

Goldstein, M. B. "Telecommunications and Higher Education: In Search of a Public Policy." In P. J. Tate and M. Kressel (eds.), *The Expanding Role of Telecommunications in Higher Education.* New Directions for Higher Education, no. 44. San Francisco: Jossey-Bass, 1983.

Gordon, M. "The Management of Continuing Education." In

Alford, H. J. *Power and Conflict in Continuing Education.* Belmont, Calif.: Wadsworth, 1980.

Gordon, M. S. (ed.). *Higher Education and the Labor Market.* New York: McGraw-Hill, 1974.

Gouldner, A. W. "Locals and Cosmopolitans." *Administrative Science Quarterly,* 1957, *1* (2), 281-306, 444-480.

Grant, G., and Riesman, D. *The Perpetual Dream: Reform and Experiment in the American Colleges.* Chicago: University of Chicago Press, 1978.

Grant, G., and others. *On Competence: A Critical Analysis of Competency-Based Reforms in Higher Education.* San Francisco: Jossey-Bass, 1979.

Groneman, C., and Lear, R. N. *Corporate Ph.D. Making the Grade in Business.* New York: Facts on File, 1985.

Guralnik, S. A. "Deploying Educational Technology at an Independent, Urban Institution." In *Technology and Education.* Washington, D.C.: Institute for Educational Leadership, 1981.

Hahn, R., and Mohrman, K. "What Do Managers Need to Know?" *AAHE Bulletin,* 1985, *38* (2), 3-11.

Harvard University Office of Career Services. *Senior Survey.* Cambridge, Mass.: Harvard University, Office of Career Services, 1985.

Hawthorne, E. M., Libby, P. A., and Nash, N. S. "The Emergence of Corporate Colleges." *Journal of Continuing Higher Education,* 1983, *31,* 1-9.

Hayes, R. H., and Abernathy, W. J. "Managing Our Way to Economic Decline." *Harvard Business Review,* 1980, *54,* 67-77.

Hefferlin, J. L. *Dynamics of Academic Reform.* San Francisco: Jossey-Bass, 1969.

Higher Education Directory 1985. Washington, D.C.: Higher Education Publications, 1985.

Hodgkinson, H. L. *Institutions in Transition.* New York: McGraw-Hill, 1971.

Hodgkinson, H. L. *Guess Who's Coming to College?* Washington, D.C.: National Institute of Independent Colleges and Universities, 1982.

Jackson, G. A. "Technology and Pedagogy: Making the Right Match Is Vital." *Change,* 1986, *18* (3), 52-57.

Jackson, G. A. "Learning Technology and Pedagogical Models in Higher Education." In A. P. Wagner and E. A. Lynton (eds.), *Educational Technology and the Adult Learner: Widening Access or Erecting New Barriers?* London: Falmer Press, 1987.

Jencks, C., and Riesman, D. *The Academic Revolution.* Chicago: University of Chicago Press, 1968.

Jennings, D. M., and others. "Computer Networking for Scientists." *Science,* 1986, *231,* 943–950.

Jerath, S. "Engineering Education in Perspective." *Mechanical Engineering,* 1983, *105,* 92–93.

Johnston, J. S., Jr. "Educating Managers for Change." In J. S. Johnston, Jr., and Associates, *Educating Managers: Executive Effectiveness Through Liberal Learning.* San Francisco: Jossey-Bass, 1986.

Johnston, J. S., Jr., and Associates. *Educating Managers: Executive Effectiveness Through Liberal Learning.* San Francisco: Jossey-Bass, 1986.

Jones, T. B. "Liberal Learning and Undergraduate Business Study." In J. S. Johnston, Jr., and Associates, *Educating Managers: Executive Effectiveness Through Liberal Learning.* San Francisco: Jossey-Bass, 1986.

Jordan, B. "Differentiation in Higher Education." NASULGC *Green Sheet,* Oct. 5, 1985, pp. 12–17.

Keller, K. H. "You Can't Be All Things to All People." *Higher Education and National Affairs.* Washington, D.C.: American Council on Education, 1986.

Kerr, C. *The Uses of the University.* Cambridge, Mass.: Harvard University Press, 1963; and 3rd ed., 1983.

Kerr, C., and Gade, M. L. *The Many Lives of Academic Presidents: Time, Place and Character.* Washington, D.C.: Association of Governing Boards, 1986.

Kurland, N. D. "Current Uses of Technology in Adult Education and Training." In A. P. Wagner and E. A. Lynton (eds.), *Educational Technology and the Adult Learner: Widening Access or Erecting New Barriers?* London: Falmer Press, 1987.

Langfitt, T. W., and others (eds.). *Partners in the Research Enterprise.* Philadelphia: University of Pennsylvania Press, 1983.

Law School Admission Data Bulletin. Newtown, Penn.: Law School Admission Services, Inc., 1986.

Lindblom, C. E., and Cohen, D. K. *Usable Knowledge: Social Science and Social Problem Solving.* New Haven, Conn.: Yale University Press, 1979.

Loacker, G., Cromwell, L., and O'Brien, K. "Assessment in Higher Education: To Serve the Learner." In C. Adelman (ed.), *Assessment in American Higher Education.* Washington, D.C.: U.S. Department of Education, 1986.

Locke, E. A., Fitzpatrick, W., and White, F. M. "Job Satisfaction and Role Clarity Among University and College Faculty." *The Review of Higher Education,* 1983, *6* (4), 343-365.

Lovett, C. M. "A Broader, More Generous View: Reflections on the Working Lives of Faculty." Paper presented at the annual meeting of the American Association of Higher Education, Mar. 14, 1986.

Lowenthal, W. "Continuing Education for Professionals: Voluntary or Mandatory?" *Journal of Higher Education,* 1981, *52,* 519-538.

Ludmerer, K. M. *Learning to Heal: The Development of American Medical Education.* New York: Basic Books, 1985.

Lusterman, S. *Education in Industry.* Report no. 719. New York: Conference Board, 1977.

Lusterman, S. *Managerial Competence: The Public Affairs Aspects.* Report no. 805. New York: Conference Board, 1981.

Lynton, E. A. "Colleges, Universities, and Corporate Training." In G. G. Gold (ed.), *Business and Higher Education: Toward New Alliances.* New Directions for Experiential Learning, no. 13. San Francisco: Jossey-Bass, 1981.

Lynton, E. A. "A Curriculum for Tomorrow's World." In J. W. Hall and B. L. Kevles (eds.), *In Opposition to Core Curriculum.* Westport, Conn.: Greenwood Press, 1982.

Lynton, E. A. "A Crisis of Purpose: Reexamining the Role of the University." *Change,* 1983a, *15,* 18-23, 53.

Lynton, E. A. "Occupational Maintenance: Recurrent Education to Maintain Occupational Effectiveness." *CAEL News,* 1983b, *7* (1), 6-8, 19.

Lynton, E. A. "Occupational Maintenance: Recurrent Educa-

tion to Maintain Occupational Effectiveness." *CAEL News,*
1983c, 7 (2), 4-7, 15.

Lynton, E. A. *The Missing Connection Between Business and
the Universities.* New York: ACE/Macmillan, 1984.

Lynton, E. A. "The Pause That Refreshes: Handling the Interrupted Education." *Educational Record,* 1986, *67,* 29-33.

Lynton, E. A. "An Agenda for Reflection and Action." In A. P.
Wagner and E. A. Lynton (eds.), *Educational Technology and
the Adult Learner: Widening Access or Erecting New Barriers?* London: Falmer Press, 1987.

Lynton, E. A., Elman, S. E., and Smock, S. M. "Rewarding Professional Activity." *Thought and Action,* 1985, *1* (2), 101-
108.

McHenry, D. E., and Associates. *Academic Departments: Problems, Variations, and Alternatives.* San Francisco: Jossey-
Bass, 1977.

MacVicar, M., and McGavern, N. "Not Only Engineering: The
MIT Undergraduate Research Opportunities Programme." In
S. Goodlad (ed.), *Education for the Professors: Quis Custo-
diet . . . ?* Guildford, England: Society for Research into
Higher Education and Nfer-Nelson, 1985.

Masnick, G., and Pitkin, J. *The Changing Population of States
and Regions.* Cambridge, Mass.: MIT/Harvard Joint Center
for Urban Studies, 1982.

Moore, W. *The Professions.* New York: Russell Sage Foundation,
1970.

Morse, S. W. *Employee Educational Programs: Implications for
Industry and Higher Education.* Washington, D.C.: Association for the Study of Higher Education, ERIC Higher Education Research Reports, no. 7, 1984.

*The National Guide to Educational Credit for Training Pro-
grams, 1982 Edition.* Washington, D.C.: Program on Noncollegiate Sponsored Instruction, American Council on Education, 1982.

National Institute of Education. *Context for Learning: The Major Sectors of American Higher Education.* Washington, D.C.:
National Institute of Education and American Association
for Higher Education, 1985.

National Research Council. *Engineering Undergraduate Education.* Washington, D.C.: National Academy Press, 1986.

National Science Board. "University-Industry Relationships: Myths, Realities, and Potential." Fourteenth annual report, National Science Board. Washington, D.C.: National Science Foundation, 1982.

National Science Foundation. *Development of University-Industry Cooperative Research Centers: Historical Profiles.* NSF report no. 84-29. Washington, D.C.: National Science Foundation, 1984.

National Science Foundation. *Academic Science/Engineering: Graduate Enrollment and Support, Fall 1983.* NSF report no. 85-300. Washington, D.C.: National Science Foundation, 1985a.

National Science Foundation. *Science and Engineering Personnel: A National Overview.* NSF report no. 85-302. Washington, D.C.: National Science Foundation, 1985b.

Newman, F. *Higher Education and the American Resurgence.* Princeton, N.J.: The Carnegie Foundation for the Advancement of Teaching, 1985.

Nussbaum, B., and Beam, A. "Remaking the Harvard B-School." *Business Week,* Mar. 24, 1986, pp. 54–58, 61, 64, 66–70.

O'Keefe, M. "Statement by the General Rapporteur." *Policies for Higher Education in the 1980's.* Paris: Organization for Economic Cooperation and Development, 1983.

Organization for Economic Cooperation and Development. *Education Statistics in OECD Countries.* Paris: Organization for Economic Cooperation and Development, 1981.

Organization for Economic Cooperation and Development. *The Role and Function of the Universities: Main Policy Issues.* Paris: Organization for Economic Cooperation and Development, 1986.

Outlook and Opportunities for Graduate Education. National Board on Graduate Education, no. 6. Washington, D.C.: National Board on Graduate Education, 1975.

Perry, W. *The Open University: History and Evaluation of a Dynamic Innovation in Higher Education.* San Francisco: Jossey-Bass, 1977.

Perry, W. *The State of Distance-Learning Worldwide.* Milton Keynes, England: International Centre for Distance Learning of the United Nations University, 1984.

Peters, L., and Fusfeld, H. *Current U.S. University-Industry Re-*

search Connections. Washington, D.C.: National Science Board, 1982.

Peters, T. J., and Waterman, R. H., Jr. *In Search of Excellence.* New York: Harper & Row, 1982.

Phillips, L. *Status of Mandatory Continuing Education for Selected Professions.* Athens, Ga.: Center for Continuing Education, University of Georgia, 1986.

Piore, M. J., and Sabel, C. F. *The Second Industrial Divide.* New York: Basic Books, 1984.

Prewitt, K. "Scientific Illiteracy and Democratic Theory." *Daedalus,* 1983, *112* (2), 49-64.

Project Athena: An Introduction. Cambridge, Mass.: MIT, Oct. 1983.

Raben, J. "Computer Applications in the Humanities." *Science,* 1985, *228,* 434-438.

Regents Guide, 1980: A Guide to Educational Programs in Non-Collegiate Organizations. Albany: State University of New York, 1980.

Reich, R. B. *The Next American Frontier.* New York: Times Books, 1983.

Rhodes, F. H. T. "Reforming Higher Education Will Take More Than Just Tinkering with Curricula." *Chronicle of Higher Education,* 1985, *30* (12), 80.

Riesman, D. *Constraint and Variety in American Education.* New York: Doubleday, 1956.

Riesman, D. "Society's Demands for Competence." In G. Grant and others, *On Competence: A Critical Analysis of Competence-Based Reforms in Higher Education.* San Francisco: Jossey-Bass, 1979.

Riesman, D. "Professional Education and Liberal Education." Unpublished address delivered at Carnegie Mellon University, Oct. 5, 1981.

Riesman, D., and McLaughlin, J. B. "A Primer on the Use of Consultants in Presidential Recruitment." *Change,* 1984, *16,* 12-23.

Robinson, L. "The Computer: An Enabling Instrument." *Current Issues in Higher Education,* 1983-84, no. 1, pp. 3-13.

Rorty, A. O. "Socrates and Socratessa Take the Philosophic

Turn." In A. Cohen and M. Dascal (eds.), *The Institution of Philosophy*. Totowa, N.J.: Rowman & Allenheld, forthcoming.

Rudolph, F. *The American College and University*. New York: Random House, 1962.

Rudolph, F. *Curriculum: A History of the American Undergraduate Course of Study Since 1636*. San Francisco: Jossey-Bass, 1977.

Rudolph, F. "Response." In J. D. Koerner (ed.), *The New Liberal Arts: An Exchange of Views*. New York: Alfred P. Sloan Foundation, 1981.

Sanger, D. E. "The Electronic College Is Still a Dim Prospect." *New York Times*, Jan. 5, 1986, pp. 50–51.

Schein, E. H., and Kommers, D. W. *Professional Education*. New York: McGraw-Hill, 1972.

Schön, D. A. *The Reflective Practitioner*. New York: Basic Books, 1983.

Schön, D. A. *Educating the Reflective Practitioner: Toward a New Design for Teaching and Learning in the Professions*. San Francisco: Jossey-Bass, 1986.

Schwartz, H. J. "Monsters & Mentors: Computer Application for Humanistic Education." *College English*, 1982, *44*, 141–151.

Science, Apr. 26, 1985, *228* (entire issue).

Science, Feb. 28, 1986, *231* (entire issue).

Scott, P. *The Crisis of the University*. London: Croom and Helm, 1984.

Shanker, A. "HEL Clarifies Education Issues: A Major Resource in National Debate." *New York Times*, Apr. 13, 1986, p. E9.

Shapley, D., and Roy, R. *Lost at the Frontier: U.S. Science and Technology Policy Adrift*. Philadelphia: ISI Press, 1985.

Signs of Trouble and Erosion: A Report on Graduate Education in America. Washington, D.C.: National Commission on Student Financial Assistance, 1983.

Smith, H. L. "Comprehensive Universities and Colleges: Synthesizers of Liberal and Professional Education." *Liberal Education*, 1978, *64*, 469–484.

Stark, J., Lowther, M., and Hagerty, B. *Responsive Professional*

Education: Balancing Outcomes and Opportunities. Association for the Study of Higher Education, ERIC Higher Education Report, no. 3. Washington, D.C.: Association for the
Study of Higher Education, 1986.

Steele, R. L. "The Campus of the Future." Discussion paper,
University of Pittsburgh, June 1983.

Study Group on the Conditions of Excellence in American
Higher Education. *Involvement in Learning: Realizing the
Potential of American Higher Education.* Washington, D.C.:
National Institute of Education, 1984.

Suppes, P. "The Uses of Computers in Education." *Scientific
American,* 1966, *215,* 206.

Sweet, P. R. *Wilhelm von Humboldt, A Biography.* Vol. 2.
Columbus: Ohio State University Press, 1980.

Tate, P. J., and Kressel, M. (eds.). *The Expanding Role of Telecommunications in Higher Education.* New Directions for
Higher Education, no. 44. San Francisco: Jossey-Bass, 1983.

Tobias, S. "Peer Perspectives on the Teaching of Science."
Change, 1986, *18,* 36–41.

Trends in Adult Student Enrollment. Washington, D.C.: The
U.S. Department of Education, National Center for Educa-
tional Statistics; Prepared by the Office of Adult Learning
Services, The College Board, 1985.

Trow, M. (ed.). *Teachers & Students: Aspects of American
Higher Education.* New York: McGraw-Hill, 1975.

Truman, D. B. "Foreword." In D. Bell, *The Reforming of General Education.* New York: Anchor Books/Doubleday, 1968.

Truxal, J. "Learning to Think like an Engineer: Why, What, and
How?" *Change,* 1986, *18,* 10–19.

Tucker, M. S. (ed.). "Computers on Campus: Working Papers."
Current Issues in Higher Education. Washington, D.C.: American Association for Higher Education, 1984.

Turner, J. A. "A Personal Computer for Every Freshman: Even
Faculty Skeptics Are Now Enthusiasts." *Chronicle of Higher
Education,* Feb. 20, 1985, pp. 1, 14.

Turner, J. A. "Private Companies Turn to Academe for Super-
computer Time and Expertise." *Chronicle of Higher Education,* June 11, 1986, p. 41.

University of California at Davis Committee on Public Service. "Why Public Service: A Guide for Faculty at the University of Davis." Davis: University of California, 1985.

Veysey, L. R. *The Emergence of the American University.* Chicago: University of Chicago Press, 1965.

Veysey, L. R. "Is There a Crisis in the Undergraduate Curriculum?" *Change,* 1981, *13* (8), 20-25.

Wagner, A. P., and Lynton, E. A. *Educational Technology and the Adult Learner: Widening Access or Erecting New Barriers?* London: Falmer Press, 1987.

Waldrop, M. M. "Personal Computers on Campus." *Science,* 1985, *228,* 438-444.

Walsh, J. "Computers in Class at the Awkward Age." *Science,* 1986, *233,* 713-715.

Weick, K. E. "Educational Organizations as Loosely Coupled Systems." *Administrative Science Quarterly,* 1976, *21,* 1-19.

Weick, K. E. "Contradictions in a Community of Scholars: The Cohesion-Accuracy Trade-Off." *Review of Higher Education,* 1983, *6,* 253-267.

Whitehead, A. N. *The Aims of Education and Other Essays.* New York: Mentor Books, 1949.

Williams, M. E. "Electronic Databases." *Science,* 1985, *228,* 445-456.

Wilson, R., and Melendez, S. E. "Down the Up Staircase." *Educational Record,* 1985, *66,* 46-51.

Wofsy, L. "Biotechnology and the University." *Journal of Higher Education,* 1986, *57,* 477-492.

Woodward, K. L., and Kornaber, A. "Youth Is Maturing Later." *New York Times,* May 10, 1985, p. A31.

Index

A

Abernathy, W. J., 76, 77
Ackoff, R., 77, 79
Adamany, D., 19
Adams, J. M., 92
Adelphi University, mission of, 10
Adult education: and attendance patterns, 93-97; and lifelong learning, 96-97
Advanced Technology Centers, and technological innovation, 20
Alabama at Tuscaloosa, University of, technical assistance by, 38
Alexander the Great, 125
Alpert, D., 50
American Association for Higher Education, 145
American Association of Medical Colleges, 92
American Association of State Colleges and Universities, 23
American Association of Universities, 145
American Banking Institute, and degree programs, 107
American Council on Education, 70, 106
American Federation of State and Municipal Employees, 102
American Federation of Teachers, 27

Anderson, J. R., 125
Aristotle, 4, 125
Arthur D. Little, and degree programs, 107
Ashby, E., 7, 12
Ashworth, J. M., 57
Assessment, implications of career programs for, 82-83
Association for Media-Based Continuing Education in Engineering, 117
Association of American Universities, 9
Astin, A. W., 12, 59
AT&T, breakup of, 115

B

Bacon, F., 4, 84, 85
Baker, W. O., 17, 30
Baldridge, J. V., 49
Barton, P. E., 102
Baylor University, mission of, 10
Beam, A., 77, 80
Beeman, W. O., 120, 126, 128
Benjamin Franklin Partnership Program, and technological innovation, 20, 21
Bess, J. L., 49-50, 54
Blumenthal, D., 167
Bok, D., 122, 124, 125, 129-130, 131

Bolter, D. J., 130
Botkin, J., 19, 20, 21, 22
Bowen, H. R., 54, 138, 147
Boyer, C. M., 42
Boyer, E. L., 96, 104, 105
Boyle, C. F., 125
Branscomb, L. M., 104, 111
Brokering and negotiating, as extension function, 35-36
Bromley, A. D., 23, 28
Brown University, computers at, 121
Bruce, J. D., 75, 95, 96
Burn, B. B., 76
Bush, V., 18, 23

C

California, small "universities" in, 9
California, University of, extension delivery by, 37
California at Davis, University of, Committee on Public Service at, 147
California at Los Angeles, University of, 70
California at Santa Cruz, University of, multidisciplinary programs at, 48, 53-54
Career and professional programs: and adult education, 95; analysis of, 69-85; and assessment implications, 82-83; background on, 69-72; criticisms of, 72-77; and joy of knowing, 83-85; and new conception of practice, 77-80; teaching related to, 80-81
Carnegie Council on Policy Studies in Higher Education, 8, 9n, 10, 15, 16, 136
Carnegie Foundation for the Advancement of Teaching, 70, 89
Carnegie Mellon University: computers at, 121; D.A. degree at, 143; Robotics Center at, 20, 21
Carnevale, A. P., 70, 102, 104, 107, 110
Chautauqua, and adult education, 94

Cheit, E. F., 71
Chicago, University of: graduate internship at, 141; science teaching at, 61-62
Chmura, T., 23, 37, 38
Claremont Graduate School, D.A. degree at, 143
Clark, B. R., 12, 28, 47, 49, 53, 54, 132, 139
Coast Community Colleges, and telecourses, 119
Cohen, D. K., 25
Cohen, M. D., 48
Coleman, J., 92
Columbia University, breadth and depth at, 65
Competence: and adult education, 94-95; analysis of, 56-68; background on, 56-58; career-oriented programs for, 69-85; concept of, 56-57; and experience, 59-60; extended major for, 65-68; liberal education capstone for, 63-65; and multidisciplinary programs, 64, 67-68; and parallel educational systems, 102-103, 104; in science and technology, 60-63
Computers: for drill and practice, 123-124; as instructional tools, 121-126; for simulation and game playing, 124-125; tutorial mode of, 125-126; as word processors, 123
Conference Board, 76
Consortia, research and development, 19-20
Consultation: in extension, 41-43; rewards for, 152-153
Continuing education: and corporate education, 108; dilemma of, 97-100
Cooperative Extension, programs of, 38
Cornell University: mission of, 5; professional education at, 85
Corporate education, role of, 102, 106-107
Council on Graduate Schools, 143, 145

Crecine, J. P., 121
Cremin, L. A., 6, 80
Cromwell, L., 82
Crosson, P. H., 147

D

Delivery, as extension function, 36-38
De Sola Pool, I., 125
Dewey, J., 4, 80
Digital Equipment: collaboration with, 20, 150; and Project Athena, 20
Dimancescu, D., 19, 20, 21, 22
Dirr, P. J., 118
Down, K. S., 117
Dressel, P. L., 139, 143-144
Dunham, E. A., 12, 139, 143
Dunlop, J. T., 102

E

Eddy, E. D., Jr., 6, 29
Edgerton, R., 62, 63
Education, training distinct from, 104
Education system: nonacademic providers in, 101-103; parallel, 102-103, 104; university role in, 101-112
Elman, S. E., 82, 146, 148, 151, 156, 160
Employers: adaptations needed by, 110-112; educational needs of, 101-112; and nonacademic systems, 101-103; and training, 103-105
Engineering, career-oriented programs in, 74-75, 81
Eurich, N. P., 13, 101-102, 107, 117
Evaluation, of faculty, 157-160
Extended university: concept of, 4-7, 15; funding sources for, 167; future of, 165-169; model of, 161-164; and technology, 129-131
Extension: for accessibility of knowledge, 30-44; background on, 30-32; bridging mechanisms for, 32-33; brokering and negotiating function of, 35-36; consultation in, 41-43; delivery function of, 36-38; functions of, 33-38; funding and staffing for, 40-41; information function of, 33-35; for scholarship, 27-29; student participation in, 43-44. *See also* Service

F

Faculty: adaptations by, 136-138; age distribution of, 136; alternative degrees for, 142-145; analysis of expanded roles for, 132-145; background on, 132-136; categories of professional activity by, 151-154; clergy model of, 134; compensation issue for, 154-155; content of study by, 139-140; and corporate education, 108-110; demands on, 133-134; dissatisfaction of, 54-55; documentation of activities by, 155-157; evaluation of, 157-160; and instruction, 133; for knowledge society, 132-160; and leadership, 163, 166; pattern and timing of study by, 140-142; preparation of, 138-142; reward system for, 146-160; satisfaction of, 160; and scholarship, 132-133, 134-135, 144
Fano, R. M., 95, 96
Fisher, B. M., 102
Fitch, J. T., 117
Fitzpatrick, W., 52, 54
Flexner, A., 4, 80
Fusfeld, H. I., 19

G

Gade, M. L., 165
Gaff, J. G., 57, 58
Gamson, Z. F., 57, 62
General Electric, courses by, 106
General Motors: courses by, 106; technical assistance for, 38

George Mason University, industry collaboration by, 38

Georgia Institute of Technology, industrial extension service of, 37

Germany: reform in, 135; university mission in, 5, 6

Gibbons, J. F., 117

Gilmore, P. C., 104, 111

Goldstein, H., 102

Goldstein, M. B., 120

Gordon, M., 99

Gouldner, A. W., 54

Grant, G., 56

Groneman, C., 141, 142

Guralnik, S. A., 117

H

Hagerty, B., 72

Hahn, R., 58

Harvard University: and computers, 122; graduate study at, 92; Kennedy School of Government at, 153; newsletters from, 26-27; and service, 150, 153

Hatch Act of 1887, 6

Hawthorne, E. M., 107

Hayes, R. H., 76, 77

Hechinger, F. M., 96, 105

Hodgkinson, H. L., 11-12, 91

Hofstra University, mission of, 10

Hutchins, R. M., 4

I

IBM: collaboration with, 20, 150; and Project Athena, 20; and word processors, 123

Illinois Institute of Technology, and telecommunication, 117

Industry, university collaboration with, 18-21, 32, 37-38, 164, 168-169

Information: function of providing, 33-35; transformed into knowledge, 24-27

Instruction: analysis of needs in, 56-131; in career-oriented programs, 69-85; for competence, 56-68;

priorities for, 2; professional activity related to, 80-81; and student attendance patterns, 86-100; technology for, 113-131; university role in, 101-112

J

Jackson, G. A., 123

Jencks, C., 11, 71, 73

Jennings, D. M., 115, 127

Jerath, S., 75

Johnston, J. S., Jr., 72, 74

Jones, T. B., 71

Jordan, B., 13

K

Keller, K. H., 166

Kerr, C., 4, 9, 30, 165

Kincheloe, W. R., 117

Knowledge society: aspects of, 16-17; and career-oriented programs, 69-85; competence for, 56-68; educational needs of, 56-131; extension programs for, 27-29, 30-44; faculty for, 132-160; information transformed into knowledge in, 24-27; joy in, 83-85; leadership for, 161-169; multidisciplinary programs for, 45-55; scholarship for, 16-55; and student attendance patterns, 86-100; technological innovation in, 17-21; technology in, 113-131; and technology transfer, 21-24, 29; and university role, 101-112

Kommers, D. W., 73-74, 78, 79

Kronaber, A., 93

Kurland, N. D., 120

L

Land-Grant Act of 1862, 4

Law School Admission Services, 91-92

Leadership, for knowledge society, 161-169

Lear, R. N., 141, 142

Lewis, D. R., 42
Libby, P. A., 107
Liberal education: capstone for, 63-65; and career-oriented programs, 71-72; for competence, 56-68; for empowerment, 62; and experience, 59-60; extended major for, 65-68; science and technology in, 60-63
Lindblom, C. E., 25
Loacker, G., 82-83
Locke, E. A., 52, 54
Louisville, University of, work load reviews at, 149
Lovett, C. M., 134-135, 138, 141, 149
Lowenthal, W., 103
Lowther, M., 72
Ludmerer, K. M., 80
Lusterman, S., 76, 102, 107, 110
Lynton, E. A., 13, 42, 65, 70, 75, 82, 87, 88, 93, 95, 99, 101, 103, 104, 107, 110, 131, 146

M

MacArthur Fellowship, 155
McGavern, N., 43
McHenry, D. E., 47
McLaughlin, J. B., 165
MacVicar, M., 43
Major, extended: for competence, 65-68; and intermittent attendance, 88
Management, career-oriented programs in, 75-77
Manufacturers Hanover Trust, courses by, 106
March, J. G., 48
Marketing, for extension, 34-35
Maryland at College Park, University of, industrial extension service of, 37
Masnick, G., 90n, 91n
Massachusetts at Boston, University of, McCormack Institute at, 153-154
Massachusetts Institute of Technology: and Project Athena, 20, 127-128; and service, 150

Melendez, S. E., 9
Memphis State University, mission of, 10
Michigan, University of, D.A. degree at, 143
Middle Tennessee State University, D.A. degree at, 143
Mission: analysis of, 1-15; and continuing education, 98; diversity of, 7-11; and faculty interests, 54; as framework, 14-15; and knowledge needs, 1-4, 13; and leadership, 163-164, 166-167; traditional, 4-7; and values and aspirations, 11-13
Mohrman, K., 58
Moore, W., 78
Morse, S. W., 13, 101
Multidisciplinary programs: analysis of, 45-55; background on, 45-46; challenges and benefits of, 53-55; and competence, 64, 67-68; dilemma of, 47-49; and personnel decisions, 46, 51-52; and resource allocation, 46, 50-51; second-stream approach to, 49-52

N

Nash, N. S., 107
National Institute of Education, 10
National Research Council, 21, 81, 168
National Science Foundation, 9, 19, 22
National Security Council, 150
National Technical University, and telecommunication, 117
Netherlands, broadcast instruction in, 120
New Jersey, consortium in, 20
New York State Board of Regents, 106
New York Telephone Company, courses by, 106
New York University, and broadcast instruction, 118
Newman, F., 57, 59-60, 90

Newman, J. H., 4
Nobel Prize, 155
Northern Colorado, University of,
    D.A. degree at, 143
Nussbaum, B., 77, 80

O

O'Brien, K., 82
O'Keefe, M., 24
Open University (Netherlands), and
    interactive videodiscs, 120
Open University (United Kingdom),
    and broadcast instruction, 119-
    120, 130

P

Pennsylvania, consortium in, 20, 21
Pennsylvania State University, Penn-
    sylvania Technology Assistance
    Program (PENN-TAP) at, 37,
    154
Perry, W., 118, 119
Peters, L., 19
Peters, T. J., 76, 77
Philip of Macedon, 125
Phillips, L., 103
Philosophy, extended major in, 67
Physical and life sciences, extended
    major in, 66-67
Piore, M. J., 76
Pitkin, J., 90n, 91n
Prewitt, K., 27, 62, 63, 66, 75
Profession, concept of, 78. See also
    Career and professional pro-
    grams
Project Athena, and technological
    innovation, 20, 127-128

R

Raben, J., 123
Reich, R. B., 76-77
Reiser, B. J., 125
Resource allocation, for multidisci-
    plinary programs, 46, 50-51
Reward system: adapting, 150-159;
    analysis of, 146-160; background

on, 146-147; and categories of
    professional activity, 151-154;
    and compensation issues, 154-
    155; for consultation and techni-
    cal assistance, 152-153; criteria
    in, 157-159; for directed or con-
    tracted research, 152; documen-
    tation for, 155-157; evaluation
    process for, 159-160; and multi-
    disciplinary programs, 46, 51-52;
    for public information, 154; for
    service or scholarship, 147-150;
    for targeted briefing and didac-
    tic activities, 153-154
Rhodes, F. H. T., 46, 85
Riesman, D., 11, 12, 56, 62, 71, 73,
    165
Robinson, L., 123
Rochester, University of, Center for
    Advanced Optical Technology at,
    20
Roosevelt, F. D., 18
Rorty, A. O., 67, 72
Roy, R., 18, 78
Rudolph, F., 6, 96
Rutgers University: Eagleton Insti-
    tute at, 153; multidisciplinary
    programs at, 53-54

S

Sabel, C. F., 76
San Diego State University, mission
    of, 10
San Francisco State University, mis-
    sion of, 10
San Jose State University, industry
    collaboration by, 38
Sanger, D. E., 127
Schein, E. H., 73-74, 78, 79
Scholarship: accessibility of, 30-44;
    analysis of responsibilities for,
    16-29; background on, 16-17;
    bridging mechanisms for, 32-33;
    extension for, 27-29; informa-
    tion transformed into knowledge
    by, 24-27; for knowledge soci-
    ety, 16-55; and multidisciplinary
    programs, 45-55; priorities for,

2; and service, rewards for, 147-
150; and technological innova-
tion, 17-21; and technology
transfer and knowledge absorp-
tion, 21-24, 29
Schön, D. A., 78, 79-80, 88
Schuster, J. H., 54, 138, 147
Schwartz, H. J., 122, 125
Science: competence in, 60-63; ex-
ternal and internal frontiers of,
23, 28
Scott, P., 6, 12
Service: concepts of, 148; and
scholarship, rewards for, 147-
150; and work loads, 149. *See
also* Extension
Shakespeare, W., 61
Shanker, A., 27
Shapley, D., 18, 78
Silbert, W. M., 95, 96
Simmons College, D.A. degree at,
143
Smith, H. L., 11
Smith-Lever Act of 1914, 6
Smock, S. M., 146, 148, 151, 156,
160
Smullen, L. D., 95, 96
Social sciences, extended major in,
66
Stanford University: Center for In-
tegrated Studies of, 20; and ser-
vice, 150; telecommunication
by, 116-117
Stark, J., 72
Stata, R., 19, 21, 22
State University of New York,
Rockefeller Institute of, 37
State University of New York at
Buffalo, multidisciplinary pro-
grams at, 53-54
Steele, R. L., 128, 130
Students: adult education for, 93-
97; attendance patterns of, 86-
100; background on, 86-88; career orientation of, 70; continuing education for, 97-100; and
demographic trends, 90-91, 164;
extension participation by, 43-
44; financial burdens of, 90;

graduate, 91-92; intermittent at-
tendance by, 87-88; maturation
of, 92-93; opportunity costs for,
91-92; younger, 88-93
Study Group on the Conditions of
Excellence in American Higher
Education, 57, 60, 88-89, 140
Suppes, P., 125
Sweet, P. R., 135

T

Technology: analysis of potential
of, 113-131; assessment of, and
liberal education, 63; background on, 113-114; competence in, 60-63; of computers,
121-126; and extended university, 129-131; innovation in, and
scholarship, 17-21; and networks,
126-129; second-order effects of,
75; of telecommunication, 114-
121; transfer of, 21-24, 29; and
wired campus, 126-129
Telecommunication: broadcast instruction by, 117-121; as delivery system, 114-121; narrowcast
and broadcast, 115; for off-
campus, distance learning, 116-
117
Texas at San Antonio, University
of, industry collaboration by, 38
Tobias, S., 61-62
Training, education distinct from,
104
Trow, M., 12
Truman, D. B., 65, 68
Truxal, J., 63
Tucker, M. S., 121, 124, 129
Turner, J. A., 121, 127

U

United Automobile Workers, 102
United Kingdom: broadcast instruction in, 119-120; capability
in, 56; university mission in, 5,
6
U.S. Bureau of the Census, 89

U.S. Department of Education, 168
U.S. Department of State, 150
Universities: adaptations needed by, 107-110; binary system of, 168; broad approach of, 112; career programs in, 69-85; categories of, 7-11; changes for, 31-32; as disinterested, 26, 167; and education, 105-107, 112; faculty for, 132-160; framework for, 14-15; growth of, 7-11; industry collaboration with, 18-21, 32, 37-38, 164, 168-169; instructional needs of, 56-131; and knowledge needs, 1-4, 13; leadership for, 161-169; matrix structure of, 49-50; mission of, 1-15; multidisciplinary programs in, 45-55; networks for, 126-129; and nonacademic systems, 101-103; priorities for, 2-3; regional, 11; role of, 101-112; scholarly responsibilities of, 16-29; traditional mission of, 4-7; and training, 103-105; values and aspirations of, 11-13, 146-147. *See also* Extended university

V

Values and aspirations, 11-13, 146-147
Van Hise, C. R., 7
Veblen, T., 4

Veysey, L. R., 5, 6
von Humboldt, W., 4, 135

W

Wagner, A. P., 131
Waldrop, M. M., 121, 122, 127
Walsh, J., 122, 125
Wang Institute, and degree programs, 107
Waterman, R. H., Jr., 76, 77
Weick, K. E., 49
White, A. D., 5
White, F. M., 52, 54
Whitehead, A. N., 4, 57, 64, 83-84, 85
Williams, M. E., 128, 130
Wilson, R., 90
Wired campus, technology of, 126-129
Wisconsin, University of: adult education at, 94; extension delivery by, 37; mission of, 6, 7
Wisconsin at Green Bay, University of, nondisciplinary program at, 47-48
Wofsy, L., 167
Woodward, K. L., 93
Worchester Polytechnic Institute, Manufacturing Engineering Application Center (MEAC) at, 21, 32
World Bank, 159

The Wonderful Worlds
of
WALT DISNEY

WORLDS
OF NATURE

Photographs and Illustrations
by The Walt Disney Studio

GOLDEN PRESS · NEW YORK

The photographs in this book were taken by: Rutherford Platt; Elma and Alfred Milotte; James R. Simon; Warren E. Garst; Hugh and Mary Wilmar; Robert H. Crandall; Stuart V. Jewell; Edward B. Prims; George A. Prims; N. Paul Kenworthy, Jr.; Tom McHugh; Art Riley; William and Mary Carrick; Herb and Lois Crisler; Alfred Holz; Roy Edward Disney; Cleveland P. Grant; Fran William Hall; Sarasota Jungle Gardens, Florida; American Museum of Natural History; Mac's Photo Service, Anchorage, Alaska; Fouke Fur Co.; Claude Jendrusch; Florida State News Bureau; Henry B. Kane; Josef Muench; Lloyd Beebe; Fred Kopietz; R. C. and Claire Meyer Proctor; Murl Deusing; Cecil Rhode; Tilden W. Roberts; Olin Sewall Pettinghill, Jr.; Arthur S. Carter; Norbert Witkowsky; Camera Clix; Hawaii Natural History Association; Milwaukee Public Museum; Dr. Vincent Schaefer; William A. Anderson; Don Arlen; Dick Borden; Dr. Walter J. Breckenridge; Joel E. Colman; Jack C. Couffer; Conrad Hall; Al Hanson; Bert Hartwell; George Mushbach; Tad Nichols; Walter Perkins; William M. Harlow and Hubert A. Lowman.

CONTENTS

THE ARCTIC WONDERLAND • By Rutherford Platt • Based on the motion picture series "True-Life Adventures" 4

THE MOUNTAIN STRONGHOLD • By Rutherford Platt • Based on the motion picture series "True-Life Adventures" 36

PRAIRIE HORIZONS • By Rutherford Platt • Based on the motion picture series "True-Life Adventures" 62

DESERT MIRACLES • By Rutherford Platt • Based on the motion picture series "True-Life Adventures" 74

SECRETS OF BEES • Adapted by Rutherford Platt from the original film narration by James Algar 86

SECRETS OF ANTS • Adapted by Rutherford Platt from the original film narration by James Algar 98

MYSTERIOUS AFRICA • By Rutherford Platt • Based on the motion picture series "True-Life Adventures" 106

CREATURES FROM A LAND APART: The Platypus, 122; The Kangaroos, 124; The Tasmanian Devil, 127; The Emus and Cassowaries, 131; The Wombats, 133. By Vezio Melegari 122

ANIMALS OF THE AMAZON: The Jaguar, 134; The Ocelot, 139; The Great Anteater, 140; The Puma, 142; The King Vulture, 143; The Harpy Eagle, 144; The Caiman, 146; The Emerald Tree Boa, 148; The Squirrel Monkeys, 151; The Douroucoulie, 157; Marmosets, 158; Spider Monkeys, 160; The Uakari, 162; Capuchin Monkeys, 164; The Sloths, 168; The Tapirs, 172; The Pirarucu, 173; The Jaguarundi, 174; The Tayras, 175 • By Vezio Melegari 134

WONDERS OF THE ANIMAL WORLD: The Silver Hatchet, 176; The Sharks, 178; The Turtles, 180; The Iguanas, 184; Useful Snakes, 188; The Hares, 190; The Crabs, 192; The Golden-eyes, 195; The Boobies, 196; The Albatrosses, 199; The Gulls, 202; The Parrots, 206; The Barn Owls, 211; The Pelicans, 212 • By Vezio Melegari 176

THE ODYSSEY OF AN OTTER • By Rutherford Montgomery • Illustrated by Hamilton Greene 214

THE BABY COUGARS • By Rutherford Montgomery; adapted by Kathleen N. Daly • Illustrated by Robert Magnusen 252

In the faint, eerie light of the arctic sun, a polar bear cub climbs onto a floating ice pan, looking for fish for his supper.

THE ARCTIC WONDERLAND

IN THIS fantastic land the sun rises once a year. At that moment the drama of life, awakening out of frozen seas, raw rocks, and bitter winds, is enacted on a grand scale. A few weeks earlier a red glow appeared over the southern horizon, dimming the aurora borealis, whose streamers had shed an unearthly white light for months over an utterly silent, motionless, and apparently dead landscape. The red glow had been gradually getting brighter until, at the moment of the beginning of our story, a flaming disk suddenly slid above the horizon.

On the first day the disk seems to hesitate before so great a task as warming up an empire of ice, where the thermometer stands at 60 degrees below zero. It does not rise above a half circle before it sinks back, to become

The great hole in this towering iceberg was made by an underground river that flowed through the part of the glacier where the ice was forming.

a bright spot like a huge bonfire at the edge of the sea. Then again it glides up with a momentum that carries it into the clear in all its roundness. At this moment sunrise and sunset are combined into one event—and the grip of the long polar night is broken! The empire of ice will be shattered by sunlight.

During the weeks that follow, great miracles occur. Continuous darkness is replaced by continuous light. The sun goes around and around the horizon without setting. Instead of an unbroken flat expanse of whiteness, brittle as glass and hard as steel, patches of deep blue water appear, widening and sparkling in the sunlight. Instead of utter silence (for even the great winds of the north pour through space in silence, there being no trees or buildings or wires to make them roar and whistle) there is the grinding and crackling of ice, the splashing of water falling off cliffs, the barking of seals, the squawking of countless birds. Back of all these local sounds the deep voice of the

polar region can be heard. This is the sound of unlocking glaciers and icebergs when tensions deep within the ice are released by the warmth of the sun. Usually the sound is heard across a vast distance like the booming of faraway thunder. Close by it is appalling. This wild booming occurs when a big iceberg is calved at the face of a glacier, or when an iceberg afloat suddenly explodes into a million pieces.

The miraculous strangeness of the arctic is heightened when the sun shines from due south at noon, then circles around to shine from due north at midnight. There is no frost or dew, no moon or stars—there is just immense space made out of sea, rock, ice, and snow. Without familiar objects like trees or buildings for comparison, it is impossible to judge distance or size. A huge iceberg looks like a speck, a tremendous cliff looks easy to climb, a roaring torrent cutting a

canyon looks like a silver thread, a pile of boulders with rocks up to ten feet in diameter looks like an ordinary sand dune. Islands and mountains shrink; they seem almost as small as those on a map. The space of the arctic is continuous with the space of the sky. This is the greatest untouched wilderness of nature on the face of the earth.

WORLD OF FLOWERS

Bleak monotony is not the truth, or the whole truth, about this land.

All over the arctic and right up to the edge of the Polar Sea are scattered some of the healthiest, most freely blooming, and brightly colored wildflowers in the world. They include fireweed, poppy, saxifrage, mustard, arctic rose, chickweed, and bluebells. They grow so fast that they fairly ex-

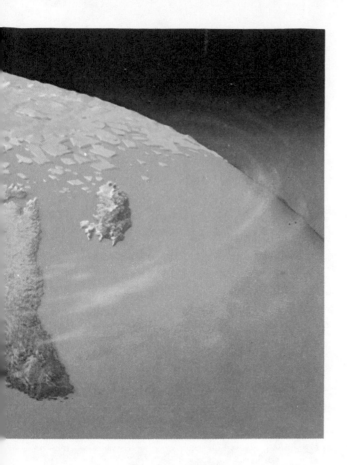

The top of the world, still in the Ice Age, is an untouched wilderness of nature. Every year numberless birds and animals invade it to reach their breeding grounds. And here on the arctic tundras grow some of the healthiest and most colorful wildflowers in the world.

AN ICE-AGE ANIMAL·

With such a wealth of plants in the arctic wonderland there should also be animals, and there are. Yet we only half-believe that any animal can live where the musk ox lives. This beast, which belongs in the storybook of prehistoric monsters, really exists—we can hear it snort and see its wool, three feet long, waving in the arctic winds. This living monument of the Ice Age, ragged and humped up, does not run and jump gracefully like a deer, but clumps along on stumpy legs. It looks like a crazy combination of a bull and an oversized sheep. Most of the time it is patient and friendly; but when danger threatens, it bucks and kicks.

Musk ox, with its big shaggy head turned toward the ground like an American buffalo's, pays no attention to the millions of birds that come to its country to nest in the spring. And in the summertime there is plenty of room in the numberless arctic valleys for both caribou and musk ox; so they do not war on each other.

plode out of the ground after the sunrise in April, and bloom vigorously all summer. In a land where everything is on such an immense scale, arctic plants are miniatures. They do not cover the ground except in patches, but they are scattered in cracks of granite and snuggle under boulders. There are no trees as we think of trees, but birch, poplar, and willow grow as flat as though a steamroller had ironed them out. These strange trees are able to collect a great deal of sunlight because they are only a few inches in height and spread out widely. As there is no fertile soil, they make their own soil out of their brown leaves of previous years, which pile up at the top of the root, where they hold moisture and sun warmth.

In mid-winter, a hungry tundra wolf stalks his prey along a desolate, snowbound river.

When the caribou troop southward in the fall to where trees give hospitable shelter at the edge of the open tundra, the musk ox turns in the opposite direction. It moves up into the mountains where the cruel gales, which would freeze almost any other animal to death in five minutes, keep the ground clear of snow. It saunters to the northernmost point of land in the world—Cape Morris Jessup, only 380 miles from the North Pole. There, in the winter, the animal munches serenely on dead plants, frozen berries, and woolly lichens, to keep its blood warm through the fury of the polar night.

In the desolation and loneliness of mid-

At the head of a rugged fjord on the coast of Greenland, a glacier meets the sea. Here huge icebergs are "calved" when, with a roar and a crash, they split off the dazzling ice face and plunge into the water.

winter, the musk ox lives undisturbed. Its natural enemy, the white wolf, has learned—the hard way—to respect a herd of musk oxen. The herd backs together, big heads facing out, to form a hollow square like the military formations of old wars. Cows and babies take their places in the center, or sometimes young calves get under the bellies of the bulls and hide behind their woolly curtains.

And now, while waiting for the wolf to charge, the oxen do a strange thing. They stoop down and rub their heads against their forelegs. A powerful odor from scent glands just below each eye is released; it carries three hundred feet beyond the formation. The purpose of this scent is a mystery. It may be to warn an enemy of trouble ahead, as does a skunk's, or perhaps it is a means of rousing good-natured animals to action. At the first whiff the musk ox is trans-

formed into a nimble, aggressive animal. It charges out swiftly, gives a swipe with its horns—murderous blades that curve down and then up—and then backs quickly into formation.

If a musk ox is grabbed by a wolf, he bucks and kicks like a steer in a rodeo, then leaps and, turning in the air, crashes down on his side to crush the wolf. If the wolf or any other offending animal stumbles or is trapped, the musk ox will gore and trample and fling the miserable creature to death. But all this is pure defense, for the musk ox, living in a country where there is very little prey, gets all the food he needs from the small arctic plants.

This lonely animal that thrives in the land of the midnight sun has a protective coloring. The shaggy fur is mottled with dark colors, with black spots below, so that when the animal stands still in the light of the summer sun it blends with boulders. From a short distance it is almost invisible. A stroke of genius in the camouflage is a patch of white on the broad back and high saddle—a perfect imitation of a boulder with snow on top! Perhaps this effective camouflage is left over from the time when the musk ox had the company of many other animals which have since vanished from the earth.

About 20,000 years ago, a sheet of ice some two miles deep buried Canada and reached down into the United States nearly as far as Cincinnati and St. Louis. The western mountains of our land were buried in vast ice fields. Musk oxen grazed across the snowy plains in front of the glaciers, where Kansas and Pennsylvania are today. With them were reindeer, wolves, mammoths, and many other animals. But as the climate of the world grew milder, the glaciers melted back and retreated over the northern horizon. The glaciers in the western mountains

Lichen plants make barren rocks colorful.

During the short summer season, the cinquefoil plant produces a single delicate blossom.

Brilliant clumps of yellow cinquefoil and white saxifrage grow in rocky crevices.

shrank up into the highest valleys and ravines, and forests soon covered the slopes. This marvelous transformation took place in a few thousand years, and left the world as we see it. The woolly mammoths and the mastodons, perhaps too big and clumsy to keep moving with the times, died out. The mountain goats, which enjoy rocks, ice, and snow, advanced to the mountain tops. Foxes, rabbits, wolves, caribou, and polar bears followed the retreating ice sheet.

The musk ox, with its rare formula for living, has kept its place right in the middle of the Ice Age through the thousands of years. It has the hollow-square defense and self-rousing battle odor against its one natural enemy, the white wolf. It is easygoing and doesn't rush around frantically getting into trouble. It can live simply on the tiny plants under its feet, whether fresh or frozen. And in a country where it is impossible to dig a lair, it can stand out in the full force of a gale, in intense cold, blanketed by those efficient woolly curtains.

As the arctic summer melts glaciers and snow, and the land is uncovered, flowers and grasses spring up, advancing to the edge of the ice.

While the musk ox is the great land survivor of the ancient Ice Age, the ancestors of some animals of today were disporting themselves in the oceans of the last Ice Age—and millions of years before that.

The sea has always been an easier place to live than land. World-wide ocean currents keep the temperature of sea water fairly even. Even when the sea freezes over, the ice crust averages only four feet thick—maximum seven feet—and underneath that crust is plenty of water with temperatures well above freezing. An animal can become a giant in the sea, moreover, and still travel easily. The body of a whale need not be suspended from its backbone, as in land animals. The water around the whale, not the backbone, holds up its great weight. The whale can move its tonnage by simply floating with the currents, or swimming with a lazy flip of a fluke. The sea, like the air, allows its creatures to move in all directions and travel long distances at will; swimming and gliding under water are similar to flying and soaring as ways of going places without much effort.

The largest monster on record was not reconstructed out of fossil bones millions of years old: it was a blue whale, caught in 1948. This animal weighed one hundred fifty tons, as compared to fifty tons for the biggest known dinosaur, and it was almost ninety feet long. Such whales are also the animals that pack the greatest power. One harpooned whale towed a whaling steamer (with engines going full speed astern) at eight miles per hour for seven hours before it tired. It must have been capable of about four hundred horsepower to do that.

No big animal in the world is so fortunate as the whale in getting food. An elephant needs a square mile of jungle to keep its stomach filled, and the square miles of jungle

Musk oxen live closer to the North Pole than any other land animals. Protected by their shaggy warm wool coats, they can withstand the coldest arctic winters.

are shrinking. But whales today have seas as vast as they ever were. When the cruising blue whale opens its mouth wide, a few thousand gallons of water pour through the rows of whalebone hanging from the upper jaw. These strain out tiny shrimp (called krill), herring, and countless other kinds of seafood. The strained water is jettisoned (a whale doesn't drink salt water). The gullet will not pass anything bigger than herring, but a whale can still enjoy a ton of fish chowder per meal.

Whales in their present form have lived in the sea for some 25 million years. Before that, for more millions of years, their ancestors were running around on land. When the climate changed and there was not enough food on land, these animals took to the sea. Other land animals were the ancestors of seals, dolphins, walruses, and other mammals.

The whale is not a fish. The front flippers are forelegs and still have five fingers, though now the front flippers are used only to keep the whale from rolling over, and to help steer. The whale is propelled by huge horizontal tail flukes, which are flapped up and down by very powerful muscles, as one sculls with an oar at the rear of a boat. The whale's hind limbs have disappeared except for one leg bone, about ten inches long, buried in the body and no longer attached to the backbone.

The whale lives comfortably in cold water without getting chilled, because its frame is covered with an enormous layer of fat, as much as twelve inches thick, called blubber. Blubber also makes the whale buoyant. To dive, the whale must use its tail flukes.

Blubber also is an elastic covering that helps the whale's body to bear the enormous underwater pressures when he dives deep. A whale can go down 3,200 feet. The pressure at that depth is almost a hundred times greater than on the surface, and would crush a blubberless whale.

A whale takes a breath much as it takes a mouthful of fish broth. From a breathing hole at the highest point of its head, the breathing pipe leads into huge lungs that expand like rubber balloons. When the whale dives, the nostrils close, and the animal can stay down from thirty minutes to an hour.

When the whale surfaces for a breath of fresh air, it lets go with such a giant sneeze that a spout of vapor shoots twenty feet into the air, making a rushing sound which can be heard a mile away. This is not a waterspout, although it looks like that from a distance. It is warm air from the whale's big lung vaporizing when it meets the cold air, as when you "see your breath" on a cold day.

At the edge of the Labrador tundra, pipewort can be found growing in shallow pools. The matted, low green growth is the crowberry plant—a favorite food for many of the region's animals and birds.

THE LITTLE WHITE WHALES

There are also little whales, ten or fifteen feet long, weighing a ton or so. When summer is in full swing and the arctic ice pack is only "broken white china" scattered along the shore, open blue water is cut by the fins of beautiful white whales. These never travel alone, like their giant relatives. In droves they scoot along just below the surface, the water boiling across their backs. One of the greatest wild animal exhibitions ever witnessed was put on when eight hundred white whales came leaping like a beautiful ballet into the St. Lawrence River.

Such a performance looks gay and carefree. Actually, the whales are going after their dinner—a school of herring. The whales must travel faster than the herring, and dive at terrific speed.

They never collide, never break the beautiful rhythm of the school, never get con-

Leaping and diving in perfectly co-ordinated rhythm, white whales travel in herds, hunting schools of fish.

fused. This amazing co-ordination is possible because of built-in echo-sounding equipment. Lacking external ears, whales have sensitive hearing canals for use under water. Here a school of white whales utters sounds: trilling calls like canaries, rapid clicks, rusty-hinge squeaks, and harsh cheers—their sounds of communication. Sometimes it's like an orchestra tuning up; at other times it sounds like children at play in a distant schoolyard.

THE TRUE UNICORN

A thousand years ago, perhaps a Viking touring the far arctic ran across the narwhal, forgotten cousin of the whale. He took its horn home and started the legend of the unicorn.

Small compared to a whale, the living unicorn is much larger than the horse on the English coat-of-arms which has the horn coming out of its forehead. The ash-gray body is flecked with dark spots. Out of the face protrudes the huge spear of spiraling ivory. Few land animals could ever manage such a heavy projection thrust straight out.

The narwhal is lonely but secure in its fiord hideaway. The killer whale doesn't go that far north, and the polar bear concentrates on small seals and baby walruses. No one has ever seen narwhals fencing or whacking at each other with their spears.

Arctic explorers report that the narwhal's spear is fine for catching the animal's favor-

ite food—halibut, a flat fish that rests on the ocean bottom in shallow water. They point out that the spear saves a lot of frantic chasing, snapping, and tussling with the fish. A short sudden thrust, and the halibut is dangling at the tip of the spear. The narwhal now swims straight ahead, and the halibut turns around and around on the spear, moving down the spiral, until it pops into the narwhal's mouth.

WALRUS

The whale is magnificent and imposing; the narwhal is fat, lazy, and lucky to have a spear. What can be said about the walrus, cousin to both of them?

This is another warm-blooded animal of the land which, in the invisible depths of time, turned into a sea animal. It has retained all four limbs, each with five digits. To sit down, the walrus folds its hind legs forward, sits on its haunches, spreads its fore-flippers and leans on them.

It looks like a wise elder statesman, with two drooping tusks two or even three feet long. Small eyes and nostrils are pushed up to the top of its head. Its wide muzzles have big, long quills sticking out all over them. Its body, which is almost hairless, is wrapped in huge, ungainly folds of skin.

This monster is certainly one of the ugliest animals on earth, but that is not all. People who have looked into its watery eyes after it has been harpooned see an expression of

The narwhal's long spiral horn is used in spearing fish for dinner.

amazement and disappointment that there is such cruelty in the world.

Those big, drooping tusks are used more energetically than a narwhal's spear. When the walrus is hungry, it takes a deep breath and sinks fifty to three hundred feet to the bottom of the sea. Standing on its head, it brings the tusks into a horizontal position to rake up the bottom. It digs out clams, tears mussels off rocks, and rakes up snails, shrimp, starfish, sea urchins, and anything else on the ocean floor that can't swim away.

The front flippers of the walrus are so short that it cannot use them to push food into the mouth. When the food is raked together in a pile by the tusks, the animal feeds by working the big quills on the muzzle-like fingers.

Walruses travel under water singly like whales and seals, but when they climb out to sleep on ice pans or rock they like to herd together. A pan of ice is white in the sun, but with walruses it looks black, as though loaded with coal. Those are well-fed walruses in a heap, sometimes fifty or even several hundred of them. They may travel fifty miles on the moving pan while asleep.

Walruses take turns at guarding against a polar bear or a savage killer whale. One head in the pile is always up watching for trouble. When it is tired of looking and grows sleepy, down goes the head, striking the next walrus. There's a grunt and another head comes up to look around. When this head goes down, it strikes another with its tusks. The movement of one disturbs the next, which grunts, looks, and lies down. So, the word is passed around and each takes its turn as sentinel.

The walrus uses his long tusks for gathering food. With them he rakes clams from the mud and scrapes mussels and snails from the rocks. His huge appetite leaves his body covered in a layer of fat that keeps him warm.

Sensing danger—perhaps a polar bear—a walrus lookout has crawled over the bodies of the sleeping herd and wallowed into the sea. Now the others awake and make ready to follow.

When anything suspicious turns up, the walrus on guard climbs over the bodies of those around him and slides off into the water. This stirs up all the others and off they slide. Each weighs a ton or more, and the slithery, squashy mass movement into the water may tip over the pan. When it up-ends, it dumps the pile of giants into the sea with a big splash.

THE PRIBILOF MONSTERS

The loneliest place in the world, so desolate and so remote that it is almost unreal, is a group of islands on the fringes of the arctic. These islands are hidden behind storm-battered reefs shrouded in fog, and chilled by gales laden with snow and sleet. They are the tops of ancient volcanoes thrust up in the middle of the Bering Sea. Two of them, about thirty miles apart, are called St. Paul and St. George—attractive names for fragments of the earth's crust that took the men who deliberately sought them twenty-one years to find!

Captain Pribilof, master of a Russian sloop, whose name this group of islands bears, must have passed near the islands unknowingly many times. Finally, in the summer of 1786, in a fog so thick he couldn't see the length of his ship, his old sloop ran against the cliffs. Suddenly he heard "sweet music" coming through the fog from a mile or so distant, and he knew that the search was over.

A bull fur seal commands his harem at the arctic breeding grounds, to which the herd of seals returns on schedule year after year.

The "music" was not like the singing of sirens but it sounded just as mythical. It could have been taken for a riot among millions of animals fighting to their death and having a picnic at the same time. They roared, barked, snarled, whistled, wailed, and chuckled, and mixed in with this unexpected medley was a weird *choo-choo-choo*, like a steam engine starting. This clamor, which came from the breeding grounds of the great Alaskan fur seal, shattered the deep silence of the arctic.

A female polar bear creeps up on the herd of seals, hoping to catch an unwary pup.

Polar bear cubs, like most young animals, are not required to hunt their own supper. They can romp and play, unconcerned, while mother bear goes hunting for seal.

Fur seals seem to consider the Pribilofs the ideal breeding spot in all the world, and maybe it is. Between the cliffs are miles of shelving, smooth rocks, not too steep, which feel good for a moist squashy body to slide over. The climate is ideal also, because during the summer nine days out of ten are foggy and rainy. That keeps fur wet and makes for privacy. Because of the furious gales, even blood-sucking mosquitoes and black flies shun the place. Moreover, the islands are a hundred miles below the edge of the permanent ice floe at its farthest extent in winter, so they are not often visited by polar bears hunting baby seals. Wolverines, weasels, and brown bears do not trespass from the mainland. The offshore reefs keep out the killer whales, so young seals can have safe water for swimming lessons.

No animal ever chose more wisely, or found a better place to serve as a breeding ground through thousands of years. How the seal found this eerie hideout and first took title to it, no one knows. This probably happened when the reefs and beaches first emerged from under the retreating Ice Age glacier.

The fur seals share ownership only with the birds, which breed by the millions up in the crevices and chinks of the volcanic rock. Seals are fish eaters, and they do not molest bird eggs. On their part, the little auks, murres, and puffins do not bother with the big brutes on the rocks by the shore, but become the audience of the bull fights and the swimming lessons of the young seals.

Although whales and walrus babies take to the sea as soon as they are born, seals have kept more of the instincts of their land ancestors. Seal babies are all equipped with flippers but they have to learn how to use them, how to breathe for long submersion,

After the polar bears have eaten their fill, an arctic fox moves in to finish the carcass.

and how to catch live fish. They must have a couple of months of lessons before they can go to sea on their own.

Mother seal, very patient, goes through the motions of the lessons in clear water where the young ones can see her. A whale swims by using its tail as a propeller, but a seal moves through the water with powerful strokes of its front flippers. The hind flippers float to the rear and are used as a steering sweep or rudder. A hind flipper strongly resembles a human foot, drawn out to about twenty-one inches in a full-grown seal, with flat instep and usually five toes.

For eight months every year the Pribilof herd of three million seals is scattered through the North Pacific. Since the children born on the Pribilofs during the summer are too young to stand the cold northern waters in winter, they and their mothers swim three thousand miles south, arriving in December to spend the winter far off the coast of mid-California. The tough old bulls, which don't mind the cold stormy waters of the North Pacific, travel only a few hundred miles down from the Aleutians, sleeping on the sea, riding the Pacific currents, catching tons of herring.

In the spring the mysterious call of the arctic is felt by these animals, scattered far and wide across the Pacific. Wherever they are, they all head north with one accord.

Swimming on his back with his webbed hind feet, the sea otter has a leisurely meal.

The assembling of millions of these creatures year after year, for centuries, always on schedule, is one of the great mysteries and wonders of life.

What is the nature of the summons? How can the animals know exactly where they must go? What guides them on their weeks-long voyages to pinpoint locations in the vast north, to the channels through the Aleutian chain which lead directly to their fog-bound rendezvous? How do they navigate such a course of several thousand miles through gales and fog, always arriving at the right spot at the right time?

Snug on a floating ice pan, this ringed seal pup lies close to its mother.

The bulls are scheduled to arrive first. A few begin turning up early in May. They survey the coast from offshore for a week or so, and then climb out onto the rocks. Hundreds of heavy bodies roll through the surf and lift themselves onto the land. They have returned to the same locations where they were the year before, but not always to the same rocks.

The bulls are swollen with much feeding. Their necks, chests, and shoulders, two-thirds of their total weight, are enormous. The biggest and strongest are the beachmasters, the bosses. They look around, and each stakes out his claim for a space on the rocks about seventy-five feet long and one hundred feet deep. This is the territory where he intends to keep a harem. From the moment a bull has laid claim to his plot of ground, he rules according to the laws of the jungle. With all his great brute strength, he will defend it. in bloody battle.

From the 12th to the 14th of June the females arrive, and in the midst of a great hubbub, roaring, snapping, and fighting, they slide into places in the various harems.

A surplus of young males, called bachelors, is climbing ashore during all this excitement.

GROWING UP

When one of the bachelors feels that he
has grown big and strong enough to command a harem of his own, he leaves the narrow path, barges into the crowd, and challenges a beachmaster. This promptly brings
on a terrible battle between heavyweights.
Giant bodies writhe and swell with rage.
The stored up energy of those huge necks
and shoulders fires the enormous muscles.
The hoarse roars of the monsters, intermin-
gled with shrill whistles of pain and raw terror, echo from the hills. Hair flies. Blood
streams down.

The animals fight until one is so badly
torn that he cannot keep up the battle. If
the beachmaster in charge before the battle
started is the victor, he has won the right to
his harem. However, if he loses, the others
drive him to the rear, to sit in loneliness and
disgrace among the bachelors. He must stay
in the background until he dies, which will
probably not be a long time away. He is
beaten in battle and finished. A new beachmaster has taken his place and assumed all
the rights and responsibilities of the harem.

Soon after the arrival of the fur seals on
the Pribilofs in June, the seal cows give birth
to the year's crop of puppies. These are
black and tiny, only eight to ten pounds
each—small for animals that will grow so
large. In a couple of months they will be
fighting each other in imitation of their giant
fathers.

During this first summer the babies grow
fast while feeding on their mothers' milk and
on the fish caught for them. This is their
best chance to enjoy being land animals.
They gallop to patches of flowers, sleep in
the sedge, or roll in the saxifrage.

They are neither strong enough nor experienced enough to set up their own harems.
The big old bulls are in full charge of that
and, besides, there is no more room available
on the seashore rocks. So the bachelors slith-
er through the crowd and take their places
higher up on rocks away from the water,
where they sit day after day looking over
the situation and waiting their turn, which
comes when they are about seven or eight
years old. Whenever these lonely bachelors
want to reach the sea for swimming and
fishing, they must use a single narrow path
which passes through the harems.

Compared to the noisy bulls, the cows are almost silent. Occasionally they snarl and fight a bit, and after the babies are born their mothers talk to them with a hollow, prolonged baaing. The pups reply with a little bleat, like a lamb's.

The father pays no attention to his family. In fact, mother and child have to be on the alert to move out of the way when the big bull wants to lie down and go to sleep, or the little fellow will get crushed.

The big bull fur seal arrives at the Pribilof breeding grounds a few weeks ahead of his harem of cow seals. They mate early in June.

The beachmaster holds the fort for perhaps six weeks. Always on the alert for trouble, always ready for a fight, he does not swim, and he has nothing to eat during that time. When summer ends, he is a mere shadow of his former self. He has been living and fighting on the fat energy stored in his big bull neck and in his mighty chest and shoulders. It is a thin, battle-scarred, and hungry bull that at last slips into the water.

At about the same time, millions of other fur seals—big bulls, slender mothers, little youngsters—slide away and scatter. St. Paul and St. George are now deserted—just desolate rocks chilled by icy sleet, shrouded in mist. It is not easy to believe that this lonely place was recently the home of millions.

But it is only a chapter that has come to an end. Come next June, the story will resume. The seals will be back on schedule.

The polar bear swims out to floating ice pans when hunger sends him hunting for seals.

THE HAUNTED TUNDRA

The spruce and fir trees that mark the northern tree line of our hemisphere face a vast bog which stretches on and on over the horizon until it meets the glaciers and granite mountains of the polar region. This bog is the tundra. Here the ground is permanently frozen, but in summer the top few inches thaw out to form endless expanses of ponds, among which mossy swamps and thickets of crowberry and blueberry bushes develop. Here, when sunlight sweeps the tundra, bringing the spring thaw, all at once a bleak land is converted into the biggest flower garden in the world.

There is no roar or rush of water, no cracking and grinding of ice, as in other parts of the arctic. But of activity there is plenty. The tundra becomes a tremendous mixing bowl of excited life. There are visitors not only from the border areas, north and south, but also from the skies, where an endless number of birds are rushing in, honking and squawking, after curving over half the world to get there.

This multitude of visitors among the wealth of flowers and berries of this wide, weird land, catching the long days of sunlight, shows the sweep of life, and how living things depend on each other. The musk ox comes down onto the tundra from his polar mountainsides; the caribou emerges from his protected winter haunts in the edges of the forest; and the wolverine, ermine, and brown bear also come out of the forest to run on the fringes of the tundra.

During the past winter the tundra was swept by blizzards. Snow poured across it, piling up immense dunes. In the dim light this land looked like the surface of a planet where life has not yet been created. Then

This young seal, learning to swim in the icy waters, has ventured too far from his parents.

during a clear night between storms, when time seemed to be holding its breath, the light of a full moon showed something moving into the tundra from the sea coast.

The white fox traveled during the winter on the ice pack, sleeping most of the time in crevices where ice was broken and piled up by pressure. When the white fox got hungry, it woke up and feasted on the remains of a carcass of seal left by a polar bear. The restless polar bear usually leaves half of its catch uneaten. Lucky is the white fox who finds itself on an ice floe with a polar bear. The bear has a keen sense of smell but poor eyesight, and the fox has no trouble keeping out of sight, downwind. He comes out only to clean up the dishes after the king of the polar seas has had his fill. Thus these two, the big white one never suspecting the presence of the little white one, travel slowly southward on the ice pans.

Suddenly the polar bear pounces, stunning the seal with a sudden swipe of his paw.

The large black birds, sitting on nests raised high off the marshy tundra, are cormorants. Overhead fly a flock of ring-billed gulls.

The arctic fox is brown until snow begins to pile up on the tundra. Then his coat becomes lighter. Not only hunted animals, but hunters too, benefit by such color changes.

In February, the white fox leaves the pan and heads inland. A curious thing has happened to it. The tip of its tail has turned dark brown. Until now it has been all white except for three black spots—its two eyes and nose. Later it will turn all brown, so that it can hide among the bushes and the mosses of the tundra.

The brown tip of the tail is the first sign that the tundra is going to wake. In some mysterious way it seems to give the fox new energy. He sleeps less and lopes for miles across the snow with his nose down. The deeper into the tundra he gets, the more excited he becomes. He pauses in front of an extra-deep snowdrift with paw uplifted, like a pointer dog. His nostrils quiver as he tests the scent from the hollows, where branches of bushes are sticking through the snow. Then, with a little quick whine, his head goes down· under the drift, and snow flies out from his fast-moving paws.

THE LEMMING

The target of the little white fox's efforts is the lemming, whose cities lie deep under the snow. Other animals, too big to find shelter when the thermometer is fifty below, take to the woods south of the tundra. But the lemming is the tundra's permanent winter resident. There it remains after other animals have been driven away by the bitter cold.

This is a friendly little animal you could hold in your hand. Although he looks like a flat, fluffy field mouse, he is rounder and fatter. Fur covers his ears and the tail is so short it hardly shows. A lemming looks about five inches long, and fat, with tiny head and small bones under its fluffy fur. It can glide easily through a one-inch hole. When the snow comes, it can vanish deep underneath that wonderful white insulating blanket. It lives among sap-filled twigs and sphagnum mosses, whose cells are like fresh springs of water. They do not freeze, because they are packed in the warmth of decaying vegetable matter.

The lemming has no need to come up into the air while the snow is on the ground. No matter how bitter the cold above, it is mild down there under the snow, among the twigs and dried leaves. The lemming runs in tunnels that extend for long distances. It rests in cubbyholes anywhere. There is always plenty of bark and dried berries in the labyrinths. Passages lead in all directions, and are exciting to explore.

The lemming eats no meat except an occasional dinner of minute insects and larvae that dwell among the grasses and roots. There is also a wealth of roots, seeds, leaves, frozen berries, and bark, and the lemming eats them all. For clipping and gnawing plants it has teeth like a buzz saw's.

To be healthy, to find food and a mate, and to seek company, the lemming must be able to run around. It has four mouse feet, and claws that can tunnel through soil or debris like a power drill. The network of tunnels, totaling thousands of miles, indicates that this little animal is the fastest snow-removal machine on earth.

In their need for warmth and food, saxifrage plants and grasses grow close to boulders. These arctic plants have no soil whatever to grow in, but send roots into cracks between boulders to tap the mineral-rich waters the melting glacier leaves behind.

Caribou are a type of arctic deer with short tails, shaggy fur, and towering antlers. Herds of caribou are sometimes tended by Eskimos.

thaw year after year until they become loosened and lifted up above the permanently frozen ground. In this way a lot of edible vegetable matter turns into a hummock full of nooks and crannies and passageways, like a sponge. With some easy remodeling, these domes will hold any number of ball-shaped nests about five inches in diameter.

The lemmings' nests are lined with grass and saxifrage flowers. The more luxurious are lined with the fur of fox, caribou, or musk ox which the lemmings found on bushes or on carcasses before the snow came. The air in the tunnels is still, and the homes are doubly insulated by snow and by grass, leaves, and hair, and warmed by energetic bodies. Let the winds howl and the temperature drop to fifty below—it's a long way off, above the four or five feet of snow.

A far-flung system of winding, many-branched tunnels runs under the snow between the hummocks. There may be a connected pattern of tunnels running hundreds of miles over the horizon. But lemmings who are raising families do not roam far from home. Each has its own nest and, if it scampers around among neighboring hummocks, it finds its way back home by its own odor. When lemmings pass one another in a tunnel, they stop to touch noses.

In the comfortable, secure, well-fed cities under the snow, there is no awareness of numbers—of the millions and millions and millions of lemmings, of how the population is mounting across the tundra. And then one year something terrible happens.

Swimming through loose snow is different from digging through packed soil. Accordingly, during summer, when there is no snow, the lemming is equipped with long sharp claws on the two middle toes of its front feet. These enable it to dig around roots. When the ground freezes and the snow comes, the claws begin to grow wider and, instead of being sharp, they are now flat and double the summer size. They have turned into snow shovels!

On the level tundra, masses of live roots, dead leaves, and clumps of sphagnum moss, growing in wet soil, alternately freeze and

The huge timber wolf has killed a caribou that was too old to keep up with the herd. Wolves have been known to trail their victims for more than 100 miles.

After this pair of timber wolves has singled out a caribou, they will continue tracking it for hours, exhausting their victim, then rushing in for the kill.

THE DEATH MARCH

In winter, the tundra is still a vista of motionless space, and it gives no outward warning of the approaching catastrophe. Beneath the snow, individual lemmings still touch noses when they meet. Now and then one grows curious about the strange world above the snow and runs a tunnel upward. At the top he blinks at the strange, cold world, then slips back down his tunnel fast—back to the nice warm nest.

By March the lemmings are not meeting singly and touching noses. Now perhaps ten or a dozen are meeting at a time, and they crowd past each other with angry squeaks and nips. When they go visiting in nearby

The timber wolf drags part of the caribou carcass back to his den for his cubs to feed on. Wolves often make their homes in dens abandoned by other animals.

In summer, the weasel's fur is brown, helping him conceal himself in underbrush and dead leaves as he hunts for mice, birds, snakes, squirrels, and rabbits.

In winter, the weasel's coat turns completely white, making him almost invisible in the snow, except for his black-tipped tail. Then he is known as an ermine. In the arctic, weasels feed on snowshoe rabbits and birds and take heavy toll of the lemming population.

hummocks, they find crowds of new nests. They must go farther and farther for fresh roots and grass. By April, spring thaws have uncovered hummocks far and wide across the tundra. The lemmings come out and scamper around, chewing the buds on the bushes. They cut grass, gather it into sheaves four inches long, and take it back into their burrows.

Rich brown fur makes a lemming almost invisible among the red shadows thrown by the low sun. The brown coat has another use: it protects the animal's skin from the cold water which is kept away by the air bubbles caught in the fluffy fur. The bubbles also make the lemming buoyant so that it swims and floats easily. Lemmings cross the ponds of the tundra by paddling furiously with their hind legs while steering with their front paws. Ripples make a long series of V's, and there is a trail of seething bubbles from little paddling paws as though from a small outboard motorboat. When a lemming climbs out it shakes itself like a dog.

Such a pleasant life is the usual thing, but this is the year of trouble. When the lemmings come out from their overcrowded galleries, they see, not wide-open spaces of fresh grass and quiet pools, but other lemmings putting out their heads from thousands of other holes. Groups are already out and rushing around in circles, splashing in the ponds, dancing in a sort of frenzy, snarling and fighting. There are too many lemmings and the future is beginning to look hopeless for this animal community.

As more and more lemmings pour up from their homes and tunnels, they become panic-stricken. They run around, eat less, and exhaustedly fall asleep in the open—not in the safety of their homes. But a lemming asleep in the open, curled up like a baby porcupine, is doomed. Suddenly, there is the shadow of huge wings, and the snowy owl with outspread claws strikes like lightning.

The panic of the lemmings spreads across hundreds of miles of tundra. It is felt in the polar region to the north, and along the coast where the ice floes are breaking up. It reaches the dark spruce forests to the south. All the life of the arctic is set in motion.

Not one fox, but thousands, appear from mysterious hideouts. These have lost their beautiful white coats and are mostly brown, with a few white patches—like the brown tundra moss mottled with patches of snow. Wolves that have been stealthily stalking the caribou now stand on the tops of hills, heads upraised, sniffing the air, moved by an irresistible call from the tundra.

Out of the forest bordering the tundra, otters, martens, and ermines come running. Brown bears turn over stones on the tundra, looking for panic-stricken balls of bright brown fur. The polar bear climbs ashore to try a diet different from seal.

The frenzied lemmings are forming squads —regiments—armies. They pay no attention to the rapidly increasing raids of the animals with queer squinting eyes and soft paws. They ignore the fast-moving shadows and fierce talons from above.

An older male lemming rushes out of its hole with a shrill squeak and sets off as though it knows exactly where it is headed. Others nearby stop milling around and follow. The leader keeps well out in front, with a dozen or so lemmings at its heels. Back of this advance party come scattered bands of twenty or thirty. Maddened by the crowding in their underground homes and on the tundra, they now press tightly together and surrender all their accustomed little ways of life. Their only urge is to press on.

The snowy arctic owl swoops down on many small furry animals. He is especially fond of rodents, and his northern visit never fails to coincide with the lemmings' panic-stricken migration across the tundra.

Northern animals—like this arctic fox cub—can keep warm by ruffling up their fur, and trapping their own body heat in an insulating jacket of warm air, even when lying on a snowdrift.

Safe from the cold and fury of the arctic blizzard, the female lemming places her young in a warm, grass- and fur-lined nest deep under the ground.

When the tundra becomes too crowded with lemmings, hordes of little animals begin jostling one another and running, in panic, to the sea.

The rippling brown patches move in the same direction. Millions and millions of little feet patter on and on for countless miles. The armies flow together, growing larger.

The other hungry armies are closing in by land and air. Their raids are multiplying, but the lemmings do not retreat under ground. They only squeak and snap helplessly at the huge beasts that fall on them; the most furious fight that a lemming can make has little effect against its attackers.

On and on the lemmings go, traveling by night at first, and curling up to sleep by day. But as this appalling river of fur flows on the lemmings grow more excited. Now, instead of taking time out to eat and let laggards catch up, they press on, not even stopping to rest by day. A few mouthfuls at most are grabbed on the run.

Often the march ends before the sea is reached—because there are no more marchers. The foxes and snowy owls, the weasels and wolves forget each other to get a share of the gluttonous feast.

But sometimes millions of lemmings do win the sea. Without hesitation they plunge through the surf, or, if they find themselves on a cliff overlooking the sea, they dive off. The bubbles in their fur make them buoyant, and the cool water feels good. They swim on and on, perhaps for miles. Bubbles foam out behind. But these bubbles are not entirely from paddling feet; the fur of the lemmings is losing its buoyancy. The big cities on the tundra will be deserted now.

BIRDS OF THE POLAR NORTH

Hard on the heels of spring, the sky fills with the whir of wings, and the polar valleys

Before they reach the shore, many fall prey to hungry animals and birds. This lemming has been caught by a weasel.

echo with the honking and squawking of millions of new arrivals. For a few weeks the ragged old musk oxen, the white foxes and hares, and the tragic little lemmings will share their savage and beautiful land with the birds who own the world.

The birds heard the call of the north in faraway places. They heard it in their homes in New Jersey, Virginia, North Carolina, California, and around the Gulf of Mexico. Below the Equator they heard it—in the Amazon Valley, the pampas of Argentina, the Falkland Islands, Tierra del Fuego, and at the very bottom of the world in Antarctica. They heard it in Gibraltar, Italy, the Azores, the Canary Islands, and Algeria. The call was heard far at sea in the Humboldt Current off the shores of Peru and Chile, and in the Guinea Current along the coast of West Africa, and in Borneo, the Moluccas, and the Arabian Sea.

Birds living in all corners of the world suddenly felt far from home. They belonged to the granite, glaciers, and tundra of Alaska, and around the Arctic Ocean. Wherever they were, unaware of others doing the same thing, they responded to the call and took to the skyways that lead to the north.

What signal did they receive? How could all act in the same way at the same time? They abandoned homes and food and familiar surroundings as though a trumpet had sounded, and set out to cross open sea and continents—thousands of miles—without hesitation. They headed for the same spot where they had spent the previous summer; they traveled the same course their kind have followed for hundreds of years. They broke through walls of dense fog to fly toward their goal. They arrived on time regardless of the weather encountered on the way.

The snowshoe rabbit's wide, furry paws help him run over the deep snow—serving as snowshoes. His white fur helps him to hide.

This ptarmigan has moulted nearly all of his reddish-brown summer plumage. When winter comes he will be entirely white.

When hidden against a background of ice and snow, these white-furred polar bear cubs will not be easily seen—not even by hungry timber wolves constantly on the prowl for food.

All other animals of the earth spend their winters at or near home. The Olympic elk lives on the Olympic Peninsula; the buffalo's home place is the prairie; a beaver winters in the home pond; every elephant holds its territory in the jungle, and every lion its territory on the high steppes; many birds—including sparrow, blue jay, meadow lark, and bobwhite quail—never get more than ten miles from their nests.

But everywhere on the ledges of the arctic, beside the boulders of polar beaches, in patches of saxifrage in sun-catching hollows out of the wind—everywhere right up to the ice floes and pressure ridges of the polar sea are nested the birds whose territory is the whole round world.

THE MARVELOUS VOYAGE OF THE TERN

One nest is that of an arctic tern on Cape Columbia, America's farthest north point of land, on the tip of Baffin Island only a few degrees from the North Pole. A couple of chicks are snuggled in the nest, healthy and happy in their fluffy down as they look over the rim, waiting for their mother to come back with something to eat. A pile of new-fallen snow surrounds them, but when the mother or father returns, it will soon be scooped out. To the family, this is not alarming; they feel perfectly at home.

This nest in the farthest north is utterly hidden in an empire of rock and ice. Even in spring the place is buried often in furious blizzards. Yet, surely, easily, and on schedule, the parents of the chicks flew eleven thousand miles from their other home on the Antarctic Continent, close to the South Pole. Storms over half the world did not deter them; the length of the Atlantic and the immensity of four continents did not cause them to lose their way. With no navigating instruments but the organs and nerves in their small bodies, they flew above the Western Hemisphere to the same spot where they had nested a year ago.

For many years the voyage of the arctic tern was one of the greatest mysteries of life on our planet. Were the terns in the far north really the same individuals seen in the

Snow goose goslings explore the marshy tundra in northwestern Canada. They must learn to fly quickly, so that they can practice for the long migration to the south.

far south? The exciting truth was discovered when some birds were caught, tagged, and released so they could fly where they wanted. Each tag had a code telling the date and place where it was fastened to the bird's leg. The tag also asked anybody picking up the bird to report to the United States Fish and Wildlife Service when and where it was found.

As time passed, reports of the recovery of a few terns began to come in. More were tagged and there was more patient waiting. Banding started in 1913, and by 1948 enough reports had been received to make clear the story of the tern.

Leaving their birthplace in the ice and pressure ridges that surround the North Pole, the terns head southward around the first of August. They fly over Kane Basin, where many polar expeditions have been destroyed by the ice. The eternal glaciers of Baffin Island can be seen on the right, while those of

Lesser snow geese (white with black wingtips) and blue geese, with newly hatched goslings, at their breeding grounds in the arctic. Their nests are found over a huge area that stretches from Siberia to Baffin Island. Although differently colored, they belong to the same species, and interbreed.

north Greenland are on the left. The terns follow the coast of Greenland to where the shores of North America fade from sight across Davis Strait. After fifteen hundred miles they reach the southern tip of Greenland, where they turn east to pick up Iceland and then head south again. The Orkneys and the British Isles pass below and the terns pick up the coast of France.

On they fly. A tern on its voyage pauses only briefly to circle over the water with beak pointed down, as though taking aim, and when a fish is spotted near the surface,

This goldeneye duckling will feed on a diet of mussels, crayfish, and insects. Adult goldeneyes are called "whistlers" because of the sound their wings make when they are flying.

When this peregrine falcon chick is full grown, he will have gray-blue plumage on his head and back, and a barred breast. This bird is usually known as the duck hawk.

he closes the V of his tail, snaps his wings tight to his body, and dives straight as an arrow.

When the west coast of Africa comes into sight, the terns follow it to the westernmost bulge, where they have a choice of routes. Some fly westward, picking up the easternmost cape of Brazil, and then continue southward along the coast of South America to Tierra del Fuego and Antarctica. Others may choose to follow the coast of Africa all the way to Cape Town—and then head two thousand miles across the South Atlantic to Antarctica.

How do they do it? How can a bird find its way over an exact and specified course—from point to point? Much of it is seeing perhaps, but they travel mostly at night. And what about fogs and the storms that blow them off course? How does a bird rec-

ognize the coastline and the landmarks? Who gave it a chart and told it how to use the chart? How does it time a flight that lasts for weeks so as to arrive at the goal on a certain day? If it goes from one visible point to another, how does it steer its course when it is flying miles above the sea?

Many days of the amazing flight of the arctic tern are spent far out of sight of landmarks, crossing oceans as unerringly as though they were lakes. The golden plover, which is not a sea bird and cannot rest on the water, flies the Pacific—over two thousand miles of open ocean—between Alaska and the pinpoint islands of Hawaii. The greater shearwater nests in one tiny place, an island named Tristan da Cunha, which is located in the middle of the South Atlantic. From there, the bird flies to its nest in the distant arctic.

All sorts of explanations have been suggested by people whose curiosity knows no bounds—and any one of them is plausible, because nature is full of miracles. One idea, not respected by many bird experts, is that the long-distance flyers are guided to their spot in the arctic, and then on a certain day back to their spot around the world, by magnetism. Men use magnetic compasses, but these have to be corrected. When man takes his compass far north, he gets above the magnetic pole and his compass points backward. He has to correct it with some complicated mathematical figuring. Nobody knows whether nature gave these birds compasses that are self-correcting!

Birds have a sense by which they correct their direction when they are following the lines of magnetic fields that sweep around the earth. This sense, or instinct, is beyond anything we can imagine. It is not merely a matter of aiming at the Magnetic Pole, as does a compass needle; this would not take birds to their goals, which are scattered all over the arctic. The North Magnetic Pole is located just above Hudson's Bay and birds would have to fly north of it, or east and west to reach their nests.

Another suggestion is that the birds can feel the rotation of the earth in their ears just as you can feel the rotation of a merry-go-round. Perhaps this feeling keeps them exactly on course. If birds can steer themselves from hemisphere to hemisphere by "listening" to the rotation of the earth, they are way ahead of us in guided missile development!

The best explanation is that the birds are guided by light. We know that bees can reach a distant point by steering according to the angle of sunlight. Why not birds, too, on a much bigger scale?

It is sunlight that calls to the birds. This is what they seek in the far north. Their inner mechanisms are quickened by long days. They have the urge to mate and lay eggs.

On the Newfoundland coast, amidst a flock of black-backed gulls, is a skua (left foreground). Skuas will often steal another bird's freshly caught fish.

The ultraviolet rays that are strong in the arctic also help them to make more lime for egg shells. So the birds that fly from far corners of the world into the arctic are called by light, and they are reaching for the sun.

Except when the arctic tern passes from the antarctic to the arctic and back again, it experiences very little darkness. Most of its life is spent where the sun never sets. The arctic tern, who lives both at the top and at the bottom of the earth, is thus the only creature in the world that enjoys almost continuous sunlight.

THE BIRDS WHO OWN THE WHOLE WORLD

Birds of many kinds fly to their places in the arctic when spring comes. All hear the same summons, all have the same urge—to lay eggs and raise families where the days are long, where there are plenty of fish and seeds to eat, and plenty of room without much danger from enemies.

Eiders make the most comfortable nests. They raise chicks safely on an exposed low rock in the midst of the polar ice pack, which is swept by bitter gales that would freeze a big animal or blow it off the rock. All that an eider needs is a small depression out of the wind, and brimful of sunlight. It plucks down from its breast and lines the nest with this fluffiness that lets sunlight filter through but captures its warmth in dead-air pockets. An eider's nest is warmer than the air above. Little chicks, however, don't seem to mind coming out from under their eiderdown quilts.

Eiders are the only birds that cultivate plants. They fertilize a circle in the hollow of a rock, and after a few years a dense growth of grass forms a beautiful living rim for the nest.

Each year the rim grows wider and deeper from the addition of new grass pressed into it. The eiders and their descendants return year after year to the same big nests. These are like old family castles of the eiders clustered together on rocky islands of the polar region where they remain undisturbed for years.

Murres stow away their eggs on crannies and ledges of the steepest cliffs. No fox could ever climb up there. They do not build real nests but simply push a few stones around so that the eggs will not roll off the bare rocks. They crowd together almost shoulder to shoulder—thousands on the face of one cliff.

A murre does not move, once it has established its breeding spot. It sticks to that square foot of ledge, and the same murre turns up on the same ledge year after year.

The rocks in the vicinity of the murres

After stealing an egg from the nest of a ring-billed gull, this weasel bites through the shell and begins his feast. Weasels will eat young birds in the nest, if they can find them.

ring with the hoarse mating call of this bird —ha-ha-ha—ha-ha-ha—over and over again.

Above the murres the little auks, or dovekies, make their nests. Where the murres swarm by the thousands, the dovekies swarm by the tens of thousands. Let a mysterious alarm be sounded—perhaps a school of herring has turned up in the water at the base of the cliff—and dovekies come off the cliff in clouds. Caught in the light of the low arctic sun, they sparkle like snowflakes above the cliffs, blood-red with lichens.

Dovekies are not so light and airy when they plump down onto the water. They bob around heavily, low in the stern. It is quite a job to be airborne when you're so low in the water. A dovekie may have to boil along like a motorboat for a hundred feet or more before it can rise.

The phalarope is the ballet dancer of the arctic bird community. While father does the baby-sitting, mother swims in circles upon the surface of very shallow waters. This circling looks very pretty and rhythmical, but that is not why the phalarope does it. She is stirring up the bottom to bring little tidbits up nearer the surface, where she can eat them without diving.

The puffin may have arrived on the scene after other birds had laid claim to the cliffs and windy islands. So the puffin digs hollows and raises its family underground. It likes the tundra better than the rocky cliffs, especially along the coast where it faces the sea for fishing. Puffins are related to the auks and murres, but you would never guess it. The puffin's bright colors and oversized triangular beak make him look clownish.

Canada geese go north high in the sky, in a perfect elongated-V formation, while the deep honking resounds afar. The geese travel overland to their places in the tundra.

Jaegers, the hawks of the arctic, head in from the sea, but are silent. The jaeger likes to have terns and gulls do the fishing for

The American golden plover builds its nest on the Alaskan and Canadian tundra. The speckled eggs are well camouflaged among the stones and grasses. In the Fall, most of the plovers fly all the way to Argentina.

him. When it sees one rise, fish in mouth, it swoops down and strikes. The fish falls, and the jaeger dives under and catches its dinner in mid-air.

These are some of the birds who own the whole world—and move into the arctic all with one accord.

Recently hatched cormorant chicks lie in a nest of sticks, feathers, and seaweed. They feed on fish by thrusting their bills deep down into their parents' open gullets.

THE MOUNTAIN STRONGHOLD

The Rocky Mountains rise abruptly from the almost level Central Plains. Their steep slopes, leading up to glaciers and snow, are the eastern rampart of the great mountain stronghold of forests and animals in the Northwest. The opposite rampart of this fabulous area fronts the Pacific Ocean, which is seven hundred fifty miles to the west.

Between these boundaries the mountains contain huge trees, marvelous animals, primitive wilderness. Here are many trees that are totally unlike the familiar ones east of the Mississippi River. Hundreds of years of undisturbed growing have raised the columns of Douglas fir — trees ten feet thick — two hundred feet into the air. Sitka spruce has

Eastward from the Pacific, through the Rockies, stretches the wilderness of the mountain strongholds. Here, on the Olympic peninsula in Washington, a Sitka spruce (center) is outlined against the sea.

been drawn from its home in Alaska, as though by a magnet, to join the coastal part of the forest. Red cedar, elsewhere small, here carries its lacy branches up hundreds of feet.

The growth on the Pacific side forms a mysterious rain forest. In the filtered twilight an elk can vanish by simply standing still. A squirrel is almost invisible when it runs up the huge column of a tree trunk. Big ferns curve and stand motionless. Every fallen giant has quickly become a slender green garden of moss and fern, ghostly bright in the misty air.

Westerly winds blowing across the warm water of the Japan Current bring in great loads of moisture. The cool mountain barrier causes these winds to spill much of their water into the rain forest and then, farther eastward, to release the rest as snow on the mountains. This snow becomes locked in hundreds of glaciers which are the sources of streams that carve deep ravines and leap down the mountains in roaring waterfalls. White peaks and black forests stretch from the plains to the Pacific, interrupted by patches of green woods where bigleaf maple, aspen, and alder grow along the quieter waterways in the valley bottoms.

In this virgin wilderness are the hideouts of primeval animals, created by time along with the trees and glaciers. They are the animals of a massive world of big dark forests and ice and rock. These animals, in a fierce, raw land inherited from the mammoths, must be strong and mobile, or peculiarly skilled, to survive.

VERTICAL MAGIC

Here, the mountain tops of snow, rock, and ice are fragments of the arctic that retreated northward long ago. Animals as well as the land prove the comparison. The mountain goat resembles the easy-going musk ox that now lives on the shore of the Arctic Ocean. Both animals have a hump filled with fat—reserve energy for the bleak months of winter, when grazing is poor. Both have streamers of wool, blanketing them against below-zero gales that would freeze ordinary animals to death in a few minutes.

The zones of life which follow northward across the face of the earth are, in fact, similar to those which follow one above another on a mountain. In temperate regions, a climber starting at the foot of a mountain travels about three miles north for every ten feet of height. Imagine looking up at a spot only a hundred feet higher along the trail and realizing that it is miles north! The top of the mountain, clearly visible in the sky ten thousand feet up, is the kind of place that might be found three thousand miles north!

Huge bears lurk in the shadows of the dense rain forest of the Rocky Mountains.

Bare rocky peaks, high above the timber line, are the home of the sure-footed bighorn and the mountain goat.

This vertical magic is one of the astonishing secrets of the mountain stronghold. The zones are alike—from light-green woods that drop their leaves, to evergreen northern forest, to treeless but flower-strewn tundra, to arctic rock and ice. Zones that run northward across the horizons are, of course, vastly wider than those that run up a mountain.

Climb to an arctic ledge with the mountain goat. Look down a thousand feet upon a treeless slope strewn with rocks and flat junipers and a wealth of bright glacier lilies, saxifrage, poppies, and gentians. This is the mountain tundra, to which the mountain

goat often descends for a good graze. Below that, scattered clumps of small whitebark pine and spruce turn into the compact forest of evergreen spires. Far below the forest, light-green patches can be seen in the lowest valleys, showing faintly through a blue mist. That may be only a few miles away, yet it is an unknown and mysterious world to the animals of the mountain arctic.

THE BIGHORN

Far above the spires of the giant trees, fresh snow on a dangerous ledge shows the prints of cloven hoofs. A bighorn has passed this way, but where did it go?

You have reached the ledge after hours of struggle with clumsy mountain-climbing gear. You can track that bighorn only a few steps. The trail vanishes at the end of the ledge. It is no use to peer over the edge, looking for the smashed body of the bighorn at the foot of the precipice. The animal has chosen to run upward over the face of the cliff, along that narrow cleft. With luck you may catch sight of the big fellow looking down serenely from a pinnacle a few hundred feet overhead.

The bighorn likes it up among the steepest, rockiest crags, where there are snowbanks in the shady spots, and ledges with clumps of arctic flowers. There he can snooze undisturbed in a sun-warmed place out of the wind. With his wonderful eyesight he can pick his routes anywhere, up or down, and go where he will. When he wants to lie down, he paws two or three times and settles himself on the rock. Animals normally paw the ground before lying down to make a little hollow, or perhaps to clear away sticks and stones or small animals that would be uncomfortable to lie on. The bighorn paws bare rock just because that is the right way to lie down.

MOUNTAIN BOUNCING

The bighorn is a mountain bouncer rather than a mountain climber. The sole of each foot has big, soft, elastic pads that spread apart under pressure to make extra-wide contact with the surface of a rock. The shallow, cuplike hoof contains the pads and provides suction to prevent slipping. But the bighorn's feet are also pliant and sensitive, and operated by powerful muscular springs. He can bounce six feet straight up to a ledge, or sixteen feet across a chasm.

In these mountains there are no absolutely smooth and perpendicular cliffs. The steep slopes always have little ridges and footholds. Bighorns can go where they want to go.

Once a herd of twenty-five bighorns was cornered where walls of rock rose hundreds of feet straight up. The only exit appeared to be blocked. But the bighorns picked out a fold in the rock and one after another, with-

With no scent to betray him, and spotted with a dappled light-and-shade pattern, the fawn can hide by merely standing still.

The huge spiral horns of the bighorn grow more curved every year—sometimes turning upon themselves to complete a circle.

out a pause, they bounced this way and that up the fold and disappeared over the top. These were two-hundred-pound animals, and a second's pause would have sent them crashing on the rocks below.

Among his arctic heights, the bighorn has little to fear from natural enemies. Only the

The mating season of the bighorn begins in late October. Then the mountains and valleys echo with the battles of the rival rams.

eagle can look down on him, and the eagle is respectful. The ewe, or mother bighorn, is constantly on the alert for the fierce bird

A bighorn ram charges his adversary, and the two animals smash together head on. They butt, kick, and jab. Sometimes the loser—as in the bottom picture here—is pushed off a cliff, perhaps to his death on the rocks below.

that dives out of the blue to snatch a lamb. While father goes off by himself to bounce among the mountains, mother stays with her young.

She teaches the lamb how to run up and down cliffs and cracks, how to bounce across ravines, and how—if the lamb is a male—to butt another male lamb. The little bighorn also is taken to a place safe for falling, and here he practices bouncing. Often the mothers and their lambs slide down slopes, and bounce up again, bucking each other, and learning to hook, jab, and parry.

About the middle of October the bighorns start down to lower pastures. Days of loafing on high mountain ledges, among fresh, delicious flowers, are ending. The mating season is on. Suddenly each bighorn ram is mad at every other bighorn ram. In the open, stony glades between scattered clumps of whitebark pine and alpine larch, terrible collisions are about to take place.

BATTLE OF THE BIGHORNS

In fighting for a mate, bighorns obey strict rules of combat. They do not slash and tear at each other in blind fury. They take positions, make certain sounds, and follow the procedures by which their ancestors always fought.

The two rivals first stand side by side, facing in opposite directions. They make a few sudden passes at each other, kicking out sidewise and trying vicious uppercuts with their front hoofs. Bighorns are usually silent animals, but now they grunt and snort—perhaps as signs of rage, or perhaps each animal is giving the other a last chance to quit.

The mountain goat's fur stays white all year. His eyes are golden yellow; hoofs, horns, and lips are black.

and may measure four feet in length and fifteen inches in circumference at the base. The dynamic spiral form is used by nature in many growing things, including shells, pine cones, and unwinding ferns.

In summer the bighorn grazes on flowers and grass on the high mountain peaks. In midwinter he retreats to lower forest zones for a few weeks. There he paws the snow like a horse to get at the grass. His emergency rations, if the snow gets too deep, are the buds of aspen, spruce, Douglas fir, willow, and juniper.

Even the greatest bouncers alive find it hard to live in deep snow in the forest. Then Mother takes over. The snow may be above their backs, but she leads her family, single file, with fifteen-foot bounds, the others leaping exactly in her tracks. The children, born last March, are now big enough to keep up. The family will welcome spring, when they can bounce up again to the high ledges.

OLD MAN OF THE MOUNTAINS

The bighorn on a far, high ledge, silhouetted against the sky, crowned by huge horns, is every inch an emperor. But he is not the greatest mountaineer. That title is held by the mountain goat, who goes even higher among the glaciers and lives all year above the tree line. The bighorn's colors blend with rocks and pastures, but the mountain goat is all white, blending with snow and ice—all white except for his round, solemn yellow eyes and jet-black, daggerlike horns and hoofs.

He seldom hurries except when gaining momentum for a steep climb, or when the pull of gravity makes him hurry down a cliff.

After ten minutes of this, the animals walk about twenty paces in opposite directions. Suddenly they wheel, rear up, run at each other, and crash head on. The heavy, hollow horns resound with a crack that can be heard a mile. Recovering from the shock, the rivals may call the whole thing off and walk away together from the scene of battle, or they may separate and repeat the crash.

Sometimes bighorns are badly wounded, even killed, by the battering. Jabbing hoofs can cut out deep slivers of flesh. Noses bleed. Horns are splintered and pieces are even broken off, never to grow again. Occasionally a bighorn is pushed over a cliff.

The big, spiraling horns—apparently useful only in the mating battles—are unlike the elegant antlers of the wapiti, which grow fresh every year. The horns keep growing year after year during thirteen or fourteen years of the bighorn's life. Spirals on an old bighorn may more than complete the circle,

If the cougar can dodge the razor-sharp horns of the mother goat, he may catch a fat kid for supper.

He walks deliberately like an old man on stiff legs. When he hooks his hoofs over a ledge and, with long white beard waving in the wind, gazes down at the puny world, he is the Old Man of the Mountains.

Icy blasts, broken crags, treacherous ledges are no bother for the mountain goat. With his hump of reserve energy and his deep, warm fur, he can ignore bitter gales as does the other true arctic animal, the musk ox. The mountain goat has feet equipped like the bighorn's, and he is the most sure-footed animal in the mountains. Instead of bouncing, he climbs like a monkey, the front feet taking hold and pulling up. His three hundred pounds will scoot up steep slippery rock or ice where a man would hardly be able to budge without ropes, axe, and holding pegs; this agile mountain animal can also clear a twelve-foot crevasse with ease.

During winter the Old Man of the Mountains seeks out the most exposed ledges and slopes that are clear of snow, and there grazes on the dead, frozen remains of plants. Any kind of plant materials, no matter how old and dry, can be turned into the muscles of this mountain climber that chews a cud. The first of his four stomachs is a collecting sack, or market basket, which he fills with grass, leaves, and twigs. He can take all day to do this and then find a sunny, windless spot to ruminate—that is, chew over the contents of his market basket. This material wads up into a cud and is pushed into stomach number two, where it is mixed with digestive juices. Then it is raised up to the mouth, chewed, mixed with saliva, and swallowed into stomach number three. After a good kneading there the cud goes into stomach number four, where the plant mash is finally turned into mountain goat.

This easygoing creature has few worries. Occasionally in summer a cougar will slink above the tree line and try to jump him. Then the goat may use the two straight black daggers on its forehead. These weapons, as sharp as meat skewers, may go in to the hilt and send the big cat away screaming with pain.

When spring thaws come, the mountain goat must keep a sharp eye out for avalanches, rock slides, and sudden water. He can usually scramble higher up on the mountains to get above the avalanches and rock slides. Or he may leap to a safe ledge and give a little grunt as he watches the avalanche roar by.

Of all the wonderful animals of the mountain stronghold, the Old Man remains the most mysterious and the least observed. To disappear he has only to stand still—which he does most of the time anyway. Then he is but a little patch of snow among the rocks.

THE BEAVER

Far below the arctic heights there are quiet streams wandering through woods of aspen and willow. And there are ponds where an extraordinary animal is hard at work.

The beaver is cutting down trees, building dams and canals, causing a series of events

If the beaver cannot find a pond that remains three feet deep all year long, he dams a stream. The dam has a spillway to keep the water level constant.

that will affect all neighboring plant and animal life. Frogs and little fishes, water birds, muskrat, mink, and even the giant moose will come where the industrious beaver has created a pond.

The beaver's pond is his fortress, and he could not survive without it. Many wild animals have horns, claws, stingers, kicking feet, or tearing teeth with which to fight for their lives against the sudden death that lurks behind every tree or rock, in every shadow.

Some animals can bluff, like a puff adder when it blows out its head and hisses, or a bear when it growls and stands its hair on end. Some animals can take to their heels—darting, scurrying, scampering, running up a tree or disappearing into a hole. But the beaver has none of these resources. Waddling along, lacking the sharp quills that protect the equally fat and slow porcupine, it is easy prey for wolf, coyote, bear, bobcat, cougar, lynx, and wolverine! Its weapons are limited to a fine set of teeth, useful only on smaller animals. It can't scare anything with a snarl. Its legs are capable only of a clumsy gallop. It has no tunnel in the ground, and is slow in climbing a tree. So it has to have the pond. When danger threatens, the beaver can disappear under water and not be seen again. It can dive and live happily out of sight even all winter, without making telltale tracks in the snow—and all the time it is breathing air and living like a land animal.

All depends on the beaver's having a certain depth of water the year around, and plenty of trees. Aspens are first choice, but red maple, beech, willow, cherry, alder, or birch will do. Such a situation is hard to find. Most ponds get low in dry seasons and are so shallow that they freeze solid in winter; no air-breathing animal can live under the ice. Streams are usually too swift, or they dry up. So the beaver makes a pond that will remain about three feet deep through the dry weeks of summer and the flood time of spring. The beaver makes the situation just right by damming streams that flow among the trees it likes to eat.

Beaver dams are marvels of engineering.

The beaver's four orange front teeth are sharp and strong as chisels. With them he can feed on the smooth green bark of the aspens, or cut down trees for his dam. His forefeet are not webbed, and can be used much like hands to grasp and hold logs, stones and branches, and to plaster chinks in his dam with mud and twigs.

When the tree crashes to the ground, the beaver will trim off the branches and float the log.

Supplies of branches are weighted down with stones, and sunk for winter food.

TREE FELLING

Beavers are small animals for the job of lumbering. Adults average three feet long and fifteen inches high, and weigh around forty pounds.

A beaver can cut down a tree five inches thick in a surprisingly short time. It tackles all sizes of trees. The biggest tree known to have been felled by beavers was a hundred and ten feet tall, with a stump five and a half feet across.

To fell a tree, the beaver stands on its hind legs and grips the bark with the sharp curved nails on its front claws. It spreads its hind feet wide and braces itself with its tail. While the front teeth drive into the wood like a holding fork, the lower teeth cut a deep notch three inches below. Then the beaver tears out the chunk of wood between.

The beaver does not control the direction of the tree's fall by cutting on a certain side. But most trees are on ground sloping toward the water and so they fall in that direction, which is the right way for the beaver. Occasionally the tree falls on the beaver and kills him.

When the cut begins to crackle, the beaver stops, looks, and listens. If the tree doesn't fall, a little more cutting is necessary. When it really starts to go, the beaver freezes. No cry of "timber!" is heard—only a loud cracking in the stump and a swish of branches high in the air. The instant the tree crashes to the ground, all beavers in the neighborhood disappear under water. Then they put their noses out and listen for a while to make sure that no dangerous visitors have come to see what the noise is all about.

Teams of beavers will often work together when building their houses, cutting logs and repairing their carefully constructed dams.

Although the beaver's house keeps him comparatively safe, on land he is slow-moving and may fall prey to a prowling coyote.

DAM BUILDING

A beaver fells a tree for two reasons. He loves to eat the tender bark of the topmost branches. He will use the trunk and larger branches for dam building and repair. The timber is cut into convenient logs, averaging around five feet. The length depends on the distance that the log has to be nudged and dragged to the nearest water. The longer the distance, the shorter the log.

A beaver moves logs to the dam site by floating them there, and if necessary he will build canals to do the job. A beaver pond that has been in use for some years, so that all nearby trees have been cut down, will have canals leading as far as five hundred feet into the surrounding land. A beaver may be almost as busy building canals as he is building dams.

Logs floated to the dam site are green wood that will easily get water-logged. The beaver sinks them into place on the dam by piling on mud and stones. Logs and sticks are laid parallel to the flow of the stream, although often rushing waters push them askew. Stones, twigs, mud, wet leaves, and perhaps the discarded antlers of a deer are thrown on. Before long a beautiful dam has risen, backing up the water deep enough so that the beaver can come and go under the ice in winter.

A beaver dam's length depends on the

On land the beaver can only waddle about, but his streamlined shape is perfect for speedy and graceful underwater travel.

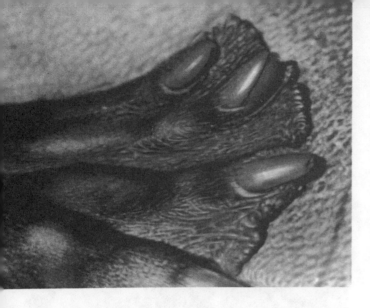

Only the beaver's webbed hind feet are used for swimming; forepaws are folded to his chest.

size of the stream. Most dams are not over three hundred feet long. A record dam in Montana was over two-fifths of a mile long.

BEAVER HOUSE

An animal that does not live in a deep hole in the ground or in a hollow tree must have some place where it is safe to raise a family. The beaver has it. His site may be a clump of willows or some large bush surrounded by the water of the pond. To this he hauls brush, sticks, mud, and stones, and piles them on—with an architectural plan in mind. The foundation must be securely

made, with extra amounts of stones, mud, and waterlogged sticks. The floor is built on this foundation, a couple of inches above water level. Over this is raised a dome of thatched brush. This is not sealed with mud, like the dam, because the beaver family, which will occupy this house all winter when the pond is frozen, likes fresh air and does not mind a dripping roof.

A secret passageway leads from the floor of the house down into the watery cellar. Having extra-large lungs, beavers can hold their breath fifteen minutes if need be. They can easily come and go under the ice through the passageway without surfacing.

The house is big enough for a man to hide in. John Colter, who discovered the marvels of Yellowstone Park, escaped from death at the hands of the Blackfoot Indians in 1809 by diving into a pond and crawling up inside a beaver house. There he hid until the puzzled Indians went away.

A beaver is covered by two coats of hair— coarse guard hairs on the outside and the fine fur that makes up the famous beaver skin. Both these fur coats are oiled. After swimming under water, a beaver gives his fur a good combing with the toe of his left hind leg. This toe, split to form a fine-tooth comb, cleans the beaver's covering of fur.

Whether lumbering on land or towing logs along a canal or across the pond, the beaver is always alert for an enemy. Sensing trouble, he stops and listens. If the trouble seems real, he slaps his tail on the water, and all beavers hearing this warning sound vanish.

In the depth of the woods, the sounds of crashing trees and the slapping of heavy flat tails are the sounds of beavers. Sometimes the gentle wailing of young beavers can be

The beaver's tail can be a rudder, an oar, or a danger signal. When he smacks it loudly on the surface of the pond, beavers half a mile away hear it and take cover.

In winter, the beaver is kept warm by the pad of fat he has stored up, and by his glossy pelt. Still later, when the weather gets colder and the surface of his pond is covered with a thick sheet of ice, the beaver can no longer leave his house in search of food. Then he must stay inside, feeding on the branches he sank to the bottom of his pond in summer.

heard coming from the beaver house. The adults, mostly silent, occasionally speak to each other with low mumbles and whines, sometimes an angry hiss.

Nature gave the beaver unique skills for cutting down trees to build dams and houses. He is the busiest animal in the mountain stronghold, and one of the happiest.

THE WAPITI ELKS

Enclosing the green valleys of the beavers and towering over them, the forests of the giant evergreens roll across the mountains. In these forests is the heart of the stronghold. Higher up, winds roar among the crags and drive snow wildly in all directions, but only the spires of the trees quiver when winds hit them. Beneath the spires, the air stirs gently among immovable pillars, and snowflakes filtering down weave a white gauze among the branches. The forest holds a silence so profound that even the sound of water falling a thousand feet over a precipice is muffled.

When the nights are growing longer and the frosts are heavier on the mountain tundra, just at sunset an unearthly sound echoes across the forest. It comes not from the depths within the trees, but from a commanding point overlooking a valley. It starts as a hoarse, guttural roar of tremendous volume, like the safety valve of a big engine suddenly letting go. It rises in pitch with a bugle-like tone, higher and higher, growing more shrill until it soars up to become a screaming whistle; then it breaks and drops, becoming guttural again, and suddenly fades. There is silence, then one loud grunt.

Up in the high pasture, the great American elk, called wapiti by the Shawnee In-

With the beavers safe in their winter stronghold, the coyote must look for other game.

dians, has challenged all the world to a fight.

More than any other animal of the mountain stronghold, the wapiti reflects the grandeur of the primeval forest. His tall body is carried on long, powerful legs; his shoulders and neck are massive. When, in the fall, he leads the females to a high spot to let the world know he is ready for a fight, he seems to challenge even the great trees. He fills his lungs with an enormous breath of the mountain air, raises his muzzle toward the sky, and pours out his bugle call.

This is the time when the wapiti's royal antlers have reached their full growth. Those antlers are one of the miracles of nature. Growing them, and then finally brandishing them while he bugles, seem to be the whole purpose of the wapiti's existence.

Every year at the end of winter the antlers break off from a knob that sticks up an inch above the skull. Both antlers fall off at

The wolverine climbs trees hunting for birds' eggs. This ravenous hunter also eats young birds out of the nest. He is the largest member of the weasel family.

about the same time. The knobs get fuzzy, and two weeks later they have swelled up several inches higher. Antler growing continues rapidly; in a month they are a foot high. The thick velvet is filled with blood vessels that put down the bone which will become the antlers. In about four months, they will be the most magnificent antlers of the animal kingdom.

The main stem, called the beam, turns back over the elk's head and one day, at the right time and place, two spikes come out on each beam. They point forward over the elk's brow and then turn up at the ends like a cowcatcher. Meanwhile the beams sweep backward and then upward, branching and rebranching until the full-grown antlers stand as high as four feet above his head.

By late summer the antlers are finished, the blood stops flowing around them, the velvet dries. The wapiti, who seems in a hurry to have his antlers polished and neat, plunges them into bushes, pawing the ground and shaking his head up and down until all the velvet is scraped off. In September, he is ready for a duel.

DUEL OF THE WAPITI ELKS

The place is a high meadow surrounded by clumps of evergreens, with mats of juniper underfoot and rocks strewn here and there. Our bugler seems to be waiting for something. He is standing apart from the harem of a dozen wapiti cows, who are grazing indifferently.

Presently a few more cows turn up, and the herd is joined by some other males with tall new antlers.

It is high time.

The challenger bugles again. Another male utters a harsh bark that sounds like "Enough!" He steps out of the shadows of the trees and walks slowly toward the challenger.

The manes on the two animals rise. Their big necks throb. They put their heads down and advance upon each other. Antlers meet and creak like branches of trees scraping together in the wind. Each warrior spreads his feet and gives a couple of powerful pushes.

No reckless charge, no crash of antlers, upsets their royal dignity. If one elk feels the other has the greater strength, without more ado he walks off the field of battle. The victor takes the harem, while the loser goes off alone, perhaps to ponder the fact that he must be getting old.

The bull elk shed his antlers in January. A new set replaced them in early spring. During the summer they are in the "velvet" stage (as here) and become sharp and hard by fall, at the beginning of the mating season.

But if they are evenly matched, they will keep on pushing and twisting and grunting. Once in a while they pull apart and glare at each other with an angry snort, and back off about thirty paces to come together again. One may get a bloody nose and some gashes.

Sometimes the pushing contest goes on for twenty minutes or so. The rivals are so busy that they do not notice their audience walking out on them. The males who held back when one of their number accepted the challenge divide up the harem, and everybody leaves.

The pushing contest, however, may have a tragic ending. Antlers of wapiti elks are not just bumpers. They are tough and springy, and they have complicated branches which do not exactly meet. As they are pushed together and twisted this way and that, they may become hopelessly locked. Then all the power of the big animals cannot pull them apart. Locked together, they will die of starvation in a few days. Bleached skeletons with antlers intertwined have been seen on the high pastures of the mountain stronghold.

Wapiti are the most dignified occupants of the mountain stronghold. The nose bridge is wide and strong, the eyes big and wise, the throat deep and heavy with hair. And the finest antlers in the world look more like royal symbols than vicious fighting weapons. Wapiti usually stride deliberately on their long legs, though a cougar striking from an overhanging limb will send them sprinting off at thirty-five miles per hour, whistling like an engine coming to a crossing.

THE WAPITI HERD
DESCENDS THE MOUNTAIN

All summer the herd has been feeding on the lush flowers and grass of the high mountain tundra. Now, as the nights grow longer, a sudden storm covers the grazing area with four inches of snow.

This is no problem to the long-legged wapiti. He paws the ground like a horse, clearing a spot for good eating. Flowers and grasses here, like those of the far north, stay fresh right up to the solid freeze of winter. The grasses keep flowering and the flowers keep opening their buds, displaying delicate stamens and pistils as they do only in the springtime down in the green valleys. To the wapiti such plants uncovered under a light snow are cool and fresh and good to munch.

But four inches of snow on the mountain meadow is a signal. By age-long custom, the herd must start south. Day by day, now, they feed lower and lower, while animals come together from across the valleys and the herd grows larger. Perhaps nature has taught them that there is safety in numbers—safety from the cougar and the bear, for example—as the elk travel far from their accustomed haunts. Or perhaps these animals simply enjoy rubbing shoulders when they migrate. Whatever the reason, the harems come together into herds, and little herds join to make big herds, and a big parade fills the downward trail. If a heavy blizzard strikes and piles up several feet of snow, the travelers push on faster, their long legs kicking aside the light, fluffy snow. In the face of snow and enemies they push on, passing through dangerous defiles, crossing angry streams.

When snow lies too thick to be pawed from grass and leaves underfoot, the wapiti elk feeds by browsing on twigs, bark, and evergreen shoots.

The timber wolf stalks the elk herd in winter, waiting for calves to stray away from their mothers, or for an old elk to tire and lag behind the main group.

At last they reach a low valley, protected from high winds, where the ground is often clear under the bushes and trees. They have gone perhaps thirty-five miles in all—not far as migrating birds measure distance. The distance varies with every herd. However, the vertical distance multiplies the horizontal many times. Taking advantage of the vertical magic of the mountain stronghold, the elk have reached an entirely different kind of country—in the hope of finding good grazing all winter.

The greatest danger to the herd comes when snow covers plants so deeply that they cannot be reached by pawing, or when a hard freeze follows a thaw and the ground is under a coating of ice as hard as steel. Elk are not made to cope with frozen ground and thick ice. Their hoofs are quickly worn; their noses get cut and bloody from trying to reach grass under a heavy crust; their leg muscles, not powered for continuous effort when the snow is five or six feet deep, eventually crumple under them.

Under these conditions the desperate herd turns from grazing to browsing—eating twigs and buds on the evergreen trees and aspens as high as they can reach. Such things are sticky and bitter compared to green leaves; they are emergency rations at best.

As the lower branches of the forest dwindle, these animals, which started their march down the mountains big and strong, with a good supply of reserve fat in their swollen necks, get thinner and thinner. Cougars gather in the dark forest, waiting for low-cost dinners on carcasses of exhausted, starved animals that have dropped in their tracks. The fine wapiti herd is close to calamity.

The herd is saved only by the first balmy wind of spring and the thaw that makes the massive snow and cruel ice vanish into thin air. Then antlers fall from the heads of the bulls, and survivors head back up the trail to the high pastures where wapitis are happy.

THE COUGAR

All animals in the mountain stronghold are afraid of the cougar, who lurks everywhere—from plains to tundra. At the slightest hint of this killer's presence, the mountain goat darts up to his highest hideout. The bighorn's kingly crown is useless when the big cat strikes, and the tall wapiti with his beau-

tiful antlers is easily brought crashing to the ground. Down in the valley, a beaver is crushed by the cougar's blow as though struck by a falling tree. Where a herd of mule deer is browsing in an open glade, one is suddenly, without warning, struck on the shoulder by an animal projectile weighing one hundred fifty pounds. The survivors wheel in terror, flashing white patches on their rumps, and making off in every direction.

Only the lazy porcupine and the sober little skunk have tricks ready for the cougar. Porky twitches his tail, and the big cat's nose is a pincushion. After each needle has stabbed deep, a tiny barb juts out, and now the fierce needles cannot be pulled out without tearing the cougar's nose to shreds. He will not be able to eat for a while.

The skunk's trick is not deadly, but it hurts the big cat's pride and spoils his fun.

The cougar glides among the mountains as silently as the shadow of an eagle. He is one of the most beautiful creatures that ever lived. When he prowls, his lithe body elongates and the skin ripples with smooth, muscular power underneath. When he crouches and freezes, just before a spring, his huge paws are gathered under his body, his shoulders expand with bunched muscles. He springs as though shot from a gun, with two long bounds and a short one, onto the back of the victim.

The tail, wonderfully long and sensitive, steers the animal in the air like feathers on a giant arrow. A cougar hits the bull's-eye. When the cat springs on a mule deer, its outspread claws hit the shoulder at a certain angle. The head snaps back, breaking the neck, and the carcass of the deer is tossed twenty feet by the blow.

The cougar is the best athlete among the big animals of the mountains. Only twenty-six inches at the shoulder, he is low enough to scoot under branches and fallen trees—an

All the forest creatures fear the giant cougar, or mountain lion. He can spring 40 feet from a branch, breaking the neck of his victim.

advantage in a forest obstacle race. His body, all muscle and unburdened with fat, elongates to seven feet. A white-tailed deer is faster in a burst of speed, but a crust on the snow will trap or cut the deer's legs, while the cougar can spread its great paws like snowshoes. The cougar can broad-jump thirty feet from a running start, and forty feet from a rise or from the limb of a tree. He can pour himself off a ledge sixty feet high, landing on his feet and legs which make perfect shock absorbers.

He is stealthy. Twigs rarely snap under him. Leaves do not rustle as he glides past. He does not hiss, grunt, or snort. All his ferocity is pent up in muscles. Occasionally only a mysterious, wailing shriek breaks the

After the mother cougar finishes training her young, they go off hunting on their own.

silence of the forest from some far-off, high, rocky ledge where the cougar has a cave. This is the voice of the strange and wonderful animal that haunts the mountain stronghold and is the terror of all its inhabitants.

THE COMFORTABLE BEAR

While wapiti elks are struggling in the deep snow, reaching desperately for bitter twigs and pine needles, black bears are dozing in their dens. They are the most comfortable animals in the deep forest.

The black bear can eat whatever is handy —flesh, fish, green leaves, fruit, or insects. The male eats and sleeps while the mother feeds and brings up the children. A black bear in the wild forest spends his casual life within five miles of the place he was born.

Even the deadly cougar is not a great worry. Bear meat is a third or fourth choice on his menu. In summertime the cougar is chiefly occupied with deer. The bear, which seldom pursues an animal but stands and waits near a trail, is a genius at turning into a shadow and fooling even the wily cougar.

The black bear comes in various colors that blend with his environment. His coat may be a deep, glossy black, except for a white patch on his chest, copied from a lonely sunbeam filtering through the trees. He may be cinnamon-colored—like an open forest of ponderosa pine, where the bark is made of red plates and the floor is carpeted with red needles. Black bears may also wear fur coats that are brown, yellow, or blue-gray.

In the fall the bear grows steadily fatter. As he eats and eats, the food forms a blanket of fat all over him, until the bear is enormous. At the same time his hair grows longer. In late November, when he gets drowsy, he can lie down and sleep, warm and safe in his four inches of fat and four inches of fur.

The colder the weather, the sleepier the bear. If the male tires of looking for a cave among rocks, or for a hollow in a tree, he may just lie down to sleep in the lee of a fallen trunk or under the dense crown of a tree or in a clump of bushes. But his sleep is not deep, like that of the woodchuck, ground squirrel, or bat. The bear's temperature does not fall, but stays around 98 degrees. Now and then he gives a little grunt, a whine, and a jerk. He may snore loudly—and the next minute, if the air is warm for winter, stand up and shake himself and perhaps take a walk. Only half asleep, he is ready to scent danger or, if need be, look for another den.

The mother bear's den has been carefully selected. If it is a cave, she will floor it with leaves. If it is an overturned tree giant, she hollows out a den at the base, where the roots are up-ended, and lines it with grass, pine needles, leaves, and bark.

Her big warm body almost fills the place. Nothing could be warmer and cozier for the

Bear cubs climb trees hunting for birds' eggs, insects, nuts, fruits and honey. They will stay with their mother until their second summer, learning all the hunting tricks and woodland ways that their anxious parent can teach them. After that, she will desert them.

While her twin cubs (left) are busy learning how to climb a tree, the mother bear (right) creeps up on a porcupine—a great delicacy. Then she calls her cubs to show them how she flips the little animal over on its back, and eats it without getting her nose full of quills.

Young bear cubs explore hollow tree stumps with eager paws and noses, looking for honey.

to do, and the babies don't wander away and get into trouble. They squeal and kick a little, but they too are mostly dozing.

After six weeks the cubs have grown to four times their weight at birth. Each is a foot long and covered with silky black down. Now the den is getting a bit crowded. But this is according to nature's timetable. Spring is coming over the mountain, and they can all come out and stretch in the open air. At four pounds, each of the little bears stumbles out on wobbly legs to get his first taste of bear food, which is about anything. For their first feast, the mother may root up a nice fresh skunk cabbage.

During their first six months, the cubs trot along close behind the big, rolling rump of their mother. She teaches them how to dig up wild onions, lily bulbs, wild parsnip, sweet flag, and bear grass. She shows them

babies when they arrive in January. Usually twins, but perhaps triplets or quadruplets, they are surprisingly small to be born of a five-hundred-pound mother. They weigh about half a pound and they are blind, toothless, and hairless.

The nest is less than thirty inches across, but big enough to give the cubs room to grow. The new babies grow fast on their mother's rich milk, which her body makes out of the deep fat that surrounds it, while she gets thinner and thinner. All the time, mother hardly wakes up. She has no hunting

Squirrels are sometimes tricked by wily cubs— for young bears often climb trees, and shake down all the nuts from the branches, stripping them of the squirrel's favorite food.

how to recognize the whiff of chipmunks, mice, marmots (called *woodchucks* in some places), and ground-squirrels, and the best way to dig them out of their burrows. She stands guard while they develop their muscles in games of tag, somersaults, wrestling, and boxing. When a porcupine drops to the ground from his perch in a tree, the babies learn that a black bear is one of the few animals smart enough to enjoy porcupine meat. He just puts a paw under the slow, stupid porcupine and tips it over. The soft underparts present no trouble such as the cougar encountered.

Often a deep snow descends on the mountain forest in spring. The little family is now too big to go back into the den for protection and, besides, bears are happy-go-lucky and can usually find a way to have some fun. In this case they all decide to take a walk. Mother bear breaks the trail by jumping, making a big deep hole at every leap. The little ones must jump into these holes or get hopelessly buried. When the mother gets well out in front, she sits down and waits patiently for them to catch up, floundering

Bears are expert fishermen, wading into streams to catch a fine fresh salmon.

and whimpering. If she were a grizzly she would carry on a conversation with her cubs on walks through the forest, grunting and whining to advise them and urge them on to greater efforts. Being a black bear, she is silent most of the time, teaching by the power of example.

Observers have told us that, when danger is suspected, she says, *"Rough—rough!"* This means, "Stop whatever you are doing!" A single *"Rough!"* means "Get up that tree fast!" Let a little bear delay and it gets a cuffing that it will remember all its life.

Once bears are up the tree, they dare not come down until they hear the grunt from their mother which is the all-clear signal. If she chooses, they may stay there a long time while she goes off to pick berries or have a few hours of freedom from her children.

Once taught by the mother, bears climb trees better than any other big animal. They do no feeding among the limbs, but the sense of security felt when they were very

young stays with them and makes them enjoy climbing. A bear of several hundred pounds will sprawl on a slender limb and go to sleep with his legs hanging down.

A good-sized tree makes a good bear bulletin board. When a black bear discovers the lair of an enemy, a lush patch of berries, or a hollow tree with a store of honey—anything that makes news—he may head for a certain tree, usually an aspen, which has smooth bark. This tree is known to all bears in the area as a message center. The bear stands on his hind legs and, reaching up, sinks ten front claws deeply into the bark.

Bear trails are well-beaten paths. But a man cannot follow them as easily as he can follow wapiti trails, which have plenty of headroom for high antlers. Bear trails run under fallen trees and through low tangles of brush. They lead to and from berry patches or drinking water or places where the fishing is good. Many generations of bears have used them, and no bear would deviate the least bit from the trail which the first one took. Later, a bear might find a shorter cut to take, or it might be easier to go around the end of a fallen tree than to squeeze under it. But wherever the trail leads, every bear will go.

Bears like to prowl close to home, usually hunting over a range of 5 or 10 miles. The mother bear is stern with her cubs, and cuffs them when they disobey.

BEAR SCRATCHING

Like all furry animals, the black bear wears two kinds of hair. The outer coat is coarser and longer, and the inner is fine—fine enough for the bearskin hats of the famous Grenadier Guards in England. The beautiful, shining coat is shed every spring. Ordinarily the best-groomed animal of the forest, the bear seems annoyed when his coat starts to come out and looks ragged. For a few weeks bears do everything they can to hasten the unsightly shedding. They rub and rub, scratch and scratch, against trees—hour after hour, day after day. Bark is rubbed off as well as hair. The bears jump into thick bushes and scratch back and forth and from side to side. This must feel wonderful, and a lot of hair is left behind.

Bears are crafty fishermen. A black bear stretches out on a log and lets his arms hang in the water with paws open. He waits in that position patiently, not moving a muscle. He may even catch up on a little sleep. Finally fishes can't keep away any longer from that big paw, which is nice and greasy. Then—*Splash!*

The bear sits up with a fish squirming in his paw. He bites off the head and lays it carefully on the log beside him while he makes a delicious mouthful of the rest, bones and all. At the end of the day a little mound of fish heads lies on the log.

A mother may leave her cubs sitting on the bank while she wades in and stands stock-still, belly deep in water. When she feels a fish brush against her sides she makes a lightning grab—and the little cubs are handed a treat.

Bears love to eat nuts that are ripe in the fall, and they know the best way to gather them. Just climb the tree and shake the branches vigorously. Then climb down and pick up the nuts.

A beehive in a hollow tree is the most exciting discovery of all. In goes the huge paw, and out it comes dripping with honey. Of

In summer, bears have no definite home; they sleep when and where they like.

During their first summer cubs are playful, while mother bear does most of the hunting. But their mother prods them to learn how to find and dig up edible roots, where to find berries and honey, and how to catch mice, woodchucks, and other small animals.

course the bees are in a panic when this terrible thing happens to them. The golden honey is their most precious possession. There is nothing to do but call out the suicide troops and attack the bear.

A bee has a stinger with a fishhook prong, so that it cannot be pulled out. One sting and the bee dies. Yet, to protect their hives, bees will go after a monster bear with utter ferocity. Their stingers cannot touch his skin under the deep fur, but they find his nose. The giant roars with pain, but he goes right on licking the honey off his arms. Bees are licked off, too. Everything of the comb and its little bees disappears.

A black bear shuffles off through the tangled underbrush. Seen from the rear, his high round rump bounces and rotates as though separate from the rest of him. Certainly, he *does* look funny. But nevertheless he is the most intelligent, and the most leisurely, of all the great animals in the mountain stronghold.

PRAIRIE HORIZONS

ON THE prairie there are few shadows to hide in and almost no trees to climb. Everything above ground is exposed. But nature has created special animals to live and bring up families here. Instead of climbers of rocks and trees, and hiders in shadows, prairie animals are runners and diggers. The vast flat spaces favor super-runners, and the deep soil invites unlimited digging and tunneling, so that an animal can travel underground mile after mile without appearing in the upper world.

The prairie is the wide-open middle of America. It begins where the eastern woods and hills stop. It reaches westward to the base of the Rocky Mountain rampart, north into Canada, and to the Mexican border on the south. The deep soft grassland of southern Wisconsin, Illinois, Missouri, and Iowa; the rich plains of eastern Texas, the wide fertile levels of the Dakotas and Nebraska; and the sunbaked plains of Montana, Wyoming, Colorado, and southwestern Kansas—all these merge to form the vast continuous space over which pronghorns and coyotes run, and under which ground squirrels, go-

phers, and prairie dogs thrust their tunnels and build their underground cities.

THE BUFFALO

Go back one hundred fifty years.

Here on the face of the prairie a massive mammal moves in thousands. The buffalo, or bison, has short thick legs—he cannot run fast like an antelope. He has heavy cloven hoofs—he cannot dig like a prairie dog. But he has his own special ways. Instead of running away, he runs towards his enemies. No animal can withstand his fearful roar and crushing power. The huge armies of buffaloes raise clouds of dust which can be seen hundreds of miles away.

The first white man to see a buffalo described it as three animals in one. It had a camel's hump; a lion's high flank, tufted tail, and tremendous mane; and the horns, cloven hoofs, and mad attack of a bull. This was na-

The vast, treeless prairie stretches without a break from horizon to horizon.

ture's greatest animal experiment in America
—a monster too heavy to climb, too big to
hide, yet able to survive in the wide-open
spaces.

The buffalo's strength and terrible looks
are concentrated in front. The heavy head
seems to sag, but the buffalo is not tired. He
is occupied mostly with grazing on grasses
and herbs, and chewing his cud. The position of the head is best for that.

The horns are hollow and curved, wide at
the base and tapering rapidly, made for tossing. But the buffalo kills only when another
animal makes him mad. With a quick motion of his horns, he can pitchfork an enemy
—wolf, coyote, or any other offending animal
—out of his sight.

The buffalo's wide head is set under a
huge mane. Hair dangles over his eyes and
cheeks. A full beard waves back and forth
below the chin. That is the way a monarch
who is unafraid, unhurried, and slow to wrath,
should look.

*The great central plains sweep westward from
the Mississippi to the foot of the Rockies.*

The buffalo is not startled by an unexpected fright as so many other animals are. If he
senses something wrong he stops grazing, he
stares, his nostrils expand, he sizes up the situation. If the suspicious object stands still,
he will turn away and go back to grazing. If
it moves toward him, he will put down his
head, paw the ground, utter a few rumbles,
and drive forward to the toss.

The buffalo, very nearsighted, depends on
keen smelling and hearing. He can smell
water many miles away. But poor eyesight is
a handicap in the charge. He may stop at intervals and cock his head to take another
look. Then on he comes again.

A buffalo walking is like a heavy two-
legged animal in front with a smaller two-
legged animal behind, pushing. The two legs
of the front animal swing slowly, carrying
most of the weight and doing the steering.

In winter the herd follows the lead buffalo as he breaks a trail through the snow-drifts. Heavy robes protect them from the icy gales.

The weight shifts between those front legs with each step. When this front animal throws his weight forward onto the front legs, the two legs of the light rear animal lift off the ground. The hind hoofs dig into the ground with backward strokes that push the animal forward.

The buffalo does not paw the ground like a horse, but when he wants to uncover grass under snow or sand, he pushes with his muzzle and roots for it like a pig. Also, he never rears up. When excited, he tips forward with head down while the hind legs kick up.

LITTLE BIRDS
FOLLOW ALONG

While the buffalo grazes, blackbirds trail him. They feast on insects which he stirs up in the grass. Some birds flit onto his backbone, where they sit in a row, snapping at flies and mosquitoes that graze on the buffalo. On cold nights the birds snuggle into the fur over the bufflalo's neck and warm their toes.

These blackbirds of the western prairie are cowbirds. They build no nests of their own, but lay eggs in other birds' nests. They may throw out other eggs to make room for their own. When the cowbird eggs hatch, the babies are raised by the other bird, who doesn't seem to know the difference.

ROLLING TROT

There are times when even a buffalo is in a hurry. When he is thirsty and smells water, or when trying to escape a blizzard, he moves in a rolling trot. He leans to the right while the right front leg takes most of the pounding and the right rear leg does most of the pushing. Then he leans to the left. Half of him is working at full power while the other half rests. So the huge animal can cover miles without tiring.

In the fall, blizzards swoop down on the plains, but this great animal was made for cold weather. Under his magnificent robe he takes winter in stride. At night he faces directly into the blizzard, for his massive front has the longest fur. He sits down and lets the snow drift over him. When the gray light comes over the eastern horizon, he shakes off the snow, eats the grasses and herbs from the bare spot where he rested, and rolls southward again.

THE PRAIRIE FIRE

The biggest animal on the prairie recognizes one deadly enemy—the prairie fire. Fire can cut off his watering place and drive him mad with thirst.

In an extra-dry year, scattered fires may surround a herd. Then some old bull starts moving and the others follow. What starts as a few frightened individuals soon becomes a swift river of rippling brown backs—a stampede.

There is nowhere to run but into the wall of fire and smoke. Many plunge and fall, while others hurry over their roasting bodies. Frantic bellowing mingles with the roar of flames. If the stockade of fire is not deep, some survivors emerge on the other side, with hair burned off, some blind, groaning—standing on black ground where wisps of smoke grow instead of grass.

THE BUFFALO GALLOP

A prairie fire calls forth marvelous speed from monsters usually slow to move. The impulse to stampede shoots like an electric current through the herd. A buffalo sitting on its flank, with legs stretched out, utterly relaxed, when it feels this impulse will spring up and spin in a tiny circle and be off like a deer.

Buffalo calves are born in April and May. In a day or two they become strong enough to follow the herd, close to their mother's side.

The buffalo uses a gallop more than a run. He plunges with head down, vaulting on his front legs while the light hind feet kick up and down. In the flight of full panic the hind feet push back, making the sand fly, then lift and swing forward together, crossing the front legs as with racing dogs.

In July and August, during the mating season, dueling buffalo bulls shake the prairie.

THE BUFFALO WALLOW

When the fur robe falls off in midsummer and the buffalo stands naked from hump to rump, thousands of mosquitoes alight on this juicy mountain of meat. If the buffalo can find a willow or a few cottonwoods, he will rub and rub, as bears do in the mountains. But the few trees may soon be rubbed down.

A tormented buffalo may mount to the highest knoll and stand with his face in the wind. Or he may go to low grounds and root around with his head until he finds the softest, wettest spot. The feel of mud on his muzzle will delight him and fill him with energy. He will push and sway and pile up the earth. If water filters into the hole, he will take a cooling bath.

A buffalo in a wallow is one of the happiest animals on earth. His huge body rolls from side to side. He rotates, enlarging the pool. He sinks deeper in the mud until only his head and the top of his hump show. He keeps up a low happy rumbling. When at last he climbs out, mud is plastered all over his body. Now he is a hideous monster indeed!

CORKSCREW SEEDS

In July, a buffalo may sit down to chew his cud among speargrasses which are just now releasing their seeds. Each seed bears a corkscrew bristle. When moistened in the night air it uncoils, and in daytime it coils up, boring like a corkscrew through grass and into the ground. But it does not recognize the difference between the ground and the body of a buffalo. Revolving about eight times an hour, it bores through the new wool on the buffalo and finally reaches the skin. Now the buffalo gets an itch worse than that from mosquitoes.

THE BIG MIGRATION

In spring, when the dry northern prairie is changing from dingy brown to pale green, a few lonely buffalo appear. Perhaps these are scouts, which send back scent signals from post to post. Or it may be that the herds to the south catch the fragrance of fresh grass.

Buffaloes gather at the river to drink and wallow in the mud—a favorite occupation.

Pronghorn antelopes search the plains with eyes eight times keener than man's.

These herds, constantly growing larger, head north, over worn trails made by their ancestors.

The column of march, twenty miles wide and fifty long, flows northward like a great brown river. The animals travel by day and rest by night. Sometimes they break apart and spend a day grazing. They may be in straggling lines, six or eight abreast, or in long lines in single file, each two feet behind the one in front. Then, as though a bugle were blown, each herd will wheel together and lope along for a few hours.

Without grunting or confusion, individuals take positions as if sergeants were marshaling them, the youngest up front and the oldest in the rear. Mothers and children take places in the center. Little buffaloes cavorting among the legs of the bigger ones are flashes of golden brown in a dark forest of legs.

When they sit down to rest at night, all muzzles point into the wind, and a few bulls remain on guard, pacing a wide circle. There are wolves beyond, waiting for a chance to pounce on a young buffalo. But the prairie monarchs are ready to toss any

wolf on their horns, leaving the carcass for a coyote to dine on.

The buffalo, it seems, owns the prairie. Always, he and his descendants will wander there, noses to the ground, followed by little blackbirds. They will wheel into line to travel north for fresh pastures in the spring. They will move south from the blizzards in the fall. There will always be millions of buffaloes.

But this was one hundred fifty years ago.

The buffalo did not reckon on the white man, his fences, and his guns.

THE PRONGHORN

All around the buffalo herds, pronghorns watched—to see what pastures the giants were occupying, where they were headed, whether they threatened to stampede. Reports flashed across the prairie from pronghorn to pronghorn over an amazing signaling system.

On each rump of a pronghorn, at the rear, there is a patch of fluffy hair like a huge powder puff, called a rosette. When the animal's big round eyes see something suspicious, perhaps miles away, the hairs in the

rosettes stand up and the pronghorn starts to run. When another pronghorn sees a pair of white patches flashing like lanterns, he also erects his rosettes and takes off. Quickly the prairie is dotted far and wide with the white flashes.

The pronghorn is attractive prey for a wolf or a coyote. Depending on keen eyes, sensitive nostrils, and tall ears, the pronghorn must see, smell, and hear from one horizon to the next. Also, he can sprint nearly a mile a minute and, over long distances, hold a pace of forty miles per hour.

September is the time for raising a family; then the exciting fall races of the pronghorns are on. The slender little doe streaks through the grass at top speed, followed by the bigger and stronger buck. Perhaps the doe does not want to hold her top speed, for presently she is overtaken.

Pronghorns are forever running. Two may start a race on impulse at any minute. Little pronghorns play enormous games of tag—tearing off in one direction for a quarter of a mile, then in another for half a mile.

A newborn pronghorn has very big eyes and ears and very long legs, all on a thin, trembling little body. For a few hours it can hardly stagger around. When less than two days old, it can run at twenty-five miles per hour.

Chimney Rock, rising from level ground, stands stark and lonely against the prairie sky.

Pronghorns have no homes, but each herd has its territory. Fawns are often born on top of a rise—a conspicuous place, but safer than the lower slopes, where heavy-footed buffaloes graze. Once in a while the fawn runs with a playmate, but mostly lies on the ground, long ears folded down flat.

The coyote keeps up a constant search for this delicious dinner, and a golden eagle may wheel overhead. But the little brown heap, exactly the color of the prairie floor, is invisible to all except its mother. It has almost no odor, so the sniffing coyote is baffled. Even the eagle, which hunts with its eyes, is usually thwarted.

The mother is a good protector. She returns to nurse the baby, and although she must graze and gather food, she is never out of sight. If an enemy is spotted, she flashes her rosettes and comes back as fast as the wind. Or she may lead the coyote away by prancing slowly in full view, perhaps limping a little, inviting it to chase her.

The coyote knows he cannot catch a pronghorn in a straight race. He can make forty miles per hour in a sprint and twenty-four on a long stretch, but that is not enough.

A coyote stalks the prairie for antelope.

When coyotes want pronghorn to eat, they must figure out some team play. They must make the champion runner take a zigzag course.

Three or four coyotes can take their stations without being seen, because the coyote is just the right size to travel on the prairie invisibly. His twenty inches at the shoulder does not overtop the grass and bushes as he glides swiftly among them. His size is just right, too, for running in arroyos, the dry stream beds which fan out all over the prairie. Many arroyos are shallow, cut down about two feet, with vertical sides. It seems as though arroyos were made to fit coyotes.

Coyote 1 creeps up in the open as near as he can, against the wind. He may be within a hundred feet when the pronghorn suddenly sniffs, stares with big curious eyes, and takes off.

Coyote 1 pursues. His object is to keep the pronghorn running, for even a superb animal runner must grow tired sooner or later.

When Coyote 1 tires, Coyote 2 springs from behind a bush and takes up the chase. The pronghorn changes course, slowing momentarily, and then is off again.

In the second mile, the desperate animal begins to tire. Coyote 3 and maybe 4, too, now dash in to join the zigzag chase.

The climax comes suddenly. The tuckered pronghorn slows to just below twenty-four miles per hour.

From a distance, a cloud of dust is seen rising from the prairie, instead of two flashing white rosettes.

OUTWITTING
A PRAIRIE DOG

The prairie dog is perhaps the most fortunate of the group of little diggers which includes rabbits, gophers, mice, and even the burrowing owl. He has the deepest and best system of tunnels, but he spends much of his day above ground feeding on grasses and weeds.

He builds a circular mound, as much as two feet high and four feet in diameter, around the opening of his tunnel. There he sits as a sentinel, constantly turning his head to watch the surrounding world. If he sees a coyote lurking near, he utters a series of squeaky barks and tumbles over backward into his hole. Duly warned, prairie dogs all

Twin antelope kids are born early in May. In ten days they can run as fast as their mother.

Full-grown prairie dogs are not afraid to venture from their burrows when food-hunting.

over the neighborhood tumble into their holes. None has ventured more than a hundred feet from the home mound.

Prairie dogs are always alert. Even those that are feeding do not leave all the watching to the sentinel on the mound. About every eight seconds each prairie dog stops eating, climbs a clump of grass, rears up, and takes a good look.

To catch a prairie dog, the coyote must use teamwork completely different from that of making the pronghorn zigzag.

The trick takes two coyotes and can be worked only when an arroyo leads close to one of the prairie-dog mounds. One coyote parades openly, letting itself be seen. Comes the warning bark and the prairie dogs dive.

The coyote pays no attention; he acts well fed—not interested in prairie dogs.

After a while the prairie dog which is about to be caught peeks out. He sees the coyote just loafing around, a safe sixty feet away. He does not see another coyote sneaking up close through the arroyo.

The prairie dog gives the all-clear signal and climbs out of the hole.

The trick has worked.

THE VOICE OF THE DESERT

The coyote is at home on the open range because he is cut to size and keeps his tail down. He is very friendly with other coyotes. When they meet, they touch noses.

The coyote's cousin, the fox, who lives in woody places, holds high his bushy tail, but the coyote must drag his to keep from being seen. When he is running at top speed, however, the gorgeous tail streams out behind, his ears are flattened, and his long sharp muzzle is thrust far out in front. He makes a streamlined pale yellow streak.

An active coyote needs a lot of food, but he prospers because he can eat almost anything. He has the biggest appetite on the prairie—for all kinds of fish, flesh, and fowl, dead or alive. Because he cleans up the prairie, he has been called a health officer and a garbage man.

At the end of the day, a well-fed coyote gives up the role of unseen hunter. He wants everybody to know he is there and proud of it. At sunset he mounts a rise, points his sharp nose straight up, and lets go. He begins with one low bark and a few whines like an orchestra tuning up. The barks and whines grow louder. Suddenly they change to a drawn-out, quavering wail that rises higher and higher, soaring through two octaves—the call of the wild prairie.

THE HIDDEN FAMILY

After this blood-curdling outcry, the coyote retires to his den for some sleep. He has picked out a soft place behind a bush and dug a hole about fifteen inches across. The tunnel may be ten to twenty feet long, depending on how lazy he is. It leads to a den that is three feet across.

In late February, the coyote may bring his mate home, and the den becomes a nest for six well-furred puppies with closed eyes. At that time mother takes over, and father goes off to dig himself another den.

For two months father must live alone, but he never forgets his family. He will try to bring them a carcass ever day, laying it at the mouth of the den where mother and babies are hiding. There they are safe from eagles and wolves that would love a mouthful of coyote puppy.

At the end of two months father is allowed to come down to his den again and meet the family. The children are getting big, ready to go out and learn to hunt. Judging by the barking and scampering of father and puppies, this is the happiest time in a coyote's life.

Nobody must know where the coyote family lives. Father never goes straight to the mouth of the den. He circles first, and may even hide behind another bush a long way off. When he thinks he is being observed, he goes straight to another den which he has dug for this purpose, and lays the food there. That den is empty, but how is a wolf or owl to know?

When the father has reason to believe the home den is discovered, he works all night digging another hideout. By next morning, the family has moved.

THE MIRACLE DIGGER

A prairie dog's hole goes straight down, as much as sixteen feet, and the owner goes down headfirst. But he doesn't crash at the bottom. The hole at the top is like a funnel, narrowing quickly from about seven inches to four. It is probable that the prairie dog can slow his speed by bunching up to make himself fatter.

He usually stops about three feet down, at a shelf or little room called a guardhouse. Here he can safely pause and consider. If the danger is great, he can go down deeper for more security. If, however, he was startled by a false alarm, he can quickly get back to his mound.

How can the prairie dog dig such a deep vertical shaft? He attacks the ground with big sharp claws on his front feet, and kicks dirt backward with his hind feet. That does not explain how he gets dirt, often gravel,

The mother prairie dog, guarding her young, is always alert, ready to bark a warning.

At mating time, the male sage grouse inflates his throat sac and fans out his tail. Then he and the other males strut and dance together, trying to impress the females.

ten to sixteen feet *up* a four-inch shaft. Does he back up the shaft, pushing the dirt? Does he turn around and push it upward with his head? No one knows the solution to this mystery of the prairie.

All we know is that he does get the dirt and gravel up and arranges it in a circular dike to keep water out of the hole and to make a lookout perch. He tamps down the dirt on the mound with his broad forehead and flat nose. Somehow he doesn't get dirt in his eyes.

From the bottom of the plunge shaft he runs a tunnel slanting slightly upward to keep it dry in case water gathers in the diggings. At the end of the tunnel, ten to twenty-five feet long, he builds a round bedroom nine inches in diameter. This is lined with grass cut in short lengths and shredded

The sharp-tailed grouse lives on the plains from eastern Canada to Alaska, and as far south as New Mexico.

wood. He builds another room off the tunnel for a toilet. No other animal on the prairie has such a safe, comfortable and clean home to live in.

When the sun is shining he goes up the shaft and sits on his mound, or eats grasses and bushes, caterpillars, beetles, and grasshoppers. About the only real exercise he gets, besides galloping and diving into his tunnel at every alarm, is to leap and hop around after grasshoppers.

This miracle digger never stores up food. He eats all he can lay his sharp teeth on, including roots and bulbs as well as tender leaves and flowers. But let it be cold and windy, or wet and dark, and he stays below without eating or drinking. His body gets water from the sap of plants and the blood of insects. As to food, he can live a long time off his own fat.

The prairie dog as he sits on his mound makes chirring small talk with thousands of friends all around. Prairie dogs like each other's company. They build networks of villages across hundreds of square miles, each village occupying two or three square miles, with a mound every ten steps.

WORLD'S CHAMPION DIGGER

The pocket gopher is one of the world's champion diggers. This little creature that

weighs about one pound can go through the soil like an underground torpedo.

The gopher builds himself a labyrinth that goes far and wide under the prairie, but he can always find his way home. This home is a ball-shaped room about ten inches in diameter, where he dumps grass and leaves to eat while lying in bed.

The tunnels that go everywhere around the bedroom actually go nowhere. Many are used only once. They are made while the animal is collecting grass roots and underground parts of plants. The gopher almost never comes up into the world of the open air, except at night to gather grass, and also when, obedient to instinct, he leaves his home and visits another burrow to mate.

One little pocket gopher can dig a vast tunnel system. Spreading his hind feet far apart, he works his forelimbs—which have long sharp claws like sawteeth—faster than the eye can see. Each strong downward stroke cuts the soil down and pushes it back under his stomach. When the accumulation crowds him, his hind feet come into play and send the dirt flying to the rear.

A pocket gopher turns around in his tight-fitting tunnel by pushing his head between his hind legs. With a twist he faces the other way. This somersault is necessary only when digging, for if he is simply traveling through a tunnel he can run forward or backward with ease. For guidance he has a sensitive nose at the forward end and a sensitive tail tip at the rear end; with this equipment he can find his way in either direction.

He builds a storeroom and stuffs it full of food. For this purpose there are two big outside pockets on his cheeks—not merely big cheeks for holding things, but true pockets with outside slits. Working fast with his forelimbs, he stuffs first one pocket and then the other full of dead grass and flexible roots. When he gets to the storeroom, he pushes with his forelimbs, beginning at the rear, so

Prairie dogs run for their burrows when a falcon with outstretched claws drops from above.

that the food comes out of the cheek pockets like toothpaste being squeezed from a tube.

The seasons move across the vast sea of grass, and the prairie changes from green to brown to white. It gives little hint of the big populations of diggers that live successfully beneath its surface—prairie dogs, ground squirrels, burrowing owls, marmots, mice, badgers, and gophers. The prairie is a world mostly of the unseen.

DESERT MIRACLES

LAND teeming with life is green. So with the tundra in summer, the mountain stronghold, and even the grassy prairie. But the desert floor is white in the glare of sunlight. Its narrow valleys are drowned in blue haze. Slopes are streaked with black sand or black rock from ancient lava flows. The flat-topped mountains are purple, red, yellow, and pink.

These are the colors of raw elements, the spectrum of pure sunlight. These were the colors of the land before plants grew on the hot earth's crust before animals came out of the sea to live on green leaves, fruits, and seeds—to run on grass and hide in the forest.

Some of the deserts in our Southwest were

Dark fingers of the giant saguaro cactus reach 50 feet up into the sky. When storage chambers are full of water, after a heavy rain, the huge plants may weigh 10 tons.

created when the mountains of California were pushed up and caused rain-bearing clouds from the Pacific Ocean to drop their moisture before it reached far inland. With little rain, desert land can show but little green. And with little plant life, there can be little animal life.

The pioneers loved the prairie and even the mountains, but when they saw the desert, they shuddered. They ventured across the desert on Indian trails connecting the few water holes, but they shunned the rest.

DEATH VALLEY

In one place the heart of the desert—Death Valley—lay directly across their path. The valley lies along the east side of the Sierras under the rain shadow of Mount Whitney, the highest point in the United States. A "rain shadow" is just the opposite of what it sounds like: there is no shadow, no rain. The mountains catch the air-borne moisture from the Pacific and store it up in

The Great American Desert stretches for hundreds of miles between the massive ranges of the Sierra Nevada and the Rockies.

A tiny elf owl has pecked out a comfortable home high up in a giant saguaro cactus.

deep snow fields. At Death Valley the rain shadow is deepest, and so this is the driest place in our country, and the lowest—280 feet below sea level. For days without a break, the thermometer may stay around 120°. In July 1913 it hit 134°, the record high on earth. All this within eighty miles of snow fields!

The pioneers crossed Death Valley as a short cut to California during the gold rush

Spines of the barrel cactus guard the plant's precious stores of water. Many thirsty desert travelers have stopped to tap these plants and drink. In the background is a grove of thorny, low-growing mesquite.

of 1849. Many died of thirst and heat. But they did not give up the search for gold and for something far more valuable—water.

Salt flats, glaring in the sun, mark places where lakes disappeared into the sand long ago. But in Death Valley a spring was discovered. Named Stove Pipe, after the piece of rusty hardware left by a pioneer to mark the spot, it saved many lives. One prospector, Two-Gun, saw to it that a shovel was always left beside Stove Pipe so that a thirsty traveler could dig out the spring.

Instead of finding gold in Death Valley, prospectors found a cleansing and antiseptic salt called borax. Someone thought up the famous twenty-mule-team wagon, and soon it was crunching over the oven floor of Death Valley like a freight train. Driven by one man on a high seat, the wagon was pulled by ten pairs of mules. Sometimes the animals would go mad for water, and there would be a chaos of rattling harness chains. Behind the wagon, a trailer carrying big water barrels was followed by a disgruntled group of spare mules—reserve power to get the outfit over ninety miles of desert.

THE STONE TREES

The desert is very old, and among the signs of its great age are the bodies of large trees sprawled here and there. From a distance, they look as though they had just been felled. Some are 150 feet long; others, quite short. A few are light-colored, like pine wood. But these logs would make a poor campfire, for they are solid stone—mostly agate, with the brilliant colors of the rainbow.

Once upon a time these trees grew in a swampy forest. That was about 160 million years ago—before the Sierras rose and made the desert. The trees were of a kind that no longer grow in our country. In that forest lived crocodiles eighteen feet long and giant salamanders weighing five hundred pounds. In the forest ponds were fishes that breathed with lungs instead of gills—fishes whose teeth are today found among the stone logs.

As the mountains rose up in the west and the desert formed, the forest withered away. But some of the old tree trunks were preserved as ancient streams buried them in mud, sand, and salt. The trunks rotted away, bit by bit, and water percolating through them left bits of mineral to replace the rotted parts. The trunks thus slowly changed to stone. Later, running water and wind removed the earth above them and exposed them for us to see today.

MIRACLES OF DESERT LIFE

The desert looks as if nothing could live there. So the pioneers thought when they were blinded by glare and tortured with thirst while crossing Death Valley. They heard no sound of life, saw nothing moving except "dust devils"—tiny whirlwinds which run across the desert and suddenly disappear like ghosts.

But on higher ground, above the salt flats at the bottom, grows a strange plant that was one of the first attempts of nature to make something alive out of sunshine shining on hot sand. Mormon tea, or the Ephedra bush, looks like nothing more than a few straight leafless twigs attached to a heavy stick. This queer old bush proved that plants can live in the desert if they don't try to look and act like ordinary plants.

Elsewhere plants depend on having water all the time, whether from rain or ground water. Ordinary plants, growing in normally moist soil, operate as water-lifting machines. They grow fast and big, making food, circulating sap, and discarding water through their leaves.

To live on the desert, a plant must be able to live on very little water and to wait for it—months or years if need be. Such a plant must not evaporate it into the air. It must have roots long enough to tap moisture far below the surface. The root cells must be able to hold moisture and also to act instantly to pick up water near the surface of the desert when rain does come. Finally, desert plants must contain airtight, watertight storage tanks.

The ugly Mormon tea plant has no leaves. Its chlorophyll, for food-making, is in the stems. These do not lose water, because they are sealed with quartz crystals from the sand. In other words, the plant is covered with glass, which lets the light reach the chlorophyll. This weird bush grows so slowly and irregularly that it can hardly be seen to change size at all.

Sagebrush, a member of the thistle family, came over from the prairie to pepper parts of the desert with deep-plunging roots. Its little leaves are covered with wool to keep their surfaces shady and hold whatever moisture there is in the air.

Greasewood is a member of the pigweed family that also learned the trick of deep roots. The little leaves of greasewood are thick and waterproof. They seal in water instead of letting it escape through holes.

The creosote bush, related to rubber trees, is an astonishing desert success. Its little green leaves look all the brighter because they are covered with resin that seals up their water.

The bobcat has the miraculous ability to climb over the cruel thorns and balance himself on the giant saguaro.

NEITHER TREE, NOR BUSH, NOR FLOWER

The greatest plant miracle here is the cactus, which seems to be neither tree, nor bush, nor wildflower. All cactuses grow differently and look different from other plants.

The pincushion cactus is round. The barrel cactus is barrel-shaped. The prickly-pear cactus is the shape of pancakes stuck together at their edges. The organ-pipe cactus, just as its name indicates, consists of big pipes going straight up. The living-rock cactus has projections and humps, exactly as though carved out of one of the stones among which it grows.

The teddy-bear cactus, also called cholla, looks soft and fluffy. The soft fluffiness comes off in clusters of sharp needles. When you try to pull them off, they stick painfully—and persistently—into your fingers.

GREATEST OF ALL

The greatest cactus of all, the biggest living thing on the desert, is the saguaro. The whole cactus may be in the form of a giant candelabrum, with arms coming out at the same height and turning up. The plant may rise forty feet without an arm. The arms may bend at the elbow as though beckoning, or turn at crazy angles.

The outside shell is rich green and smoothly waxed with resin, which makes it watertight. The shell does the job of leaves in making food out of sunlight, water, and earth. Deep parallel ridges run along each arm, with vicious thorns closely spaced along the crests. These ridges look hard, but they can fold and unfold like an accordion.

This green tower is a reservoir for water. When a downpour comes, the plant expands to hold more water. In a long dry spell, the pleats fold in and the plant shrinks.

The ocotillo (center) is not a cactus. It drops its leaves in dry spells, and releafs when it rains. Truly cactuslike, the prickly pear at left and the cholla at right, have no leaves.

Sooner or later it will rain, probably quite heavily. Half the rain of a whole year may fall in one night. The next morning, the surface sand is dry, the pools have vanished, the stream beds are dry and eroded-looking again. But the saguaro was prepared. Its roots are spread flat and wide, as a big water-collecting net, just below the surface in the sand.

Saguaro roots remain idle for months, seemingly baked to cinders in the sand—then go into action the moment they feel the touch of water. They keep on collecting as long as the wetness is there. One cloudburst may fill the plant so full that it can last on its personal water supply through four years of drought.

The greatest danger to a saguaro would be a continuous water supply, for this plant has no way of stopping its own intake of water. Let the desert turn into a wet place and the

The Joshua tree is the largest member of the yucca family. Its strange haphazard patterns are a familiar feature of the desert scene.

saguaro would fatten to its limit, explode, and die.

The saguaro stops its leaks ingeniously. Its spongy, pithy cells are tiny water bags with thin walls through which the water seeps. The outer cells contain a sticky substance like mucilage. When the outside shell is punctured, the mucilage is touched by air, hardens, and coats the inside of the hole—stopping the leak.

The saguaro has one more problem to solve: standing upright. A fifty-foot plant may weigh six tons. So the saguaro must have a strong skeleton. This is formed by a framework of hardened cells running the whole length of the trunk. These cells are buried in the water cells just beneath the outer shell.

The resin that makes the skeleton also

makes the sharp thorns. These are some of the toughest plant material ever created. They do not disintegrate when scorched endlessly by the sun, and are practically unbreakable. Their colors—bright red, pink, purple, yellow, orange, brown, and white— are very attractive.

DESERT TOM

The bobcat lives among the trees and ledges of the canyons. He's a night runner that loves to pounce on little animals which come out when all is cool and dark. He goes up the saguaro after woodpecker eggs, or just to rest up there and scan the desert.

How can the bobcat run up over the saguaro's ruthless thorns? He has some way of dealing with sharp things. Perhaps the pads under his toes are puncture-proof. Or else he places his feet so as to push against the sides of the prickers instead of their points.

In January and February, when calling for a mate, the cat may pierce the quiet night with caterwauling worse than any you hear on a back fence in the city. Let wood rats,

The king snake is a friend to man because of the many rodents he eats. But he is the kangaroo rat's chief enemy.

jack rabbits, lizards, toads, turtles, kangaroo rats—and all the company that pop out from underground and run around the desert at night—beware! Yet he is more dangerous when he travels silently.

When the cat meets prey that puts up a good fight, he forgets all about strategy and becomes an animal typhoon. He screams, spits, hisses, and scratches.

The fight with a bobcat is quickly over. Fortunately for the other animals, this aggressor in the desert is only after a meal. When that is eaten, he retires.

The big population of little desert diggers, on the other hand, do not disturb the peace by fighting among themselves. They are out of sight in daytime, when most great animal fighting takes place. When they come out at night, they walk and hop on the desert's vast expanse. They are not apt to bump into each other, for they are little and the desert very big. At dawn, they vanish again into holes.

PYGMY KANGAROOS

The kangaroo rat of the American desert is a handsome mouse, about twelve inches long from nose to tail tip. About seven inches of that is a long strong tail, with a brush at the end that acts as a balance for the rest of the body and as a rudder when sailing through the air. When he puts his heart into it, the mouse can clear eight feet of hot sand —more, in proportion to size, than the giant kangaroo can do in Australia.

Some of the bigger kinds of kangaroo rats dwell in the driest, hottest heart of the desert—Death Valley. They *never take a drink.*

How can this be? A camel may go a month without water because it has an extra stomach which holds gallons of water in reserve. A desert toad, buried like a living mummy under the sand, can live off its own blood forty-six weeks or more. Seeds of plants live for years in their waterproof coats. But sooner or later all these living things must renew their supply of water or they die. Why not the kangaroo rat?

This little fellow not only had his limbs redesigned for desert jumping, but also had his insides redesigned to perform a chemical miracle. He nibbles on the driest seeds and on dead stems; he does not even have to eat anything damp, like a leaf.

DESERT-STYLED ANIMALS

A rabbit is the color of gray sand and stones, and he comes with long hind legs for jumping. But the form of his body makes him sit high and in that position he can't eat. To nibble on grass and seeds among the stones on the desert floor, he must put his head way down. His fine big eyes may then miss a hawk, coyote, or fox sneaking up. But nature has pulled the desert rabbit's ears far out. When his head is down, the super-tall ears stick up—tuned in on the surroundings.

The horned lizard (which people call a "toad," although it isn't) goes for ants and caterpillars on the ground. Accordingly its own face is near the ground. Its wide, flat body, colored and spotted like the desert floor, is almost invisible. In case a snake does come upon it, the horned lizard is armed with spines and prickles like a cactus.

The desert is full of things that seem to call for the wildest imagination. One is the Gila monster (pronounced "Heela monster"). This lizard, about a foot and a half long, lies in the sunflecked shade of a creosote bush, fat and limp as a sack of grain. He drags himself along slowly, looking for centipedes and millipedes which run past on little legs that follow each other like the wheels of a long freight train. A quick motion and the train disappears. The lizard lets the centi-

If this kangaroo rat recovers from fright before the sidewinder strikes, he will scratch sand into the snake's eyes, and make his escape on swift jumping legs.

pedes and millipedes roll along, however, when he sees snake or lizard eggs.

The Gila monster was converted into a desert model by being covered with a beautiful piece of natural insulation. This consists of many tiny bones, rounded on top like polished beads. These are bright salmon pink, yellow, white, and jet black, in designs like Navajo Indian beadwork. They make the monster almost sunproof. If he lies in the thin shade of a bush, perhaps it's because he can find more centipedes and millipedes there!

MORNING ON THE DESERT

By the time the sun is above the mesa on the eastern horizon, the desert's various night runners are under the sand. Now the daylight squads suddenly appear. They will be in more of a hurry than the others, who had all night. In an hour, it will be too hot to hunt. But the night runners will have an-

The roadrunner—a kind of cuckoo—is one of the few creatures quick enough to outwit a rattlesnake. Darting and feinting, he tires the snake, pecks out his eyes and eats him.

THE RUNNING MACHINE

Rabbit, lizard, and rattlesnake jump to attention when something that resembles a long-legged hen sprints between two creosote bushes. This "hen," really the roadrunner cuckoo, is a creature of the desert as truly as the kangaroo rat. He gets all his water from meat. He can build a nest in a cholla next to the cactus wren, or in a thorny mesquite or any other thorny scrub. His speed is dazzling. He runs across a gap here, and over there, and suddenly he is far away.

The roadrunner can fly a short distance, in a sort of extended bounce. His wings are short and round, designed to send him over the desert fast by taking weight off his feet. He spreads his wings and sails right over cactuses, mesquites, and creosote bushes. His powerful muscles favor his legs. He runs entirely on tiptoe, with heels bent back and held high. Knees and thighs, short and buried in the body feathers, work like strong springs, the upper part of the legs vibrating while the feet take long strides.

THE TAIL OF THE LIZARD

The little gray lizard, a champion runner himself, can flex his body and swing his long tail so as to swerve, turn sharply, double back without changing pace, and elude capture by almost any pursuer. But the roadrunner is expert at twisting and turning.

If the roadrunner grabs the lizard's tail, this may break off, allowing the lizard to escape. (The lizard will grow another tail later —not as good, but useful enough.) But the lizard will probably end up in a nest in a cholla, there to be swallowed headfirst by a baby roadrunner. The young bird, beginning with the head, chews slowly, and the tail of the lizard—if any—will droop from its mouth for a long time.

other chance when the sun is low in the west.

The desert rabbit sits beside a stone, his tall ears straight up as he jerks his head around to get a good listen of the new day. The little gray lizard is at the edge of a mesquite shadow, stretching up to see what goes on out there where the sun is brightening the sand. Suddenly the face of a young rattlesnake is caught by the daylight at the entrance to a little cave. He opens his mouth in a fangy yawn after a good night's sleep.

High above, at a dark hole in a saguaro, another face appears. A woodpecker surveys the desert. He has made an air-conditioned room for himself in the saguaro. His technique was to drill around the thorns until they fell off.

Lacking a true tree, the cactus wren chooses the thick, writhing arms of the cholla cactus. His house must have floor, walls, and roof, and how he does the whole thing among a hundred stabbing spears is a wonder. Working furiously, he somehow gets a mass of material for the nest wedged down among the spines.

ROADRUNNER VERSUS RATTLESNAKE

What should a rattlesnake fear? When it moves into the burrow of a kangaroo rat or a rabbit, the owner moves out fast—if it can. When the snake comes out in the morning to lie in the sun, all the neighbors keep at a safe distance. Nothing on the desert dares to challenge the dictatorship of the rattlesnake —except the cactus-crested roadrunner!

The roadrunner regularly eats centipedes, grasshoppers, bugs, crickets, and spiders. But one day he feels like a change. He lifts his tail straight up and drills a rattler with a look from his round, bright eyes. The rattler lifts his head high, and his tongue quivers. He coils and gives a dry, menacing rattle.

His strike is so swift it's invisible, and a prick from the pair of deadly needles would finish the roadrunner. Yet the snake is out maneuvered from the start. The roadrunner dances around, keeping always just out of reach. He dodges the deadly fangs—teases the snake to go on striking into thin air. At last the head of the snake wavers, its strike becomes feeble. The bird swiftly closes in. Two pecks in the eyes, and it's all over.

The hungry roadrunner swallows the limp rattlesnake head first.

THE TARANTULA AND THE WASP

When the egg of a pepsis wasp hatches, the new little larva needs something to eat. In fact, it needs fresh tarantula meat. But a tarantula is a monster—big, hairy, powerful, with poison fangs that spell death. And how can tarantula meat be kept fresh for ten days in desert temperatures? If the meat is the least spoiled, the baby wasp will die.

The mother goes forth to hunt a tarantula.

The female pepsis wasp is called the "tarantula hawk" because she is the spider's deadliest enemy. She wins battles by paralyzing the spider with her poisoned sting.

Around the base of its single shaft of white lilies, the yucca grows a clump of dagger-sharp leaves.

The tarantula's castle is a burrow about an inch wide and a foot deep, lined with silk to prevent sand and stones from falling out of the sides and also to give footholds for climbing. Here the spider spends most of its time, four of its eight eyes gleaming alertly in the dark. (The other four don't gleam.) The top of the hole is surrounded by a parapet about an inch high. On this the tarantula may sit motionless, waiting for crawling prey, such as a beetle, to come along. From the parapet, the tarantula can leap down.

The wasp must wait until she can catch the hairy monster up there in the open. If she can get her needle into just the right spot and inject just the right amount of poison, her victim will be not killed, but paralyzed. That is a wasp's substitution for refrigeration. The right spot is the nerve center on the hairy chest of the tarantula. For the wasp to reach that, the spider must be walking on its eight legs, instead of having them folded over its thorax.

When her chance comes, the slender wasp, antennae and wings quivering, charges the spider. She grips its hairy corselet with her jaws and tries to swing herself up. When astride the monster, she can curve her abdomen and slip the end of it under the spider's thorax at exactly the right spot.

The spider has a target of its own—an exposed spot on the neck of the wasp. It rears like a bronc and throws off the wasp. They spar. One thrusts with its face, the other backs into action. The wasp jumps high, buzzes its wings, tries to dive onto the back of the spider. The spider feints with its abdomen, then suddenly sidesteps.

After a while, the big tarantula is lying on its back, quivering. The wasp has grasped the spider, but she can drag this enormous load only a short distance. Soon she drops it and digs furiously. Then she grabs a leg, pulls and hauls, folds and pushes, until the tarantula is all tucked into the hole.

The wasp now lays one egg. She glues it to a certain spot on the spider's breast. The spider can move its legs in its sleep, but at this spot the egg is bound to be safe.

The work of the pepsis wasp is completed.

THE LITTLE WHITE GHOST AND THE LILY

Where higher ground above the desert floor folds into a canyon, the sand is studded with bunches of bayonets. Some emerge from a point on the ground and stick out in all directions as if from pincushions. Others grow on Joshua trees, which have balls of bayonets radiating from the ends of big writhing branches lifted some twenty feet high.

Both are yucca lilies. Although the leaves are long and slender, like ordinary lily leaves, they are thickened for water storage and are airproofed with wax. In the spring a mighty stem comes forth from the pincushions, quickly grows to heights of from two to ten feet, and releases a skyrocket of white lilies. White lilies also burst from the Joshua trees. This is a miracle that has been understood only in recent years.

One night, when yucca lilies open and release their wonderful fragrance on the desert air, little white ghosts appear among them. These are pronuba moths, which have been months underground, wrapped up like small mummies. The flowers' fragrance pulls them like magnets in the darkness.

The female pronuba moth makes straight for the stamens that are bursting with pollen. She scrapes together a wad of pollen exactly three times bigger than her head. Holding this load with her mouth, she flies to another yucca plant. Still holding the ball of pollen, she backs down to the bottom of the flower, drills a hole with her egg-laying needle, and deposits a clutch of moth eggs inside the green pod at the base of the pistil. Next she climbs to the top of the same pistil, where there is a cavity exactly three times bigger than her head. She stuffs in the wad of pollen, which fits perfectly. Nature does the rest.

While the pronuba eggs are getting ready to hatch, the yucca's seeds are ripening. When the moth's larvae come into the world, they find themselves surrounded with their special kind of food—green yucca seeds, all moist and fresh. They do not eat all of the great numbers of seeds in the pod; they leave plenty of extra seeds to raise more yuccas—and more pronuba moths, too.

Where did the pronuba learn the art of plant breeding? What inspired her to drive home the right amount of pollen in the right spot? How can it be that she does everything in the right order? The desert keeps all the answers secret.

THE FLOWERING DESERT

During months, perhaps years, the desert does not change its appearance. The air is pure, the sky blue, white clouds sit on distant mountains. Cactuses, mesquite, creosote bushes, and sage stand without changing color or size, as though painted on the desert floor. Everything can wait—it doesn't seem to matter when the rain comes. But when some day the rain does come, a magical spectacle occurs.

Countless billions of seeds have been scattered invisibly across the sand. Each contains the germ of a poppy flower, packed with a tiny bit of moisture, in a sunproof case. These sparks of life wait in the desert.

Now the rain comes, and the sand is soaked and cooled, and this buried life suddenly awakens. A bright red and yellow carpet unrolls across the desert. Nothing on earth can match the splendor of the desert at this hour. This is the miracle of the desert.

The low-growing beavertail cactus is free of thorns. Instead, the joints of its stems are pitted and pocked.

SECRETS OF BEES

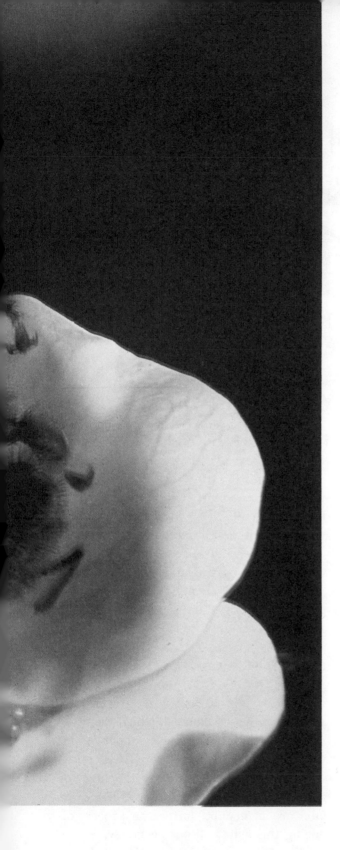

Brilliantly colored flowers spread banquets of nectar and pollen for bees.

A HONEY BEE is the most remarkable creature on earth. Everybody likes to see a bee capering among the flowers. It stands out in a crowd of insects because it is bigger than most of them, makes a bigger buzz, and never stops working.

But people are afraid of being stabbed. A bee's stinger is a spear that shoots from its rear. It has nine barbs on each side, split down the middle. The two halves slide back and forth on each other. This double spear is enclosed in a sheath worked by a strong muscle. The two halves slide back and forth with a pumping action. When the spear enters the flesh, the barbs hold fast. A bee is light and can't take hold strongly with its tiny claws. It could not sink its spear through tough skin at one blow. Instead, the spear must pump itself in.

When the bee tries to pull away, it is fatally wounded, tearing itself away from its own stinger. Bees are not anxious to sting people. They sting only when scared or angry. When the ordinary honey bee stings it dies; the barbs cause the spear to remain in the body of its victim, and as the stinger is torn away, it pulls the bee's vital organs along with it.

Few people know the exciting mystery hidden in that black-and-yellow ball of buzz. It packs a lot of life power. A drop of honey is a high-octane fuel that drives the bee to flower after flower, while it sparks their seeds. Bees and flowers are two parts of the same life, like heads and tails of a coin. This amazing creature-and-plant team, coordinated to an almost unbelievable degree, is one of nature's most wonderful creations.

A bee is the only flying creature built to carry heavy freight. It has storage space and lifting power to transport syrup, pollen, and varnish. It easily manages the heaviest airborne cargoes. All other fliers (birds, bats, and other insects) carry only themselves through the air, except for light air mail

The bee sucks up nectar through a tube, and stores it inside its body.

such as twigs and worms which birds carry in their beaks occasionally.

Man's freight planes carry a pay load of about 25 per cent of their weight. A bee can carry almost 100 per cent. Man's planes have enormous wings for lifting and gliding, but they do not have power to move forward. They lift only when the plane is going fast enough to make suction on top. The bee has short wings on a fat body. It cannot glide, but it can move up, down, or stand still in mid-air. It does not have to move forward for its wings to lift it. It needs no propeller or jet, because the wings both lift and drive it forward in flight.

This is done by a marvelous mechanism. The short, wide wings beat at high speed with a weaving figure-8 motion. By changing the shape of the figure-8, the bee can drive itself forward, or stand still in the air in front of a flower and look it over.

The stubby wings can fold in a second when the bee dives into a flower or into one of the tightly fitting cells of the hive. It would be in a fix if it had long, rigid wings like a dragonfly's. A dragonfly never folds its wings, but it never dives into flowers; it just loafs on them. The bee has two pairs of wings, but even if you watch carefully, you would never see them. They are so close together their edges almost touch. For flying, a row of hooks on the forward edge of the rear wings fastens into a pleat on the edge of the front wings. This doubles the wing-spread. They can be quickly unhooked and folded up like a lady's fan, or unhooked when the bee wants to whirl them as an electric fan, instead of using them for flying. Often a group of worker bees will use their wings as fans for ventilating the hive, or to warm it in winter, or to drive off the excess moisture in nectar, during the process of reducing this watery liquid to honey.

This flying machine has three places for storing cargo. One is the tank inside, which it fills by sucking up nectar syrup through a long tube from the inside of the flower's body. The other two are the baskets on its hind legs for carrying pollen. Who ever heard of a plane carrying freight on the landing gear? But the bee has been doing this since man first wrote about it in 3,000 B.C. It hasn't changed its equipment for carrying freight since.

The bee carries freight in one direction only. Outward bound, it needs only a speck of honey for fuel, enough to reach the goal, where it can find plentiful stores of honey and refuel. Honey is so powerful that a pinhead-sized speck of it will whirl the bee's wings for about a quarter of a mile.

If nectar is flowing strong and anthers are bursting with pollen, a bee can suck up a load of syrup in a minute. It can build two big, bulging loads of pollen in the baskets on its hind legs in three minutes. Often it may carry water in its honey tank, if the hive is thirsty. It may scrape resin off sticky buds and twigs, especially poplar, horse-chestnut,

willow, and honeysuckle buds, and load this into the pollen baskets. This resin will be made into varnish to coat tree hollows, making all surfaces perfectly smooth, even at the points where the hive is attached. Resin is used also to stop up cracks and crevices.

When it has a load, the bee flies home at fourteen miles per hour with a tankful of nectar inside, and two bulging bags of pollen swung below that keep it flying upright. A loaded bee cannot fly upside down. It is no acrobat like a housefly, which can run about on the ceiling and can even manage to fly upside down with ease.

The tank can be filled by sucking nectar through a tube. But how can the bee attach the loads of pollen to the outside of its hind legs without the help of a well-trained ground crew? It isn't just a matter of scooping up pollen grains and tossing them into baskets the way you gather apples. To keep

Pollen clings to a bee's hairy body just as dust clings to a shaggy mop.

loads from blowing away or falling out in mid-air, pollen must be moistened, pressed like a snowball, molded, tamped down, and evenly balanced on each leg. Moreover, it must be collected from many flowers. The way a bee can collect and load its pollen baskets in three minutes is an everyday accomplishment in his world, but it is a true marvel of animal skill.

To collect pollen, a bee dives into a flower, scrambles around, rolls over like a child playing in the surf. The splashing throws pollen grains all over its body, where they stick to feathered hairs. When the bee dives for nectar, it doesn't have to cut capers. Its body picks up pollen just by brushing past the pollen boxes that are usually held out in front of the flower on long trembling stems.

This honey bee rapidly fans its wings to drive moisture off nectar.

The bee leaves the flower, and, while hovering in mid-air, or swinging below the flower and hanging by one claw, it combs its face, the top of its head, and the back of its neck with its front legs. Even the bee's eyes collect pollen, as hairs grow out of its eyeballs. The bee has a special soft brush to remove this pollen. A reverse gulp brings up a speck of honey from the honey tank to moisten the pollen. The middle legs scrape off the middle of the body, reaching up over the back. Rapid combings and passings to the rear get the pollen onto the hind legs. The scrapings are caught in a comb with nine rows of bristles. The bee doubles up its legs. A huge rake passes through the rows of bristles, pulling the pollen into a press made by the knee joint. When the bee bends its knee, the jaws of the press open; when it straightens its leg, the jaws close, and the pollen is pressed and pushed up into the pollen basket. The pollen basket is a shallow trough in the

middle of the hind leg, located just where it widens like the blade of a paddle. To hold the load securely in place, there are many curving hairs around the edges. They serve to hold the bee's bulging load of pollen securely in place, just as stakes are used to contain a full wagonload of hay.

There is a single rigid hair in the center of the basket that makes it possible to build twice as big a load. As the pollen ball grows bigger and bigger, the curving hairs surrounding it are pushed apart, and the load mounts above them. The long rigid hair in the center gives the load a core. It holds the big swelling ball of pollen together like a pole planted in the middle of a haystack.

All this skill and equipment is useless unless the bee can get to the right place at the right time. Bees do not spend the night among the flowers. They wait in the hive until sunrise. They do not know which flowers will open pollen boxes and gush nectar the following morning, or where they will be located. Flowers bloom in different places every day. Every morning ten thousand flying freight cars get ready to go out and load up.

They will not start until they know the kind of flowers, and the direction and distance to those flowers. Somebody must give them flight instructions. This will not be the queen, as she never issues an order. Entirely occupied with laying eggs, she would not know about flowers, pollen, or nectar. She might spend a year in the hive and go out into daylight only twice in her life. The job of gathering nectar and pollen belongs to the worker bees.

Now perhaps a dozen bees go out in different directions and scout the countryside. They fly around in the vicinity of the hive in ever-widening circles. If there is an apple orchard, a field of poppies or alfalfa, or a garden of beans or peas close by, or a meadow blooming with clover, great is the

excitement in the hive, and the whole army will be on the wing and ready to travel in a few minutes.

But the day's plunder may be some distance away. The scouts may have to search across miles of countryside. When one of these returns, it will tell the others exactly what kind of flowers are open, and give them a compass bearing for the direction and announce the distance to the spot. Many other creatures can communicate, but few can equal in clarity and usefulness the language that the honey bee has invented.

This sounds like a fairy tale, but life is that way, especially with bees. The fact that bees can talk to each other and give complicated instructions to a group of workers in the hive is a recent and startling discovery.

When a scout strikes it rich, it fills its tank, packs its baskets, and flies back to the hive. Others crowd around, pushing back like police lines to clear space for the scout. If it begins with a weaving dance, turning left and right, it is saying, "Plenty all around! Go and get it!" In that case, the bees crowd up excitedly, touch the dancer with their antennae to pick up the odor of the flowers they must look for, and fly off.

But if the treasure is a long way off—perhaps a single tree or a small patch of flowers—that would be like finding a pinprick on the map, and the searchers could easily get lost. So the scout, instead of weaving, runs along a straight line, wagging its abdomen. At the end of the line—only an inch or so long, as not much space is cleared in the crowd—it turns left and circles back to the starting point. It runs straight forward again along the same line, circles right—and then repeats its message!

The straight line points directly at the flowers. The speed with which the speaker circles tells the distance. The farther off the flowers are, the slower it circles back. If it makes ten circles in fifteen seconds, the flow-

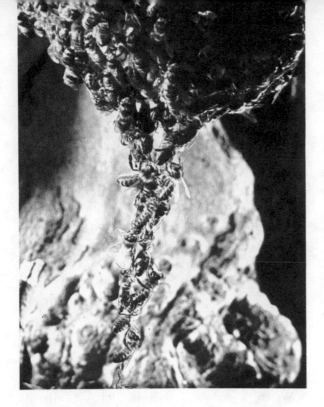

is a thing of sunshine and fresh air, and its buzz is the song of a summer day. It fits so beautifully into our world, and does such a fine job sparking the seeds of flowers, that it is hard to believe what a different world bees live in—the strange world of the hive.

The whole hive is like one animal, living in a beautiful home, with rows of six-sided rooms built of wax that looks like marble. In this building clusters a throng of bees. A small hive has twenty thousand, a middle-sized hive seventy-five thousand, and a big hive, two hundred thousand members.

This is not a city of many families; it is a single life. One extra-large bee that lives in the heart of it has produced all the bees of the hive. This is the queen who slaves to lay up to one or two thousand eggs per day. Before we speak of her, let us see how the bees build the white bee building.

The trick is performed by younger bees under seventeen days old, which have not yet reached the stage of flying off to gather honey and pollen. If the comb is new, and there is no old comb to enlarge, they hang themselves in festoons from the roof of the hive or the hollow in the tree. One hooks its claws to the roof and another hooks on to the hind legs that dangle down. They look like watch chains looped from the ceiling. More and more bees hook their front legs to the hind legs of those above. The chains grow longer. As they sway and touch, the bees hook on right and left, forming a living curtain. Nobody knows why they hang up in this way, but the wax seems to come faster when the body is stretched out.

On each side of the abdomen are four wax pockets. After twenty-four hours of hanging, tiny slips of wax begin to appear, like letters stuck in their pockets. When a bee feels its wax ready to come all the way out, it takes

ers are about 300 feet away. If it moves in slow motion—two circles in fifteen seconds—the flowers are around four miles away! The amount of honey or pollen is told by the wagging of the abdomen. If it shakes vigorously, the supply is abundant. If it shakes lazily, there is only a little, and just a few bees should go. The others, in that case, will wait for another scout's arrival.

This marvelous briefing of a big audience of bees was discovered by a patient scientist named Karl von Frisch. He spent years figuring it out.

This little ball of life with its great flying power, its weird equipment for plundering flowers, its big eyes (two globes with 6,300 eyes in each bulge occupy most of its face) and its ability to communicate, does not have a life of its own.

We have been watching it by itself in order to get a close-up view of its secrets. But it does not exist that way. Unlike other creatures, it does not have babies and raise its own family, build its own home, eat its own food, or fight for its own life. The honey bee the letters out of its pockets, chews them, and pats on the wax where the comb is to be built. Sometimes the wax scales come fast, especially if many bees have hung themselves up at the same time. Wax scales litter the floor. The bees swinging on high regard this supply of wax as workmen would regard a load of lumber dumped near their job. The bees do not delay this building until the time the waxmaking is fully completed. Instead, the lowest let go the legs of those above, drop to the floor, pick up the wax slabs and buzz up where the walls of the hive are rising.

Honey bees enjoy the reputation of being architects and engineers because they build many rows of little rooms the same size, each one with three pairs of walls facing each other, so that they are six-sided. Such a building has a pattern like lattice or wallpaper, and it forms mysteriously under the feet of six-legged insects who run around and work constantly. They have no drawing boards, compasses, or rulers, but the job is well-measured and very strongly made.

Wax is reinforced by drawing long thin threads of varnish through it. The wax hardens around the threads, like concrete reinforced with wire. Varnish is also used on rough places in the hollow tree the bees brush against, going and coming. Cell walls are only 1/350th of an inch thick. It would be impossible to see a thread so fine. This makes a sharp edge—even for the feet of the bees—and since bees constantly run around on their comb, the top edges must be thickened. Extra wax is dabbed on, giving the walls a rounded coping. The outside of the building becomes a comfortable screen for them to run around on.

The secret of the bees' skill lies in the way they use natural forces. Soft materials

A worker bee rams pollen into a storage cell, packing it tightly with its head.

like putty, clay, or warm wax will become very thin when you push against them from opposite sides. If a lot of holes in the soft stuff are pushed against each other at the same time, they form six-sided walls, particularly if the walls are extremely thin.

Bees start by just piling on wax, laid on like mud when a swallow builds a nest. The holes begin as rough cups, pressed in by the bee's body, and the cells will always be that size and exactly fit the shape of the bee. The work of shaping and finishing the cells is done by lots of bees in lots of holes, all pushing simultaneously against each other. They use heads, feet, bodies—smoothing, scraping, and ramming home the wax, which is kept warm by their bodies.

When nature pushes fluid materials together, they form six sides. That shape makes them cling the closest together without spaces between. Crystals are made this way. Snowflakes are all six-sided or six-pointed. You can see flat, six-sided surfaces between soap bubbles where the round bubbles touch when sticking together. It is a strange and wonderful law of nature. It is this that makes the fine architecture of bee

Nurse bees are kept busy feeding the grubs of baby bees.

combs, when bees build the soft wax together, all working at the same time. It is simply the result of the bees getting into the little round cups they have made and pushing them together.

Bees never rest inside their cells. They lead most of their lives crowding the face of the comb and flying out to fetch nectar and pollen. Cells are used to raise babies and to store honey and pollen. Storage tanks are capped over with a neat little lid of wax when full. No attention is paid to them except in winter when food is scarce. Then the cap is torn off and honey or pollen, according to which the tank holds, is used by all the bees. The bee which takes honey out of a cell passes it around.

To prove that a bee never digests its food all alone, but rather that the whole hive di-

gests food together, scientists fed six bees in a hive of 24,500 radioactive honey. After two days, all the bees in the hive were radioactive, from passing the treated honey from mouth to mouth.

Bees are ever busy collecting from flowers, building their wax home, storing up honey and pollen, and passing around food. But a few extra-big bees never do any of these things. While the others are so busy that they never stop working, the drones, or male bees, are idle. They don't even take the trouble to reach into a tank of honey or pollen for food. They ask other bees passing food around to give them some. The drones are waiting to fly off into the sky just once, chasing after the queen. That is all the drone bee ever does in its entire life. It has no pollen baskets, but it does have bigger wings for flying power and bigger eyes to see the queen when she is a tiny speck flying through the air.

There is only one queen in the hive. Like the drones, she never collects from flowers, builds with wax, or passes food around. She is not lazy. She is as important to the hive as a heart is to an animal. The other members of the hive must depend on the queen bee if the life of the group is to continue.

The queen is a special invention. Other bees work so hard that they don't have time to have children, so nature invented the queen who is different from all the others and who can have all the children.

To keep a hive of many thousands of bees strong and healthy, several thousand babies must be born every day. For although the queen may live for five years, worker bees live only forty-one days, and it is the endless job of the queen to replace them as they die

The large queen bee is surrounded by attendants who constantly feed her royal jelly.

off. She spends most of her time walking across the face of the comb, and as she passes one six-sided cell after another, she pauses for a few seconds and drops in an egg. Her job takes so much energy that she must have attendants to feed her constantly.

When the queen is laying eggs, she is surrounded by a retinue of twenty-two bees making royal jelly. They face her, surrounding her like spokes of a wheel. Their entire job is to keep feeding her royal jelly. As they pass the twelve-day-old mark, they are replaced with younger bees, probably six-day-olds. For royal jelly can be made only in the heads of adolescent bees.

The queen is not allowed to do any other work. In a day she can lay two thousand eggs, four times the weight of her own body. How can this be? She doesn't disappear and she is just as heavy, and ready to lay two thousand eggs more on the following day.

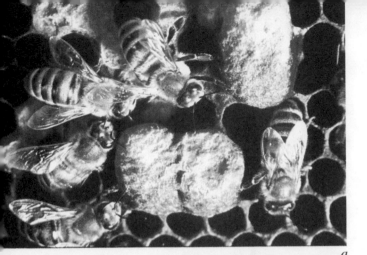

a

b

c

This is a strange secret of bee life. We find the answer in the mysterious power of royal jelly. This food looks like sticky cream, and the only place it can be made is in the head of a young bee. A bee must be the proper age to make royal jelly—from six to twelve days old. During that week, it chews pollen from the tanks in the comb, and mixes it with a peculiar kind of saliva to produce royal jelly. Wherever the queen turns while egg laying, the surrounding royal jelly feeders turn. Every twenty minutes she stops, and one of the retinue pumps her full of royal jelly, which makes her lay many eggs. The meal lasts three minutes. As the chief ingredient of royal jelly is pollen, we see how the dust that sparks plants turns into baby bees! And just as many plants would never mature their seeds without the bees to bring them the needed pollen, so some of this very pollen helps the queen bee lay her eggs.

If a queen dies or isn't laying enough eggs, the bees make a new queen. First they build an extra big cell. This queen cell is roughly dabbed together in a hurry. This special cell is peanut-shaped, and it is hung to the outside of the comb. The bees take an egg from a regular cell and put it in the queen cell. Sometimes they take a new-born baby bee. If it isn't over three days old, it is not too late to turn it into a queen instead of letting it hatch as a regular worker bee. This baby is fed all the royal jelly it can eat. It takes fifteen days to produce a queen, if the workers start with a fresh-laid egg. If they start with a one-day-old baby already hatched, they can have a full-grown queen bee in no more than eleven days.

The queen has a fine pair of wings, but she uses them only about twice in her long life: once to fly off on a mating flight, and again to fly away from her hive forever with a swarm, to start a new home. The grown-up queen stands around getting her bearings, and stretching her wings for three days. The bees keep feeding her royal jelly, but she can lay no eggs until after she has flown up into the sky with the drones and returned from her mating flight.

Meanwhile the drones have bestirred themselves for the first time in their lives. They prance around, clean their antennae again and again, clean their big eyes (the drones have 13,090 little eyes in each globe, more than twice as many as the ordinary bee has). If the weather is fair, around four o'clock in the afternoon of the fourth day after she became mature, the queen dashes off into the sky, with the drones after her. She returns to the hive a half hour later, ready to lay eggs for the entire colony of bees for the rest of her life.

When the drones return to the hive, demanding honey, the workers refuse to feed them and they starve.

If there is one time when a queen gets angry, it is when there is another queen around. This happens when a fresh queen has been produced while the old queen has not yet left the hive with a swarm. Then the two queens fight it out to the death.

The stinger of a queen is long and curved, and has no barbs. The queen can pull it out without killing herself, and sting her enemy again and again. A duel of queens is a terrible battle, with each trying to drive home the poisoned spear first. The bees understand that nature has decreed that a hive can have but one egg-layer. If a queen turns away, the others push her back to the attack. Fighting queens are not allowed to stop until one is killed.

When there are two queens in the hive, they often sound a high, clear note as a battle cry. The note of a queen who is

Two queen bees, piping shrilly, battle fiercely until one of them is dead.

fighting mad is called the piping of the queen. It is probably made because she is breathing hard in her excitement. The piping is made by forcing air through ten little holes in her sides. It is like the high note of a flute.

Often the older queen does not fight it out with the young queen, but when she finds out a new queen is being made in her hive, she prepares to leave and take along whatever portion of the population will follow her and establish a new hive.

There is great excitement when a swarm is being stirred up. The hive neglects to go out and gather honey. Its whole routine is upset. The swarm may be a terrifying ball of thirty-five thousand bees. It shoots out of the hive, swirls around crazily and heads off. After roaring along, it comes to rest on a limb of a tree. It waits there for scouts to bring news of a protected place to build a comb. Then it flies there, starts taking wax letters out of its vest pockets, and bee life buzzes along again in its remarkable way.

SECRETS OF ANTS

TAKE A GOOD look at an ant. It is made like three tiny bugs fastened together in a row on a piece of pipe. The one in front is the head; the middle one is the chest, or thorax; the one on the rear end, the abdomen, is the biggest of all.

If the ant is broken apart, each segment can go on living for a little while. Each has its own blood supply, its own breathing tubes, its own openings into the outer air closed by its own valves, and separate nerves to operate the muscles of each part. After

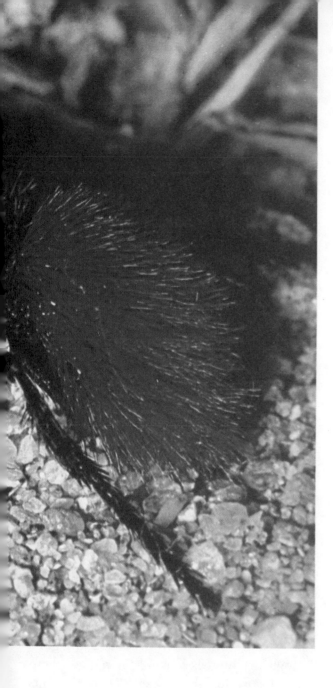

The fearless black ant (left) *prepares to attack a velvet ant much larger than itself.*

Ants have the biggest population of any dry-land creature in the world, as they can fit themselves into any situation. They don't have to live in a certain kind of place, like a bee. Any soil anywhere in the world makes a home. A bit of rotten wood in a fallen log will do; or cracks in your house or barn. Ants are not particular. Bees eat only pollen and nectar, so that if there are no flowers around, there are no bees. But ants will eat many different foods found in large quantities everywhere.

Their chief food is dead insects, and of these there is an endless supply. One man watched a large family of ants all morning, patiently counting the dead insects he saw lugged and pushed into the nest. The number averaged 28 per minute, or 13,500 bodies of all sizes in one eight-hour working day for the dinner table of that one family.

If dead insects are out of season, ants will readily turn to other varieties of food.

An apple or any fruit bruised by falling to the ground makes a luscious dish. Ants like food to be soft and squashy. They will not chew through the stretched, polished skin of an apple. They love seeds of grasses and berries. They wait for decay to cook them because seeds have tough coats. Some ants plant seeds, and when they start to sprout, bite off the root tip to keep them from growing, and they have a garden of fresh vegetables, available in endless supply.

Ants pass up fresh pollen, which is a kind of crystal and hard. They cannot make pollen mush like bees, but they like honey. They lick sweet juices off leaves, and sap coming from a wound in a stem, and sweet syrup off other insects. They take nectar from flowers if they can, but flowers seem to know this, for many put up obstacles to ants crawling in. These flowers keep their nectar

the head is cut off, its jaws go on biting and its feelers go on feeling. The middle part, with six legs, can go on running and kicking. The rear part can continue to do what it was doing, whether laying eggs, stabbing with a stinger, or performing as a bottle of honey. Ants get into terrible fights. Because they have this type of body, if an ant is beheaded or its rear is torn off, the other two parts keep on fighting ferociously.

only for bees. They erect bristles that stop crawling ants like a barbed-wire entanglement. Some flowers defend nectar with gummy places, for no little insect can walk if its feet are stuck. Others dangle flowers from shaking, slippery stems, which knock off an ant before it can get to the flower. Ants are not bothered when they cannot obtain nectar from flowers, because they have so many varieties of food to choose from.

Suppose we watch an ant take a dead moth home. The fat body is twenty-seven times as big as the ant, and to make matters worse, stiff wings stick far out on each side. The route lies through a thicket of grass. The ant cannot follow a path down on the ground, because the grass stems would block the outstretched wings. It has to be up high with more open space, where the moth can be tipped up or down, turned this way and that. The job the ant is doing can be compared to a man's carrying an airplane through the thick treetops of a dense, matted jungle.

It is difficult to know how long the process will take. As the ant gets closer to home, perhaps others will smell the food and come out to help their companion with the terrible job of pulling the huge moth through the towering jungle and out onto a clear pathway leading to the anthill.

It is thickness of muscle, not length, that gives strength. The strong man has bulging muscles. An ant's muscles are thick and short. But more than strength is needed to get the moth home. The ant does not try to carry it. It drags, pushes, pulls, up-ends the load. It runs from side to side, in front or behind, working like a demon, never pausing. It has six legs to brace against the grass while it nudges the thing with its head. It can take a stand with three legs and use the others to support the load or as levers. It keeps up a rapid fire, tapping the moth's body and the grass with its feelers, sizing up the situation every instant. The moth mys-teriously keeps moving—bumping and lurching toward the very place where the ant wants it to be.

With its long legs spread apart, and its body hung low, an ant is built for super-leverage, strong bracing, powerful dragging, pushing, and pulling. It even uses its elbowed feelers for support.

Its six legs—two pullers, two supporters, two pushers—make it easy to understand why ants are so strong for moving heavy loads. They may work singly or tackle a major problem together. They can quickly bring pebbles from underground—pebbles which a man, if he were the size of an ant, would use a bulldozer to move. Ants can maneuver the rocks to clear their tunnels, and also make circular walls around the home entrance for protection. For ants are the world's greatest tunnelers and diggers, and their underground galleries and rooms are built to last for years, with special chambers built on various levels, to be used as apartments and storehouses for ant eggs or surplus supplies of food.

Ants protect themselves from enemies better than any animal on earth. Even a keen-eyed bird has trouble picking up a target that disappears while you look at it. An ant is not helpless even when a beetle, an earth-worm, or a snake burrows into the nest. One small snake, called a worm snake, will glide through ant tunnels looking for rooms where the ant's babies are hidden. Then the ants carry their babies through the connecting galleries into rooms deeper underground. Others attack the monster without hesitation. Although they are pigmies in comparison to the enemy, they put up a terrific fight: kicking, biting, stabbing, slashing, and cutting. For ants will attack anything that attacks them, regardless of size.

Often ants meet grasshoppers in the grass. The grasshopper has its eardrums down its forelegs, so that it can hear every little

sound in the grass. When the big fellow looms up and stares down at them, the ants are maddened. One may point its rear end at the grasshopper and use its stinger like a firehose. It squirts a silent, invisible spray of stinging poison as far as eighteen inches. Then it is time for the grasshopper to become maddened, and to pull the springs of his mighty hind legs, and leap out of sight. Ants, with their tearing jaws and hidden stingers, have many ways of making giants mind their own business, and never hesitate to use any of their fighting equipment.

The endless series of galleries and rooms in which ants live may house several hundred thousand creatures. Called a colony, it is more like a family, because the throng often consists of children of one queen. Ant queens do not murder another queen if she turns up, as do queen bees, so ant nests may have several families living together. But they must all smell the same way, because this smell is paid out along their hunting

With six legs, strength and skill, ants are able to carry pebbles many times their size.

trails. No matter how many trails crisscross, each ant can find its way back to the underground home from which it set out.

Ants that are busy digging tunnels, hauling food, and running trails never have wings. But in August, certain ants sprout wings! These are males and queens, going off to lay eggs. On a clear, calm afternoon these winged ants fly off on a mating trip into the sky. After this flight, the males drop to the ground; they can't hide, with their wings. They must hobble around until another insect or a bird finds them and eats them.

The queen also drops to the ground, but nature has attached her wings so that they can be easily torn off. She grabs them with her jaws and front feet and soon she is helpless and alone, far from the anthill where she has been carefully tended by nurses and workers.

Because she came through the air, there is no odor trail to find the way home. She must dig a hole as fast as she can. She is not a tunnel digger, so it is hard work. Her jaws are worn down, her hairs scraped off, her smooth armor scratched and bruised. She must dig before a bird spots her. When the hole is deep enough, she pulls a stone or some dirt over her and snuggles down and lies there for eighty-seven days in the quiet darkness until all her eggs have hatched. After that she has many children to do the digging, and real tunneling can start.

Ant tunnels are clean, round tubes. They are used as subways for the ants to get to rooms where they lay eggs or store food. The idea is to make it easy for the worker ants to carry their eggs and babies from one room to another if an enemy turns up.

Ants live a long time compared to other insects. A bee dies in six weeks, but ants live for years. The colony can grow hundreds of thousands of ants with a vast system of tunnels, if not disturbed. Four months after the first eggs hatch, a new crowd of stronger tunnelers appear. Their swiftly passing polished bodies smooth the tunnels. These ants arch roofs of rooms and flatten floors. Two years later the large operation needs special guards. These turn up from the eggs that never stop hatching, and soldier ants stand

In case of battle, ant larvae are carried from room to underground room, out of danger.

at the entrances. Three years after the lost queen first dropped to the ground, some ants sprout wings, another flight goes off into the sky, another queen drops to earth, and starts furiously digging away for a new nest. Soon she will have established another flourishing colony of ants just like the one she left behind—the formula nature uses to scatter ant nests all over the world.

The giants that invade the ants' tunnel systems are not their most dangerous foes. All the cruel weapons, their fierce strength, and their stabbing and poisoning equipment are chiefly used against well-organized armies of other ants.

Great battles take place between ants again and again in summer. Let us watch a family of familiar black ants going about their business, running their maze of tunnels, raising hundreds of children, lugging in dead insects, and preparing for that great event when the winged ones will fly off on their once-in-a-lifetime flight into the blue sky, so another ant queen can begin a new ant colony.

One day an ugly stranger turns up at the tunnel of these black ants. He knows there are hidden rooms filled with white bundles of black ant babies. The stranger is richly colored, brown-red tinged with purple. His jaws protrude far out on each side of his head like enormous curving scimitars, made to slash and pierce the armor of ants. This is the face of the horrible Amazon ant, and the black ants know it spells trouble for the whole colony. For he will soon return, bringing an army of enemies with him.

When they know the red ants are nearby, the blacks begin to stop their holes with stones and dirt. They scatter pebbles and debris so that they will not give away the location of their entrances.

Perhaps 200 feet away over the hill, the red ants are seething with excitement. Their scouts, searching the countryside, singly or in squads of four or five, leave an odor trail back from the front door of the blacks' hideout to the door of the home nest. This is the trail the red marauders will follow as they begin their march.

Now the reds pour out of their tunnels and line up in compact regiments. The column moves straight toward the home of the blacks. Arriving on the scene, the reds break ranks, ferociously pulling out plugs and tearing covers off tunnel entrances. They probably find the holes with their sense of smell. When the tunnels are opened, there is panic underground. The reds invade the galleries and snatch up babies. The blacks also snatch up their babies and carry them from room to room, trying to find a safe place for them.

Soon both reds and blacks pour out of the tunnels. Many have jaws full of white bundles. These are babies (pupae sound asleep) easily mistaken for eggs. The blacks are wildly looking for a place to put their bundles, while the reds form a single column and head straight for home, still holding the white bundles tight in their jaws.

The desperate battle begins.

The blacks do not let the reds keep their single-column march. They attack, and a terrible battle is joined. Reds and blacks slash with scimitars, stab with stingers, squirt poison vapors, bite off heads and legs. The two parts left after the head is cut off go on fighting. The field of battle is littered with pieces of ants and white bundles fallen to the ground. The chances are the blacks outnumber the reds and will drive them off, pick up the babies, and put them back in the nest. Then they remove the dead bodies, and put the anthill back in order again.

Another kind of red ant, the red formica, makes war in a mob, instead of forming columns. They form a waving front several feet or yards across and ripple along, searching for black ant nests. They have been seen to go out raiding forty-four times during July and August. On six raids they found no nests, but from twenty-five expeditions they brought back great numbers of white bundles of babies. The reds bring them up as red ants, and the captured babies will work the same way and just as hard as they would for their own family.

Ants are quick to forget, and soon after a battle, life goes on as usual.

PARASOL ANTS

People are proud of their vegetable gardens. But when it comes to the most delicious and nourishing vegetable cultivated in any garden, the prize goes to the ants. Not all ants, just a few that have learned to produce a vegetable so rich in protein and sugar that they can give up eating insects and live on the garden crop. No other animal lives on food exactly like the food of these leaf-cutter, or parasol, ants.

Since ants are underground dwellers, they pick a special kind of plant that can grow in darkness. Mushrooms thrive where it is dark, damp, and cool. The underground part looks like cotton, and the ants prune it so it never grows the mushroom umbrella we see above.

This mushroom cotton makes luxurious gardens. The gardens look like bath sponges, full of holes where ants run in and out, and where fresh air can circulate. Mushroom cotton, treated with chemicals from the mouths of ants, causes clear, shiny heads of a mysterious vegetable to bubble out. The ants snip off these bubbles and eat them. They lay eggs on the cottony threads and when they hatch, it is as though they were lying in a bed of cabbages. The babies devour the crop all about them. Since this mushroom cotton grows only on fresh leaves fertilized in a particular way by ants, they keep cutting round pieces of leaves and carrying them back to their galleries. The parade of ants holding round green bits of leaves high overhead is the curious sight that gives them the name of parasol ants. The ant mushroom garden must be kept clean and pure. Dust must not spoil the delicate flavor of its vegetables, and germs would bring all sorts of weeds, spores, and bacteria into their neat vegetable garden. So while bigger ants are out cutting and carrying leaves, little ants

Mushroom cotton grows on leaves the ants have hung from the ceiling of the cave.

are continually cleaning both the trees outside, as well as the underground tunnels, where the leaves are hung, covered with their growth of mushroom cotton.

HONEY CASK ANTS

Indians digging in the dry Southwest struck what looked like little green grapes. As they dug deeper, they kept finding more grapes down to about six feet. The grapes were juicy and sweet. But how in the world could they grow buried in the ground? The answer tells one of the strangest secrets of life in the darkness of ant caverns.

The juicy things were not grapes. They were storage bottles for honey. These bottles had feet that could wiggle, and bodies and heads attached, with waving feelers. Primitive man made wine bottles and water jars out of leather. But the bottles the Indians found were live animals. They were ants which had agreed to drink all the honey brought to them, until they were round as a ball, and to give a drink to other ants.

These honey ants live on honey alone, but honey dew is plentiful for a few weeks only. Ants get it by stroking the backs of aphids—plant-sucking insects that make syrupy honey dew—or from gall lumps. Gall lumps are nests of insects which suck sap from oak trees, and turn it to honey dew. The syrup these insects make oozes out of the gall in droplets, during the night.

The ant family which depended on honey dew as its only food would die of starvation when honey was out of season unless some way were found to store it up. Ants cannot build wax reservoirs, like bees, so some of them became honey bottles.

A honey bottle ant is called a replete, meaning "filled up." In a big family of honey ants, 300 repletes may be filled with honey syrup. They are ordinary workers, and are not born with special equipment for this job. We do not know whether a boss selects them or whether they step up and offer their services. From the time they start becoming repletes, they never go outside their caverns. Other ants locate and collect the stores of delicious honey dew, for the repletes are little more than living storage bottles.

An ant starts turning into a honey bottle when young, before the armor of its body hardens. Then its skin can stretch. The honey stomach is in the rear, or abdomen. Its head and chest remain the same, but as more ants bring it a drink, its rear swells and swells until it is as round as a grape. It hangs itself up to the roof of the cavern, holding on with the claws of its front feet. Dangling there, it can only wave its legs. It is too fat to move. If the honey bottle gets accidentally knocked off, other ants use strength and skill to carry it up and hook it to the ceiling again. The others take good care of their honey bottles, who may live hanging patiently from the ceiling for years, supplying their anthill with its favorite food, whether honey dew is in season or out.

Living casks of honey hang from the ceiling. Workers look after them.

Most of the time, the lion is quiet and dignified, as one would expect a monarch to be. He
is very much like a large house cat, enjoying
nothing more than to lie in a comfortable heap,
drowsing the hours away, and blinking thought-
fully at goings-on around him.

MYSTERIOUS AFRICA

FAR away, beyond the curve of the earth, a huge block of granite—a section of the earth's crust—is lifted about a mile above sea level. This block, straddling the equator, makes a plateau known as the high plains of eastern Africa.

The plateau is broken by a diagonal crack twenty miles wide and three thousand feet deep. It has been punctured by a few volcanoes with high peaks, now white with snow, and shoulders hundreds of miles across. So vast is the granite block that the mountains are only isolated landmarks.

On top of the plateau, vistas of red grass are peppered with yellow rocks and thorny green acacia trees. Termite nests thrust gray cement fingers above the grass. Gullies fan out with secret trails, and scattered water holes sparkle here and there. White peaks float high in the purple air like pictures in a fairy story. In midday the sun blazes straight down. At night the stars and the moon are

Jungle, rolling hills, and white-crowned, majestic mountains are all part of the varied landscape of mysterious Africa. In the background of this picture is Mount Kilimanjaro.

over-bright in the clear air of the heights.

But the most astonishing thing about this plateau is the story of its animals.

RETREAT FROM THE ICE AGE

Once upon a time a vast variety of animals ran and jumped, roared and charged, snorted and fled over all the continents. America, Europe, and Asia were the homes of elephants. Rhinoceroses plunged through thickets as far north as the arctic. Lions and leopards stalked across Europe and Asia. Wart hogs built their villages in England. Giraffes browsed in the tree tops of Greece and China. Wild horses dashed over the plains of America.

Lands and seas were different in those days. America and Asia were connected; so were Africa and India. The Sahara, now a desert, was then green and fertile.

But conditions changed. Land bridges between the continents sank, or the continents drifted apart. Areas to roam in, as big as continents, were divided as the Rockies, Alps, and Himalayas rose higher. In northern

The lioness is a powerful, expert hunter, and the contented, protective mother of a fairly well-behaved family. Later, the male cubs will have shaggy manes and tufted tails.

Africa the grassland and shady groves, crossed by animal trails, turned into sandy desert.

Competition for food in the animal kingdom became more savage, and the animals had to fight to live. Those that ate the flesh of other animals became expert stalkers and hunters. Some mammals ate only plants, but to survive, they needed sharper eyes, longer ears, and faster feet. A few animals ate both plants and flesh.

Wonderful runners and jumpers developed. Teeth, claws, tails, and legs changed. Eyesight improved. Noses lengthened and were even pulled out to become trunks. Necks also became astonishingly long, as in giraffes.

Then lands in most of the world grew colder. Animals perished or retreated before the creeping glaciers of the Ice Age. But the high plains of eastern Africa, straddling the equator, were a refuge in the chaos of the Ice Age. As the animals retreated south before the ice, they were funneled into mid-Africa.

They came from the north and the east. On the high plains they found rolling grasslands to graze on, dry gullies to hide in, parklike groves for dozing in the heat of day, piles of stones for lookouts and dens, jungles with trees for safety, and water holes for all. It was a perfect place for the refugees of the primeval world.

Then another great geological event happened. With the breakthrough of the Mediterranean at Gibraltar, the rise of the Atlas Mountains, the creation of the Sahara Desert, and the separation of Arabia from Africa, the big continent with the animals on the high plains was cut loose from the rest of the world—by a sea of sand on the north, and by seas of salt water in all other directions.

KING OF BEASTS

A great variety of animals live together on Africa's high plateau—but how can this be? Why don't bigger ones kill smaller ones, until only elephants and rhinoceroses are left? Somehow they have been sorted out by the ages, and organized to carry on together.

Here on the African plateau, the lion is truly the king of beasts. Because of his great strength and noble bearing, almost all the animals show him tremendous respect. Only the giants, the elephant and the rhinoceros, ignore him.

In daytime the lion is lazy, sleepy. He hunts only at dusk and in the night. Then his great roar signals the start of the hunt. The herds are alerted, keyed up, ready to run. Animals at water holes stop drinking. If the lion shows up to take a drink, he has the place to himself. The others will return later.

Why does the lion roar when about to kill? Perhaps because his lioness often does the killing. She has sneaked up on the other side of the herd, about a mile away, and his roar will drive the prey toward her. Sometimes he roars after making a kill—perhaps just to let off steam. Or the roar may be part of a warming up for a supreme effort. Animals bark, bellow, and howl for many reasons, but the lion's roar usually means he is hungry or angry.

In the daytime, and any time he is well fed, the lion is mild, tolerant, and good-natured. He sits in a comfortable heap, paws extended to one side, like a big house cat. His lioness and children purr contentedly to each other. But the lion is also curious. He will stare with big eyes and get up and walk slowly to examine anything he doesn't understand. He is not easily upset. He seems always to be thinking things over.

He stands high, his mane waving in the breeze like a king's flag. But when he stalks, he crouches low, with elbows high and stomach to the ground, invisible in the grass. This huge, elastic body, over ten feet from nose to tip of tail, has mighty power in its steely muscles and tendons. But the lion exerts himself little. He may kill only once a week, to eat, and never for the fun of it.

The lion lurks on the fringes of the herds, coming up on them with the feel of the wind on his nose. He focuses on one animal and stealthily approaches foot by foot. Suddenly comes the rush, a few giant bounds, and hurtling through the air is an animal projectile that never misses. The sweep of a giant paw breaks the backbone, or one front

A mother lion carries the remains of her kill to a more comfortable dining place in the shade. Four cubs trail her, while a fifth impatiently paces around the dinner.

paw placed on the doomed animal's neck and the other around the face will jerk the head back and snap the neck.

The other animals are now safe. They may graze in peace. The lion is feeding.

ANTELOPE HEADQUARTERS

The high plain is antelope headquarters of the universe. Here antelopes, running by thousands, form the largest herds. Here antelope horns become more astonishing than any other horns in the animal world.

Some horns rise from the top of the head and undulate backward over the shoulders. Others stand straight up—long, slender, and spiraling. Those of the hartebeest wave up from the top of his forehead. The eland wears a crown like curving, unraveling straps. The sable antelope holds aloft a pair of crescents. Most stately of all are the lyres of the greater kudu. Antelope horns are hollow, except for a bony core near the base from which they continue to grow as long as the animal lives.

When a giraffe drinks, he must do a split because of his long legs. Here, while two giraffes are drinking, the others keep watch.

The gnu looks like a bit of mixed-up evolution. His body is slender and long-legged like a horse's, his horns are short and heavy as those of an ox, his head and shoulders are massive with mane and beard like a bison's, and his motions are unique. He trots daintily on tiptoe, suddenly he wheels around, looks back, flourishes his long horse's tail, puts head down and seesaws on his front legs, kicks his heels in the air, and gives a snort that resounds with a metallic ring. After that he takes off with long, stiff-legged strides, hardly seeming to touch the ground. Gnus can travel all day at this trot.

If gnus in a herd notice a peculiar motion in the grass, or have a feeling that something is stalking them from a gully, they halt and have a good look around. The leader heads toward the danger, followed by the herd in single file. When all are facing in the same direction, they stop. If the marauder is sighted, it is gnu custom for two of the biggest males to warm up for battle. They bow their heads and kick each other furiously for a couple of minutes as if to prove their ferocity and the appropriateness of their other name—wildebeests.

When animals herd together, it may be because they feel safer that way. A herd grazes, clatters over the plain, wheels in its course, and gets panic-stricken all as if controlled by one nervous system. It makes more noise, raises more dust, looks more threatening than individuals. If it knew how to fight as an army, it could kill its strongest foes easily. But this it does not do. After all the display of mass strength, when the attack comes only one gnu fights; the others run away.

Does each survivor in the herd feel it has been saved by the crowd? All still appear to have a sense of security. True, one of their number is missing, but few saw it happen, and they don't call each other by name. They turn back to eating and drinking.

One of the handsomest members of the antelope family is the graceful impala. The body is built for speed. As in many other hunted animals, the eyes are large, protruding, and set at the sides of the head, so that danger from any direction will be seen at once.

The grasslands—from the American prairie to the African veldt—support a variety of life.

ANIMAL SKYSCRAPERS

From a tower—his neck—the giraffe looks down on the plain. He stares over the top of a tree, from which he has just lassoed a leafy branch with his eighteen-inch tongue. As he chews, his lower jaw goes round and round, as if being unscrewed.

The giraffe wants no part of the business of runners and hunters, but he may become involved if the lion begins thinking about having giraffe steak for dinner. Sensing danger, the stately, easy-going giraffes, perhaps a hundred strong, will take off and gallop for miles. They bring their hind legs in front of their forelegs, like coyotes and jackrabbits.

Strangely, the giraffe has the same number of neck bones as other mammals, including a mouse or a man. The miracle of the neck is achieved by lengthening each bone. In the same way, leg bones are lengthened. It all adds up to a towering creature that can enjoy fresh leaves and twigs, high on a tree, with little effort.

A giraffe makes good use of its fine view of the landscape. It gazes and gazes with big clear eyes, under beautiful heavy eyelashes. It takes note of any suspicious movement in the long grass; it sees down in the gully a tawny shoulder which is hidden from shorter animals. In fact, the giraffe has a reputation as a good lookout. When other animals see giraffes at a water hole, they come trooping over.

Nature made the giraffe's neck to stand up, not to swing all the way down. To drink, the giraffe must spread his legs far apart. Then his mouth can just barely reach the water. But in that awkward position he is helpless; he can't suddenly rear up and dash away. He has to pull his legs back slowly. So only one or two giraffes drink at a time, and the others keep a lookout while waiting for their turn.

With all his immense neck, the giraffe has no vocal cords. He cannot express feelings with a roar or a whinny. He can only stare at the world in silence. Except that sometimes after a long, long drink, air comes out of his mouth with a soft *"ah!"*

With giraffes as lookouts, zebras crowd into the shade of a tree to avoid the noonday sun.

STRIPES AND BARS

Next to antelopes, the commonest herd on the mysterious plateau is composed of zebras. These look like little toy horses, the more so because their vivid stripes suggest a circus. Sometimes they trot along with their heads nodding in unison, wheeling and parading, as though showing off.

The stripes are a miracle of camouflage, for the critical time in the life of a zebra is the hour around sunset. That is when the dozing lion wakes up, stretches, utters a mighty hunting roar, and begins looking for dinner. Nothing will please the lion more than a zebra. But at this time of day the grasses and the clustered acacia trees throw long bars of sunlight and shadow across the ground. Where they fall, the zebra has only to stand still and vanish.

Shadows running through grass are broken, and so are the stripes of the zebra. The animal's bars all break through its outline. If they followed its outline, they would make the animal more conspicuous. The stripes cut over its back line and under its belly like hoops; they make rings on its neck and legs, and chevrons on its face. And this masterpiece of camouflage is, to repeat, most effective at sundown.

In daylight zebras are more conspicuous. The white fur between the dark stripes brilliantly reflects the light, and the animals look white on the plain. But the lion is not hunting now. When changing from one shady place to another, he may saunter casually through the herds. Then antelopes and zebras pause for a moment in their grazing, glance in the lion's direction, shift positions to give him a path, and calmly turn back to grazing.

THE TRUE NATIVE

The zebra, with its wonderful stripes, is a true native of the high plain. Lions, antelopes, elephants, giraffes—almost all other animals in the African ark—came from foreign lands, as well as possibly from Africa. The lion was well known in Greece, Syria, and Asia Minor. But it seems that zebras have never lived in any other place.

The first wild horses on earth, some fifty-five million years ago, were American. They were dog-sized inhabitants of the forests of North America before the Rocky Mountains were up-lifted. These animals had four toes on each front foot, and three useful toes on each hind foot. As time went on, the number of toes decreased until thirty million years ago the foot of the horse had only three toes. Horses that run on one toe developed about twenty million years ago. This single toe became the hoof of the horse.

Legs on those American wild horses grew long and slender—giving better leverage for faster running. The hock of a horse, which looks like a knee turned backward on the hind leg, is actually an ankle. This shows how long and slender the foot is.

As ages rolled by, the miniature wild horses of America grew larger. When they migrated to Africa, they were probably about the size of wild asses which live in eastern Asia today. On the high plain some evolved into zebras—fat, striped, and with sleek hair. The burros and donkeys of our day, with their sharp little hoofs that can cling to stony paths up the sides of the Grand Canyon, are bred from the wild asses of Asia and North Africa. No tame animal has ever been bred from the zebra.

Far from being toy horses, zebras are pure wild animals. Nervous and alert, keen-eyed, they have a murderous kick. Efforts to tame them for harness and saddle are vain. Perhaps the individual is lonely and needs the herd. On the high plain they do always run in herds, whinnying together and kicking each other for a place at a water hole.

A peculiar layer of fat under the sleek zebra coat seems to make the animal cold-proof and heat-proof. Zebras are always plump. They drink a lot of water and never get more than five miles from a water hole. Other animals seem to know this and follow the zebras around when they are thirsty. The lion follows the striped herd, too, but only because he likes zebra meat for his dinner.

WORLD'S FASTEST RUNNER

While hunters are stalking the main herds, some superb races are taking place elsewhere. A small young antelope, a little zebra, or a rabbit, for example, will spot a cheetah and take off for dear life. The cheetah, spotted like a leopard, does not use the leopard's spring from a tree or rock onto the back of his victim. The cheetah depends on open-field running.

The cheetah is a cat, yet a little doglike. He sits high like a dog, with front legs planted like pillars. His claws are fixed like a dog's and cannot be retracted like a cat's. His legs are long, shoulders high, head small

Catching its breath after the chase, the big cat settles down to a dinner of fresh antelope.

This cheetah raced one of the fleet-footed antelopes of the high plain, and won; for the
fast-moving, long-legged cheetah can streak
after a victim at a speed sometimes reaching as
high as seventy miles per hour. Notice the doglike
appearance of this member of the cat family.

with piercing eyes, and tail long. With a graceful combination of the long stretch of a greyhound and the springy swing of a monkey in full stride, this swiftest animal on earth in two seconds can get up to forty-five miles per hour, and with a *real* burst may hit seventy miles per hour. The little antelopes and the rest may, however, win the race if they get a good start. The cheetah tires fast.

TALKATIVE NEIGHBORS

A little way apart from the heavy drama of the African ark three astonishing animals are finding happiness—baboon, elephant, and rhinoceros. They are not bothered by the two big problems of hunters and hunted: how to eat and how not to be eaten. They find plenty of their kinds of food. Only one, the baboon, has an escape problem, and he has solved it in a peculiar way.

The baboon, being a monkey, is supposed to be a tree dweller. But African trees are the hunting place of the beautiful, slender leopard, which relishes baboon. So the baboon (no peabrain he) left the trees and became a monkey that walks on the ground. Baboons moved into caves of rocky cliffs along

Two baboons, with the typical loops in their tails, go fishing in an African stream.

streams, and into the piles of big boulders on the hills. Here they are safe while the leopard hunts among his tree branches in the moonlight.

Baboons live in clans of about fifty and are very sociable. They have the sharpest eyes on the high plain—eyes said to equal eight-power binoculars. When they see a trespasser, they all chatter and jeer.

Baboons look like long-nosed funny old men walking on all fours, but their stiff-legged, sidewise gait is fast. They sit down anywhere and amuse themselves by turning over stones, picking up the surprised ants and centipedes, and licking them off their fingers. Beetles and ants' eggs are especially favored, but these long-nosed fellows can live on all sorts of food, animal or vegetable.

When baboons are disturbed, they just talk loud and scamper off. Little baboons who can't keep up hitch rides on their mothers, where they look like bronco-busters. Or they grab the hair on mother's stomach and hang on upside down.

THE LARGEST
LAND ANIMAL

Behind the scenes the elephant is the most peaceful and happiest of the wild animals. He pays no attention to the others. Their hubbub does not bother him. The lion detours around the elephant, and the two seldom meet. The elephant's only encounter might be with a pack of wild dogs insane enough to gang up on him. In that event he curls his precious and delicate trunk up under his chin and, towering over the pack, lets them yap and dance around until they are tired and go away.

The elephant can stand still and reach far out in all directions with his trunk to collect an immense amount of food—about a quarter

The ridges on the underside of an elephant's trunk help in grasping. Not only males, but females too, have tusks, which are most- ly for rooting in the ground. Elephants are among the more intelligent mammals, but sto- ries about their memories are exaggerated.

of a ton of green fodder every day. Without stretching his neck he can pick leaves almost as high as the giraffe can reach. With two little lips at the tip of his trunk, he pinches off tender twigs as delicately as though he were picking daisies.

The elephant has a way of reaching twigs and leaves beyond the reach of giraffes. If he takes a fancy to fresh leaves that are far up on a tree, he puts his forehead against the trunk and pushes. Down comes the tree—though its trunk may be two feet thick.

That elephant trunk, an elongated nose which coils and waves like a colossal snake, can reach down as easily as up. After a little plowing in the ground with tusks, the elephant will pull up some tasty roots. If the tall grass around is going to seed, the trunk can touch the tassels gently, sniff in seeds, and then coil under and blow the seeds into the mouth. Or, if the tall grass has become dry hay, the elephant has huge teeth that act like grindstones. Like a long arm his trunk sweeps together an armful of grass into his eager mouth.

Though the elephant collects food on three levels, he needs a square mile to keep his stomach filled. So elephants sometimes have to bestir themselves. A herd may travel fifty miles in a night looking for water and trees, or reed pastures. Little elephants, which always trot along close to their mothers, are unable to go more than ten miles an hour, so mothers with children may get separated from the big old males. But elephants have a mysterious way of communicating and, somehow or other, they are able to find one another again.

The elephant's six-ton body is as well balanced as an antelope's. With its head, trunk, and tusks (perhaps three hundred and fifty pounds of ivory) in front, the animal is balanced like a seesaw. When the trunk is held forward, the hind legs carry less weight and can push. The giant can move some twenty

This elephant's trunk is curled around his next mouthful of grass. Despite his enormous strength, he does not kill to eat; he is a complete vegetarian.

Elephants sometimes strip whole branches from the trees while feeding, stuffing themselves with huge quantities of grass, fruits, leaves, and twigs—eating as much as half a ton of green fodder every day.

miles per hour, crashing through thickets as if they were tissue paper.

Sometimes elephants, usually very solemn, feel playful. If there is a steep, high bank by a river, they stand on the edge to cave it in. Then they sit on their tails and toboggan-slide down in a cloud of dust. In the water they roll over and sink, putting up their trunks like snorkels to breathe through, with their heads under water. They suck up water and blow it over their backs and between their front legs at their stomachs. They love to roll in the mud.

JACKALS AND HYENAS

As grazing herds travel with the weather, back and forth over the high plains, with lions following, other animals are drawn into the strange procession. Among them are jackals and hyenas, seeking the carcasses which the lions leave. When the lion has eaten his fill, the jackals are first to close in.

The jackal hunts at night for small wart hogs, baby baboons, and rats. When he yaps at night at the big antelopes and zebras, perhaps he is calling a lion to come and do some killing.

The hyena is no hunter. Evil-looking and slow, he sneaks in at the end of a kill to

A lion killed an antelope, fed, and went on. Now, the African wild dogs take their turn.

Although bad-tempered, and dangerous when he charges, the rhinoceros is a plant-eater, active mostly at night. His eyesight is poor, but his sense of smell is exceedingly keen.

Intelligence, speed, and powerful horns characterize the African Cape buffalo. The base of the sharp horns forms a thick, bony helmet.

finish whatever is left. Even the jackal hates the hyena, who comes in and pushes him aside. If tough hide, stringy hair, and skull and bones are all that is left, these suit the hyena. His powerful jaws and teeth will crunch the bones with loud cracking noises.

The hyena laughs at a carcass. His horrible laugh is that of a ventriloquist; it seems to come from the wrong direction. A ravenous pack of hyenas will produce the worst uproar on the face of the earth—a chorus of barks, squeals, hisses, wails, and shrieks. The lion pays no attention; but other animals may be scared away, for only the wild dogs are rough and tough enough to deal with hyenas.

THE WILD DOGS

The wild dogs, most ferocious animals of the African high plain, have big ears, long legs, and spots like a hyena's. They hunt in large packs, a leader out in front and the pack following in line about a half mile back. They hunt tirelessly day or night, not for food alone, like the lion, but with a lust for killing. Against them even the giant eland, weighing a ton, has no chance. It has been said that they will even gang up on a lion, driving his majesty from the kill. A pack may surround a lion and tear him apart, though not before some dogs have been torn apart first. The wild dogs are the lion's only real enemy.

The wild dog is a blood-thirsty villain, yet also a stylish and impressive animal. He swings into the chase with perfect team-work, giving a clear hunting call, *hooo-o! hooo-o!* like the wail of a bloodhound. He can outrun the fastest antelopes and zebras because he combines endurance with speed. As a killing machine he has few peers.

SULKY AND DUMB

If the elephant is happy, the rhinoceros is sulky and dumb. He has a very small brain in proportion to his body. He is left over from a bygone age of giant mammals which included, about twenty-five million years ago, the *Baluchitherium*, perhaps the biggest mammal that ever walked the earth. That monster rhinoceros was 34 feet long and 17¾ feet high. His shoulders were higher than the head of the giraffe is today!

The rhinoceros of the high plain is not greatly disturbed by animal hunters. He just sits around near his mudhole, surly, making sounds like a giant having bad dreams. He may stretch flat out in the mud like a pig, panting and foaming. But around sundown he scrambles to his feet and finds other rhinoceroses. If the night is moonlit, they squeal and snort, gambol, and boost, shove and try to upset each other. Some of them even bound into the air. It is disgraceful.

A rhinoceros has a marvelous instinct for finding water. He seems to be able to smell it under the ground. Then he digs like a dog, sending the sand flying out between his hind legs. Other animals, even the elephant, get to depend on the rhinoceros as a water finder and a well digger. This is one of his contributions to life in the African ark.

The high plains of Africa—the greatest roaming ground for mammals in the entire world.

CREATURES FROM A LAND APART

THE PLATYPUS

LONDON, 1798—One day a tall sunburnt man, swaying a little in his walk as sailors do, waited patiently to see a famous professor. Luckily, he did not have to wait long. At a sign from the professor, he put a package down on the cold marble table. He opened it unhurriedly. And there "it" was, between the two men. It was an unknown dead animal, a sort of big mole with rumpled fur and

an odd beak, like a duck. The professor took up a magnifying glass and the sailor started to talk. He said that he had come from a far place, a new continent, Australia. Yes, that animal had been captured at Hawkesbury, in New South Wales. It lived there with others like it, by a stream. The natives say that the female lays eggs and that the male has spurs on his hind legs that can cause serious wounds by injecting a poisonous liquid.

The professor looked at the sailor, went back to the animal, and then rendered his decision: Humbug!

This was a time of sensational discoveries and hoaxes. The newspapers printed stories about sailors cheated by Chinese embalmers who sold them fabricated mummies, at fabulous prices. Some of the sailors had even brought back "mermaids" manufactured from the cadavers of monkeys, to which fishtails had been skillfully sewn. This duck-billed creature must be the work of a forger. Such was the opinion given, with great calm, by Mr. George Shaw, eminent professor of the British Museum. Since the sailor insisted, the professor was kind enough to promise

The platypus (left) is one of the curiosities of the animal world, hatched from an egg like a snake or a bird, but nursed on milk like a mammal. Once hunted for its furry pelt, it is now protected in Australia, the only country where it is found.

Using its four webbed feet as paddles, the platypus plunges into streams, lakes, and rivers to dine on small crabs, worms, and mollusks. When underwater, it swims with its eyes and ears shut, searching out food with its very sensitive beak.

him to make a more detailed examination. He would consult a learned colleague. If the sailor could possibly arrange to come back a few days later, he would get his answer.

And the sailor came back, to be told that his animal had gone off to Göttingen for definitive study by one of the greatest scientific authorities of the time, Johann Friedrich Blumenbach. He was a shining light of medicine and zoology, and one of the fathers of modern anthropology. And Blumenbach confirmed what Shaw had come around to suspecting: the remains were those of a genuine animal. That is how, at the end of the eighteenth century, the existence of the platypus, or ornithorhynchus, was discovered —the egg-laying mammal, which can give fatal wounds with the poisonous spurs of its hind legs. Actually, it probably only kills its own kind, and then only in battles among males that humans have imagined but that no one has reported seeing.

In 1809 the French scientist Lamarck classified the platypus and the other animals of the same order in a class belonging to neither the mammals nor the reptiles.

The platypus continues to live its mysterious life and tries to avoid man. And man, the animal's great enemy who waged an unrelenting war upon it to get its silky fur, is now protecting it.

The platypus makes its burrow among the roots of trees, in skillfully concealed grottoes with several entrances. But the female is not satisfied with this communal dwelling; she requires another for herself when it is time for her to lay her eggs, in order to protect her brood. This nest is set in the bank above the level of a lake or river, and is carpeted with wet eucalyptus leaves. When everything is ready, the female closes all the entrances of her retreat and, in the darkness, lays two or three eggs no bigger than those of a pigeon.

When the incubation period is over, the young one about to be hatched uses its egg-tooth, a hard excrescence on the maxillary bone, to split the shell. Birds usually use the egg-tooth on their upper beaks for that purpose, but the platypus has no beak at birth. The beak forms later, when the young platypus stops feeding on its mother's milk, and when it must learn to dive under the water in search of small crabs, worms and mollusks. During these dives it closes its eyes and ears, and seeks food with its sensitive beak.

This animal is very much affected by noise. It is said that platypuses have been killed by loud noises. One of them, being sent to Winston Churchill as a gift, died on board ship just outside of Liverpool, during World War II, killed by the sound of an explosion.

From just this much of it, we might take the animal pictured on the left to be a deer. In fact it is a young kangaroo, another of the animal curiosities that are found naturally today only in Australia and Tasmania.

THE KANGAROOS

THE first European to see kangaroos was the Dutch seaman Pelsart, in 1629. His ship was wrecked on an Australian reef; he got to land exhausted and lay down to rest in the grass. Suddenly he saw a fleeing herd of animals with heads like dogs, making huge leaps. He had just time to see that they had very small front legs, enormous hind legs and long muscular tails.

When he finally got back to Europe, he described these strange creatures. Other adventurers after him confirmed his report. And so the existence of these Australian animals became known in Europe. But their name came from the English Captain James Cook, the famous explorer who wrote in his journal in 1770, in Australia: "(This animal) has the light color of a mouse, the build of a greyhound and quite the appearance of that dog, with a long tail, which he carries in the same manner . . . except for his way of walking or running, which is like the leaping of a hare or a deer." He asked native Australians the name of this surprising beast. He asked them in English, of course, and the

After it outgrows its mother's pouch the young kangaroo, or joey, adjusts itself happily to the number of positions in which a kangaroo finds itself comfortable.

These kangaroos seem to be eating peacefully now, but at the first threat of danger they will be off, bounding away at nearly thirty miles an hour.

Accommodating is the word for the mother kangaroo, for a while. Until it outgrows the space, the young kangaroo, or joey, has a home in its mother's pouch, which it enters soon after birth. Usually kangaroos have just one young, or sometimes two.

aborigines answered in their language, "Can ga ru," meaning (more or less), "I don't understand." Cook took this as being an answer to his question, and the name kangaroo has been used ever since.

The natives' name for the true kangaroo is walaru or wallaroo and they have retained it. These are the large kangaroos. Those that Cook had seen were wallabies, the smaller kangaroos. But whether large or small, and there are a number of very different species, all of the animals that we call kangaroos belong to the family of marsupials. (Most marsupials, except the opossums, are found only in the southern hemisphere.)

The name marsupial comes from the Latin word for "pouch," and was given these animals because in almost all, the females have an abdominal pouch in which their young pass the first months of their life. Even after they have started to come out and look for their own food, they still use their mother's pouch as a shelter from danger.

This pouch contains the teats at which the young feed for several months. When the little kangaroos are born, the mother licks a path on the hairs of her abdomen up to the pouch, which they can then find with ease. The young kangaroos, or joeys, continue using their mother's pouch until they outgrow it. The female usually gives birth to one, but sometimes two, young.

It is thought by some scientists that kangaroos lived in trees originally. It is not known how or why they came down to the ground to live. However, one group, the tree kangaroos, have returned to life in the trees, sleeping and feeding there.

Kangaroos, unlike many other animals, have no lairs or burrows. They get along without any shelter, roaming freely and leaping with those tremendous leaps that so impressed the first explorers of Australia. These broad jumps, which may measure as much as twenty feet, give them remarkable speed, up to twenty-five miles an hour. They rest on their powerful hind legs, and use their tails for additional support. An adult great gray kangaroo male may measure almost seven feet from the tip of his nose to the tip of his tail, and can weigh over two hundred pounds.

Although it is hard to keep the big kangaroo in captivity, there are many zoos throughout the world. They have even been bred in some zoos.

The tree kangaroos are not over three feet in length. Unlike the terrestrial kangaroos, their front and hind legs are almost equal in size. Their big strong tails are used as rudders when they jump to the ground from the trees in which they live, sometimes from a height of sixty or seventy feet.

The best-known wallabies, because they are the most apt to be seen in captivity, are probably the rock wallabies. They vary in size; there are several species. The soles of their hind paws are protected by a pad that keeps them from slipping. In Australia they can be seen in rocky areas running and leaping, searching for the vegetation they feed on, such as leaves, grass, roots, and bark. Nothing is more graceful than a wallaby's leap; even the smallest can make tremendous jumps.

Since foxes and dogs have been introduced into Australia, the smaller kangaroos have mortal enemies. They escape by jumping, and do not hesitate to jump into trees, using their front paws, like velvet-covered hands, to hold on to the branches.

All kangaroos are herbivorous; most of them eat leaves or grass. In order to get leaves, the tree kangaroos climb trees, bracing themselves with their tails. They may spend long hours during the day sleeping in the fork of a tree.

Rat kangaroos feed on grass and tubers and are sometimes a nuisance to farmers. They are about the size of rabbits.

THE TASMANIAN DEVIL

TASMANIA is an island about the size of Ireland, one hundred and fifty miles off the southern coast of Australia. It was discovered by the Dutch explorer Abel Tasman in 1642.

In Tasmania there are low mountains, forests, swift rivers, and lakes. The eastern part of the island has areas of grassland. Settlers came to Tasmania from Australia in the nineteenth century and began farming in suitable parts of the island. Today about three hundred thousand people live on the island and it is part of the Commonwealth of Australia.

There are two unusual mammals living in Tasmania which are not found anywhere else in the world. One is called the Tasmanian devil; the other is the Tasmanian wolf. They are marsupials, or pouched mammals, as are many of the Australian mammals. Unfortunately so many of them were killed by the early settlers that they are rarely seen in their native home.

The Tasmanian devil may have been called that by the people who first came to live on the island because the little animal's fur is black with white spots. Or, it may possibly have been so named because of its angry expression when cornered.

The head and shoulders of the Tasmanian devil are proportionately larger than the rest of its body and are strong enough to enable the animal to kill creatures larger than itself. It has short legs, and walks with the same swinging gait that a bear does. It is about three feet long.

Native to the oceanic island of Tasmania, this little animal, the Tasmanian devil, was hunted almost off the face of the earth 'by the early settlers of the island, who feared it.

The Tasmanian devil makes its home along rivers. It eats birds, lizards, snakes, frogs, rodents, and large insects. And, because it sometimes raided their chicken yards, it was often killed by farmers.

These animals mate in early spring and the young are born several months later. There are usually four babies which the mother carries about in her pouch. When they get too big to fit in the pouch, the mother builds a nest for them, in which they live until they are ready to be on their own.

The Tasmanian devil generally hunts at night and sleeps during the day, often curled up in a hollow log. Its cries have been described as being whines and snarls.

The Tasmanian wolf, the other marsupial unique to this island, looks like a dog with brown stripes running across its back.

It eats small mammals, even wallabies which are bigger than itself. Early settlers killed Tasmanian wolves in large numbers because these animals not only killed chickens but also sheep. Now the few remaining Tasmanian wolves live only in the wildest hill regions, if any still exist. They hunt at night and sleep during the day.

The female Tasmanian wolf has four young at a time. She carries them in her pouch until they are too big for it; then she hides them in a den. Her pouch, unlike the kangaroo's, opens to the back.

Scientists believe that at one time both the Tasmanian devil and the Tasmanian wolf also lived on the continent of Australia along with the many other marsupial animals found there. Marsupials are considered to be among the more primitive of present-day mammals. Their young are in an early stage of development when they are born and must continue their further development within the mother's pouch. Most other mammals give birth to young which are much more advanced in growth than the marsupial babies.

The Tasmanian devil is a nocturnal animal, sleeping by day, hunting by night, and, like many other animals of that part of the world, a marsupial, carrying its young in a pouch.

The relatively large head and shoulders of the Tasmanian devil enable it to overcome animals bigger and stronger than itself.

Native to the inland plains of Australia, the emu is a large and flightless bird, standing five and a half feet in height when full grown, and covered with long shaggy feathers.

THE EMUS AND CASSOWARIES

THE EMU is one of the two very large flightless birds which can still be seen in the wild in Australia. It lives on inland plains.

Emus have brownish-gray feathers which form a heavy coat over their bodies. Only two patches of bare blue skin on their necks and their heavy legs are not feathered. They are as tall as a man, adults reaching five and a half feet in height, and weigh as much as one hundred and twenty pounds. They are the second largest birds in the world; only the ostriches of Africa are larger.

During most of the year emus travel about in small flocks in grassland regions of Australia. They eat plants, fruits, insects and small animals.

When nesting time comes in February and March they pair off. Each pair builds a nest on the ground out of grasses and leaves and the female lays from seven to ten eggs. The eggs are big—each may be five and a half inches long and weigh as much as a pound and a half. Only the father sits on the eggs; he has to incubate them for about two months. When the young emus finally hatch, the father alone takes care of them.

Baby emus do not look like their parents; they have striped yellow and brown down at first. This probably helps protect them from predators, because it is very difficult to see them in their native habitat. It takes about two years before young emus become adult birds and raise families of their own.

Emus are rather gentle birds. They are curious about any strange creature which appears and will sometimes come up to men and stare with large pale-brown eyes.

The early settlers in Australia killed emus for food and also ate their eggs. Even now the farmers and emus are not on good terms. The big birds eat the farmer's crops and crash through the fences which have been built to keep them out of cultivated fields. At one time the men who were trying to raise wheat in western Australia asked the government for help against emus, and a small number of soldiers was sent out to shoot the birds. Emus can run very rapidly and can also swim well, and the soldiers were unable to kill very many of them on the birds' home ground, so the "Emu War" was a failure. Since then a fence five hundred miles long, supposed to be secure against emus, has been put up in the interior region of the country and it is constantly checked to make sure that emus do not break through it.

Fortunately Australians, like Americans, are now beginning to value the original wildlife of their country. There are plans for setting up wildlife sanctuaries where emus as well as other rare Australian animals can live in peace.

Emus do well in captivity—as a matter of fact they do so well in some zoos that the flocks have grown to greater numbers than the zoos have room for.

According to scientists who have studied fossil remains, other species of emus lived in the Australia-Tasmania area as long ago as a hundred thousand years. Now there is only one species left.

The other big flightless bird of Australia is the cassowary. There are also other species of cassowaries found in New Guinea and on surrounding islands. The Australian cassowary lives in forests in the northeastern part of the continent.

Unlike the emus, adult cassowaries are not friendly. They strike out with their powerful clawed feet and are capable of killing a man. In zoos they often fight with each other, and even males and females have to be kept in separate pens. In spite of this bird's

Practically everything about the emu is large, from its stride, which carries it at speeds up to an estimated thirty miles an hour, to its eggs, which, laid seven or more in a clutch, average over five inches in length.

aggressiveness, some of the primitive peoples of New Guinea keep captive cassowaries and use their feathers as money.

Cassowaries have a strange bony covering, which looks like a helmet, on their heads. The exact purpose of this is not known, but scientists think it may protect the bird's head as it travels through the thick underbrush of its forest home.

The skin of cassowaries' heads and upper neck is featherless and is bright red and blue. Some species have long folds of skin, called wattles, which hang down from their necks. Other than serving as decoration, these strange wattles seem to have no particular function.

The plumage of adult cassowaries is black and quite heavy. The birds stand about five feet tall; the female is somewhat larger than the male.

Shy birds seldom seen in their native forests, they can run at rapid speeds through the forest undercover and are also excellent swimmers. They eat fruits, insects and small animals. Their calls are a combination of grunts and bellows.

At nesting time the pairs build large nests of leaves on the ground and each female lays from three to six dark-green eggs. Then she departs and the male takes over, sitting on the nest until the young birds hatch. At first the young are striped, but their later feathers are brown and eventually, when they are adults, they have black feathers.

Other big flightless ground birds still found in the world today are the ostriches of Africa and the rheas of South America.

THE WOMBATS

THE gentle little wombats are sometimes called the "badgers of Australia." However they are totally unlike the tenacious, carnivorous badgers in almost every respect. The only habit the wombats and the badgers share is that of digging burrows.

The wombat uses its sharp claws to dig a long and rather large burrow in the earth. During the day the wombat rests in its burrow. At night it comes out to feed on grasses, tree bark and roots.

The wombat looks rather like an outsized guinea pig. It has only a tiny tail and short legs and its whole appearance is round. The average wombat is about three and a half feet long. Some may weigh as much as eighty pounds.

The wombat is a marsupial. The female has one baby at a time and the young wombat passes the first few months of its life safe in its mother's pouch.

There are two species of wombats in Australia. One has coarse grayish-black or yellowish-brown fur and a bare nose. The other has soft gray fur which extends over its nose.

At one time in the long distant past a wombat the size of a large bear lived in Australia. Scientists know this because they have found fossil remains of this wombat.

The wombat is another marsupial, and lives only in Australia and Tasmania.

ANIMALS
OF THE AMAZON

THE JAGUAR

THE jaguar is one of the most powerful felines in the world, and the largest one in the New World. It resembles the leopard very much in appearance, character, and habits. In the Amazon jungle, the jaguar is feared by other animals and man. The jaguar is well equipped to get itself food in abundance; with its powerful and accurate attack and with the strength of its claws, it seldom misses its prey. Almost before the victim is aware of the shock, the jaguar's claws have penetrated to a vital part of its body and it is dead.

At night, the jaguar is often on the watch near a stream where other animals might come to drink. Like all cats, large and small, it moves gracefully and silently, even in the dense vegetation of the tropical forest.

As to its relations with man, opinions differ and even contradict each other. To some observers, the jaguar is only a big cat, who is afraid of man—both those who hunt with only primitive lances and arrows and those who are equipped with the most mod-

ern rifles. According to others, this cat will attack a man as fiercely as if he were a tapir or a capybara.

Among the animals of the Amazon jungle, the jaguar, a solitary predator, is the undisputed master. Even the fish, it seems, are not safe from the cat's unfailing claws. That sets the jaguar off from the other big cats, except for the true tiger of India. Only these two big cats have no aversion to water.

That is one of the few similarities between the American *el tigre* and the true tiger.

South American Indians tell stories about the way the jaguar fishes—probably not true, but certainly picturesque. They maintain that the jaguar spits into the water: the saliva floats to the surface and attracts the unwary fish; a quick stroke of the paw and they are on the bank. According to another version, the jaguar uses its tail as bait, letting it hang down into the water. Actually, the fishing procedure of the jaguar is probably a good deal like that of cats trying to catch goldfish in aquariums.

All the fables told about it show the passionate interest and extreme caution that the jaguar inspires in the Indians of the South American jungles. In legends, the jaguar is

The jaguar, shown here crouched and ready to spring, is the largest and most powerful member of the cat family in the Americas.

often represented as a captive—which is a way of trying to believe that this animal can be overcome.

The Tupi Indians believe that the jaguar is afraid of thunder and lightning, and interpret the animal's unrest as a sign indicating the coming of a storm. Most likely this is just the usual excitement shown by all animals, including domestic animals, when sudden atmospheric changes occur.

Here is one of the most popular Indian tales told about the jaguar:

"One day the Jaguar came upon the Lightning, who was making a club. The Jaguar came up from behind and the Lightning did not see him. He leaped at the Lightning but could not get to him. He thought the Lightning was an animal and wanted to eat him. The Jaguar asked the Lightning if he had any strength, and the Lightning answered that he had none. Then the Jaguar said, 'I am not like you. I have great strength and I can break all the branches. Just see!' And he climbed a caimbé tree and broke all its branches. Then he climbed a parica tree and broke all its branches, too. Then he came down to the ground and tore up all the grass. Finally he got tired and rested. Panting, he said, 'See how strong I

The young of a cat are its kittens, as even the junior jaguar shown here, and woe betide the man or animal who threatens to come between a mother and its young.

am! I am not like you!' And he sat down alongside the Lightning, turning his back on him.

"The Lightning took his little club, waved it, and everything happened at once: thunder, flashes of lightning, wind and rain. The Jaguar climbed a tree, but the Lightning knocked down all the trees and the Jaguar fell to the ground. The Lightning took him by the paw and swung him around. The jaguar escaped and hid under a rock, but the Lightning caught up with him, struck the rock and forced him to come out. Then he climbed another tree, but the Lightning knocked down that tree. The Jaguar fled to a cave, but the Lightning caught up with him there too, and made the earth cave in. And the Jaguar had no more peace; the Lightning was always pursuing him. Then it became very cold, with wind and rain, so that the Jaguar was chilled and could not run any longer, and finally curled up on the ground. When the Lightning saw him in such a sad state, he said, 'You see, my friend, what I am like! I am strong, too! You are not the only one that is strong; I think I am stronger than you are!' And he went off. The Jaguar went back to his den. But ever since then, all Jaguars are afraid of thunderstorms."

This legend confirms the popular reputation that the jaguar has for courage and aggressiveness. Some Indian tribes will not even use the skin of a Jaguar that they have killed, as if the death of this predator was enough of a blessing and it would be dangerous to try to make further profit from it. Certain tribes, however, make use of jaguar teeth; they burn them and grind them into powder, using the powder as a remedy for toothache and other dental problems.

Sometimes a jaguar is unwary and is caught in a trap, generally a big and deep pit, covered with branches. The cat is then brought to a zoo in a strong cage. It may resign itself to imprisonment if it is well fed, but it retains its proud, untamable spirit.

Neither water nor the top of a tree is a safe refuge from the prowling and predacious jaguar. But it was probably the quest not of prey but of comfort that brought the oddly matched pair at left (a black jaguar is rare) to dunk themselves in the river.

Elegant in motion, fierce in battle, and always wary, the ocelot is a skilled and cunning hunter which often sets upon its quarry from a well-concealed ambush.

THE OCELOT

Like many cats, the ocelot does its sleeping by day and its hunting by night.

MEN have called certain cats "mysterious" because of cats' impenetrable gaze. The domestic cat used to be considered an ally of sorcerers, and even as a bit of a sorcerer itself. The adjective "lazy" might be applied to its blissful way of stretching and yawning when it is sleepy. If the perfect proportions of its body are considered, as well as its admirable adaptation to nearly all circumstances, the adjective "elegant" could certainly be used. Mysterious, lazy, elegant—a cat is all of these and many other things besides. But above all the cat is a predator, an efficient and well-armed hunter, a professional in the art of ambush. The only cat that hunts on the run is the cheetah.

All cats have the same highly specialized teeth. They lack the crushing molars, but the incisors, canines and premolars are perfectly adapted tools for cutting the flesh of their prey. Cats' curved, pointed claws are fearful weapons. And, since these claws are retractable, except in the cheetah, they do not wear down because of constant contact with the ground. In addition to these weapons, cats have remarkable senses of smell and hearing. They also have a keen sense of sight and can, of course, see in the dark. But not all cats have the same degree of perfection of these natural aptitudes.

The cat is an individualistic, reserved animal, which always guards its independence. These feline characteristics are all found in the ocelot, in the wild state. Naturalists do not know too much about the behavior of the ocelot in its natural habitat because it is a very difficult animal to observe. First of all it is exclusively nocturnal in habit. During the day it sleeps in its den. Then it chooses the most remote sections of the forest for its refuge. There it has practically no rivals.

The area over which the ocelot occurs is from southern Texas, where it is now rare, through Mexico to Central and South America. There are several different races of ocelots which vary in size and color.

The ocelot is a patient, wily and able hunter. It finds its prey among small mammals. It will also eat snakes, birds and even monkeys when it can catch them. The mating period is not definitely known, but it is probably in early summer. The litter is usually limited to two cubs. Ocelots are sometimes killed for their magnificent fur, which is highly valued. Capturing adults for zoos is difficult; the ocelot scents the traps and passes warily by. However, young ocelots are supposed to be easy to tame.

The ocelot is usually about three feet long including its tail. It has a bright pink nose.

THE GREAT ANTEATER

THE great anteater is a very strange-looking animal. It almost looks like a mistake of nature, as do most anteaters. None of the parts of its body seem to go with the others.

Its very long head ends in a long nozzle-shaped snout. At the end of its snout is an inconspicuous slit, less than half an inch wide, which is its mouth. Another remarkable feature of the giant anteater is its tongue. It is round like a tube, twelve inches long and half an inch wide. This tongue is covered with a sticky substance.

The giant anteater's four-foot-long body is borne on four legs that do not match: the front ones are strong and short, the hind ones longer and larger. The front legs have strong, sharp, curved claws—the middle claw may measure up to three inches in length. These claws make an effective weapon for defense.

When it walks, the giant anteater bends the claws of its front legs and walks on their outer surface. At night it waddles clumsily through the forest, pretty much at random, snout to the ground, searching for ants and termites. It has weak eyes and depends on its sense of smell to lead it to anthills and to termite nests, which it demolishes with powerful blows of its claws. Then it gathers up hundreds of these insects with its sticky tongue. After its meal, the anteater retires to a shelter under dense foliage, rolls itself up into a ball and covers its body with its bushy tail. It sleeps peaceably most of the day.

Adult females have a single offspring each year. The baby anteaters are carried about on their mother's back at first, and stay with her for about one year.

However strange an animal may seem to us, there is always a reason for it. The long narrow head and sticky eel-like tongue of the great anteater equip it to do best the thing for which it has been named: eat ants.

THE PUMA

At one time found in most parts of the United States, the puma has been hunted to the edge of extinction.

THE puma is a carnivorous mammal, a member of the cat family which includes such magnificent animals as the jaguar, the lion, the tiger, and the leopard.

Other names for the puma are cougar, mountain lion, and catamount. It is only found in North, Central and South America.

This large handsome cat has a solid-colored tawny coat, without spots, and is almost as big as a lioness, being thirty inches high at the shoulder and almost seven feet long, including twenty-five to thirty inches of tail. It weighs up to two hundred pounds. Its head is small and graceful, and its golden eyes are very expressive. The solid muscles of the puma's body give it a rapid, powerful spring.

In western United States it usually lives in rocky terrains. It climbs trees well. Pumas live a roving solitary life, walking abroad at dusk under the cover of the brush or trees. It attacks small mammals, elk, deer, and sometimes even domestic farm animals. At one time pumas were found in most parts of the United States. Now, however, they have been hunted to extinction in most parts of the country. As a result, their normal prey, such as deer, have multiplied to the point where they cannot always find enough to eat. Many deer die of famine in the winter.

The puma or cougar of South America lives in jungles as well as in mountainous areas. It hunts monkeys in the forest, chasing them through the trees.

In the early spring litters of from two to five young are born. They have yellow fur with dark spots during the first six months of their life. They stay with their mother for about two years.

The puma is curious about man, but seldom if ever attacks him.

THE KING VULTURE

Not until it is four years old has the king vulture its many-colored adult plumage.

THE king vulture is distinguished from the large number of other vultures by its brilliant plumage and its unusual appearance. Most American vultures are brown or black; the king vulture is a striking cream and black. It lives in Central and South America, usually in rather forested regions.

The Andean condor, which is much larger than the king vulture, is also found in South America but mainly in the Andes. This condor has a wingspread of about ten feet. The wingspread of the king vulture is about seven feet. Both birds, needless to say, are impressive in flight. The contrasting colors of the king vulture's naked head are amazingly beautiful. The black of the beak becomes a

clear reddish at the end. The rest of the skin on the head is a mixture of reds, purples, and yellows. Only adult birds have this vivid head coloring. The feathers on the back, the abdomen and the thighs are a soft cream. The lower part of the wings and the big tail feathers are a dark, iridescent greenish-blue.

King vultures, like other vultures, wait for the sun to warm the air before they begin their circling flight. Soaring on thermal updrafts, they are constantly on the lookout for dead animals. Because of their relatively weak feet, they cannot catch their own prey. When they spy carrion on the ground, they come down to feed. Many vultures will often feed at the same time and roost together at night in the same trees. Like all the members of their family, they perform a very useful job of sanitation.

The harpy eagle, found from southern Mexico to northern Argentina, is a menace both to the animals that run on the ground and to the monkeys that inhabit the forest tops.

THE HARPY EAGLE

THE harpy eagle may be named for the Harpies of ancient Greek mythology. The Harpies were creatures with the heads of women and the bodies of birds of prey. These legendary Harpies were sent to punish people by carrying off their food. However, this superb bird of Central and South America does not really resemble the Harpies.

Their strange name may come from the Greek "harpazein" which means "to seize." The Greeks called falcons and kites "harpe." The Roman naturalist Pliny calls the vulture "harpe" as well.

The harpy eagle, like these other birds, is a bird of prey. It is about three feet long, and its body is covered with magnificent plumage. The head and neck are soft gray; the crest, wings, tail and upper part of the body are a handsome slate-gray; the underparts are white, as are the feathers on the legs. The beak and claws are dark and the skin of the legs is yellowish. The birds' bright eyes are constantly alert. The harpy eagle's head has a double crest of feathers which the bird can raise or lower at will.

Small creatures of the jungle are defenseless against the lightning speed of the harpy eagle, and few animals are able to enter into competition with it. It flies tirelessly above the tall trees or perches on a high branch, almost hidden in the dense foliage. When it has sighted its prey, whether this be a macaw, a monkey, or a sloth, the eagle drops down on it with incredible speed through intertwined branches, lianas and bushes, and seizes it in its strong claws. The eagle's feet and talons are so big that they almost seem out of proportion with the rest of the bird's body.

Thus armed for the struggle, this constant struggle that puts natural selection into operation at every moment within the teeming life of tropical forests, the harpy eagle probably dies a natural death, unless some disease or injury weakens it so that it becomes the victim of another predator.

Most of the Indian tribes in the basin of the Amazon regard the harpy eagle as an honorable enemy. The blood, fat and droppings of the bird are used as bases for native medicines, supposedly good for a number of diseases. The Indian who is skillful or lucky enough to bring down a harpy eagle does not let anyone forget the fact. He adorns his head with the big strong feathers from the wings and tail of his trophy.

Finding a nest of this bird is a very difficult enterprise, although the nest is large and sturdy. The harpy eagle nests in as high a tree as possible, in well-hidden, almost inaccessible spots. The female lays two eggs. As with most eagles, the young stay in the nest for a long period before they are able to fly. Both parents help feed the young. The harpy eagles do well in captivity and are found in many zoos.

THE CAIMAN

Some animals seem impossible to classify at a glance. One of these is the caiman. A traveler, finding one near a stream in a Brazilian forest, might scream, "A crocodile!" and flee. The caiman is not a crocodile, although it belongs to the order Crocodilia. It also belongs to the sub-family Alligatorinae. Crocodiles are found in Asia, Africa, Australia, and tropical America; one species of alligators lives in the United States and one in China; caimans live in Central and South America.

There are more than one species of caiman. A distinction must be made among the spectacled caiman, the jacaré caiman and several others.

The spectacled caiman has a kind of armor on its back that seems to be made of heavy coins, thick enough to resist bullets. If one has to be killed, it must be shot in the side, where its armor is weakest. The adjective "spectacled" was given to it because the transverse ridge above its eyes gives the illusion, when seen directly from the front, that the caiman is wearing a pair of spectacles with frames on them. Its eyes can be seen at once, whereas its teeth can not. It has them though, eighty of them—and very strong ones.

The caiman stays on land during the day for hours on end, without going very far from the water—the river, lake or pond that is its hunting ground. Half-buried in the tall grass, it sleeps for hours, only getting up when it is hungry again. It gets into the water with the slow clumsy gait that is characteristic also of crocodiles and alligators. At first the caiman does not seem to be a good swimmer, but appears to be content with staying on the surface, letting the upper part of its head, the eyes and nostrils,

emerge. The slow and quiet movements are only a feint. If the caiman went through the water at full speed, as it does sometimes when it has to, there would be a good chance it would not catch anything it cared to sink its teeth into; while, if it is motionless, it arouses no suspicion. Those eight feet of floating scales, with no sign of life, look remarkably like a log. Many a fish, mollusk and small amphibian continue their quiet life in the pool with no fear whatever, until they are within reach of the huge mouth that swallows them immediately.

Then the caiman will turn again and go slowly up the bank. It has sighted a marsh bird preening its feathers, feet out of the water. There is hardly a flutter of the bird's wings, as the enormous animal makes its killing with incredible speed. However, things are not so easy on land for the spectacled caiman. It is up against faster animals that are very dangerous to it. There is the jaguar, for instance, who treats the reptile as it would any big lizard, and sometimes kills it. And then there are men, with their dangerous firearms or even simple nooses.

Capturing a caiman is not a simple task. A stout rope has to be placed around the animal's neck and then pulled tight. Thereafter, the caiman may be taken to a zoo.

If the noose has been held by some of the Indians of the Amazonian jungle, the caiman may finish up as a roast. Its skin has long been valued for making fine leather goods, and there is an extensive market for it in many parts of the world.

The caiman is born from an egg the size of a duck's egg, which its mother had buried in the sand. As soon as the young animal is in the open air, it turns instinctively toward the water. Not very stable on its weak legs, it often becomes entangled in the dense tropical vegetation and has great difficulty in covering the short distance to safety. This is

the baby caiman's most dangerous time. Sometimes it will be seized in the sharp beak of a bird, sometimes by the sharp teeth of a carnivore, and sometimes it will be eaten by an adult caiman. Finally, four or five little caimans to a particular brood arrive at their watery goal, safe and sound. Most of them will end up as food for a predator within the first few years of their lives, but a few will grow up to be eight-foot-long adult caimans.

Neither crocodile nor alligator is the scaly caiman which, full grown as above, or newly hatched and hatching as below, looks quite a bit like both its relatives.

THE EMERALD TREE BOA

THE boas live mainly in the tropics of the New World. There are some fifty or more species, ranging in size from the giant anaconda, which may reach a length of thirty feet, to the small rubber boa which is only two feet long. The emerald tree boa, one of the most attractive members of the boa family, is about four feet long when it is full-grown.

The female emerald tree boa, like all other boas, does not lay eggs but gives birth to young. Young emerald tree boas are red, but the adults are a brilliant green, with yellow or white bands on their back. Since these snakes live mainly in trees in the forests of northern South America, their brilliant colors blend in perfectly with their surroundings.

In its mouth, it has long sharp teeth, from which it gets its scientific name of *Boa canina.* But a boa's bite is not poisonous. They use their teeth to hold the small animals they catch, while they constrict their prey within the coils of their bodies. They eat birds and lizards and small mammals that wander within their reach. Their jaws can be extended so that they can swallow an animal that may be wider than the width of their own heads.

Boas spend much of their time sleeping. When a boa is disturbed, it coils itself around a branch. It does not try to escape; it neither attacks nor pursues. Its only reaction is to become immobile.

Those animals which seem to be aware of the power of the boa's crushing grip may then ignore it. But the jaguar, aggressive as always, will not accept this immobility and may let fly at the reptile with a blow of a powerful paw at the snake's most vulnerable part, the head.

One of the most beautifully colored of all snakes is the emerald tree boa, which is native to the northern part of South America.

Even for a snake, the equatorial forest is full of dangers and it has no assurance of leading a long and peaceful life. Perhaps that is why boas do not seem homesick in zoos. They may not have complete freedom there, but they will not encounter their enemy, the jaguar.

The Cook's tree boa resembles the emerald boa in certain ways, especially in its habits, but it is a golden-brown color. It hides so well among the leaves and branches of trees that it can hardly be seen.

The most famous boa is probably the ten-foot boa constrictor, which lives in Central America and northern South America.

The anaconda, not only the largest boa, but thought also to be the largest snake of the New World, lives in the tropical forests of South America. It is usually found near water, either along rivers or in marshes. It eats mammals as well as birds and reptiles.

There are even two boas found in western United States. One, the rosy boa, lives in Southern California and Mexico. It is a small striped snake about three feet long. It makes its home in dry rocky areas and eats rodents. The other boa, the rubber boa, is smaller. It also eats rodents and lizards. This brownish-gray boa lives mainly in forests of the Northwest but its range extends to California.

The jaws of the emerald tree boa, shut or wide open, are less of a menace than the long green body trailing after them which, coiled around a branch is harmless enough, but coiled around an animal can kill it.

The squirrel monkey is omnivorous in diet, eating everything, including insects, fruit, and even small birds.

THE SQUIRREL MONKEYS

"It has, I think, now been shown that man and the higher animals, especially the Primates, have some few instincts in common. All have the same senses, intuitions, and sensations,—similar passions, affections, and emotions, even the more complex ones, such as jealousy, suspicion, emulation, gratitude, and magnanimity; they practise deceit and are revengeful; they are sometimes susceptible to ridicule, and even have a sense of humor; they feel wonder and curiosity; they possess the same faculties of imitation, attention, deliberation, choice, memory, imagination, the association of ideas, and reason, though in very different degrees. The individuals of the same species graduate in intellect from absolute imbecility to high excellence."

Thus wrote the famous naturalist Charles Darwin, author of the theory of evolution, in his book *The Descent of Man*, published in England in 1871.

Darwin's observations form an appropriate introduction to the New World monkeys, which are pictured and described here in the following pages. For, as he says, the attributes that man shares with all the higher animals are most evidently, and in by far the greatest degree, shared with those known as the primates, of which the monkey is one.

To primates, as the name itself suggests, zoologists give the first place in the order of the animal kingdom. In doing so they recognize that it contains the most complicated and highly organized living creatures. Of the eleven major groups into which the primates can be divided, only two exist exclusively in the New World and are generally included in the term New World monkeys.

A more precise name is *platyrrhini*, which comes from two Greek words meaning flatnosed, which, broadly, is a distinguishing characteristic of all New World monkeys.

The Old World monkeys are also known by another name—*catarrhini*—which comes from two Greek words meaning curvednosed, and describes the less flat and less widely separated nostrils evident in the primates of the Old World, as opposed to those of the New.

It is generally believed that the catarrhini represent a higher stage of development in the evolution of life than their New World relatives, the platyrrhini. The latter show characteristics that the former have apparently "grown out of." Yet, for all that, the platyrrhini represent a high form of life.

One of the features unique to the New World monkeys is their "fifth hand" as it is sometimes called—their prehensile, or grasping, tail, which none of the catarrhini possesses.

Yet not all of the platyrrhini are so equipped either. The squirrel monkey, one of the most common of the New World monkeys, cannot grasp or hold anything with its tail, although its tail is long.

The squirrel monkey is about ten inches in length from head to toe, and its tail is about fourteen inches long. It has a small expressive face and large eyes, and is arboreal in habit, like most of the platyrrhini. That is, it lives and spends most of its time in bushes and trees above the ground (*arbre* is French for tree, hence arboreal—tree-living) and does not usually descend to the forest floor.

This is a matter of security, not one of taste, for all manner of dangers are to be found on the forest floor, and the greatest safety lies in the lush leafy thick of the forest high above ground.

When the squirrel monkey does descend, it does so in great groups, all at once, to the accompaniment of much crashing and chattering. This makes its coming sound at least more fearful for others than it actually is.

The squirrel monkey is found in the tropical forests of Central and South America, ranging from Nicaragua to Bolivia and Peru. It does not usually live in the deepest, darkest parts of the forests, but prefers the sunlit edges, the river banks of the valley of the Amazon, and the scrub woodlands that edge the great savannas.

It is omnivorous in diet, eating anything and everything—insects, spiders, small tree frogs, snails, fruit, eggs, and even birds.

It travels in troops that tend to keep close-knit, no member straying very far away.

There are six kinds of squirrel monkey found in South America. All are subspecies of *Saimiri sciurea*. The face is greenish white, the head dark gray or black, and the body greenish-golden in color. The greenish-golden coloring is produced by fine hairs that are yellow at the base and black at the tips. The arms and hands and feet are ruddy yellow, and the tail is gray with a black tip.

If any feature of the squirrel monkey is reminiscent of the other animal from which it draws its name, it is its movement, which is quick and scampering and accomplished on "all fours." It is not like the squirrel in color, shape, or habit.

More appropriately, the Tupi Indians of the Amazon called the squirrel monkey saimiri, which in their tongue means only "small monkey."

Like all monkeys the squirrel monkey is acclimated to the tropics and to the hot moist tropical forests. It does not like cold, and physically cannot stand it. The greatest obstacle to keeping one in captivity is this sensitivity, and many of the thousands shipped out of the jungle die for this reason. Cold, dryness, or absence of sunlight for any prolonged period of time can prove fatal to these little monkeys.

Hardiness is less common in all the New World monkeys than it is in the Old World monkeys, some of which stand captivity reasonably well.

At about the same time that the squirrel monkey and most other monkeys of the tropical forests are settling down for the night in their various ways and protective concealments, one species is just starting out on its rounds.

The squirrel monkey is appropriately named, for it scampers in the trees just like a park squirrel, running on all fours. It is not able, as some other New World monkeys are, to make use of its tail for grasping.

THE DOUROUCOULIE

THE douroucouli monkey or *Aotes* is unique among the New World monkeys in being the only one that is truly nocturnal—night living.

Uniqueness in nature is not a matter of chance or caprice, as it may sometimes seem to man, but is the result of selection and specialization for survival. In the douroucouli it is the eyes that are specialized: too sensitive to be exposed for long to the full light of day, but so sensitive that even in full darkness it can see such tiny objects as insects, one of its sources of food.

This determines the douroucouli on a night course in life. When the squirrel monkey is just contentedly snuggling its furry tail around itself and going to sleep, the douroucouli is emerging from the hollow tree trunk where it has spent the day sleeping. It is starting out to look for the insect and animal fare upon which its life depends.

The sleep of the douroucouli is not profound by day, however, for there are many dangers abroad then. It must sleep half-alerted to them, so that when danger threatens, it can retreat to a safer spot.

In size the douroucouli is a little smaller than an ordinary cat. It is colored a neutral shade of brownish-gray, which blends in perfectly with the twilight and night colors of the forest in which it moves, and with the

Not as large as a house cat, the douroucouli sleeps during the day in a well-protected retreat, coming out only at night to hunt for the insects and animals on which it feeds.

shadows among which it catches its hours of half-sleep by day.

The name *Aotes*, by which it is also known, comes from a Greek word meaning "earless," which is at least the impression one gets from its face, the ears being small and covered with hair and lying close to the head.

The douroucouli's face is dominated by a pair of large, round, orange-yellow eyes, which give the animal a strangely soft and gentle expression. And, indeed, it is said to make a good pet, friendly though placid. It is prized in some areas of South America for its thoroughness in tracking down roaches and other insects in homes.

The douroucouli, when it hunts in woods at night, calls in a wide variety of voices. It can twitter and squeak like many other monkeys, and it can sound a gong-like booming noise that is loud and far-carrying and is like that of no other monkey.

Like the squirrel monkey, to which it is related, the douroucouli is not one of those monkeys that can use its long bushy tail for grasping.

It is, however, extremely able with the hands it does have, which possess, as do man's, thumbs that can be placed opposite to the fingers. Holding its food in one hand, the douroucouli can tear it apart easily with the other hand.

The douroucouli, in common with certain others of the platyrrhini, often bears twins. Many other monkeys have only one offspring at a time.

Another New World monkey that often bears twins is the marmoset, which also is not a "true monkey." However, in many respects it conforms more to what monkeys are thought to be than do some of the true monkeys themselves.

MARMOSETS

Marmosets belong to the family Callithricidae, as opposed to the true monkeys, which belong to the family Cebidae. Yet marmosets have been described by one eminent naturalist as "the most perfectly adapted of all Primates for arboreal existence."

Their movements are quick and jerky, and are carried out with such suddenness that they can disappear in the blink of an eye. This, actually, is the only defense they need against a stronger adversary with whom one may find itself suddenly confronted. Its tactic is to stare at its enemy and hope that, while the latter is trying to make up its mind how to attack, some momentary distraction may catch its eye for a second. In that second the marmoset will have leaped to new cover and safety.

Like most monkeys and near-monkeys, marmosets travel in bands—males, females and children of a family together.

The marmoset's diet is made up mainly of insects, which it obtains with characteristic quick movements.

It is one of the paradoxes of the marmoset that while being relatively limited in its facial expressions, it is thought by many to be among the platyrrhini that most closely resemble man.

It does not grimace or smirk or make faces the way many monkeys do. To convey its anger or displeasure it can only pull back its lips and bare its teeth. This is about the limit of its expressiveness and yet in composure the face of the marmoset is much more like man's than those of some of the more imitative monkeys. The marmoset has sharp pointed teeth which can easily pierce human skin. Yet as a rule it becomes a pleasant pet, friendly to those it knows, though something of a danger to strangers who approach too close.

According to Edward Bartlett, a famous naturalist who explored the Amazon animal world, the Indian women of Peru make pets of marmosets.

Marmosets were brought back to Europe from the New World in the middle of the sixteenth century and though they were not classified by naturalists for another two centuries, they almost immediately became the prized pets of the royal and the wealthy aristocrats. Perhaps the most prized and popular was the beautifully pelted silver, or black-tailed, marmoset, which takes its name from its silvery-white coat.

Marmosets are distributed over the vast regions of the equatorial forests of South America, with different species concentrated in specific areas. The silver marmoset, for example, is said to be distributed in "a marginal strip along the right bank of the Tapajos and the left bank of the Tocantins."

Marmosets usually have twin offspring. Sometimes, however, they have not two but three young, and then it is not uncommon for the mother to kill one of them at birth. Although this may seem cruel, it is probably instinctive, and in any event a kindness to the two that survive. The survivors, being well nourished, both have a better chance of survival in the forest than any one would have had if all three had lived.

At birth the mate assists, receiving each baby as it is born, bathing it with his tongue, and transferring it to his back, where it clings, hidden in his long hair. His services do not end there either, for he carries the children on his back, sometimes for as many as seven weeks afterwards. It is usual for the young marmoset to begin its independent acquaintance with the world at about three weeks of age, when it may climb down off its father's back and make short trips into its surroundings.

The common marmoset (*Callithrix jacchus*) is also known by the name ouistiti, which was given to it by the Amazon Indians. The ouistiti's mating cry is the same as its name.

The Indians of the Amazon naturally saw a great deal of the many different kinds of monkeys in the tropical forests of that region, and it is not surprising that many of their myths and legends, like those of the northern Indians that dealt with deer and buffalo, concern the little primates of the New World.

The Indians tell this story of the way the monkey came to behave as it does—to utter its flute-like cries, and to live so much in the trees.

"Long, long ago the Monkey and the Tapir were friends and often spent their time together. One day they decided to take a walk in the forest. The Tapir had his flute with him, an instrument that he delighted in playing much of the time. The Monkey was envious of the Tapir's flute and he talked the Tapir into lending it to him, though the Tapir was not very happy to do so. As soon as the Monkey had it in his possession he scampered up a tree and, putting the instrument to his lips, let loose a deafening squall of sounds. After a while the Tapir asked for his flute back, but the Monkey said no, he might as well forget it, the flute was his now. This infuriated the Tapir, who swore he would kill the Monkey if he ever caught him. The Monkey heard his threat and to save himself from the Tapir's vengeance, never again came down from the trees."

Science gives a less fanciful explanation of the monkey's ways, although it agrees that it lives in the trees as a matter of security. It says the monkey's vulnerability to the more ferocious ground animals requires it to live above ground, and that its specialized limbs enable it to do so. And its voice, which is developed to a fairly high degree, is not the gift of the tapir, but grows from the need it has to keep in touch with the fellow-members of its tribe, for warning of danger.

For all their monkey-like ways, the marmosets are not considered "true monkeys," the term reserved for members of the family Cebidae. One difference is the tail, which in the marmoset is not prehensile. Another is that the marmoset has claws on all of its digits except its great toe, which has a nail. True monkeys have nails on all their toes and fingers.

SPIDER MONKEYS

THE spider monkey is a true monkey. It has nails on its toes and fingers and it possesses a tail that is prehensile and in many ways more useful to it than its hands or feet.

The spider monkey's tail is its most extraordinary possession. It is longer than the monkey's body is—over two feet in length in an adult, and composed of twenty-three vertebrae, which give it suppleness and strength. It is longer and narrower than any of the monkey's other limbs and can be used to reach farther and into smaller places than can the animal's arms and legs. The monkey can hang by it, swing by it, pick fruit with it, even throw things with it.

The normal means of travel of the spider monkey is known as "brachiation"—a swinging progression from one limb or vine to the next and on to the next that is like the movement of a trapeze artist on swings.

Normally the spider monkey dwells in the topmost branches of the tall forest trees, and seldom if ever comes down to the ground.

The spider monkey travels in bands of ten, twenty, or more, often mingling with the capuchin monkey. At dawn it begins to look for food and is busiest until about ten o'clock in the morning. It feeds periodically throughout the day but not with the same intense activity with which it began.

The little spider monkey moves about by brachiation, swinging like a little trapeze artist from one limb or vine to another.

When it walks along a limb on all fours, it carries its tail arched into an S shape. If startled by something below, it will often descend to get a closer look at the intruder, emitting a barking sound that has been described as "terrier-like." It has been known to throw twigs and branches down at humans and to give other forceful signs of its displeasure at their presence.

Captivity has less dire consequences for the spider monkey than for many others, which, as a rule, do not live well in zoos or private homes. In spite of the expression of worry on its face, the spider monkey has a gentle, friendly disposition, and its constitu-tion is relatively hardy. For this reason it is much valued as a pet.

As opposed to the female marmoset, who calls upon her mate to assist her at the birth of her young, the female spider monkey withdraws from her troop shortly before she is due to give birth, and does not return to it until two to four months have passed. Then she returns, bringing her young with her. And it is she, not the male, who carries them about, first clinging to her chest, later riding on her back. In twelve months the young spider monkey achieves its full skeletal growth, though it continues to gain weight after that time.

There are four different species of spider monkeys and four times as many sub-species, each differing from the others in some degree—in color, habitat, diet, and so on.

The red uakari turns redder when it's angry, a property it shares with man. Yet anger seems far from the thoughts of the gentle-eyed creatures in these two pictures.

It fears only the eagles that soar over the forest and the few snakes that venture up from the ground.

There are three species of uakari, and two of them possess the power of blushing.

The bald or white uakari, found in the Amazon region, has a pink face and skin and a coat of lank gray hair. The red uakari, found in a neighboring region, has a vermilion face, paler skin, and a coat of long reddish hair. These two will turn even redder in the face when stirred to anger. The third type of uakari, the black-headed uakari, does not.

It was probably one of the blushing uakari that the Spaniards called "mono feo" or "ugly monkey." Bald and hairless about its head, with its long coat bedraggled-looking at best, the uakari may, by human standards, seem far from beautiful.

The uakari is particularly unsuited to life in captivity, being neither very lively nor very hardy when put in a cage. The younger ones are said to be more willing to attach themselves to keepers and to adapt to zoo life, but even they are very sensitive to climate, diet, and other factors.

Although not sociable to any degree in captivity, uakaris are normally friendly in the wild, and travel and band together with others of their kind. They do develop family groups. The males are very protective of the females and will attack a person who appears to threaten them.

The normal diet of uakaris is fruit, which may include shoots, nuts, roots, bulbs. In captivity they have been found very difficult to keep properly nourished.

THE UAKARI

A MONKEY that blushes when it is angry is the uakari, which also enjoys the distinction of being the only one of the New World monkeys to possess a short tail, a feature fairly common in the Old World monkeys.

The uakari is a cat-sized monkey with a well-developed brain and superior intelligence. Its favored habitat is among the high places of the forests, through which it travels on streets and avenues of crossing and intertwining limbs, vines, and branches.

CAPUCHIN MONKEYS

Quite different from the uakari is the capuchin monkey, which, of the many New World kinds, is perhaps the most common, most captured, and most captivating to human audiences.

The capuchin is also the most intelligent of the platyrrhini, with a brain that is highly developed and large in proportion to the size of the animal itself.

This undoubtedly accounts for the capuchin's often being seen as an organ grinder's playful little assistant, a sight that once was common in Europe, and to a lesser degree in North and South America.

Such capuchins were taught to distinguish between coins of different values, to show gratitude to the givers of larger coins, and to show contempt or even abuse to the givers of pennies.

The stories that demonstrate this little monkey's intelligence are numerous. They will sit with attention and watch a movie, showing reactions to animals appearing on the screen, such as fright at snakes.

A capuchin can be ingenious in getting to its food, one having used a short stick to dislodge a longer stick to dislodge a still longer

The capuchin monkey gets its name from the coloring around its head and shoulders, which is reminiscent in effect of the cowl and habit of the Capuchin monks. Of all the New World species, the capuchin monkey is the most intelligent, and the most widely distributed in captivity, which it survives reasonably well. And what would the organ grinders do without this nimble little fellow?

stick that it could use to dislodge its food from a high place.

In the wild the capuchin travels in troops of from ten to fifty or more members. It does not make a home, like the douroucouli, which may return to the same resting place several days in a row, but beds down for the night wherever the end of the day may find it.

Boldness and curiosity mark the capuchin, and on occasion get it in trouble, as above, where one has mistaken a poisonous coral snake for some less dangerous variety. In the wilds the capuchins travel in bands of from ten to fifty members, keeping up a constant chatter as they go, playing and feeding most of the day, settling anywhere at night.

The capuchin takes its name from the Capuchin monk, whose cowl the monkey's head-coloring resembles. Although there are many species, differing from one another in color, the typical capuchin is about a foot and a half long, with a slender prehensile tail a few inches longer than that. It weighs only from two to four pounds.

It is found in Central and South America from Honduras to the northern tip of Argentina.

When food is plentiful the life of the capuchin in the forest seems remarkably easy.

It rises with the sun and feeds busily for a few hours, and then spends a few more hours in various forms of relaxation. The younger ones play among themselves while the older ones sit and sun themselves and chatter to one another. This siesta-like interlude is interrupted for a few more hours of leisurely feeding and then is resumed when the heat of the day becomes oppressive.

The capuchin diet is made up of fruit, insects, birds' eggs, and even small birds.

When angered, the capuchin arches its back and spits like a cat. It can also bark like a dog. Generally its humor is good and makes it a popular pet.

Whatever it is that makes one animal friendly and another unfriendly is hard to say, but the capuchin is definitely among the friendlier animals and develops an apparent affection for men.

It may well be a capuchin monkey that figures in this story, told by Charles Darwin in *The Descent of Man:*

"Several years ago a keeper at the zoological gardens showed me some deep and scarcely healed wounds on the nape of his own neck, inflicted on him . . . by a fierce baboon. The little American Monkey, who was a warm friend of this keeper, lived in the same compartment and was dreadfully afraid of the great baboon. Nevertheless, as soon as he saw his friend in peril, he rushed to the rescue, and by screams and bites so distracted the baboon that the man was able to escape, after, as the surgeon thought, running great risk to his life."

THE SLOTHS

THERE are two kinds of tree sloths, the two-toed and the three-toed. Both are found in Central and South America. They were given the name sloth because of their very slow, sluggish movements.

Unless they are disturbed, sloths spend three-quarters of the day sleeping. Normally they sleep hanging from the branch of a tree, holding on with their strong claws. The rest of the time they spend eating the leaves and buds of trees. Even their eating is done in the slowest of slow motion.

Sloths have algae, tiny microscopic plants, that grow in their long hair. During the rainy season in these animals' tropical home, the algae in the fur turn green. It is then almost impossible to see the "green" sloths among the dense vegetation of the forest. However, the keen eyes of the harpy eagle can sometimes spot a sloth and this big bird then swoops down and captures the sloth in its strong talons.

Sloths are capable of protecting themselves by slashing out at a would-be predator with their strong claws. But their greatest protection probably comes from their immobility—they are simply not seen by other animals. They are regarded as inedible by most people in Central America; in South America they are eaten by some tribes of Indians.

It is almost impossible for the three-toed sloth to move on the ground since it cannot stand upright. The two-toed sloth is somewhat more active. If they are forced into water, sloths are good swimmers and can even swim rapidly.

Scientists who have studied the sloths in their native habitat have found that these slow animals have what seems to be the lowest body temperature of all the mammals. Their temperature may reach a low of 75°F., although the normal range for them is from 85°F. to 91° F.

The coarse hair of sloths parts in a peculiar manner, compared to that of other mammals. Apparently sloths have lived upside down for so many centuries that their hair parts on the underside of their bodies and

The green tinge to the hair of the sloth is produced by minute plants called algae, which live in the hair and, during the rainy season, turn green, thus helping disguise the animal against green background.

For the first three months of its life, the baby sloth clings to its mother's fur and is carried with her wherever she goes.

ANIMALS OF THE AMAZON   169

The strong sharp claws on its toes, with which the sloth holds onto branches, are also the animal's only means of defense.

hangs down toward their backs. Most other mammals have hair parts on their backs, with hair falling down their sides.

The mating season is the one time when sloths are seen together. Normally they live entirely alone. In captivity it is not possible to keep two females together; they bite and slash each other.

The baby sloth clings to its mother's fur during the first few months of its life and is carried about in the trees hanging to her body. The two-toed sloth will actively defend her baby if she is forced to.

Sloths have lived in the world for a very long time. During the Pleistocene Epoch there were giant ground sloths living in both South and North America. They ate leaves and plants. One ground sloth was twenty feet long. In South America, remains of these ground sloths have been found in caves with man-made objects. This would indicate that these sloths became extinct fairly recently.

THE TAPIRS

At one time there were many tapirs living in the world. Fossils of them have been found in southern United States as well as in Europe.

The four species of these mammals which exist in limited numbers today have changed very little from their ancestors that lived in the Pliocene Period. They are about the size of a large hog and weigh about five hundred pounds. They have long snouts. Their legs are short and they have three toes on each hind foot and four on each front foot. They eat water plants or plants that grow near water. Tapirs are excellent swimmers and during the day often stay near rivers or lakes. At night they may venture out onto land, always trying to avoid, however, their greatest enemy, the jaguar. They are killed for food by some Indian tribes.

Most kinds of adult tapirs have very short hair. The young animals look quite different from the adults. Until they are about six months old, they have spots and stripes.

The Baird's tapir lives in the forests of Central America. The Brazilian tapir is found in the Amazon region and the hairy tapir lives in the Andes Mountains of South America. The only other species of tapir in the world is found in parts of southeastern Asia. It has black and white hair; the tapirs of the Americas are brown.

Because of the odd number of their toes, tapirs have been placed in the same order as horses and rhinoceroses.

The curiously humped tapir is much like its ancestors of the Pliocene period.

THE PIRARUCU

The pirarucu, found in South America, is one of the world's largest fresh-water fish.

PIRARUCU are fresh-water fish found in the Amazon and other rivers of northern South America. They are among the largest fresh-water fish in the world. A big pirarucu may weigh two hundred pounds and be seven feet long.

Their name comes from the Portuguese "pira" meaning fish, and "rucu" meaning red. Actually their large scales are gray and are only bordered with red. Their scientific name is *Arapaima gigas*.

Pirarucu are an important food fish for the people of South America. Indian tribes have caught them for centuries, shooting them with a bow and arrow, or else harpooning them. Then they preserve the fish by drying the flesh in the sun so that it can be used for food at a later date.

Not only human fishermen go after the pirarucu—the powerful jaguar may be successful in catching one of these big fish.

Like many fish living in fresh water in which there is a great deal of decaying vegetation, the pirarucu come to the surface to breathe air. They would die if they were forced to remain under water for any length of time. When they expel the air they make a kind of burping sound that can be heard for almost a mile.

The pirarucu are among the rare fishes that not only make a kind of nest but also take care of their eggs and the babies.

The pirarucu and other fresh-water fish found in northern South America are almost all totally unlike those found in North America. Strangely enough, these South American fish seem to be related to fish found in Africa, and even to those of northern Australia.

The jaguarundi, three feet long and weasel-like, is a relative of the ocelot and inhabits much the same regions, preying on birds and small animals. It is an excellent swimmer.

THE JAGUARUNDI

SOMETIMES the fur of this small cat is gray and sometimes it is reddish-brown. People thought that these were two different animals and called the gray cat the jaguarundi and the reddish cat the eyra. Eventually scientists found that both cats were the same, regardless of the color of their fur. Sometimes a reddish-brown female will have gray kittens in her litter, as well as kittens of her own color.

The jaguarundi lives in Central and South America. A few may even be found in the southwestern part of the United States. It is small for a wild cat, about three and a half feet long, with a small head, a long tail, and short legs. It looks more like a weasel or otter than it does like a cat. As a matter of fact in parts of Mexico it is called the otter-cat, not only because of its appearance but also because like the otter, it is an excellent swimmer.

Regardless of whether it lives in the dry deserts or in tropical forests, the jaguarundi preys on birds and small animals such as rabbits, rats and mice. Like most members of the cat family, the jaguarundi climbs trees readily. It seems to hunt during the day if it lives in an uninhabited region; otherwise it hunts at night.

The jaguarundi is a secretive animal and not very much is known about its life in the wild. It lives in much of the same area as the ocelot, and possibly has much the same food habits as its spotted relative.

THE TAYRAS

The tayra is a nocturnal animal, in shape much resembling weasels and mink, with a long sleek body and relatively short legs. But the tayra is larger, three feet in length, and its fur is black and does not change during the year.

WHEN night falls in the tropical forests the tayras, tree weasels of South America, wake up and begin their search for food. They often hunt in family packs or in pairs. They eat almost anything they can find, from small animals to fruit. Since they are excellent climbers they also raid birds' nests for eggs. Tayras are active animals and have to spend most of their waking hours getting the food necessary for their energy requirements. During the day they rest in a hidden spot.

Tayras are related to weasels, martens, and mink. They look rather like these important fur-bearing animals, having the same type of long body and short legs. However the tayras are about three feet long—twice or three times the size of a weasel. Unlike the weasels of the north that change color from brown to white with the coming of winter snows, the tayras have black fur throughout the year. Their heads are brown or light gray; their long tails are bushy.

Tayras can be seen in some zoos. They adjust reasonably well to life in a zoo, but thus far none have ever bred in captivity.

Another member of the weasel family which lives in South America is the grison. It is smaller than the tayras and has gray fur. The grison also does most of its hunting at night and sleeps during the day.

Tayras are now found only in Central and South America, but scientists think they may have originally been a North American species which gradually migrated south.

WONDERS OF
THE ANIMAL WORLD

THE
SILVER HATCHET

Iт is thought that some fishes of the depths make frequent excursions to the surface of the water at night, going down again at daybreak to the depths, which they light up feebly with their light-producing organs, or photophores. And so fishermen will sometimes find, in a squirming mass of silvery sardines, mackerel or other edible fish, some strange creature. They will throw it back or, if they are at the dock, give it to the waiting cats, so it is never identified.

Sometimes, however, fishermen get the idea of bringing the odd fish they have chanced upon to marine biological institutes. This was what happened with a little abyssal fish found—and identified for the first time— some thirty years ago off the coast of Sicily. This tiny animal, hardly two inches long, is very broad in front and very narrow in back. On the whole it looks like a hatchet, with a sort of small handle. Because of its brilliant silvery color, it was given the Latin name of *Argyropelecus,* or silver hatchet.

As is the case with most abyssal fishes, its mouth is enormous compared with its teeth. Its huge telescopic eyes look upwards.

Its anatomical features meet the requirements of the very special conditions of the fish's environment: the tremendous pressure of the water, the darkness, the problems of its search for food, the icy-cold water.

The silver hatchet has been caught in the Atlantic Ocean and in the Mediterranean Sea. It swims at various depths, from about ten thousand feet to about three hundred feet, probably in pursuit of its prey. It would not come to the surface unless caught in ascending currents that it could not resist. There near the surface await the fishermen's nets, from which museums of natural history sometimes can enrich their collections with a silver hatchet.

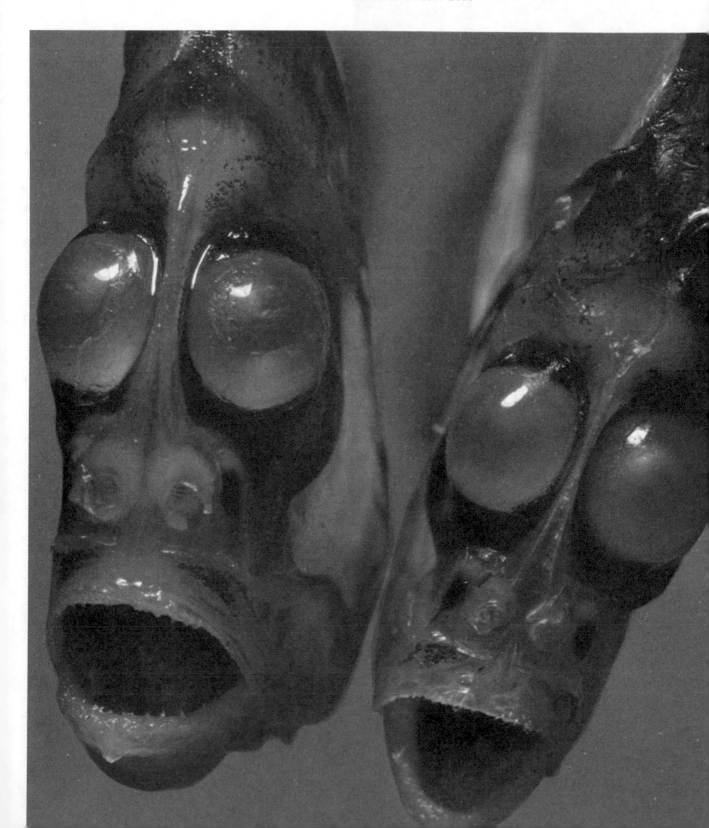

THE SHARKS

SHARKS are classified as fishes although their skeletons are cartilaginous; that is, made of gristle, rather than bone, as are the skeletons of most other fishes. They also differ from bony fishes in many other ways. Most sharks give birth to live young, although a few lay eggs. There are more than two hundred species of sharks.

The great white shark is one of the largest sharks. It can be up to thirty feet in length and weigh about two tons, although the usual length is about ten feet. Its head has the typical shape of the species, terminating, well below the snout, in an enormous transverse mouth. Within its very powerful jaws are triangular teeth like those of a saw. With this equipment and an insatiable appetite, it is not content with mollusks and plankton, but is armed to attack all kinds of animals from man to seals, and spreads terror in the world of fishes.

The white sharks, and all sharks in general, are elongated and spindle-shaped. They have great muscular power. This power and the large fins give them tremendous speed, matched by few other aquatic animals.

The bad reputation that all sharks have was actually earned by just a few kinds. For all there are in the ocean, only relatively few sharks approach shore, and they are not apt to attack a swimmer unless provoked.

Sharks live chiefly in warm ocean waters, but there are some in colder regions. Some even go up rivers and a few are found in fresh-water lakes. Some seize anything they come across; others eat small sea animals, plankton, and plants.

The stories told by seamen and explorers have given rise to many legends about these animals, such as the myth of small ships being crushed and their crews gulped down by sharks. It is a fact, however, that some kinds of hungry sharks will unhesitatingly swallow virtually anything, and that they attack indiscriminately, even coming close inshore at beaches, terrifying swimmers. According to recent statistics, sharks have caused the death of some forty victims in the last ten years. The number of deaths seem to be increasing, possibly because of the popularity of skin diving. All sorts of alien inedible objects—wooden beams, empty kegs, and even rubber tires—have been found in the stomachs of captured sharks. The shark is guided to its prey by its sense of smell. The slightest trace of blood attracts it at once.

The tiger shark is smaller than the white shark, but just as dangerous, fierce and aggressive. It is hunted as are many sharks, for its liver. An oil is obtained from shark liver that has great therapeutic value because of its high vitamin content. The tiger shark is usually found swimming near the surface of warm ocean waters.

The thresher shark has a very long tail fin. It waves this fin back and forth in the water and thus stuns small fish which the shark then eats. Sometimes a team of threshers will work together to keep a school of fish in an inlet while the sharks feed on them. Thresher sharks are found in temperate as well as in warm waters.

The most unusual looking shark is the hammerhead. Its flat, hammer-shaped head extends out beyond each side of its body.

In general, most sharks are animals that it is well for man to avoid. The basking shark is an exception. The first one to be captured, in 1928, caused a sensation because of its tremendous size; but despite its dimensions, it does not have the predatory nature of other sharks. The average basking shark is about thirty feet long. It has many small teeth and it lives on small sea animals and plankton. It was a basking shark, a veritable sea monster, that followed the famous raft, the Kon-Tiki, for some time during its epic crossing of the Pacific Ocean. All the shark did was to escort the raft until it lost interest in this strange floating object; it made no attempt to attack the raft, no doubt much to the relief of the raft's occupants.

The skin of sharks is hard and thick. It is used to make fine leather goods. Sharks are covered with small scales, each ending in a sharp curved "tooth." The resemblance to human teeth is astonishing. Each "tooth" on a scale has a pulp cavity with nerves and blood vessels and is covered with enamel. If a scale is lost a new one grows in to replace it. Before these scales are removed from it, sharkskin is called shagreen. Shagreen is sometimes used for sanding wood.

There are two fish that have no fear of sharks. One, called the pilot fish, is often found in the immediate vicinity of sharks, feeding on the scraps of food left by them. The pilot fish is about sixteen inches long, and looks tiny alongside the shark. The other fish, the remora, or shark-sucker, has a suction disc on its head. It attaches itself by this disc to the body of a shark and hitches a ride. It also feeds on leavings from the shark's meals.

The normal feeding hours of a shark, when they are most dangerous, are around sunrise and sunset. Other times they keep to the bottom or, not infrequently, cruise near the top, with just their dorsal and tail fins showing.

THE TURTLES

THE most famous tortoises, as well as the largest, are those found in the Galapagos Islands. Individuals among these giant land tortoises have weighed four and five hundred pounds.

At one time there were great numbers of land tortoises living on the volcanic Galapagos. However during the whaling days in the South Pacific men discovered that they could be used for meat. Thousands of them were packed aboard whaling vessels and killed for food. The tortoises could go for long periods without food and water. They were slaughtered as needed to provide the crew members with fresh meat. After whaling had stopped, because of the discovery of petroleum, fishermen still continued to kill large numbers of these turtles for the oil that could be secured from their bodies.

Today the Galapagos tortoises are in danger of being totally exterminated. They ap-parently lay very few eggs and these as well as the young turtles are destroyed by the rats, wild dogs, cats, and other animals which man has introduced into these islands. Some of them can be seen in zoos, but they have seldom bred in captivity.

The desert tortoise, found in western American deserts, is related to the Galapagos tortoise but it is much smaller, only about ten inches long. These desert tortoises, like their larger relatives, eat cacti. They are not active during the heat of the day, but rest in underground hiding places. When the temperature falls in the evening they come out to feed.

During mating season the males often have battles over the females. They try to tip each other over and one is sometimes successful. With a great deal of effort a tortoise can succeed in getting back on its feet, but in the meantime the victor has gone off with the female.

Turtles which live in a completely different environment are the sea turtles. The largest of these is the leatherback which may be six to eight feet long and weigh over a thousand pounds, although turtles of this size are rare. The green turtle, caught commercially for food, may weigh four hundred pounds.

Most sea turtles live in warm ocean waters. Their legs have become modified into flippers so that they can make rapid progress, sometimes reaching a speed of twenty miles through the water. They still need to breathe air and must come up to the surface at least every few hours.

Sea turtles return to land to lay their eggs. The female laboriously crawls up on a sandy beach and digs a hole in which she may deposit as many as one hundred eggs. Then she

Turtles are cold blooded; their body temperature is regulated by the air temperature. Thus they cannot survive extremes of cold or heat.

covers them with sand, and goes back to the sea.

The eggs hatch from one to three months later and the tiny young turtles get down to sea as fast as they can. Many young are lost to predators such as gulls, ospreys and large fish. In some regions turtle eggs are considered to be a great delicacy, and people dig them up. Because of the decreasing numbers of sea turtles, an effort is being made to protect them, and it is unlawful in many places to disturb their nests.

There are also turtles which live in fresh water. One of the most fascinating of these is the alligator snapper, which lives in the southern part of the United States. The alligator snapper may measure more than two feet in length and may weigh one hundred and fifty pounds. It spends its life almost entirely in the water; only the female comes out to lay her eggs on land.

The alligator snapper has its own built-in fish lure—a projection on the front of its tongue which looks like a wiggling worm. Any fish that investigates this lure is apt to become food for the turtle.

Turtles are the oldest living order of reptiles. Their ancestors were on earth two million years ago, even before the dinosaurs, and present-day turtles have not changed

During the mating season, the male desert tortoises fight among themselves for the females. Victory in such battles goes to the one that succeeds in tipping its opponent over on its back, as pictured above. This predicament, although difficult to recover from quickly, does not have the fatal consequences that frequently attend the battles of males of other species.

very much since then. It is thought that their shell has aided their survival.

All of them lay eggs and all of them have shells. This shell, covered with horny plates in most species and with leathery skin in others, is the turtle's defense against its enemies. Because of this heavy shell, a turtle moves slowly on land. A tortoise can travel about one quarter of a mile in an hour, if it does not decide to rest on the way. Turtles are cold-blooded, which means that their body temperature is regulated by the temperature of the air. For this reason they are not found in very cold climates, and must hibernate during the winter months in temperate regions. Those that live in hot climates cannot stay in the sun—they would die if exposed for any length of time to a temperature above 110° F.—and must hide in shaded or cool spots during the day.

Yet with luck, turtles can live to be older than most other animals. There is a record of one tortoise in captivity that lived to be one hundred and fifty years old. In the United States the word turtle is usually used to refer to those species which live largely in water; the word tortoise to those species which live entirely on land.

There are about two hundred species of turtles found in the world today.

Although it is adapted to life in the water, the sea turtle must come up to the surface to breathe air from time to time.

The desert tortoise is not equipped to outfight or outrace an enemy: when danger nears, its only defense is to retract within its protective shell and wait for the situation outside to improve, a tactic that assures it great longevity.

THE IGUANAS

IGUANAS are those lizards that belong to the Iguanidae family. There are about seven hundred species of them. They are found only in the New World, in certain islands in the South Pacific, and in Madagascar.

In eastern United States the most common iguana is the fence lizard. It is grayish-brown but has blue scales underneath its body. It was given its name because it is often seen running along fences or resting in the sun on them.

Western iguanas include the horned lizards, the sand lizards, and the utas. The

Having a fierce and foreboding expression, the Galapagos land iguana is four feet long when fully grown. It has been unfortunately reduced in number by the activities of men, and dogs and pigs which root out its eggs.

horned lizards, or horned toads as they are sometimes called, may, if frightened, squirt a small amount of blood from their eyes. The utas are among the smallest iguanas, the adults measuring only about five inches in total length.

Another interesting iguana of the Southwest is the chuckwalla. If an enemy threatens it, it hides in between rocks and inflates its body. The enemy finds that it is almost impossible to pull the inflated chuckwalla out of its hiding place.

The anoles are a fascinating group of iguanas. They are found in tropical or sub-tropical regions. Depending on the temperature and light, they can change their color from brown to green. The males have a red skin flap on their throats which they inflate during courtship or as a warning to other males to keep out of their territory.

The largest iguanas are the common iguanas which live in tropical Central and South America. They may be as long as six feet including their tails, but the tails account for about two-thirds of the total length. They look like animals which have survived from the earliest days of the earth.

Common iguanas are vegetarians; they eat leaves and fruit. With their strong claws they can easily climb to the highest limbs of the tropical forest trees. The females lay their eggs in the ground; the young iguanas hatch in about two months.

People who live in the regions where the common iguanas are found consider them to be a great food delicacy. The iguanas, however, are not easy to capture since they can escape by climbing, by running, or even by swimming.

Two of the rarest iguanas live in the Galapagos Islands off the coast of South America. The first of these is the marine iguana, the only iguana which feeds on seaweed. One of its favorite foods is sea lettuce. They are excellent swimmers, but usually feed close to shore at low tide. After they eat, they spend the rest of the day basking in the sun along the rocky coast.

Most of the marine iguanas are blackish like the volcanic rock on which they live. However, on some of the islands the iguanas have patches of red or green during the mating season. At this time too, there are apt to be head-butting battles between males and even between females looking for places in the sand where they could lay their eggs. Each female lays only two eggs—some other species of iguanas may lay as many as eighty eggs—which hatch in about two and a half months. Newly hatched marine iguanas are about ten or eleven inches long; adults may be from three to four feet in length.

The other Galapagos iguanas are the land iguanas which are from two to four feet

Scattered upon the surface of a seaside ledge, motionless in the heat of a brilliant noonday sun, are many hundreds of the darkly colored marine iguanas, native to the Galapagos.

long. They live on cacti and other plants. Their numbers have been greatly reduced by dogs, by pigs which eat iguana eggs, and by humans who use them for food.

There are two species of land iguanas found on different islands of the Galapagos. In one species the males become red and yellow during certain seasons; in the other species there is no color change from the usual yellowish-brown.

In 1964, leading scientists of many countries established the Darwin Research Station in the Galapagos. One of the purposes of this biological station is to find out, by studying various plant and animal interrelations, what conservation measures are necessary to save the rare and unique animals of these islands, including the land iguanas. There are now thriving colonies of these only on two of the eight islands.

Both the marine and the land iguanas of the Galapagos were first described by Charles Darwin in his *Journal*. He visited the Galapagos early in the nineteenth century.

From these two photographs, the difference between the land iguana (above) *and the marine iguana* (below) *of the Galapagos Islands, may be easily observed.*

USEFUL SNAKES

TRADITIONALLY, snakes are animals towards which man has shown a profound aversion. This crawling animal arouses man's fear and repugnance, and seems to represent to him a menace against which he would find it difficult to protect himself. The cold, unwavering glance of the snake's immobile eyes does not inspire affection. And yet one cannot say that snakes are ugly. If man did not have such a deep-seated prejudice against snakes, he would admire their elegance, their splendid and varied colors, and their marvelous motion. Another thing which should be kept in mind is that many snakes are not poisonous or dangerous but that, on the contrary, they are very useful to farmers and are even protected in some countries.

Members of the Colubrine family, the largest family of snakes, are found nearly everywhere in the world. Most of them are not poisonous. They eat rodents, especially rats and mice. Some members of this family are even called rat snakes. There are five kinds of rat snakes found in the United States.

The bull snake, or gopher snake as it is called on the Pacific Coast, is about six feet long and is yellowish-brown in color with symmetrical brown spots. When surprised, this snake coils, hisses and even rattles its tail. If a farmer in mid-western United States is having his crops eaten by rodents, he tries to catch bull snakes and put them in his fields. After the bull snake is let loose, it is not long before the farmer's crops no longer suffer from the rodents. The bull snake follows its prey down into the depths of their burrows, crushes them in its powerful coils and eats them. Above ground it also kills its prey by constriction.

Other snakes which aid in the control of rodents are the corn snakes, yellowish-brown with red spots, the pilot black snakes and the coachwhip snakes. The coachwhip snakes were given that name because they look like whips used by coachmen.

In India, many folk tales are told about the Indian rat snake. It sometimes grows to eight feet in length and is supposed to be a welcome visitor in houses infested with rats and mice.

The rat snakes of Madagascar are of great help to the sugar plantation owners because the snakes keep the rodent population under control. Otherwise the rodents would do great damage to the sugar cane crops.

The indigo snake, handsomer and more amiable in character than the bull snake, is also entitled to the farmer's gratitude. If man could get used to these inoffensive creatures and overcome his repulsion, he would do justice to allies that make few demands on him.

The king snakes will attack and eat other snakes, including the poisonous rattlesnakes. The king snake almost always comes out the victor in these combats, especially if the rattlesnake is smaller. The king snake seems immune to the rattlesnake's venom. The king snake kills its adversary by strangling it in its coils, and then eats it, starting with the victim's head. In addition to snakes, the king snake will eat rats, small animals and birds. There are about fifteen species of king snakes found in North America.

Whatever the reason for man's aversion to snakes, it is often inappropriate, for many snakes are helpful to man.

The colors of the varying hare change with the seasons, from white to brown.

THE HARES

In early spring the European male hares can be seen doing all kinds of strange antics—leaping in the air, tumbling about on the ground, and fighting among themselves.

From the description "as mad as a March hare" it is obvious that this behavior is customary at the beginning of the hare's mating season.

Hares belong to the same family as rabbits. Hares, however, are usually larger than rabbits. Their young are born with fur and with their eyes open. Rabbits are born naked and with their eyes closed.

Hares and rabbits are very important in the balance of nature. They are food for thousands of predators, foxes, owls, hawks, snakes, weasels, coyotes, bobcats and many others. Consequently the hares are in constant danger, and only a small percentage of them live for longer than a year. They have no means of defense, although a mother hare will try to fight to protect her young. They can run very fast and sometimes escape from enemies in this way. The jackrabbit of western United States (which is really a hare) has been clocked at a speed of forty miles an hour. It can make twenty-foot leaps, too. Jackrabbits are perhaps the fastest of all the hares.

During the day hares spend most of their time resting in "forms" on their territory. These "forms" are just favorite sitting places where the hare feels protected—in a log, or a brush pile, or sometimes in the open. In the evening and during the night the hares feed. They are vegetarians and will eat almost all kinds of plants.

One of the most interesting hares of North America is the varying hare. It is also called the snowshoe rabbit because of its furred feet, with which it can walk easily on snow. During the winter this hare has thick white fur. Only its ear tips are black. However, in the spring it begins shedding its white fur, and its brown summer coat starts coming in. By midsummer it is completely brown. In the fall it begins turning white again. These color changes make it much harder for its enemies to see the varying hare in its natural habitat.

Varying hares mate in early spring and the young are born in about a month. The average size of the litter is four. The mother does not prepare a nest for them. During the day she stays near them, but she nurses them only at night. Within a few weeks they are eating grass, and are weaned when they are about a month old. They mate for the first time when they are a year old. Varying hares may weigh as much as four pounds and be as long as eighteen inches.

Another hare which changes color with the seasons is the large arctic hare. It may weigh up to twelve pounds in Alaska, where the largest ones are found. Arctic hares provide food for many of the animals of the Arctic, including the bears, the snowy owls and the foxes, as well as for the Eskimos.

The crab's hard shell serves it as armor plating, protecting the tender flesh beneath.

THE CRABS

CRABS seem to have no head because they have no neck. Their body is protected by a carapace, a shell, from which five pairs of claws emerge. The first pair of claws have pincers on them.

This very valuable carapace is also a recurrent source of danger to the crab. The crab cannot grow while it is enclosed in its shell. For this reason, periodically during its years of growth, it must molt the old shell and replace it with a new one. In the short period from the time the crab sheds its old shell until the time the new shell hardens the crab is without protection. It must also grow to a larger size in this interval—which it manages to do by taking in large quantities of water and expanding its body. Most crabs try to stay hidden until they have new

hard shells, but many are lost to predators at this crucial stage.

The crab is surrounded by enemies because its meat is sought for, not only by man, but by all sorts of animals: birds, fish and octopuses. Accordingly, it tries to escape notice as much as possible. Many crabs are camouflaged so that it is difficult to see them in their natural environment. For example the crab *Dromia vulgaris* has a large number of spines on its carapace. These become covered with little pebbles, algae, shellfish, and pieces of sponge. Thus the crab merges with its surroundings and is almost invisible.

Crabs usually move sideways, but they also walk backward or forward. When trying to escape danger, they travel quickly.

The rock crabs of the northeastern coasts of the United States remain motionless among rocks during the day or else dig a hole in the sand with their powerful pincer claws and bury themselves completely. At night they come out hunting for food. They eat a wide variety of food, both living and dead, animal and plant.

The most dangerous enemies of crabs that live in the ocean are the octopus and the dorado, or dolphin fish. The octopus paralyzes the crab with its tentacles, which cover it with a sticky liquid. The dorado uses its teeth to attack the crab's carapace; once a hole has been made, the fish eats the crab's flesh. The crab cannot defend itself unless the dorado attacks one of its claws. In that case the crab sheds the limb and escapes. The claw will grow on again at the crab's next molt. The dorado only attacks smaller species of crabs.

The largest crab known is the Japanese spider crab. Its very long legs may measure ten feet from claw to claw. Smaller species of spider crabs are found along the Atlantic and Pacific coasts of North America. They are named for their small bodies and long legs.

One of the most familiar European species is the tourteau or edible crab of the Atlantic and the North Sea; it is rare in the Mediterranean. It can be up to two feet across and weigh as much as thirteen pounds. During the Eocene epoch it was very common in all the seas of the world, and fossil specimens of it have been found almost everywhere.

Along the Atlantic coast in the western hemisphere the best crab for food is the blue crab. It lives not only in the ocean, but is also found in brackish and even fresh-water rivers along the coast. "Soft-shelled crabs" are blue crabs caught and used for food at the time of their molt; their new shells have not had a chance to harden. They are eaten shell and all.

Some crabs live on beaches, burrowing into the sand. One of these is the fiddler crab. The male fiddler crab has one very large claw which it uses to attract a mate and to fight other male fiddler crabs during the mating season. If this large claw should

be lost to a predator, it will be replaced at the crab's next molt, but on the opposite side of the body.

Fiddler crabs usually dig their burrows in the sand between the areas of the beach covered with water at high tide and dry at low tide. When the tide goes out, the crabs come out of their holes to feed. Since they eat during the day, it is possible to observe them on isolated beaches. If they are disturbed, they run back to their burrows.

Fiddler crabs eat organic matter which they find in the sand. Females use their two small claws to roll this material into little pellets. The males use only their single small claws for eating, never their large claws. Before the tide comes in, the crabs return to their holes and close up the entrances. They rest there until the next low tide.

Young fiddlers and adult females are brownish-gray, as are adult males when they first come out of their burrows. However, during the day, in some species, the males' shells gradually change so that they are almost white with orange-yellow claws. If they are caught, their color changes back to gray-brown, as it also does at the end of the day. These color changes are caused by hormones in the crabs' bodies.

Fiddler crabs are often quite small creatures. Some measure about one inch across their shell and a little less than that from head to back.

Sand or ghost crabs are also burrowing crabs. It is almost impossible to see them on sand because of their protective coloring. However, they usually come out to feed only at night when they are relatively safe from shore birds.

There are also many species of land crabs, especially in the tropics. Although they must live their early life in the sea, breathing through gills, as adults they live on land. During the day they hide under rocks and logs, coming out at night to look for food.

The hermit crabs are not true crabs because they lack shells. In order to protect themselves they use discarded sea shells such as those of periwinkles and whelks. As the hermit crabs grow, they have to find new and bigger shell "houses." When these crabs walk around, they carry their shells with them. The largest hermit crab is the coconut

The movement of most crabs on land is relatively slow and awkward compared to their movement in water, which buoys them up.

or robber crab. It is able to open a coconut with its claws and may even climb up coconut trees to cut down the nuts. It lives on South Pacific islands.

The vivid plumage of the adult goldeneye is just a promise in the duckling's down.

THE GOLDENEYES

GOLDENEYES are diving ducks which nest in holes in trees, usually near a fresh-water pond or lake. The females lay from eight to twelve eggs in the nest and cover them with down. When the ducklings hatch, they remain in the nest for about two days. Then they jump down from the tree and follow their mother to water where they can feed.

The common goldeneyes are found throughout the world in the northern hemisphere. They nest as far north as the tree line in the summer, but spend the winter in coastal waters or in fresh water that is not cold enough to be frozen.

They are handsome ducks. The male weighs about two and a half pounds. He has a dark green head with a distinctive white face patch and yellow eyes. In flight and when he is sitting on the water much of his body appears white; he has dark wings, a dark tail and dark stripes down his back. The female is smaller and is grayish-white with a brown head. She has no face patch.

The goldeneyes fly as fast as fifty miles an hour and their wings make a loud whistling sound. For this reason they are sometimes called "whistlers."

They dive for their food—crayfish, water insects, mussels, and other shellfish.

Another goldeneye found in the western part of North America, as well as in a few isolated spots on the eastern coast, is Barrow's goldeneye. It looks much like the common goldeneye, but the male has a dark purplish head and a crescent-shaped white face patch. These western birds nest along streams high in the Rocky Mountains. They, too, build their nests in holes in trees.

The blue-footed booby nests from Baja California south to Peru and on the Galapagos Islands. The young are white and downy.

THE BOOBIES

IT IS not really known exactly why boobies were given that name by sailors who first saw them and may have visited their nesting colonies on tropical islands. The sailors may have thought that the birds were "boobies" because they were so trusting. Since boobies nest, for the most part, on small uninhabited islands, they were unacquainted with men and permitted the sailors to approach without showing any signs of the fear that wild animals normally show at the approach of men.

Regardless of the reason, the six species of gannets living in tropical waters have retained the common name of booby.

Boobies are relatively large sea birds. They are white and black or white and brown, depending on the species. The colorful parts of their bodies are those covered by naked skin rather than feathers. For instance there are the blue-footed boobies, the blue-faced boobies, and the red-footed bobbies. But these colors may change between the breeding and the non-breeding seasons.

Most boobies tend to nest in colonies. It is thought that those living below the equator nest between October and April, although being tropical birds, they may also have no definite nesting season. The adult males usually arrive at the future nesting sites first and pick a territory. The females soon follow, and each accepts a particular male as her mate. Most boobies mate for life and the pair bond is strong.

Boobies generally nest on the ground, although a few species build crude nests in trees. A common display among them is for the male to offer the female a twig or pebble for the nest. Other ceremonies may include mutual neck preening and an uptilting of heads. Their cries on the nest grounds are described as trumpeting and whistling. Most boobies raise only one young each season, although they may lay two or more eggs. Both the female and the male incubate the eggs and care for the young birds. The young booby is almost nude when it first comes out of the egg, but within a short time it is

Boobies at sea fly ahead of a ship looking for the flying fish that skitter off the bow wave.

covered with white down. Both parents feed their offspring, at first with regurgitated food and later with small whole fish.

During the first days of its life the young booby is shielded from the hot tropical sun by its brooding parents. Later, however, the parents leave it for ever-increasing periods of time. Soon the young bird loses its down, and in about four to six months its first plumage of mottled brown and white feathers comes in. At last it is ready to take off to sea and fish for itself.

The young boobies wander far from their nesting sites and may travel thousands of miles. During each molt their feathers become closer to the colors of the adult plumage. Finally, after from three to five years they return to their ancestral grounds to mate.

Boobies are expert fishers. They fly above the water until they sight a fish. Then with wings closed or half closed, they dive often from heights of fifty feet or more. They can swim underwater, using both their wings and feet. They eat the fish underwater, rather than returning to shore with it.

Boobies tend to feed in small flocks in the early morning and in the late afternoon. During bright moonlit nights they may fly all night. They are often harassed by frigatebirds which make them regurgitate the fish they have been lucky enough to catch.

THE ALBATROSSES

ALBATROSSES are truly birds of the sea; only when they nest do they come to land. Gliding on long, pointed wings, albatrosses ride the winds for hours and may travel several hundred miles a day. At night they rest on the surface of the sea, often feeding on squid and other small ocean animals during that time.

Of the fourteen species of albatrosses in the world, nine live entirely within the southern hemisphere. There they are found chiefly in the region between 30° and 60° south latitude where there are strong prevailing west winds. Albatrosses depend on winds not only to help them take off but also for sustained flight. On calm days these big birds are almost unable to take off.

Albatrosses have followed ships in southern waters since the early days of exploration in the seventeenth century. Sailors call the larger species gooney birds and the smaller ones mollymawks.

Sometimes an albatross will accidentally land on the deck of a ship and for a time be unable to take flight. If it is approached by a man, it will disgorge a jet of yellow oil from its mouth, apparently in an attempt to defend itself.

Most albatrosses nest on remote islands, usually in colonies. The males arrive first and begin occupying their territories. When the first females come, each is surrounded by several male birds. The males, in turn, bow and spread their wings. After all have finished, the female selects her mate and goes off to the nesting site with him. Then the paired birds begin their courtship displays, nibbling at each other's feathers, throwing their heads up, stretching out their wings and occasionally braying.

The black-browed albatross does not often come to land, and may, between landing on land once and landing once again, soar over thousands of miles of vacant ocean. It may even travel completely around the globe out of sight of land, which it comes to only to mate and to raise its young.

Nests are used year after year although not by the same pairs. Some species build nests of mud and grasses on the ground. The male brings the material in his beak to the female and she arranges it into a small cone-shaped nest. Eventually she lays a single white egg which both parents take turns incubating for seventy to eighty days depending on the species.

When the young albatross finally hatches, it is covered with down. It is fed by its father and mother for a long period; for example, young of the largest albatrosses stay in the nest for eight months. Only then are they fully feathered and able to fly.

Once the young birds leave the nest they spend their next few years on the ocean. When they are fully mature, they join the other breeding albatrosses on islands.

The wandering albatross is the largest. It has an eleven-foot wing spread and is about four feet long.

One of the most common albatrosses of the southern hemisphere is the black-browed albatross, which has a wing spread of seven and a half feet. These birds nest on many islands, including the Falklands. Sealers and whalers used to raid their nests for eggs, as they did many other colonies of nesting albatrosses.

Most albatrosses are gray and white or black and white, but two species, the sooty and light-mantled sooty, are brownish-gray. The sooties do not nest in colonies but in pairs in hidden spots on cliffs on sub-antarctic islands.

The Laysan and the black-footed albatrosses nest on islands in the Pacific.

The black-browed albatross builds a tall nest. Some species lay their eggs on bare ground.

THE GULLS

The mewling cries of gulls soaring high in the air is a familiar sound in many coastal cities. Yet it still seems strange to see these long-winged birds circling in the air above tall buildings.

The raucous gulls are a welcome addition to harbor cities, for they are valuable scavengers. They keep the waters clean of garbage and of dead animal matter. They usually alight on the water to pick up their food, but will sometimes swoop down and pick up food on the wing. If several gulls see the same piece of food at the same time, there may be a noisy fight about it.

Some gulls also eat clams and other shell fish. However, they are not able to open the shells with their beaks, so they have devised an ingenious method of getting the creatures which live inside. The birds pick up the clams in their beaks and fly over a beach, or a concrete road or even a parking lot, and drop the clam. The shell breaks and the gull swoops down and eats the clam.

Most gulls are seen near shore. They will follow ships for a short distance to see if gar-bage might be discarded, but will turn back before they are too far out to sea. Only the kittiwake, one of the smaller gulls, is known to travel long distances at sea. It seems to follow the fishing fleets. Kittiwakes banded in England have been found later in Newfoundland on the North American coast.

Gulls are sociable birds and nest in colonies with other gulls and even with other sea birds such as terns, puffins and cormorants. However, if a nest is left unattended in such colonies, the gulls will eat the eggs and young of the other birds. Gulls usually lay two or three brown speckled eggs in a nest of seaweed on an isolated beach or on an uninhabited small rocky island. The young are covered with mottled brown down and are able to run about from the time they hatch, but stay near the nesting site for a month or more. If the baby gulls make the mistake of wandering into a neighboring gull's nest, they are apt to be killed.

It takes the larger species of gulls about three years to get their adult gray and white, black and white, or all white plum-

Swallow-tailed gulls nest on the Galapagos Islands but are found along the coasts of Peru and Ecuador at the end of their nesting period. They are the only gulls that have forked tails. In flight they look rather like their smaller relatives the terns.

If gulls can stay alive during the first year of their lives, they often live for many years. There is a record of one banded herring gull that lived in the wild for twenty-eight years.

There are forty-three species of gulls in the world and they range in size from eleven inches to thirty-two inches. The great black-backed gull is one of the largest, as is the nearly white glaucous gull. Both species are found in the northern hemisphere.

Perhaps the most commonly seen gull is the herring gull. It is a large gull, measuring about twenty-six inches in length. It has a gray back and black wing tips.

Along the West Coast of the United States the common gull is the California gull. It looks rather like a small herring gull but it

Nesting swallow-tailed gulls may be found in the Galapagos at almost any time of the year. A single egg is laid among the rocks.

age. Before that time they have flecked brown and white feathers and look very different from adult birds. With each succeeding year their plumage gets lighter in color, so that it is possible to tell the approximate age of young birds.

has greenish legs, instead of pinkish. The California gull is immortalized by a monument in Salt Lake City. When the Mormons first settled in Utah, a plague of crickets descended on their crops. These insects were eaten by flocks of California gulls, and enough of the crop was saved to see the Mormons through the next year. To show their gratitude the Mormons had a statue made of the California gull.

Another species of gull which may be found far inland from the sea is the small black-headed Franklin gull. During the summer months it lives in the interior parts of the United States, nesting in marsh areas. At the time of plowing, Franklin gulls often follow the plow, scratching up uncovered insects. However, in the fall these gulls migrate south and spend the winter in salt water along the Gulf Coast.

Two gulls nest on the Galapagos Islands, the swallow-tailed and the dusky. During the time when it is not nesting, the swallow-

which has a forked tail. A white triangle can be seen in its long gray wings when the gull is in flight. It eats squid and fish that swim near the surface of the water.

This bird nests on many of the Galapagos Islands and possibly on other small islands to the north. A single egg is laid from which hatches a downy chick. The young gulls are sometimes eaten by the Galapagos hawks.

The dusky gull is a grayish-brown bird. Like many other animals of the Galapagos it is exceedingly friendly to and curious about men who come to these islands.

Dusky gulls nest all through the year but are very secretive about their nesting sites. Their main food seems to be small crustaceans.

tailed gull makes a long trip over the sea to the coasts of Ecuador and Peru; the dusky gull, on the other hand, stays closer to home, and is seldom found far away from islands near the Galapagos.

The swallow-tailed gull is the only gull

A frequent sight at the seashore, especially near dunes where they nest, are groups of great black-backed gulls with a few darker young among them.

THE PARROTS

Parrots have been popular as pets since the days of the ancient Greeks and Romans. Old prints show Christopher Columbus presenting a parrot at the court of Ferdinand and Isabella. Robinson Crusoe had a parrot on his desert island, which he brought back with him to England. There are always parrots in pirate and sailing stories. Much of their popularity is due to the ability of these birds to imitate human speech as well as other sounds when in captivity.

Parrots are found in tropical regions around the world. There are over three hundred species that range in size from about four inches to about forty inches. The smallest are the pygmy parrots of New

Guinea. The largest are the macaws of Central and South America, and their total length includes their very long tails.

Macaws are often seen in zoos. They have raucous cries and are seldom still during the day. Their beaks are so strong they can crack Brazil nuts with them. They do not talk as well as some of the other parrots, but they are very colorful with their green, red, yellow and blue feathers. In their native homes they are said to travel in pairs rather than in flocks, as do so many other parrots.

The best talker is supposed to be the African gray parrot. It is a handsome bird with gray feathers on its body and deep red feathers on its rather short tail. It has pale gray eyes. This is probably the bird that was a favorite with the Romans.

The best talkers of the New World parrots are the amazons from Central and South America. They are usually green with touches of red or yellow somewhere on their bodies. They have short tails and sturdy bodies. If they are trained when they are still young they can often acquire a good vocabulary of words and even whole phrases. Of course, they do not understand what they say, but merely imitate human sounds.

Many families have a small parakeet, the budgerigar, as a pet. These little birds originally come from Australia where they are often found in flocks like sparrows. They eat seeds. They do well in captivity and an occasional budgie may even learn a few words. Originally they were green birds with some yellow and blue feathers, but in captivity selective breeding has produced blue, white, and even mauve birds. In England there are special budgerigar shows each year with prizes given for color and form.

In the animal order embracing parrots, there are some three hundred different species, including parakeets, macaws, and cockatoos, like the sulphur-crested cockatoo shown here.

The tongue of the rainbow lorikeet is well adapted for getting nectar from flowers.

Other parrots from Australia include the handsome cockatoos. They are big birds and have crests on their heads. Like the macaws they are not especially good talkers but are kept in zoos because of their beauty. In their homeland they travel in noisy flocks.

The rainbow lorikeets, found in Australia and the East Indies, have tongues that are especially adapted for getting nectar from flowers. These birds first crush the flowers and then lap up the nectar. They travel in large flocks.

One of the most unusual parrots is the owl

parrot of New Zealand. It has lost the power of flight and is now rare because so many have been killed by predatory animals brought into New Zealand by settlers. This parrot is about twenty inches long and is yellow, green, black and brown.

The owl parrot is mainly active at night in the beech forests where it lives. During the day it sleeps under the roots of trees or in cracks in rocks. It climbs trees to find its

The rainbow lorikeets, native to Australia, frequently travel in large flocks.

A distinguishing characteristic of the cockatoo is the crest on its head, a band of feathers that it can raise and fan forward at will.

food—fruits and leaves—and when it has finished eating it glides down.

These birds also nest under tree roots or among rocks. The two or three white eggs are incubated by both parents for about three weeks.

Another unusual parrot of New Zealand is the kea. These brownish-green birds live

Although the parrot has a reputation for ability to learn to speak, in nature it imitates no voice other than its own, which is unmusical.

above the timberline in the mountains during the summer and nest among the rocks. However with the coming of winter the keas move down to warmer areas. After extensive sheep ranching was begun by settlers in New Zealand, the keas discovered a new source of food in winter—the discarded remains of slaughtered sheep. They acquired such a taste for sheep fat that eventually the birds began killing live sheep. New Zealanders put a bounty on keas for some time, but finally found that the way to keep the birds from killing sheep was simply to bury remains of slaughtered sheep so the keas could not learn to eat meat.

New Guinea and nearby islands are the home of the tiny pigmy parrots. They have tails similar to those of woodpeckers and use them in much the same way.

Some species of pigmy parrots build their nest in the nests of termites; others nest in holes in trees. For some unknown reason it is impossible to keep pigmy parrots alive in captivity.

At one time there were parrots in the United States. They were called Carolina parakeets. Great flocks of them lived in the country east of the Rockies. Unfortunately when the country was being settled, and before the days of conservation, farmers killed large numbers of these birds because they ate the fruit on the farmers' trees. When a few birds were shot, the flock would return to see what had happened to them. It was then easy for the farmer to kill the rest of the flock. None have been seen since 1920.

Most parrots nest in holes and lay white eggs. They have strong beaks and thick tongues. They eat nuts, seeds and fruits. Some of them use their claws to hold and to bring food to their mouths, almost as if their

claws were hands. Many kinds of parrots are thought to mate for life.

The little love birds, small parrots found in Asia and Africa, make perhaps the most obviously devoted mates in the bird world. When caged, they show each other constant attention and if one dies the other is said to pine away unless another mate is provided for it.

THE BARN OWLS

Barn owls have been called "feathered flying mousetraps," which is a good description of them since they eat mice and rats almost exclusively. For this reason, barn owls are especially valuable to farmers. Of all the owls these are the most apt to take up living quarters in man-made dwellings such as barns, church belfries, and abandoned houses. Because of their weird calls they have given many an old building a reputation of being haunted.

Barn owls have the most extensive range of all the owls in the world. They are found in every country except New Zealand and certain islands in the Pacific Ocean. There are nine or ten species of barn owls. They vary in color from the black ones of New Guinea to the familiar tan and white birds of North America.

Barn owls mate for life or at least for long periods of time. In the northern hemisphere the females lay from five to seven eggs very early in the spring. The eggs hatch in about a month. The young birds are fed mainly on rodents and, like their parents, cough up pellets of the undigestible parts such as fur and bones. The young owls are able to fly in two months.

Barn owls are rather large birds, adults measuring from twelve to nineteen inches in length. Adults do not migrate but remain in the same region winter and summer.

They catch their prey by sound, not by sight, and are able to hunt successfully in total darkness. Their heart-shaped faces seem to serve as a kind of screen to help them pick up the slightest sound when they are hunting.

Noiseless in flight, hunting only by sound, and living on rats and mice, the barn owl is rightly called a flying mousetrap.

THE PELICANS

PELICANS are often seen flying in flocks in a V shape or line formation. Sometimes, depending on the wind, they fly close to the water with their long wings nearly touching the waves. At other times they can be seen circling very high in the sky.

Pelicans are large birds. The average white pelican of North America weighs from ten to seventeen pounds when it is full grown. It is from four to five feet long and has a wingspan of eight or nine feet. Brown pelicans are smaller, usually weighing about eight pounds, and having a wingspan of seven and a half feet.

These birds are found almost everywhere in warm and temperate regions. The brown and the white pelicans are the only species in the Americas. In Europe, Africa, southern Asia, and Australia there are six species. Pelicans have existed in the world for a very long time. Fossil remains date back to between thirty or forty million years ago.

All pelicans have a throat, or gular, pouch which can be extended when they are feeding. The gular pouch of the American white pelican can hold as much as three gallons. This pelican fishes from the surface of the water; the brown pelican dives into the water for its food.

The white pelicans sometimes have a community fishing arrangement. They gather in a semi-circle on the surface of shallow water and with noisy splashings drive the fish in towards shore. Then, almost in unison, they gather the fish into their voluminous pouches. Pelicans for the most part eat "trash fish," that is, fish which are not valuable to the commercial fisherman.

In March and April the white pelicans of North America begin their long migration from the Gulf Coast to their inland breeding areas. Over mountains and deserts they fly, to islands in fresh water lakes in Utah, Wyoming, and western Canada. A few nest in coastal areas, but most of the seven major breeding areas of white pelicans in North America are in fresh water.

They nest in colonies of from a few birds to several hundred pairs, depending on the local food supply. They may lay their chalky white eggs on the ground or in mounds of earth from eight to twelve inches high.

Baby pelicans are naked when they come out of the eggs, but within a week they are covered with white down. Their first feathers are gray.

When the young are about four weeks old they leave their nest and gather into groups with other young pelicans.

From the time of hatching until the young are ready to feed on their own, the parents have had to supply each one with about one hundred and fifty pounds of fish. In order to do this the parent birds may have had to fly as far as one hundred miles a day to get food.

In September and October the white pelicans fly south to winter along the Gulf Coast.

The brown pelicans follow much the same breeding pattern, but they are coastal birds and are seldom seen inland.

The white pelican: a persistent fisherman with a dip net for a mouth and an appetite to match.

THE ODYSSEY
OF AN OTTER

THE POND

THE POND was a pleasant place in the spring. It had been made by a pioneer, who had also built a grist mill run by a large water wheel. The roof of the grist mill now sagged and most of the shingles were gone, but the water wheel was still there, held motionless by a rusty chain.

No one now lived near the pond except wild creatures. A mallard and her ducklings made their home in a patch of cattails on the lower shore. A blue heron came every day to fish and to catch frogs. A buck deer came to drink. Raccoons fished for frogs and clams in the shallow water along the upper shore. Weasels, minks, martens, bobcats, and coyotes came seeking prey. They were a constant menace to the mallard and her brood, to the muskrats, and to the rabbits that lived in the nearby thickets.

This haven for furred and feathered creatures was in a well-populated area of Wisconsin, where there were many farms and towns, but no hunters ever came to it with guns or dogs. The pond was part of a wildlife sanctuary, a refuge for dwellers of the wild.

The world here, as everywhere in thicket and stream country, was divided into two classes of creatures—the hunters and the hunted. The hunted kept their wits sharp and were ever watchful against death from the air or the ground. But there were two furred dwellers of the pond who hardly fitted into either class. They were otters. True, they fished for fish and frogs. But they never attacked the mallard or the muskrat or the rabbits. The pond was a natural home for them. Even so, they would not have tarried there long, except that Mother had a pair of babies in a den nearby, and Graymuzzle would not leave without her. Otters are great travelers. They stay in one place only in the spring when their young are too small to travel.

Mother and Graymuzzle were slim animals with lithe, slender bodies, small ears, and long, powerful tails. They wore fine fur coats highly prized in the fur trade. Mother was the worrying sort. She visited Flash and Tiny, her babies, at least once every hour.

Flash was larger than his sister Tiny, but neither was much bigger than a large field mouse. Their eyes were not yet open, but they had lusty voices. This was a time of danger for the babies. They were helpless, and any passing weasel, mink, or marten would kill them if it found the nest. Even the fox and the coyote would eagerly dine on young otter. But none of the killers would face a mother otter.

On a bright May morning, a she-fox passed close to the den. She paused to listen and to test the breeze, as any good hunter would do. She had to hunt steadily, because she had a litter of pups big enough to demand meat. She was close to the upper entrance to the den, but she could not see it, because it was screened by rose brier and shrubbery. It was an exit rather than an entryway, a sort of escape route should the main entrance become blocked. The real entrance to the den was an underwater tunnel, which opened into the den from the pond. Mother always entered through this tunnel.

Inside the den, Flash was awake. As usual, he was hungry. He raised his head and called for Mother. Outside, the fox cocked an ear. She listened intently until she had located the source of the sound and knew what it was. Then she moved toward the rose brier thicket. She thrust her head into the bushes. Looking down into the den, she saw the babies. Tiny was now awake; her voice rose with that of Flash. The fox's red tongue moved back and forth over her fangs and she gathered her legs under her for a leap. She must act quickly. These little ones would not be left unguarded for long.

Just then, Mother popped out of the tunnel below. She stood for a moment looking up as the head of the fox thrust through the bushes above. She hissed defiantly and arched her back. She was smaller than the fox, but she was defending her babies, and that made her fearless. She sprang up at the fox, which leaped back and moved well away from the bushes. Mother's slim muzzle thrust itself out of the thicket. Her hiss made the fox move away fast. She wanted no battle with a mother otter. She snarled savagely, but she went away.

Mother did not try to follow. On land she was no match for the speed of a fox. She slid back into the den and cuddled her babies. They began feeding at once. She was gentle with them, licking their soft fur, slicking them up carefully. Her encounter with the fox would make her twice as watchful.

After they had fed, the babies went back to sleep. During this period of their lives, they only ate and slept, caring nothing about the strange world they had entered. They depended entirely upon Mother. As with all wild babies, this was a most important time. If they could survive it, they would be able to cope with their enemies.

The job of looking after them was all Mother's. She would not let Graymuzzle help her or even come into the cave. He would not see his son and daughter until they left the den on their first outing.

She lay close to the sleeping babies for a long time. Out in the pond, Graymuzzle was whistling to her, coaxing her to come out and play games with him or help him catch a fish. He did not like to play alone. The muskrats would not play with him, no matter how often he made friendly advances to them. And the blue heron always flew away when he tried to be friendly.

Mother heard him, and wanted to play, but she was nervous because of the fox. At last she slipped down to the tunnel mouth and dived into the water. She swam with a speed that could match that of a trout or a bass, and she swam under water, turning on her side from time to time to check the surface. She spotted Graymuzzle and darted upward.

THE DONKEY ENGINE

Mother surfaced close to Graymuzzle, and their noses met for a moment. Then Graymuzzle was off, diving deep and swimming fast. Mother followed him down into the green depths. Bubbles streamed up in their wake. She swam as strongly and as swiftly as Graymuzzle. Their speed was so great that even a trout could not escape from them in a straightaway chase. They were playing a game, but if they came upon a fish, they would take it.

A donkey engine had once been used at the mill. It had been pushed into the pond, and now it sat at an angle on the bottom. It had an upright boiler with a short length of smokestack on top of it. The fire door at the base was closed, but there was a small draft door which was open. An ancient carp made the donkey engine his castle. He was a big fellow, and very old. He could squeeze through the draft door because his scaly body was very slick. The old engine had always been a fine place for him to hide from the otters.

Graymuzzle and Mother saw the carp, and dived down swiftly. The carp saw them, too. They were his only enemies, and he was always expecting them. With a flip of his tail he was off to his refuge in the donkey engine. As the carp wiggled through the draft door, Graymuzzle's sharp fangs were nipping at its flapping tail, but he could not get a good hold. The carp escaped.

Inside the boiler, the carp turned and pushed his pumping mouth close to the opening. His round wall-eyes stared out at Graymuzzle. If a carp could laugh, he would have laughed in Graymuzzle's face. Graymuzzle lunged at the fire door. He was very excited. This time he had almost caught the carp. He hit the door hard, and the rusty hinges broke. The door slid to the bottom of the pond, sending up muddy water.

Graymuzzle darted inside the engine. The flues had been removed for junk metal, and there was plenty of room in the boiler. Mother followed Graymuzzle. They could see nothing because the thrashing of the carp and the stir they made had agitated the rust and the mud inside the boiler. Up they went, seeking the carp. They shot out of the smokestack in a cloud of rusty, muddy water.

The ancient carp was forgotten. Here was a wonderful game. Graymuzzle dived down with Mother close behind him. They shot through the open fire door and popped out of the smokestack. Around and around they went, into the engine and out. Finally Mother surfaced and listened.

She did not hear her babies. They could be asleep, of course, but something might have happened to them. Perhaps the fox had returned. She dived, swam swiftly to the underwater tunnel, and entered the den. The babies were curled up asleep in their nest, and she lay down close to them.

One after another, the days at the pond slipped by peacefully. Graymuzzle was impatient to be off on the long journey the family would make as soon as the youngsters were able to travel. He and Mother had been over the route before, a long circle of streams and lakes and ponds. The circle always brought them back to the mill pond in time for Mother to fix up the den and rest until a new family arrived.

In the den, Flash was more active than Tiny. He was developing faster. Their eyes had been open for some time, and they had looked at everything inside the den. Flash did a great deal of poking around, and one day he climbed up to examine the upper exit. He reached it after much scratching and clawing, but he could not see anything because of the shrubbery. A dead bush thrust its dry limbs outward. Flash crept out on one of the dead branches. For the first time he looked at the world outside the den. It was very big compared with the little cave where he was born, and there were many strange things to see—tall trees, big rocks, the pond. An animal sat at the edge of a thicket. Flash was not afraid of it, for he had never seen a fox before. The fox had come out of the thicket to sun herself and did not notice him.

Flash looked down at the pond. The mallard hen was swimming, followed by her brood. They were fast developing wing feathers. Flash's interest shifted to the old mill. It looked very big to him. He failed to see the big owl perched on a beam under the A of the roof. The owl was on his daytime roost, but he was always alert and ready to swoop down if he saw movement.

Flash crept a bit farther out on the limb. He wanted to see more. The dead branch snapped under his weight and down he went, kicking and crying loudly. He landed on a grassy spot and started kicking to get his feet under him. Now he was frightened, and called for Mother.

The fox and the owl saw Flash the instant he fell. Both were trained hunters and always noticed movement. The fox got to her feet and moved forward, her belly close to the grass. Here was an easy meal. The big owl dived down, his great talons open wide, his hooked beak parted.

Flash looked up and saw the owl plummeting down upon him. He scrambled toward the rose brier bushes which screened the den opening. He ran as an otter runs, twisting and dodging. This was different from the owl's usual target. A rabbit or a squirrel runs in a straight line. The owl's talons missed Flash, partly because the fox had leaped in to seize the little otter. The two hunters collided. The owl beat his wings and ripped at the fox with talons and beak. The fox lashed back with her long fangs. While fur and feathers flew, Flash struggled to push his way up through the tangle of bushes.

Mother had heard Flash's cry for help and

had entered the den through the water tunnel. Scrambling out again through the upper exit, she saw Flash burst through the screen of shrubbery. Both the owl and the fox were ready to call off their fight. The fox leaped away and the owl beat his way into the air. Mother stood over Flash and licked his face, hissing softly to him. When she was sure that the attackers were leaving, she picked him up by the scruff of his neck and leaped up to the den opening. She dropped inside and put him down in the nest. Flash was glad to be snug in the den. In a very short time he had learned about some of the dangers lurking in the outside world. His first lesson had been a frightening one. It would make him remember that danger was on the ground and in the air. Strange animals and birds were not to be trusted.

Tiny had been frightened, too, because Flash had left her. She had scurried about, crying and looking for him. She tried to climb out the way he had done, but she was not able to get up the steep side of the den.

Mother stayed and calmed her youngsters. She knew that soon they would not stay in the den when she left to play or fish. She would have to take them with her. But she wanted them to be strong enough to cope with the enemies they would be certain to meet. They would always be friendly creatures, more interested in making friends with strange animals than in fighting them. This would be dangerous if they met a bobcat or a coyote. She was sure Flash had learned about at least two dangerous killers, but Tiny had still not had her first lesson.

Mother did not leave the den until Flash and Tiny curled up and went to sleep. Their fear passed quickly, as it always does with wild animals. Once the danger is out of sight, it passes from their minds like the shadow of a cloud passing across a meadow. But from now on Mother would stay closer to the den, and she would visit the youngsters more often. After a while, she went out, and surfaced in the pond close to the old mill. Graymuzzle called to her from the far side of the pond, and she answered. But she did not move. If he wanted to fish or play with her, he would have to come to her side. Graymuzzle finally came darting across the pond. As usual, Mother had had her way.

FIRST OUTING

One day in late spring, Mother led Flash and Tiny out of the den. She took them through the upper opening. Otters are among the finest swimmers in the wild, but the young must be taught to swim. They clambered out and down through the screen of bushes. Both kept close to Mother, because everything was strange. Flash had forgotten about his first adventure, but he would remember if he saw a fox or an owl. Graymuzzle was out in the pond. When he saw his family, he swam swiftly toward the bank where they had halted. He left the water and moved up the bank toward them.

Flash and Tiny backed away, hiding in the tall grass with just their heads showing. Graymuzzle was a stranger to them, and they were afraid of him. Although he and Mother looked alike, he was much bigger.

Mother trotted down the bank to Graymuzzle, and they rubbed noses and cheeks. She called to Flash and Tiny. She was very proud of them, and wanted them to meet their father. They watched her, but they did not move, and Graymuzzle trotted up the bank toward them. They ducked past him and raced to Mother's side. Flash hissed

defiantly when his father approached. He was ready to defend Mother, but he edged around behind her. Tiny pressed against her side. Graymuzzle nudged Tiny with his nose very gently, and hissed softly. He rolled her over in the grass, and she was won over at once. Flash watched warily for a few minutes. The stranger wasn't hurting Tiny. In fact, they seemed to be having fun. He gave in and ran to join the game.

Graymuzzle and Mother were eager to teach the youngsters to swim. Flash and Tiny were now ready to learn. Water deep enough for diving is an otter's best friend and protector. No predator can catch an otter once it gets into deep water. The parents were anxious to get the lessons over with so the family could start off on the long journey.

Mother played tag with Flash. She whirled and dashed toward the pond, with Flash following as fast as he could. He expected Mother to turn aside when she reached the water, but she fooled him. She leaped into the pond.

Flash tried to stop, but the mud bank was wet and slippery, and he shot forward when he planted his feet to halt. Out into the pond he went, where he promptly sank. Sputtering, kicking, lashing his tail, he went down; his eyes and mouth filled with water. Mother was waiting. She dived deep and came up under him. She lifted Flash out of the water on her back. Flash sputtered and

hissed, and got rid of the water he had swallowed. As soon as she was sure he had his breath back, Mother dived and left Flash struggling. Once again she rescued him. This went on for some time, until Flash began to use his feet and tail as he should. He managed to paddle enough to keep himself afloat, and he liked it. He didn't try to reach shore, as he had at first.

Graymuzzle took over Tiny's swimming lessons, but the tag trick did not work with her. She always stopped well back from the water. Graymuzzle began to get impatient. He led her to a spot where the bank dropped off steeply into the pond. Tiny looked down at the water and cried loudly.

Before she knew what was happening, Graymuzzle gave her a shove which sent her tumbling into the water. Then he shot down the bank on his belly, following her. Tiny had sunk immediately, and Graymuzzle dived and brought her to the surface. He kept her out in the pond until she could stay afloat and paddle a little.

Now a new world opened for the youngsters. Flash learned to dive, and to dart about under the water like Mother and Graymuzzle. Tiny was slower to learn. For a long time she was satisfied just to paddle about on the surface.

Flash was very much interested in the underwater world. He could not stay under as long as his parents, but he could manage a couple of minutes. Things looked very different when seen from beneath the surface. The ripples on the surface made everything move and change shape constantly. The mallard and her brood, for instance, became odd-looking creatures. The part of them that was in the water was clear and natural. It was the part out of the water which did strange things.

Flash soon learned that he could approach the other creatures in the pond by diving and swimming under water until he was very close to them. He worried the muskrat, which could not swim as fast as Flash could. Flash only wanted to be friendly, but the muskrat did not trust him. And in a way, the muskrat was right. For if an otter got hungry in a place where there were no fish or frogs, he would eat a muskrat.

When the buck deer came to drink, Flash would dive and swim close. He would watch the buck from only a few feet under water. The buck's antlers seemed to waver, the body to wiggle and twist, the legs to move in and out. As soon as Flash surfaced, the buck returned to normal. Flash always popped his head out of the water a yard or so from the buck. The big fellow merely snorted and stamped his hoofs, and sometimes shook his antlers.

The garter snake was a fascinating fellow to follow and watch from below. Seen from under the surface, the snake appeared to be dancing across the pond. He seemed very long—as long as twenty feet—because it was not possible to tell where the tail ended and the wake began.

The blue heron was another creature that Flash liked to watch. He liked to approach the long-legged bird when she was fishing for frogs in shallow water. The thin legs under water would be clear and steady. The body with its long neck and beak seemed to be doing a dance. Suddenly the heron would thrust her beak and head down into the water to spear a frog that had jumped into the pond. The beak and head could then be clearly seen. But as the heron took off to carry the frog to her young, the waves set in motion by her legs would turn her into a weird creature which seemed to be writhing in agony as she vanished into the sky.

There was fun, too, on the steep bank, where Mother and Graymuzzle had a toboggan slide which was worn smooth from use. Flash and Tiny learned to romp after them when they raced to the top of the bank. Mother and Graymuzzle went shooting down the slide on their bellies, and Flash and Tiny followed. Once the slide got wet and slick, the ride was a fast one. It ended with a big splash as they hit the water. Flash and Tiny would play for hours on the slide.

Another thing they liked to do was fish for minnows and frogs. At first Flash caught mostly frogs. They were easier to overtake. When he saw one jump into the pond, he darted after it and caught it before it could burrow into the mud bottom. His first adventure with a large fish came when he met the ancient carp. The carp fled one way, and Flash fled the other. The huge fish frightened him.

Then he started chasing mud minnows, and learned he could catch them by putting on a burst of speed. And one day he caught a six-inch brook trout in a fair chase, because he could swim faster than the trout.

Mother and Graymuzzle felt the youngsters were ready for the long journey. They would leave the sanctuary and enter country where they were not protected from trappers and hunters. They would also be fishing in waters claimed by fishermen. There were lodges along the streams and lakes where men from the cities came to fish, and few of the lodge owners liked the otters. They were sure that otters destroyed game fish.

But the lodge owners were mistaken. Like the other otters, Graymuzzle and his family would not harm the fishing. They would seldom stay longer than a day or two in any one place. They would always move on seeking new places and new adventures. And they would keep on moving, until they had completed the great circle. If they survived, another spring would find them back at the old mill pond.

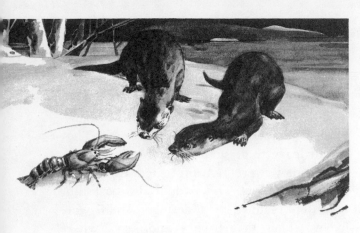

THE JOURNEY BEGINS

Graymuzzle led his family down the small stream that flowed over the dam of the mill pond. It was too shallow for anything except splashing or hunting frogs and fish. But at one point it was blocked by a large rock. The water backed up, forming a deep pool, just right for swimming. Here they all had a fine swim. After a while, Graymuzzle and Mother broke off the fun and started looking for trout. Flash took to the bank and explored a pile of large boulders.

Climbing out of the pool, Tiny sat on a flat rock. There was a crack in the rock, and at the bottom of the narrow opening, filled with water, rested a crayfish. Tiny reached down and tried to get hold of the crayfish. Her foreleg was too short to reach it and, besides, she doubled her paw into a fist. But she kept trying.

Flash sat on top of a boulder and looked around. It was the first time he had been still since arriving at the pool. He was watching Tiny, wondering what she had found. He had to see, so he jumped down and ran to her side. He pushed her roughly away from the crack and looked in. The crayfish, alarmed, was waving its big claws menacingly. Flash reached down. He left his paw open, and he had a longer reach. His claws fastened upon the crayfish, and he pulled it out of the crack.

Tiny was used to being shoved aside by her brother but that didn't keep her from being furious when she saw him making off with her crayfish. She bounded after him. And when he stopped to eat the tasty morsel, she leaped at him and nipped his ear. Flash whirled around to teach his sister a lesson. She ducked past him, grabbed up the crayfish and fled to the pool.

Flash was close behind her when she jumped into the water, and they raced around the pond. Every time Flash pulled up alongside her, Tiny would duck aside, reverse her direction, and be off. She was small, but she was agile, and could turn faster than Flash.

After a long chase, Tiny decided to share the prize with her brother. She climbed out on the bank and lay down, and Flash scrambled out after her. Tiny let him get his teeth into the shell, then jerked back. The crayfish neatly divided into two parts. Brother and sister dug the sweet meat from the shell.

Meanwhile, Mother and Graymuzzle had found the fishing very good. The pool attracted brook trout, sunfish, carp, and perch. Mother came ashore with a twelve-inch carp. Instantly Flash and Tiny dashed to her side to get their share. Mother had already eaten two fish. She had brought this one ashore for her youngsters. She sat down and watched while they tore the carp apart and devoured it.

After eating, Flash was in the mood for play. He dived into the pool and called to Tiny. But she wanted to stretch out and relax, so Flash had to play by himself. He dived deep and swam fast. The bottom of the pool was gravel and boulders. There was no mud, and the water was very clear. Everything down in the pool stood out clearly.

Looking up, Flash saw a small animal—a water mouse—swimming toward the far bank. He swam lazily after her. He thought the fat little mouse might want to play. But the water mouse wasn't interested in play. She was swimming furiously, knowing well the danger of making such a crossing. She might be spotted by a hawk, or by one of her enemies that lurked in the depths below. Flash was close to the tail of the fleeing mouse when the water boiled directly ahead. A big trout shot out of the water. Its jaws opened and the mouse vanished. Flash darted straight at the trout, which saw Flash as it dropped back into the pond. It whirled and fled, with Flash in hot pursuit. The trout quickly found a refuge in a crevice at the base of a rock. Flash could not reach it. He gave up and swam to the surface.

Graymuzzle had explored the pool and had fished in it; now he was ready to move on. He headed downstream, and the family followed. They traveled slowly, looking about and sniffing at everything. They spent a half hour watching a land turtle. They dallied at a mud bank where the clams and crayfish were plentiful. They explored both banks of the stream and quite a bit of the woods beyond.

The small stream led to a larger one, where the family had a good swim. While the others swam on downstream, Flash climbed out of the water and ran into the deep woods. He was just beginning to learn the joy of romping through dense thickets under big trees.

He was not a tree climber, but the birds in the trees interested him. When a large flicker flew to a tree and clung to the trunk rapping away with his beak, Flash sat and watched. But he could not sit still for long, and he soon loped away.

Although Flash was now out of sight of the stream, he could still hear the murmur of the water. A dense woods surrounded him. Bounding around a tree, he came to an abrupt halt. Close to him a bobcat had come out of a thicket. The bobcat stared at Flash. He was sizing up the otter, trying to decide

if he should attack the youngster. Instinct told Flash that this fellow was dangerous. He whirled and raced down the slope toward the stream. Already he knew that deep water would keep him safe from attack. The bobcat raced down the slope after Flash.

Flash burst into the open on the bank of a large body of water. This was the biggest pool he had ever seen, but he did not pause to look it over. Out in the water he saw Graymuzzle, Mother, and Tiny. That made him feel better. He looked back toward the woods. The bobcat had halted at the edge of a thicket. He was a creature of deep cover and had no liking for open country.

Flash tobogganed down a steep bank, landing in the water with a splash. He raised himself high out of the water and looked around. This big pond was a reservoir. A concrete-faced dam ran along the lower end, making a great curve from bank to bank. The dam interested Flash. He swam to it, and followed its face until it ended at a high bank.

This strange barrier needed looking over. Flash climbed the bank and walked out on the flat top of the dam. He trotted toward

the center. There he came to a large wheel which controlled the floodgates below. The wheel was attrached to a big screw, flat and parallel to the top of the dam. Flash climbed up and seated himself on the wheel. He turned his head from side to side as he looked around.

Out in the reservoir, Graymuzzle had already started for the far shore. He had decided that the stream ended here. He would lead the family over a ridge and down into another valley where they would find another stream. Flash wasn't worried. He could easily overtake them. He jumped from the wheel and stood looking down at the water. His attention was fixed upon some leaves floating on the surface in a queer manner. A large leaf was caught in a small whirlpool caused by the pull of the water escaping through the floodgate below. The leaf whirled around then disappeared. Another leaf floated into the whirlpool and vanished.

Flash had to find out where the leaves had gone. Diving off the dam, he followed the leaf down into the water. It swirled ahead of him, just out of his reach. Suddenly he felt a strong pull. He could see no creature that might be pulling at him and he was frightened. It was as though some unseen animal had seized him and was dragging him down. He fought desperately against the pull, but he could not escape from it. Tumbled and buffeted, he was swept toward the gate below. He began to get very short of breath. He had always believed that he was master of the water, that it was something meant to serve him. Now it was his master, battering and smothering him.

Suddenly he was out of the grip of the water, tossed onto a wide pool. He surfaced and swam weakly to shore. Pulling himself out on a bank, he lay panting. It was many minutes before he recovered his breath and his strength. The roar of the water spouting from the gates at the base of the dam filled him with terror. When he did manage to sit up, he looked around for Mother and called loudly. There was no answer. That was not surprising. She could hardly hear him with the roar of the water filling the air. But he was sure of one thing—he had to get away from this place and back to the family. He started downstream, avoiding the water.

Flash was half grown, and very husky for his age, and he had learned a few things. But he lacked wilderness wisdom. He still needed the guidance of Mother and Gray-muzzle. Still, he was not greatly worried. The family could not be far ahead of him. They would move as they always did, stopping often. If he hurried and did not waste time, he could catch up quickly. He was sure that they had gone downstream, for Graymuzzle had been following this stream ever since they came to it. Flash hurried along the bank. The going was slow because of brush and willow which grew down to the water's edge, and there were large rocks he had to climb. He finally took to the water, where he could travel faster. Swimming as swiftly as he could, he repeatedly called to his mother.

BONNY

Flash went on swimming all day. He found no trace of his family, and toward evening he was tired and very hungry. He moved in close to shore and dived deep. Under an over-hanging bank he spotted four suckers. They were facing upstream, fanning the water just enough to keep themselves from drifting. Their round mouths worked steadily and they pumped water through their gills. Flash shot under the bank, and the suckers scattered in hasty flight.

Selecting a large sucker as his target, Flash darted after the fish. The sucker was fat and a slow swimmer. It fled close to the bank, trying to hide. Flash was on it at once. He surfaced with the fish held securely, and paddled to shore. Climbing out of the water, he sat down and dined. He ate all of the fish except the tail and the backbone.

After he had finished eating, Flash washed his face and his light buff vest. Now he must look for a place where he could curl up and sleep. He started off along the bank at a fast trot. He sniffed eagerly, hoping to catch the scent of Mother or Graymuzzle or Tiny. A bush growing close to the water blocked his path. He romped up the bank and around the bush, then stopped. He had caught the scent of an otter. Hissing eagerly, he looked down in the direction from which the scent came.

On a small grassy shelf, just above the water, he saw an otter lying stretched out, apparently asleep. Eagerly, Flash slid down the bank. He called softly as he halted, and nudged the otter. It did not respond. Flash moved around it and his foot caught in a chain. The chain clanked, and Flash leaped back. One of the otter's hind feet was securely gripped in the jaws of a steel trap.

Flash knew instinctively that there was something wrong here. He hissed as he circled the dead otter. He avoided the trap chain, jumping over it when he came to it. Finally he turned to the stream and dived in. He raised his head high out of the water and whistled, all the while watching the otter in the trap. His whistle was answered by a plaintive cry, which came from under an overhanging bank a few yards below the dead otter. The cry sounded like Tiny's when she had hurt herself, and he swam toward the bank.

As he came close to the bank, the over-hanging grass parted and Bonny's head appeared. She was about the same size as Tiny.

Whimpering, she pushed the grass aside, and swam out to meet Flash. He thrust his muzzle forward, and their wet noses touched for an instant. Each was glad to find another otter.

The otter in the trap was Bonny's mother. And, with her mother dead, Bonny was lost and helpless. All she could think of doing was to wait, hoping her mother would wake up at last and swim away with her. Flash was also lost and lonesome, but he was better able to take care of himself. His training was more advanced than Bonny's.

The trapping of Bonny's mother was senseless and cruel. At this season her fur was worthless. The only excuse for destroying her was that she caught fish in water owned by a resort. This was not a good reason, however, because, like all otters, she caught mostly scavenger fish that preyed upon trout eggs. This more than made up for the few trout and bass she killed.

Bonny was a trim little otter, and now that she had found a friend, her fear left her quickly. And, as soon as she stopped being afraid, she was hungry. She dived and tried to catch a fish, but they easily got away from her. She was not very skillful, for her mother had always caught fish for both of them. Flash swam along with Bonny. Although he wasn't hungry, and would rather have played, he flushed a carp and caught it.

The two otters surfaced together and swam to the bank.

Flash sat next to Bonny while she ate the carp. He was taking no chances of losing his new friend. Bonny finished her meal and washed herself carefully. When Flash started for the stream, she followed. They took to the water just in time. As they swam away, the trapper came to look at his set. Fortunately, dusk was settling, and he failed to see the two small heads bobbing in the stream.

It was late to locate a place to bed down, but Flash was not worried. He picked a small knoll close to the stream, where there was a dense thicket. Here, well hidden by heavy foliage, the two little otters curled up and went to sleep.

With the first light of day, Flash and Bonny were up and moving. Breakfast was the first chore to be attended to. Again Flash caught a fish, but Bonny captured a frog and a crayfish. They shared their catch. Flash's fish was a large sucker, and made a fine meal.

After they had eaten and slicked themselves up, they went exploring along the top of the bank overlooking the stream. Bonny's legs were shorter than Flash's, and he slowed his pace so that she could keep up with him. He stayed in the lead, but she never got more than three jumps behind.

When they came to a steep bank which sloped off into the stream, it reminded Flash of the toboggan slide back at the old mill pond. He leaped over the edge and went shooting down into the water. When he surfaced and looked for Bonny, he saw her standing on top of the bank. She was calling loudly to him. Flash swam to shore and romped up the bank. He hissed coaxingly, then leaped forward and went shooting down the slide again. Bonny timidly edged to the rim, where she hesitated. Finally she made the plunge and went scooting down into the water.

They played on the slide for more than an hour. Finally Flash broke off the game, and swam out into the stream. It was time to look for new adventures. The restlessness of the otter made him move on. Bonny swam after him. They traveled swiftly, taking advantage of the current. Toward midday they halted long enough to fish and to dine on the bank.

The spot Flash picked for their lunch was at the foot of a long slope. A narrow but well-beaten path led down from the top of a hill to the stream. The high hill looked inviting, and Flash felt like exploring. He started up the path with Bonny trotting after him. The curving trail wound around small knolls and clumps of birch and willow.

Bonny was enjoying the adventure as much as Flash. Neither of them knew enough about danger to be aware that they were getting quite a distance from the stream and deep water. They bounced around a curve and came to a fast halt. There was something up ahead.

In a grassy meadow, close to the trail, a pair of kids were frisking about. The little goats were full of life and play, and Flash and Bonny watched them eagerly. When the otters moved out into the meadow, the kids stopped romping and stood staring at the strangers. Flash moved toward one of them. The kid wheeled and danced away in a circle, with Flash running after it. Bonny approached the other kid. It danced off, too, like the first kid. Bonny bounded after it.

The fun might have lasted a long time if the nanny goat had not come running up. When she saw the two animals chasing her kids, she charged with her head lowered. Flash did not know what she was about until she butted him and sent him rolling across the grass. He scrambled to his feet, hissing and snarling. But when the nanny goat charged again, he turned tail and fled down the path. He ran a long way before looking back. When he did look he saw nothing of Bonny. He sat up, making himself as tall as he could, and whistled.

He whistled again, and this time he got an answer. It came from a thicket on his right. Bonny had circled and kept to cover. She leaped out and raced toward him.

Side by side, they made their way down to the stream and dived in. They swam well out before they looked back up the slope. The nanny goat was coming down the path with her two kids romping and dancing ahead of her.

Bonny was eager to go back and play with the kids, but Flash's rump was sore from the butting he had taken. He called to her, and headed downstream. He did not intend getting close to the big goat again.

They traveled for almost a mile before they went on land again. Both were tired and ready for a brief rest. They climbed out of the stream and curled up on a grassy hummock. Bonny set to work at once picking fleas out of Flash's fur. The companionship of Bonny and Flash was different from that of a pair of grown otters. They did not know where they were going. Flash was not guided in a great circle, which would eventually take him back to the old mill pond to raise a family. The urge to be always on the move would keep them going with no fixed goal.

As long as they stayed in the stream they would have food, and some protection. Whether or not they would survive depended on luck. Of course, neither Bonny nor Flash knew anything of that. They knew only that they were enjoying themselves and having a wonderful time.

DOWN RIVER

The stream had now become a river. In it were many different kinds of fish, and Bonny had learned to catch them almost as well as Flash. Toward noon on a hot summer day, they came to a place where the river widened into a riffle. Flash was floating along, enjoying the cool water, when he saw a strange sight on shore. He flipped over and hissed a warning to Bonny.

With their heads just above water, the otters watched a farmer drive a light wagon down to the river. The wagon was pulled by two horses—strange monsters to Flash and Bonny.

The horses plodded along, and the man sat on the spring half asleep. Puffs of smoke curled upward from his corncob pipe. Reaching the river, the horses waded in and pulled the wagon after them. It bumped along over the boulders, at the spot where the farmer forded the river.

Flash and Bonny were very much interested, but they were also wary. The huge animals pulling the wagon were the biggest creatures they had ever seen. To get a close look at them, they dived and swam under water, moving swiftly toward the wagon. At the middle of the river, where the water was about three feet deep, the horses decided to have a drink. The farmer slackened the reins, and sat back puffing on his pipe.

Flash judged he was close enough for a good look. He could see the legs of the horses clearly because they were underwater, but the current rippled the surface so that he could not get a good look at the rest of them. He popped his head out of the water, and Bonny did the same thing. Their heads came out just as the muzzles of the horses lowered to drink. Flash and Bonny found themselves looking up at two huge heads that were only inches from them. Hissing wildly, they dived.

The startled horses picked up their heads. They whirled to flee, and the sharp turn cramped the front wheel of the wagon. They lunged toward the shore they had just left, and the wagon toppled over, spilling the farmer into the water.

Terrified, Flash and Bonny swam under water until they could no longer do without air. They popped to the surface, and raised their heads to look back. They saw the horses drag the overturned wagon to the shore. The farmer was splashing after them, shouting loudly. Then Flash saw the farmer's straw hat sailing toward them. He hissed a warning, and dived again. Again he and Bonny swam under water as far as their breath would allow. When they surfaced, the hat was gone, and so was the farmer, the horses, and his wagon. He had started home to make repairs.

Flash and Bonny went on. They paused several times to fish, but mostly they kept moving, carried along by the current. Soon Flash noticed that the river was getting narrower and the current was stronger. He looked ahead and saw white water.

Bonny was worried by the strong current. She swam in close to shore, until she reached calm water. Raising her head, she called to Flash. The foaming rapids frightened her and she wanted no part of them.

Like a small boy showing off, Flash headed for the rapids. Before he realized how strong and rough the current was, he was swept into the swirling waters. He fought hard, but he could make no headway. All he could do was ride along and try to keep the breath from being knocked out of him.

On the bank, Bonny called loudly as she ran along, close to the cascading rapids. Once in a while she caught a glimpse of Flash's head, and that made her run faster. But there were many big rocks along the shore, and she was not able to keep up with Flash. Still, she kept running. She leaped to a boulder that jutted out into the stream, forming a pool of quiet water. From the rock she jumped into the pool.

Flash was sitting on a flat rock close to the edge of the pool. He had already recovered from his rough trip over the cascade. He answered Bonny's eager call. She swam to his flat rock and snuggled against him. Flash did not push her away, but he wasn't going to let her think he was scared of the fast water.

Getting to his feet, he dived into the pool. He streaked across it and shot into the torrent boiling around the boulder. He knew the fast water would toss him right into the pool, and it did. Bonny joined him. She was still nervous about the fast water, and did not attempt to follow him when he made a second dive into the torrent.

They had entered water owned by Rainbow Lodge and reserved for fishing. Guests of the lodge were assured a supply of fish and game by a gamekeeper who planted game fish and birds, and who destroyed predators. And the gamekeeper included otters on his list of predators.

This, of course, meant nothing to Flash and Bonny. When they came to a partly submerged tree, Flash climbed out of the water and bounded up the trunk. Bonny followed him.

A branch rose from the trunk about ten feet from the water. It had broken off four feet from the trunk, so it was just a big snag. Flash and Bonny climbed the snag. Nailed to it was a board with a printed sign that read:

KEEP FISH AND GAME PLENTIFUL .. DESTROY OTTERS, FOXES, COYOTES AND BOBCATS
RAINBOW LODGE MANAGEMENT

Having satisfied their curiosity about the half-submerged log, Flash and Bonny scampered along the trunk and dived into the water. They swam a short distance before seeing the buildings of the lodge. These interested them very much. Flash was reminded of the old mill. Near one of the buildings was a man seated on a bench. He looked very much like the farmer they had seen. He had his back to them and was working on a power saw. Beyond him was a kennel with a run attached, and behind the netting stood two big hounds. They were looking toward the river, and they saw the otters. At once the hounds started baying loudly. Flash and Bonny had never heard such frightening sounds, but instinct told them to get away fast. They dived and streaked away.

On shore, the man laid aside the saw and stood up. He turned and looked down over the river, but he saw nothing. Flash and Bonny were darting away downstream. They did not surface until they were well below the lodge.

THE GREAT LAKE

Flash and Bonny followed the river to its end, where it emptied into Lake Michigan. The lake was so big that when they looked ahead they could see no land. Great crested waves rolled in and smashed into white foam on the dark rocks of the shore. The two otters were lifted on the crest of a wave, then dropped into its trough. Frightened, they headed toward the shore.

But when they neared the black rocks, they knew they could not reach the land this way. Swimming well out from the rocks, they finally came to a cove with calm water and a short stretch of beach. They rode a small wave in and landed on an expanse of sand. This was a strange place. There were no trees or underbrush. There were just rocks and a windy sky with seagulls banking and turning or sweeping low over the beach. A few of the gulls alighted and walked across the sand, their wild cries filling the air. Flash and Bonny turned back to the water. They plunged in and swam out into the cove, where they felt safer. Flash dived after a herring, and Bonny followed him. Down in the deep water they saw more fish than they had ever seen before. This might be a good place to stay a while. Soon they were playing water tag; their fear of the great lake was forgotten.

Flash decided to dive under the boat for a close look at the part which was underwater. He shot under the boat, moving fast so as to get past it quickly. Before he knew what was happening he found himself in a mass of flapping, twisting fish. He couldn't get through. He snapped and clawed, but the fish pressed in around him. Then he was suddenly out of water, but the fish were still all around and over him. He had dived into the fisherman's seine.

When the fisherman saw what he had caught along with the fish, he stopped working the winch which raised the net, and left it dangling alongside. He turned to the dog and called.

"Hey, Pooch, we caught us an otter."

Pooch barked loudly and tried to reach out and nip Flash. The fisherman looked at Flash with satisfaction. During the summer he was a fisherman, and during the winter he trapped. He grinned broadly. Then he slapped the dog back from the net.

"Let that otter be, Pooch. He ain't but half grown, but I can pen him up and feed him on no-good fish. He'll grow, and come winter his pelt will be prime. I'll make me some money off him."

The fisherman's name was Hank. He was not really a cruel man. He fished and hunted for a living, and to get pelts he had to kill animals. Hank never bothered to think about it. He swung the net into the boat and left it closed while he fixed a cage for Flash. He had a wooden tub aboard which would serve very well as a cage until he got home. The net would do for a cover.

Hank swung the net over the fish bin and dumped his catch, keeping the net over Flash so that he could not escape. Flash squirmed and hissed and clawed and bit, but he could not get away. Hank rolled him up in the net and dumped him into the tub. He stretched the net over the top of the tub, tying it with twine.

Near the entrance to the cove, the water was rougher. Flash and Bonny found that it was fun to ride the waves. They were having a fine time when Flash noticed a cloud of gulls swooping down on a fishing boat riding at anchor well out from the shore. The fisherman was cleaning a fish and tossing the waste to the gulls. A shaggy pup sat in the stern, watching them.

Flash was curious about the boat. Here was something new, a strange thing which needed closer inspection. The otters swam toward the boat, and when they were within a hundred yards they dived to approach it under water. There was a strong smell of fish coming from the boat. Now that they were close they could see the gulls hitting the water, snatching up waste the fisherman tossed overboard.

Then the pup saw them. It started barking excitedly, and Flash and Bonny dived deep. The man in the boat turned to look, but saw nothing. He got to his feet and started hauling in the purse seine he had set.

Flash could see out by pushing the net upward. The tub sat close to the rail, and he was able to look out into the lake. He saw Bonny bobbing up and down. He could not hear her call, because Hank had started the outboard motor. The boat started to move and Bonny's small head became smaller and smaller until it finally vanished.

Pooch sniffed at Flash, but did not try to nip him. Hank had made it clear to the pup that he was not to harm the young otter. Flash hissed at the dog, then decided that Pooch meant no harm. Being imprisoned in the tub was frightening. Flash had always been used to plenty of room and freedom of movement. He fretted and tried to push the net off the top.

When the boat docked, Hank packed his fish and delivered them. This took some time. He finally returned to the boat and carried the tub to his pickup.

Several of Hank's friends peered into the tub. They agreed that Hank would get a good price for the pelt once the otter had his growth and the pelt was prime.

"Not a blemish on him," one man said.

"Won't cost you a dime to feed him, either. After all, you got fish," another said with a laugh.

Flash crouched down and listened to the strange voices. He smelled the men and did not like the strong odor that came from them.

Soon Hank drove away from the boat landing. The tub jiggled and jumped as he turned off into the rutted lane which led to the abandoned farm where he lived. Flash stopped pressing against the net and trying to see out of the back of the truck. Hank pulled into his yard, and Pooch leaped down from his place on the driver's seat. Hank stood, looking around the yard. He had to fix a place for the otter, one with enough room to move about. His eyes rested on an old chicken coop. He could repair the mesh fence and nail boards over any holes in the coop.

Hank had inherited the farm from his father. He did not like farming, so he let the land go back to the wild. Brush and trees had overrun the fields that had once been cultivated. Deer came to the meadows, and that was all right with Hank. He wasn't above shooting a deer out of season. The venison tasted just as good as that of a deer legally taken.

Hank left Flash in the tub while he fixed himself something to eat. After he had eaten and put the scraps out for Pooch, he got busy on the chicken coop. Though he would not work the fields, Hank would work hard at anything that pleased him. Fixing an otter pen pleased him, and he got the job done quickly.

Flash just lay and waited until Hank came to take him out of the tub. Even when Hank dumped him into the chicken pen, he did not leap about. He lay still while Hank securely fastened the screen door and walked away. Only after Hank and Pooch were gone did Flash start looking for a way of escape.

PRISONER

The chicken coop had been built to house no more than several dozen hens. The side facing the screened yard was open. A row of roost poles was set over a raised floor, and nest boxes were lined up under the floor. Flash poked about in the coop, looking for a hole. He could find none, for Hank had nailed boards over every broken place.

The coop gave Flash a feeling of being confined. The walls seemed to be pressing in upon him, and there was a stale, unpleasant smell. Flash went out and ran all around the net enclosure, sniffing at the chicken wire. There was no hole big enough for him to squeeze through. He tried the door, but it was wired shut.

Pooch came trotting down from the shed where he had his bed. Flash climbed up the wire barrier, testing the netting which covered the top of the run. He looked down at the pup and hissed. Pooch wagged his tail. He had accepted the otter as a part of the household, and wanted to play. Flash dropped to the ground and thrust his muzzle against the netting. Pooch moved forward, and their noses met. Flash would gladly have romped with the pup, but the wire netting separated them. Pooch raced around the yard and came back to the netting, while Flash ran back and forth eagerly.

And so a friendship began between the shaggy pup and the otter. Flash had not forgotten his family, but he missed Bonny more than he missed them. He could not stand being shut up in such a small space. He spent hours running back and forth inside the pen. He hated the coop and never went inside, even when it rained. The rain was soothing. It was water, and he liked water. When the rain beat upon him, he romped about, flinging himself wildly from one side of the run to the other, sliding on his belly and rolling over.

His diet was fish heads, with an occasional sucker. Flash became used to the man who came to the pen every day and dumped in his food. He always had plenty to eat and he grew larger.

Hank watched him with satisfaction. He did not try to be friendly with the otter. He treated Flash well, just as a farmer treats his stock well. He did not ask for the friendship which Flash would have gladly given. Hank's only interest in the otter was in having him mature, so that his pelt would be a number one product. He judged that by the coming of the first winter snow the otter's pelt would be prime.

So the summer days passed. Flash got his exercise by running up and down inside the pen, and Pooch kept him from being completely lonely. The dog visited the coop often, always hopeful that the otter would come out of the pen and play.

Fall came, and Hank began thinking of trapping. He got his traps out of the shed where he kept his old truck. He cut new stakes to anchor the traps. He tested several bottles of scent he would use to lure his victims. And he stopped fishing. This made quite a problem so far as otter food went. Both Flash and Pooch often went hungry. But Hank did not worry about it. He expected the first snow any day now, and when it came, he planned to kill and skin the otter.

Flash spent one whole day without food. Toward evening, Hank tossed a soup bone into the pen. Pooch was with him and whined eagerly. He had gotten nothing at all. Hank looked at the dog sourly.

"Why don't you go get yourself a rabbit?" he asked.

Pooch wiggled his back end, whining again. As Hank walked away toward the house, Flash started gnawing at the bone. He stripped off a few scraps of meat and gristle and ate them. To hold the bone firmly, he pushed it up against the netting. Pooch shoved his nose through one of the meshes, so that he was able to lick the bone. Flash did not snarl at him. He would have shared the bone with Pooch if the netting had not separated them.

Pooch wanted the bone badly. He started digging close to the wire. Flash had stripped every scrap of meat from the bone, and even licked the marrow out of it. He sat watching Pooch. The pup had given him an idea. This might be a way to get out. He started digging on the inside of the netting. Dirt flew as both pup and otter dug. Each soon had dug a hole a foot deep. Pooch shoved his head into his hole. Flash, too, thrust his muzzle downward, eager to find a way out under the netting. Their noses met, but there was

mesh between them. In building the pen, Hank's father had buried the netting deep in the ground. Both Pooch and Flash gave up.

The next day, the skies were lead gray. Clouds swept overhead, driven by a cold wind, and then the snow started falling. It swirled down and the wind whipped it across the dry dead grass and weeds in the yard.

Flash raced back and forth inside the pen. The storm excited him. He did not have to be told that this was an important change of season. Instinct warned him to seek a place of shelter where he could find water that would not freeze over, and where there was food he could get at.

By midafternoon, the storm had passed. Much snow had fallen. The wind had died down before the storm ended, and now the ground was covered by a blanket of snow. Hank came out of his house. Brushing snow from a bench, he put down a whetstone, a stretching frame, and the handle from a hammer. He got out his skinning knife, started sharpening it on the whetstone. As he whetted the blade, he looked down at the pen where Flash was bounding back and forth. The otter's golden-brown fur was sleek and thick.

Pooch sat in the snow beside Hank. Suddenly he started barking loudly and leaping around. Hank stopped whetting the blade and looked to see what had excited the dog. Pooch had spotted a buck which had come out of the woods to dig for forage in the meadow below the buildings. Hank slid the knife into the sheath fastened to his belt. He could kill and skin the otter any time. But the deer might soon decide to leave, and he didn't intend to miss this chance to get several hundred pounds of meat. He walked quickly to the house to get his rifle.

As Hank walked away again, he realized that he could not take a barking dog with him while he was stalking a buck. Pooch

wasn't yet trained to hunt. Hank returned to the house and got a length of light rope. Pooch objected to having the rope tied around his neck, but he finally gave in. He followed Hank down to the hen coop, where Hank tied the rope to the frame of the pen door.

When Hank started off, Pooch set up a terrific howl—and he kept on howling. Hank turned back angrily. He pulled a red bandanna handkerchief from his pocket and stooped down over Pooch, holding the dog fast by pressing his knees against the dog's shoulders. Then he securely gagged Pooch by tying his jaws shut.

"That'll shut you up," he said gruffly.

Hank moved away fast. His plan was to circle and then approach the buck from cover in the timber. He judged that from the nearest cover he would have a two-hundred-yard shot, which was easy range for him.

Flash had watched with interest while Hank tied up the pup. He did not know why Pooch barked so furiously. The barking had been excited, but not angry. Now he watched the muzzled pup lunging at the rope, trying to follow Hank. Flash pressed his muzzle against the mesh which covered the door frame. He wanted to help Pooch, or just romp with him. Seeing the dog leaping against the rope suggested a game.

Suddenly Flash noticed that when Pooch lunged against the rope, the bottom of the door pulled outward. He thrust his head into the opening, but Pooch backed up and the door sprang back. Flash's head was trapped. He struggled and flopped wildly, bracing his hind feet on the screen and pushing. This effort wedged his head even more tightly in the opening. Pooch moved in close to watch. He shoved his nose against Flash's head, and would have licked the otter's face if he had not been gagged. Flash's breath was being slowly cut off as he pushed against the door and increased the pressure on his neck.

Then the crack of Hank's rifle rang out. The report excited Pooch, and he leaped away from the door, hitting the rope hard as it brought him up. He hit so hard that he was thrown on his back. The jerk on the door opened it wider. Flash squeezed through the opening and out of the coop.

He was free, but he had no way of knowing that he would be killed if he stayed in this place. He ran to Pooch and playfully bounded around the dog. The red handkerchief interested him and he sniffed at it.

Pooch had been so shaken by his hard fall that he had not gotten to his feet. When he did get up, he discovered that the terrific tug on the rope had pulled the noose off his neck. Flash leaped in and got a grip on the loose ends of the handkerchief. Pooch pulled and Flash pulled, and the handkerchief slipped off.

The instant Pooch's jaws were free, he started barking eagerly. He ran around the pen and off toward the meadow to find Hank. Flash ran after him. They raced down the slope, ducking around bushes. Far below, Hank had dragged his kill to a grove of trees. There he hung up the deer, so that it would be easier to dress. He heard the dog, but he did not mind, because he had his meat.

Pooch outran Flash. His legs were longer and the loose snow did not hinder him. Flash had to plow through the snow. Pooch disappeared over a ridge, and Flash kept on his trail. When he reached the top of the ridge, Flash halted to have a look around. Pooch had vanished into the grove of trees and had found Hank, but he had left a clear trail.

Flash hesitated. Below him he could see a stream, and he felt a strong desire to return to the ways he knew so well. He headed down the slope, sending the snow flying. Halfway to the stream, and away from the lee side of the slope, he was met by a strong wind. It swirled the snow into his face. As Flash moved on, the snow soon ·obliterated his tracks.

WINTER

It was months since Flash had plunged into a stream, and the sound of running water filled him with wild joy. Reaching the stream, he dived deep. He swam about, keeping close to the bottom. A sucker darted

out of a hole under the bank. Flash chased it and caught it. Then he surfaced, and climbed out on the bank to eat the fish.

A little ice had formed along the banks of the stream, a warning of what was to come. Flash ate the fish, and now instinct started to guide him. He went up the creek, back toward the country he had left with Bonny. He moved steadily along, pausing only to fish when he was hungry. Night found him a long way from Hank's place. He bedded down in a hollow at the base of a big tree.

That night the temperature dropped to far below zero, freezing any open water that was not moving swiftly. Pools were locked under ice, and every eddy froze over. Only the fast-running ripples remained free of ice.

This was the time when Flash needed the knowledge of an old winter-wise otter. If he had been with Graymuzzle and Mother, they would have led him to a place where there was shelter and he could reach deep water. They would find a pool with a stream cascading over rocks to form a doorway to the pool. Flash had no knowledge of such places. He would have to depend upon luck.

During the week that followed Flash's escape, the weather remained bitterly cold.

Flash had to travel farther each day to find open water. But he kept going. Not once did he think of staying close to a fast-running riffle. The second week brought another big storm, which lasted three days and piled up snow three feet high. Traveling was hard work. Many times Flash scooted along under the surface of the snow.

After the storm, the cold returned, and one day Flash traveled from dawn to dusk without finding open water. He did find a pool with a small airhole where the stream entered. He tried to break the ice around the edges of the hole, but it was too thick. That night he slept in a snow bank with his stomach empty.

The next day he pushed on, hunting for anything he could eat. And he was not the only hungry beast. The bobcat, the fox and the coyote were also hunting. The rabbits were all burrowed down under the snow.

On the second day after the storm, Flash met one of the killers. He was plunging through the snow at the top of a hill when he saw a bobcat working its way uphill toward him. The bobcat saw Flash at the same time. It was savagely hungry and willing to tackle even a grown otter. It bounded toward Flash, snarling.

Flash was as hungry as the bobcat, but he was more cautious. He knew at once that the cat was a killer, and that it meant to

attack him. Raising himself high in the snow, he bared his fangs and hissed. The cat halted and crouched a few yards away. Then it began to circle, hoping to get behind the otter and leap upon his back. Flash turned and kept his face to the killer. Finally the bobcat leaped. Flash dived under the snow, just as he would have dived under the water if this had been a pond. He was gone when the cat landed.

Fifty feet from where the bobcat stood, Flash popped his head out of the snow. He needed to fill his lungs with air. At once, the bobcat came charging toward him. Flash dived and made off at right angles to the path he had first taken. Again he traveled fifty feet before surfacing. This time he thrust out only his nose before diving again. And the next time he poked his head out, he saw nothing of the bobcat and moved on down the slope. In the distance he could see a large pond. It was covered with snow, but it was a pond.

Flash worked his way down to the pond, which had a circular dam at the lower side. The dam had been built by many generations of beavers, and every year it had grown taller and the pond back of it deeper. Flash approached it from the upper side. He paused for a few moments at a beaver house and sniffed at the air vent leading to the compartment below. He could smell only a faint animal scent; the house was unused.

Flash heard the sound of running water from across the pond, and ran that way. He climbed on top of the dam, following the sound to a spillway where the water flowed over the dam. There was a fair-sized opening, but it was choked with branches, and cut sapling limbs. Flash squirmed down among the branches. He twisted and wiggled, and suddenly he was in open water under the ice.

The first thing Flash thought about was fish. Within a few minutes he saw a school of brook trout, and caught one. But when he tried to get back through the spillway, he found that it was choked. When entering it he had stirred up the mass of branches, limbs, and saplings, and now he could not push his way through. He had to find a place to eat his fish and he had to have air. He started searching the pond, and this brought him to the entrance of the beaver

house. He popped up into the house, dropped the fish, and sat, panting. As soon as he got his breath, he began eating the fish.

The den had a dry bed of shredded bark. Fresh air came in through the vent above, where the roof poles stuck up through the mud-and-willow ceiling. By accident he had found a winter haven. He would have to remain here unless he could open the spillway.

He soon solved the problem of staying out under the ice. He discovered that the bubbles of air he breathed out would recover oxygen from the water, and that they always collected against the ice in a large bubble. All he had to do was breathe in the big bubble.

He spent the first few days exploring the pond. It covered several acres, and at the far end there were two other beaver houses, both in use. There were a dozen beavers in the colony. Two old he-beavers attacked him when he poked around their cache of logs in the deepest part of the pool. This was their food supply, and they were willing to fight to defend it. Flash was a faster swimmer than the beavers, and could duck and turn like a trout, so he escaped their sharp chisel teeth. But he was curious about the cache, and wondered why the beavers would defend it. He went back to it again, only to be met with the same kind of angry attack by three other beavers. After that, Flash left the beavers alone. They were not creatures to play with.

Only one other animal visited the pond— the bobcat. He stopped at the house where Flash was curled up inside on the bark bed. Sniffing at the air vent, the cat smelled Flash and began clawing and ripping at it. But the beavers that had built the house had made it strong enough to withstand the attack of even a bear. Flash was shielded by a foot of frozen mud, and the bobcat finally quit trying and went away.

There wasn't much to do in this world under the ice, but Flash did not feel cooped up as he had while Hank held him prisoner. Every day he went fishing, and after he had dined he took a long, fast tour of the pond. He spent most of the time sleeping. He was always aware of being alone, and although he could no longer remember Mother, Graymuzzle, and Tiny, he had never quite forgotten Bonny. Once freed by a spring thaw, he would be off seeking others of his kind.

As spring approached, every day he searched for a way to get out from under the ice. But the pond was still frozen over as far as he could travel, which was only a little way. The stream feeding the pond was a

very small one and very shallow. If it had not been fed by a spring, it would have frozen to the bottom.

Release came when a chinook wind swept over the woods. The wind was warm, and it melted the snow and softened the ice. It also started freshets, turning the little stream into a raging torrent. The pressure of the torrent split the ice, which broke and heaved upward. Flash found a large crack and scrambled out upon the ice. Without pausing for a backward look, he set off upcountry.

SPRING

The snow had not completely vanished from the earth. It lay in banks, wherever there was shade cast by the young leaves bursting from their buds. Flash kept to the open. He wanted no more snow and ice. He liked the smell of the damp earth warmed by the sun. Shoots of green grass were thrusting upward, and a few early flowers bloomed. Driven on by a great restlessness, he moved steadily along, making nervous hops and quick dashes.

In a deep hollow he came upon a buck deer cropping the tips from low-growing bushes. The buck's new horns were forming. They were soft and pulpy, and covered with short brown hair. The buck lifted his head and stared at Flash, his big ears propped forward. He knew that Flash was not an enemy. He dropped his head and began browsing again.

A few yards from the deer, Flash stood up on his hind legs, balancing himself with his powerful tail. His forepaws were draped over his buff-colored vest. He examined the buck closely. The buck stamped a hoof and snorted. He was in no mood for play. The winter months had been lean ones for him, and all he wanted to do was to eat and build up his strength. Flash decided to leave.

From the hollow, Flash went over a hill and down to a stream. He dived in and started fishing. He caught a large sucker, and swam to shore to eat it. Across the stream, a pair of mallards swam out of a patch of cattails. The drake had a gaudy red head and brightly marked wings. The hen, much smaller than the drake, was plain brown. They saw Flash, and they, too, knew he was not an enemy to be avoided. As they swam close to the bank where he was feeding, he looked up from his meal. He would gladly have joined them for a romp, but he did not try it. He knew that if he did, they would only fly away.

He finished his meal and moved on upstream. He had traveled less than a half-mile

when he came to a large pool. One end was shaded by an elm tree whose branches extended out over the water. Flash climbed onto a high bank and stared down at the pond. He was filled with excitement by a trim little otter swimming around in the pool. She looked very much like Bonny. Flash's memory of Bonny was dim, but it was revived by the sight of the little otter.

Hurrying down the bank, he dived into the water and swiftly darted toward the she-otter. She raised her head high and watched him. When he was close to her she hissed at him and bared her teeth. If this was Bonny, she certainly did not recognize him. Flash made eager whining sounds and moved still closer, thrusting his muzzle toward her.

She snapped at him and hissed louder. At that moment, a large dog otter surfaced beside her. He snarled angrily and lunged at Flash. Flash was so startled that at first he did not move. But the dog otter's teeth fastened upon his neck, and he began to paddle frantically. He kicked himself free, retreating as fast as he could swim. The dog otter chased him across the pool. Flash dived and darted off at another angle. When he surfaced he saw that the big otter and the slim one were rubbing muzzles.

Flash wanted to join them, but he was afraid of being attacked again. The big otter turned toward the far shore and the slim one followed. Climbing out of the pool, they started up the far hillside. Flash swam across the pool and climbed out on the bank. The two otters were moving fast, and Flash ran up the slope, eager to overtake them. Perhaps this time the big otter would not leap at him. The pair vanished into the woods. Flash ducked through a thicket and halted to listen and look, not sure which way the otters had gone.

Flash had stopped close to a wood rat's nest, a big pile of sticks and leaves and grass. Rat smell was strong on the breeze. From the nest came squeaks of fright and pain, abruptly cut off.

Flash moved closer to the nest. The wild squeaking stopped, and a long-tailed weasel came bursting out. It had been attacking the rat family and considered Flash an intruder who had invaded its hunting ground. It was a deadly killer, a creature without fear, and it was not frightened off by Flash's size. Snarling, the weasel leaped at Flash and sank its fangs into his leg. Flash tried to shake the weasel loose, but it only sank its fangs deeper. Flash gripped the back of the weasel between his teeth. He bit hard and the weasel's backbone cracked. The slim body went limp and dropped to the grass.

Flash nudged it with his nose, hissing softly. He was over his sudden flash of anger, and only curious about the small animal which had attacked him. The weasel kicked its hind feet, then lay still. Flash nudged it again, but it was dead.

Flash went back to the pool and fished, then sunned himself on the bank. Meeting the two otters had sharpened his desire to find Bonny, or at least other otters who would accept him and let him join them. Soon he got to his feet and continued his journey upstream.

Flash was now entering territory which should have been familiar to him—the territory where the lodges and resorts were located. If he had been older when he made his first trip down the river he would have remembered them. As it was, he had forgotten them completely.

He left the stream he was following and crossed a ridge. Below him lay the river, deep and inviting. He ran through the bushes eagerly, put on a burst of speed, and dived into the water from a high bank. He went down close to the rocky bottom and swam swiftly upstream. When he surfaced, he saw a man fishing. The man wore waders and was standing well out from the bank. He was using a fly rod, but he was casting with a silver-colored spinner. Flash was wary. He took a deep breath, dived, and swam toward the fisherman to get a look at him from under water.

The fisherman's legs were big and long. His body, above the surface, wavered and twisted as ripples distorted Flash's vision. Flash turned and swam away. The fisherman made a long cast, and the spinner sailed out and dropped beyond Flash. The fisherman let it sink several feet into the water before starting to reel in. The spinner seemed to come alive, flashing as the spoon revolved.

The flashing spinner attracted the otter as much as it would attract a pike or a picker-

el. Flash darted after it. He swam over it, not willing to touch it until he was sure what it was, and his body hit the line. The fisherman thought he had a strike. He gave a powerful jerk backward on the pole, and the pair of hooks attached to the spinner sank into Flash's shoulder. A stab of pain sent him darting away.

The line on the fisherman's reel spun out, and he applied the brake. He was sure he had hooked a big musky, and did not want to put too heavy a strain on his tackle. He would play his catch and wear it down before bringing it in. He had plenty of line and meant to work carefully. He kept some pressure on it, but not too much.

Instinctively, Flash knew the barb in his shoulder had something to do with the man he had seen. He fought against the line. But his skin was tough and the barb refused to pull free, so he headed across the river. At the far bank, he surfaced under an overhang of bushes and grass. He had to have air. As

soon as he stopped moving, the fisherman
started pulling on the line to get some action. Pain shot through Flash and he started
off upriver. But the pull on the line slowed
him, so he turned and doubled back. He
could swim as fast as any fish. The line went
slack, and the fisherman reeled frantically.

The downstream current helped Flash
move even faster. By the time the slack had
been reeled in, he was going at top speed.
The line snapped taut, putting a sudden
strain on the barb. It held for a few seconds,
then pulled loose. Flash swam on, and again
he surfaced under cover close to the bank.
At last he was free of the barb.

The disappointed fisherman reeled in his
line. The big one had gotten away, but he
would have a tall tale to tell his friends
when they all met at the lodge that night.
And he would return to this spot for another
try at the big musky.

Flash stayed under the bank until the
fisherman left. Starting upstream again, he
swam close to the bank. When he came to
the abandoned den of a bank beaver, he entered it and curled up. He was weary after
the battle with the fisherman. He fell asleep
and did not awaken for several hours.

Flash had never had any reason to fear
men before. Even when he had been im-

prisoned by Hank, he had not been actually
mistreated. But his experience with the fisherman had really frightened him. The pain in
his shoulder had been connected with a man,
and from now on he would be wary of men.

DANGER AHEAD

Journeying up the river, Flash often leaped
out and explored the woods along the banks.
It was in this way that he came upon Rainbow Lodge. The sound of dogs barking made
him remember Pooch, and he hurried to the
edge of a clearing. From the cover of a
thicket he looked down upon the grounds of
the lodge. The lodge itself was a large
building with a deep porch across its front.
Several men sat on the shady porch, smoking
and talking. Another was out on the lawn
practicing putting. He would tap a little
white ball with a stick, and the ball would
scurry to a hole and disappear. But the ball
never seemed to be able to escape from the
man. He always fished it out and rapped it
again.

Below the main building were outbuild-
ings—including a shed with cars parked in it
and a barn with a corral. Flash saw horses in
the corral, and remembered the farmer's
team he and Bonny had panicked. He would
not go near the horses or the men, but a little distance from the corral was a dog house

with two dogs in a screened yard. Thinking of Pooch, Flash decided that these dogs were friends and might play with him.

Flash bounded away, keeping to cover. When he was opposite the pen, he moved toward it. There was brush growing almost up to the yard. Stepping out into the open, he hissed loudly and eagerly, and ran toward the pen.

What happened next took Flash completely by surprise. Barking savagely, the dogs leaped at the screen. Flash slid to a halt and looked up into the faces of the excited dogs. Their snarls and gleaming fangs terrified him. He knew he must flee, but for almost a minute he could not move.

The gamekeeper came hurrying out of the barn. When he saw Flash, he rushed back inside to get his shotgun. Flash caught a glimpse of him, and his first thought was to seek the safety of deep water. He ran toward the river, following a well-beaten path used by hunters and fishermen.

Meanwhile, the gamekeeper had picked up his shotgun and opened the gate of the dog pen. The two big hounds burst out of the pen and raced down the path. The gamekeeper ran after them.

Flash swerved when he reached the lodge's boat landing and dashed along a row of boats. The hounds were snapping at his tail as he leaped into the water. Halting on the dock, they bayed loudly, to let their master know they had cornered the otter.

Flash dived deep and swam swiftly out into the river. Now he could neither hear nor see the hounds, and he felt safe. He swam upstream until he needed air. Looking back at the dock he could see the dogs and the gamekeeper standing beside them. Flash felt no fear, for he had never met a creature that could match his speed in the water. But he did not know about guns, which could kill from a distance.

While Flash watched, the gamekeeper raised his gun, sighted, and fired. No other

animal, except the loon and the mudhen, has such keen eyesight as the otter, and Flash actually saw the shot coming. Immediately, he dived, and the shot raked the water above him. Some of the pellets stung his back and head, and the pain sent him darting away, diving deep. It was a shock to him to discover that even in water he was not safe from man. He swam about in a panic.

On the bank, the dogs howled loudly and eagerly. They had learned that when their master fired the gun there would be game to retrieve—ducks or geese or a raccoon shot out of a tree. They leaped into the river and swam toward the spot where the charge of shot had raked the water.

Flash was forced to surface for air, and he saw the dogs swimming toward him. They barked, and the gamekeeper fired the other barrel of his shotgun. He was far enough away for Flash to dive before the shot reached him. Again he darted away under water. The gamekeeper reloaded his gun and ran along the bank, shouting encouragement

to the dogs. But compared to Flash, they were slow swimmers; he left them behind.

Flash's faith in the safety of the river was so shaken that he climbed out on the bank, heading toward the woods above the river. An old, experienced otter would have remained in the river and easily escaped. This way, the dogs clambered out of the water and raced along the bank until they picked up Flash's trail. They left the gamekeeper far behind, but he kept running, certain that they would corner the otter.

Flash jumped over a fallen log into a dense thicket. He stood there listening for a few moments, then made for a grove of trees. He ran fast, but his short legs were no match for the long legs of the dogs. Flash knew they were getting closer, and he looked about for a place to hide. He saw no holes he could duck into, no rock piles he could hide in. He ran on, going uphill, and as he neared the top he looked back. The dogs were gaining on him. They ran with their mouths open, their red tongues lolling over their white fangs, and they kept baying savagely.

At the top of the hill Flash saw that he must cross an open meadow. He did not dare to go back, even though he knew by instinct that breaking into the open would bring the dogs snarling down upon him. He raced across the meadow and ducked under the lowest strand of a barbed wire fence.

Suddenly he was face to face with a new and terrifying danger—a big Jersey bull. Flash slid to a halt almost under the bull's moist muzzle. Snorting and pawing the ground, the bull lowered its head. Before Flash could leap aside, two curving horns scooped him up and tossed him high into the air.

Flash landed with a thud on the other side of the fence. He lay in the grass, struggling to get his breath. The dogs were barking and the bull was bellowing. Sitting up, he saw the dogs chasing the bull across the meadow. Quickly he ran along the fence and down toward timber, leaping into a thicket.

The gamekeeper reached the fence and started calling to the dogs. At the same time, an angry farmer was running toward the pasture, a pitchfork in his hands. The gamekeeper called the dogs to him. After he had explained things to the farmer, he led the dogs along the fence until they picked up Flash's trail. The gamekeeper had lost some time, but he showed no sign of worry. He knew that the otter did not have a very big lead and that the hounds would overtake him.

Flash raced through the woods. He had changed his mind about the river and wanted to get back to it. On land, he would never be able to escape. Shifting his course, he went straight downhill. He had always found a river or a stream between the hills, and there had to be one here. And he had to find it soon, for his breath was coming in short, painful pants, and his steps were growing shorter.

THE DRAINPIPE

Before Flash was a ravine, deep and narrow. Without hesitating, he went shooting down the steep drop, landing in a shallow pool. A stream trickled along the bottom of the ravine, but, like the pool, it was too shallow for swimming. The hounds were already tumbling down the steep side, and Flash scrambled away down the stream. He saw almost at once that the ravine was blocked. And he could not turn back, because the hounds were charging after him. A highway crossed the ravine at the top of a fill at least thirty feet high. All he could do was to try to climb out over the fill, and he ran toward it, splashing in the stream.

Then he saw a round, black hole—the hole of the culvert that passed under the fill, made of a pipe several feet in diameter. As he paused, the hounds came up behind him, and one slashed at his rump. Flash whirled and sank his fangs into the cheek of the hound. With a savage howl, the hound pulled free and leaped back.

Flash backed into the culvert, turned, and ran for several yards. He stopped where some rocks had dammed a part of the pipe, making a pool. Sinking down into the small pool, he looked back. At the mouth of the pipe was a circle of light, and within the light stood the two hounds baying for the gamekeeper. The one with the slashed cheek stood well back, as if he had no wish to come any closer to an otter. Flash had a feeling neither of the dogs would come in after him.

After a while, the gamekeeper arrived. For a few minutes he peered into the pipe, listening to Flash hissing. Then he tethered one hound at the entrance to the pipe, led the second hound over the fill, and tethered him at the lower opening. Leaving the dogs to guard both ways of escape, he set off to get the things he needed to dislodge the otter.

Flash decided that he would try to escape. He wanted to go on down the little stream, which should take him to deep water. He crept toward the lower opening, and as the light from the opening brightened the inside of the pipe, he moved more carefully. He edged forward until he could look out, and immediately backed up. One of the hounds, lying close to the opening, leaped at Flash. Luckily, the tether kept him from entering the pipe.

Flash scurried back to the little pool, and a half hour later he tried the upper opening. Here, too, he found a dog lying close to the mouth of the pipe. The hound heard him and started howling and snarling. Flash went back to the pool and lay down in the cool water. He would have to wait until the hounds went away.

The gamekeeper returned, carrying a shovel and two poles with heavy canvas tacked to them. He set up the poles at the upper end of the culvert, so that the canvas covered the opening. He shoveled dirt upon the lower edge of the canvas, making a dam which kept the stream from flowing through the pipe. The water began backing up, and soon a pool was forming. The gamekeeper unleashed both hounds and left them at the lower opening. They knew what to expect. They had their quarry cornered, and their master was going to flush it out of the pipe for them.

The gamekeeper sat on top of the fill, watching a small pond build up back of the dam. He smoked and watched until finally

the water was above the top of the pipe. He slid down the bank, grasped the two poles, and jerked upward. The canvas was pulled free of the opening and the water gushed into the pipe.

Flash had realized he was in danger as soon as the light at the upper opening disappeared. Looking toward the lower end of the pipe, he saw the heads of two dogs thrust into the circle of light and heard their growling and barking. But he was not prepared for the flood of dirty water which rushed at him when the gamekeeper removed the dam. He heard the rumble of the water as it boiled down the pipe and started toward the lower opening. Before he could take more than a few steps, the water crashed into him. Once again, just as when he had been sucked through the floodgate under the res-

ervoir, he was in water he could not fight. He rolled along the pipe, tumbling over and over, battered by the debris in the roaring stream of dirty, muddy water.

He shot out of the pipe, and he and the roaring water hit the hounds at the same time. For a few moments there was a crazy swirl of dogs and otter and water, but somehow Flash fought his way to the surface. He took a deep breath and looked around. The water had spread out in the stream bed below; the dogs had disappeared. Less powerful swimmers than Flash, they had been sucked under and drowned.

Before he dived and darted away downstream, Flash caught a glimpse of the gamekeeper on top of the fill. The man did not see the otter. Climbing down the bank, he called for his hounds. His plan had failed. He had meant to drive Flash out of the pipe, but had built up too big a head of water back of the fill. After walking along the stream for half a mile, searching for the dogs, he gave up.

While the gamekeeper started for home, Flash was swimming on, not slowing his pace until he came to a larger stream. His fear had not left him completely, but he felt safer. He was hungry, and within a few minutes he was seated on the bank of the stream eating a fat sucker. As he ate, he often paused to sniff and look and listen. From the woods came only bird calls, little noises made by rabbits and mice, the rustle of the wind in the treetops. These were all familiar and reassuring sounds, but Flash listened to them closely. No longer was he a careless young otter. Danger had taught him to be wary and watchful.

After he had dined and washed himself, he slid into the stream and swam strongly with the current. Again he felt the old urge to find others of his kind. Once in a while he whistled hopefully, but there was no answer to his calls.

Rounding a bend in the stream, he saw a river below him. The stream he was following entered the river over a small waterfall. He darted toward it, dived over, sank deep into a pool of clear water, and came up slowly.

When Flash's head popped out of the water he was puzzled. All around him and over him was wire mesh. The memory of Hank's chicken coop came back to him. He dived to get under the mesh, but it was under him, too. He was in a trap. He swam

about furiously, looking for a means of escape. But the trap door through which he had entered had snapped shut and locked. He was again a prisoner.

JOURNEY'S END

Flash realized that it was no use fighting the trap. He lay in the water with just his head above the surface, waiting to see what would happen next. A light truck pulled up on the bank. Two men jumped down from the cab, approached the trap, and stood looking down at him.

"Got us a nice young male," one of the men said.

"Beautiful pelt," the other said.

The first man glanced at his wrist watch. "We'd better get it over with. It's getting late."

Moving close to the water's edge, the men bent down and lifted the trap. Flash crouched on the bottom. He hissed defiantly as the men put the trap into the back of the truck. They got into the cab and the truck bounced away over the rough ground.

They had been traveling for some time when Flash sat up so that he could look over

the low sides of the truck. They were going uphill through wooded country. The trail that dropped away behind them was faint and choked with weeds. The truck reached the top of the hill and started down the far slope, still following the faint trail. At last in a secluded spot, the truck stopped. Flash flattened himself on the bed of the cage. He could not see where he was, but instinct told him that this was the end of the journey. The men came around to the back of the truck, picked up the cage, and carried it a short distance.

Flash crouched inside, hissing at the gloved hands holding the trap. Suddenly the trap was tilted sharply. Flash tumbled forward, spilled out of the open door, and fell for more than six feet before he hit water. The instant he felt the water, he dived. It was deep, and he went all the way to the muddy bottom. He did not want to surface so soon, but he had no time to take a deep breath before diving. Cautiously he poked his head up.

The truck was still on the bank with the two men standing beside it. If Flash could have read the lettering on the side of the truck, he would have known that this was a State Fish and Game truck. The men were rangers, and they knew how to keep otters out of forbidden territory. They trapped

them and moved them to a sanctuary. Flash could not understand what had happened. It was puzzling. These men had caught him, but somehow he had escaped. As they turned to get into the truck, he took a breath and dived again.

This time he stayed under for three minutes. When he surfaced, the men and the truck were gone. He raised himself out of the water and looked around. There was something vaguely familiar about the old grist mill on the bank. The water wheel, too, seemed like something he had seen before.

And then he saw other otters, four of them. They had hidden under the piling of the old mill while the truck was at the pond. Flash did not recognize them as Mother, Graymuzzle, Tiny, and Bonny. All he knew was that he had found other otters, and that was enough. He swam swiftly to meet them as they paddled out into the pond. None of his family recognized him, but Bonny started to swim toward him. Suddenly she felt that she was being too friendly with this young otter. She turned and darted away. Flash swam after her, ducking when she ducked, trying to come up beside her so that he could make friends.

Graymuzzle decided it was time for a game of tag. He darted away, with Mother and Tiny after him, and Bonny joined the game. Around the pond they raced, following Graymuzzle. He swerved toward the mill

and climbed ashore on the platform which supported the water wheel.

Graymuzzle clambered up over the wheel with Mother close behind. Down below, the rusty catch creaked and then snapped. The wheel began turning, and down came Graymuzzle and Mother. Water poured over the wheel. Delighted, Graymuzzle darted around the wheel and rode it down along with the water. Mother and Tiny followed.

Flash and Bonny were the last to ride the wheel. They went down splashing and landed in the pond close together. When they surfaced, their cheeks met for a moment. Side by side, they clambered out on the platform for another ride. The game lasted almost an hour, until finally Graymuzzle got hungry. He swam away to fish, and Mother and Tiny followed.

Bonny swam away toward the far bank, and Flash followed her. They climbed out on a grassy knoll, where they sat with their heads close together. Bonny wasn't as timid as she had been long ago when Flash first met her. With a soft call she started off toward the inlet of the pond, and Flash bounded along beside her. Life was ahead of them— a life that included diving and hunting and playing and raising a family of their own. It included wandering, too. But no matter how far they might wander, they would always return to the old mill pond, where they would find a safe place to make a den.

THE BABY COUGARS

In a cave in the mountains, two tiny spotted kittens were born. They were baby cougars. One day they would be the fiercest hunters in the mountains. But now they were small and helpless, and their eyes were still tightly closed.

Their mother licked her new babies proudly. For many days she stayed close beside them, to feed them and keep them safe and warm.

At last the kittens opened their eyes.

They were still wobbly on their feet. It was a big world for such tiny fellows—but they wanted to find out about it. Clumsily, their little tails held high, they tumbled over each other and over their mother.

Mother Cougar watched her babies carefully. Day by day they were growing bigger and stronger.

At last she felt that the kittens were big enough to be left alone for a while. She must go out and hunt for food.

That very day the kittens were playing when suddenly they spied a visitor—a nosy pack rat. What a fine new game! Round and round the cave they chased him—round the cave and out onto the ledge.

There the kittens stopped in surprise. It was the first time they had been outside the cave.

High above them a hungry golden eagle saw the two tiny specks on the ledge. He folded his wings and came diving downwards.

It was lucky that Chimbica saw the eagle in time and knocked his brother Tawny out of the way. It was lucky—for the eagle had claws strong enough to carry off a baby cougar.

The kittens had learned their first lesson: Stay inside the cave when Mother is away.

There were many more lessons for the young cougars to learn.

The day soon came when their mother felt that it was time to take the two youngsters hunting with her.

She went to the cave entrance and called her cubs.

Slowly, wonderingly, they followed her out onto the ledge. It was true—she really was going to take them with her!

Joyfully, Chimbica dashed after his mother. Helter-skelter along the narrow ledge. And suddenly—down went Chimbica, over the edge and into the grass below.

Tawny soon followed his brother.

It was a big jump for two little cougars—but the grass was soft and Mother walked on, unconcerned.

Grass was something new for the cubs. It was soft and green and tall.

Chimbica and Tawny practiced stalking—hiding and creeping and crouching and then making sudden little springs.

They even tried eating the grass—and it tasted good.

Then Tawny saw a grasshopper, and off he bounded after it, making playful slaps with his big paws.

But the grasshopper was always a jump ahead of the clumsy little cougar.

Chimbica found a snowshoe rabbit lying in a thicket. It looked just like the rabbits Mother brought home for dinner. Happily Chimbica sprang in after it.

But the rabbit's big ears twitched—his eyes opened—and off he ran, with the surprised Chimbica close behind.

Once out of sight, the rabbit played an old rabbit trick on Chimbica. He circled and went speeding back to the thicket.

And run and sniff as he might, poor Chimbica could not find his rabbit.

Now Tawny had found a wonderful supply of pine cones to play with. They had been left there by a brown squirrel, who was filling up his storehouse for the winter.

When the squirrel saw Tawny near his storehouse, he came scolding and chattering down the tree to drive the cub away.

Tawny, a playful fellow, ran to meet his new friend.

The squirrel whirled and ran back up the tree, with Tawny close behind. Like any cat, he was a good climber. But once up the tree, with the squirrel far out of reach above him, Tawny clung, swaying, to a branch. How was he to get down?

Only one thing to do.

He called loudly for his mother and brother Chimbica.

Mother Cougar opened one eye, but she didn't move from her sunny flat rock. Her cubs had to learn about trees.

Chimbica came running and darted up the tree.

Now he and Tawny were on the same branch, and the ground looked awfully far away to the frightened cubs.

Still chattering furiously, the squirrel dropped a nut on Tawny.

The cub teetered madly for a second, then fell, bringing Chimbica with him. Both kit-tens landed on their mother, who snarled crossly and cuffed them both.

Then to make up for it, she gave them each a lick with her rough tongue. After all, they had learned another lesson.

Now as the sun went down it was time to begin the really serious business of hunting.

The mother cougar began moving silently towards the clearing where the deer browsed. The cubs followed, pausing to sniff the wind and listen just as their mother was doing.

All three hunters spotted the big buck as he moved into the clearing.

Mother and cubs moved deeper into the shadows and stood perfectly still.

The buck moved slowly towards them, nibbling at grass and twigs and sometimes lifting his head to sniff the breeze.

Tawny was hungry, and wondered why his mother didn't leap on the buck right away.

But Mother was waiting for the buck to come even closer to her rock. A mistake would mean that the buck would bound away and might be lost.

And Mother Cougar could not afford a mistake. Already the evening breeze felt cooler and the leaves were beginning to turn color. Soon it would be winter. Then the deer would leave the mountain and go down to the lowland. It would be a hungry time for the cougars.

And Mother Cougar wanted her cubs strong and well fed to meet the winter.

Mother Cougar never took her yellow eyes from the buck.

He came a step nearer. Then he turned his back on the rock.

This was what the cougar had been waiting for. She crouched and leaped, right onto the buck's shoulder. One snap of his neck and he was down.

Chimbica leaped a second after his mother, trying to do just as she had done. It was a good try, but his leap carried him far short of the buck.

Late as usual, Tawny scrambled after his brother.

The little family ate well that night.

When the feast was over, Mother Cougar neatly covered the remains with dirt and leaves.

The moon was going down over the mountains as Mother Cougar led her cubs back to the cave. They walked close beside her. Even Tawny was quiet.

It had been a long day and they were tired out. They had learned so many lessons.

Mother Cougar licked them both once before she too fell asleep. It would not be long now before they left her, and went to hunt on their own. And she knew they would be good hunters.

AA   BB   CC   DD   EE   FF